Night-Rider Legacy

Night-Rider Legacy

Weaponizing Race in the Irasburg Affair of 1968

Gary G. Shattuck

Center for Research on Vermont
University of Vermont

White River Press
Amherst, Massachusetts

Published by White River Press, Amherst, Massachusetts
Whiteriverpress.com

ISBN: 978-1-935052-72-2 (paperback)
    978-1-935052-80-7 (ebook)
Images

Cover: Viewed through shattered glass inflicted by shotgun wielding night-riders, three Vermont State Police officers gather evidence at an Irasburg home, July 19, 1968. Vermont State Archives and Records Administration.

Back: Vermont State Police Cpl. Howard Gary Gould who died by suicide, July 30, 1979. Vermont Historical Society.

Library of Congress Cataloging-in-Publication Data

Names: Shattuck, Gary G., author.
Title: Night-rider legacy : weaponizing race in the Irasburg Affair of 1968
    / Gary G. Shattuck.
Description: Amherst, Massachusetts : White River Press, [2021] | Includes
    bibliographical references and index.
Identifiers: LCCN 2021026378 | ISBN 9781935052722 (paperback)
Subjects: LCSH: Racism in law enforcement--Vermont--Irasburg--History--20th
    century. | Irasburg (Vt.)--Race relations--History--20th century. |
    Vermont State Police--Corrupt practices--History--20th century.
Classification: LCC HV7936.R33 S53 2021 | DDC 363.2/308900974323--dc23
LC record available at https://lccn.loc.gov/2021026378

DEDICATION

In Honor of Our Brother
Cpl. Howard Gary Gould
Jan. 29, 1942–July 30, 1979

In this most sinister of tragedies your integrity and honesty was above reproach. You were, in the most finest sense, a man and a proud example of the Vermont State Police. We loved you and pray that God takes good care of you, for you deserve the best.

Vermont Troopers Association
Winter 1980

Contents

Part I—Night-Riders

PART II—A SINISTER TRAGEDY

PART III—RENEWAL

"Sometimes revolution is forced upon people by circumstances."

Senator Stoyan Christowe, Windham County
Vermont Legislative Council, May 27, 1968

FOREWORD

PAUL S. GILLIES, ESQ.

SITED ABOVE VERMONT'S CAPITOL, on Baldwin Street, sits a large residence called Redstone, designed to reproduce a Bavarian hunting lodge. Built in 1890 by George Guernsey, Montpelier's premier architect and builder, it was the summer home of John William Burgess, the leading political scientist of his day. Set back from the highway, the building has been the source of countless stories, conspiracies, myths, and phantoms. The state purchased it in 1947.

The Vermont State Police took over Redstone that year, as a command center for the state's law enforcement department, and vacated the building in the mid-1980s. If a building reflects the character of its occupants, Redstone is a perfect metaphor. It became in those years a fortress, a castle, a bunker, isolated from the main campus of the Capitol Complex, and it kept its secrets well. That is, until Gary Shattuck decided to train his eye on two incidents that brought attention and criticism to the State Police.

In 1968, a local man shot out the living room window of a house in Irasburg that was the residence of a Black minister and his family. An officer subsequently protecting the occupants walked into the house to unexpectantly discover the minister and a white woman—not his wife—in a compromising position on the couch, which in turn led to a very public arrest of the two for the crime of adultery.

In 1979, a man who worked for the State Police in St. Johnsbury distributed router bits—seconds, he said, from his job at a local factory—to some troopers. Accusations of criminal activity persisted, and led to the tragic suicide of a trooper.

Both of these crises stained the public reputation of the State Police, as accusations of racism from the Irasburg incident and persistent and unfounded rumors of the culpability of several troopers from the router bit investigation became the subject of media coverage and public criticism of the department. The events became politicized, and led to attempts to reorganize the Vermont State Police, the Motor Vehicle Department, and other law enforcement personnel within state government into an Agency of Public Safety, administered by an appointed secretary. That proposal failed, but the idea has been revived recently in the legislature.

What we know of those two incidents has to date remained in a fog of rumor and innuendo. Until now no one has been able to penetrate that fog, as the files of the department relating to them disappeared, including the full story of how the government and leaders of inquiry participated, prompting Vermont's leading research historian—himself a former trooper—to pursue them.

Night-Rider Legacy is the result of Shattuck's pursuit of the facts of both incidents. As with his study of the work on the opioid crisis of the late nineteenth century (*Green Mountain Opium Eaters*), of what really happened in Albany in 1770 when Ethan Allen took the cause of the New Hampshire Grants into the courts of New York (in *The Rebel and the Tory*, co-written by John Duffy and Nicholas Muller), and his remarkable history of how modernity affected rural, isolated Vermont with the coming of the railroads (*By the Wand of Some Magician*), Shattuck's newest work is a monument to his persistence in locating records that otherwise remained unknown to the public.

The Vermont State Police was pilloried in the press for turning a racist incident into a racist arrest. The story got ahead of the facts, and Redstone failed to understand the impact of the Irasburg incident on the troopers. There was no support network, only blame without compassion. The tragedy of the router bit case, albeit a decade later, was another product of the vacuum of leadership on the second floor of the castle that began soon after Irasburg.

These stories cannot be timelier, as the nature of law enforcement is being challenged throughout the country, as the nation in recovery decides how much government should do for us, as we begin to understand the history and presence of racism in our culture, as the tragic schism that separates the country continues to warp public policy. They reveal the complexity of governance, and the importance of real leadership, that doesn't feint in the face of crisis. "The one thing I've learned in public life," Gov. Richard A. Snelling said, "is that when you try to clean up a mess, you're going to get it all over yourself."

One of the ironies of historic research is how difficult it is to write about recent events, given the paucity of sources, compared with the rich resources often available to those who bury themselves in the deeper past. For all our pride about public records laws, essential papers, particularly on sensitive subjects, seem to disappear. There were many sensitive incidents in the 1960s and 1970s involving Vermont state government that are just now becoming understood, including the corrupt policeman who faked drug arrests in pursuit of his ambitions, the crisis in the judiciary involving justices accused of misconduct, and the two controversies covered here. It's always wise to allow a little time to elapse before trying to understand complex matters, particularly when those subjects are saturated in secrecy, but there's a risk that with the passage of time the sources will dry up and the true stories won't be told.

The Irasburg and Router Bit stories have never been revealed in depth until now. Through Shattuck's eyes we enter an otherwise closed world, where strong personalities clash, errant officials invent their own defenses and strategies, agencies are not well governed, and incidents determine policy. The image of the Vermont State police trooper—the erect bearing, the physical conditioning, the intelligence and sensibility to deal with extreme behaviors, the uniform, the hat— was tarnished by these events, although the fault was not of their doing. It was their leaders who failed to respect the trust placed in them that led to these tragic consequences.

History isn't pretty. Human beings are not always faithful. What we're told is often not the truth. Leadership isn't found in the petty tyrant who locks himself in a turret in a castle and refuses to leave, the prosecutor who places his own ambitions over public responsibility, the destruction of sensitive public records to hide conspiracies and avoid culpability. It's the oldest story in the world that when everything goes awry, the weight of blame will be cast upon the innocent.

Paul S. Gillies, Esq.

Attorney, historian, author

Uncommon Law, Ancient Roads, and Other Ruminations on Vermont Legal History. Vermont Historical Society, 2013.

The Law of the Hills: A Judicial History of Vermont. Vermont Historical Society, 2019.

STEPHEN C. TERRY

As a reporter in Vermont in 1968, I could not have selected a more momentous year to be in the news business. At the time I was a reporter and bureau chief for the Vermont Press Bureau, the statehouse bureau for the *Rutland Herald* and *Barre-Montpelier Times Argus*. In retrospect, it seemed that every day there was an unending torrent of breaking news. In the world, the nation, and in Vermont news, stories only served to heighten the natural competitive urges of Vermont's daily papers and local television outlets. Every day there was a race to be first in print or on the air.

An American war was raging in Vietnam with many Vermonters on the casualty list. In Washington, Sen. George D. Aiken, R-Vt., was among the leading Senate doves trying to convince President Lyndon Johnson to stop bombing and wind down the war. While Johnson didn't listen to Aiken, the President shocked the nation on March 30,1968 when he announced that he would not seek re-election because of the war in Vietnam.

Meanwhile in Vermont, the state was in turmoil as local draft boards were sending young Vermonters to the jungles of Vietnam. Anti-war protests pitted neighbors against neighbors.

In April, Martin Luther King, the important voice for civil rights, was assassinated while standing on a hotel balcony in Memphis. Several months later, in June, after an election victory in California,

Sen. Robert F. Kennedy, D-N.Y., was gunned down and murdered at the Ambassador Hotel in Los Angeles.

These murders were deeply shocking for many Vermonters. They were the topical story line for Vermont reporters, especially given the fact that Democratic Gov. Philip H. Hoff was not only anti-war, but deeply committed to trying to deal with racism in Vermont.

In 1968, Hoff teamed up with New York City Mayor John V. Lindsay to create the Vermont-New York City Youth Project. The program brought three hundred urban Black youth to Vermont to live and work on projects alongside mostly rural young Vermont white people at various locations in the Green Mountain State.

The project stirred latent racial resentment in the state that came to a head on the night of July 19, 1968 when three people in a car shot up a home, near the Quebec border, in which lived The Rev. David Lee Johnson, a Black minister, his family, as well as a white woman, Barbara Lawrence, and her two young children.

The shooting dominated the state's news pages, and it attracted national media attention as the racial attack was uncommon in a small rural Vermont town.

The shooting, which became known as the "Irasburg Affair," focused initially on the racial attack. Very quickly, however, this story had not only a race angle, but was spiced up by an adultery charge, which was against Vermont law, but rarely enforced.

The Vermont State Police, while guarding the Rev. Johnson's house, said they witnessed Johnson and Lawrence having sex on a living room couch. Since both were married, the county prosecutor brought adultery charges against each of them. In short, this was a story that the media could not pass up as it attracted intense state, regional, and national interest.

In the background of these events, was the fact that 1968 was an election year in Vermont and the race for the Republican gubernatorial nomination was the top political story of the season. Liberal Republican Atty. Gen. James L. Oakes of Guilford was running against Deane C. Davis of Montpelier, a traditional Vermont Republican, recently retired as CEO of National Life Insurance Co.

The Irasburg shooting hung over the campaign like a dark cloud.

Oakes, like Philip Hoff at the time, strongly held that the attack on the Rev. Johnson was racially motivated. Davis was cautious in blaming it on racism. In his campaign, Davis ran against the more liberal Oakes by claiming that Oakes would be just another Hoff, if Oakes was elected governor. In this way Davis could be seen as objecting to the unpopular Hoff policies on race without making it his prime political platform.

Davis ended up defeating Oakes by a substantial margin in the primary. He was ultimately elected governor as Philip Hoff, who had served an unprecedented three terms, did not seek a fourth.

Now, more than 50 years later, this chapter of Vermont history—unknown to many now living in the state—has been brilliantly brought back to life by Gary G. Shattuck, a lawyer, former Vermont State Police patrol commander, as well as a former assistant U. S. attorney.

Shattuck is now an historian and from his Shrewsbury, Vt., home has done masterful and meticulous archival research about the Irasburg case.

The title of Shattuck's newest book gives readers a strong hint of its contents. *Night-Rider Legacy: Weaponizing Race in the Irasburg Affair of 1968* is a blockbuster work which covers the role of the state police and the Vermont media, and the ultimate influence of this series of events on continuing efforts to change the culture and practices of state police leadership.

It is simply a must read for anyone interested in that period of Vermont political history as well as the deeply held cultural values of the state with its monochromatic, and overwhelming majority, of white residents.

In his book, Shattuck focused not only on the Irasburg case, but uses his impressive historian's research skills to dive deep into other significant cases, including what became known as the "Router Bit Affair," which resulted in the suicide of state police officer Howard Gould in 1979 behind the Vermont State House.

The story involved state police officers who were accused of receiving router bits from an auxiliary trooper who was also working at the Lyndonville tool company. The bits were supposed to be "seconds" that were available at the company. But an internal review of the case resulted in allegations that the state police were covering up the theft. Gould's suicide and the note that Gould left behind (a copy of which Shattuck provides) only intensified and super-charged the Vermont media's coverage of the case.

I was a witness to these events then as the Managing Editor of the *Rutland Herald.* Our reporters, as well as those for our sister paper, the *Times Argus*, followed the Router Bit Affair and the suicide of Gould with blanket coverage.

Shattuck's book raises important questions for the state's media. Did our reporting, some based on leaks and our unrelenting desire to be first with the news, help drive Gould to his suicide?

In my view, as well as of others at the time, it was Gould's inability to deal with his implication in the router bit scandal that led the trooper to shoot himself in a shocking way behind the statehouse.

This part of the book, titled "A Sinister Tragedy," occurred while the state police were still reeling from the Irasburg incident. It was made even more so by the refusal of the state government to acknowledge the pain and suffering of the family Gould left behind. In my view, it is still a wrong that should be righted these many years later.

For me, a surprise of this important book is that Shattuck is convinced that despite the conventional wisdom, then and now, that the actions of the state police in the 1968 Irasburg case were not based on racism, but an overworked, understaffed, and not fully trained state police force.

While I still don't agree with that conclusion, Shattuck's historical research of the records of the case gives the reader evidence to challenge my and others' conviction more than 50 years later that racism drove the actions of the state police.

In these highly publicized state police scandals, as well as a review of a third case, based upon a book called *Mocking Justice* by Hamilton Davis, in which a corrupt former police officer, Paul Lawrence, planted drugs on people in order to then arrest them, Shattuck makes a strong case for reforming police policies.

Author Shattuck's deeply sourced analysis of highly publicized state police scandals offers readers insight into the shortcomings of Vermont state police and political leadership.

The state police top brass, and then Governor Richard A. Snelling, attempted to upgrade and reform the state police so that it would emerge from its scandals with the trust and confidence of the Vermont public. Yet, after more than a half-century, Gary Shattuck's highly readable, powerful, and informative, book serves as an historical reference for an ongoing dialogue of policing in Vermont and in our nation.

Stephen C. Terry

Former Reporter and Bureau Chief, Vermont Press Bureau 1965–1969

Sunday Editor *Rutland Herald* and *Times Argus* 1975–1977

Managing Editor *Rutland Herald* 1977–1985

Author, *Say We Won and Get Out: George D. Aiken and the Vietnam War.* Center for Research on Vermont, University of Vermont/White River Press, 2019.

SPECIAL NOTE

THIS IS NOT A STORY about race, racism, or racial prejudice *per se*, or using the N-word, in Vermont in 1968, nor in the toxic environment the nation faces in the 21st century. Neither does it address the increasingly virulent intersection of race and law enforcement during that half-century interim. Those are matters for others better equipped to inspect, evaluate and explain.

Instead, this is an account of the unintended consequences resulting from the careless use of divisive, racially-charged language lodged against a law enforcement agency when virtually no evidence of racism existed. It describes a violent event in 1968, a police investigation into its circumstances and the ensuing troubles that bewildered organization faced traceable to the use of inflammatory rhetoric impugning its work because of the presence of imagined racists in its ranks. Like the sound of a ringing bell, those first, easily spoken expressions of hate coming from others pursuing personal motives formed a potent—and ultimately fatal—mix impossible to recall.

The weaponization of words about race, and not race itself, initiated what happened in Vermont in 1968 fostering consequences impacting us to this day.

PREFACE

BETWEEN 1968 AND 1979, the Vermont public witnessed a series of events involving its law enforcement community, principally the Vermont State Police (VSP), that sorely tested the vital support that organization needed to accomplish its work. Fighting off allegations of ineptitude and racism, a rogue cop planting drugs and running roughshod over individuals' rights while others engaged in petty thievery repeatedly tested the credibility, and resolve, of the state's premier police agency. Episodes beginning with the VSP's investigation of a burst of violence against a Black family (1968), to a former trooper turned criminal setting up scores of innocent people for bogus drug convictions (1973–1974), followed by the suicide of a despondent trooper fighting off unfounded allegations of his involvement in thefts (1979) seriously damaged its reputation and the public's trust.

Taking place during a period opening and closing to the sound of gunfire, each of these scandals, identified respectively as the "Irasburg Affair," the "Paul Lawrence Affair" and the "Router Bit Affair," splashed across newspaper headlines and television and radio airwaves drawing the rapt attention of a national audience. In 1969, *Life* magazine published a version about the alleged racist motivations of the VSP, committed by southern-style hick cops, entitled "The Ruckus in Irasburg." The story provoked such concern that one New York City Black man planning a trip to the state with his family wrote to Gov. Deane C. Davis expressing his "shock and dismay."[1] Will we, he asked "be safe or require a 'Safe Conduct Pass'" before our arrival? Popular Vermont novelist Howard Frank Mosher's fictionalization of the event in 1989 in his *A Stranger in the Kingdom* prompted additional attention in 1997 with filmmaker Jay Craven's production bearing the same title. Another book released in 1978 chronicled the actions of the cop gone bad at the same time the media flooded audiences with innumerable reports concerning the thefts precipitating the trooper's sad suicide the following year.*

While the trooper-at-large received overall positive reviews and public support during each episode, their superiors did not. Disgusted at what they witnessed, prosecutors and legislators periodically rained down derision on the VSP command staff. During the Irasburg Affair one state's attorney viewed them with a bit of hyperbole as "The King and Dukes of the mighty Kingdom of Redstone," referring to their distinctive Queen Anne-style Montpelier headquarters, and then later as a "Mickey Mouse administration."[2] Recently, a former attorney general characterized a VSP commissioner and two officers during the Lawrence Affair as "bad cops" for their lying.[3] And in the fallout of the Router Bit Affair, one legislator described the department as "a real Gestapo operation."[4] By century's end, Hollywood joined in the ridicule with its farcical *Super Troopers* (2001) followed by *Super Troopers 2* (2018) further discrediting it. How could such untoward things happen in quiet Vermont, the outside world asked? There, maple trees in autumn splendor beckoned, tourists flocked year-round to recreate in its waters and on its mountains, and rural life offered its innocent and easy ways as a place of safe refuge to those escaping the madness of city life. It made no sense.

Vermonters also questioned how things could go so wrong with its chief law enforcement agency, watching it morph into a pariah among state agencies as the unseemly stories rolled out. A dizzying number of inquiries took place to get to the bottom of it aiming to institute reforms. Beginning with an investigation into events taking

---

* Author Hamilton E. Davis's *Mocking Justice: America's Biggest Drug Scandal*, subtitled *The shocking true story of Paul Lawrence, a corrupt narcotics cop, and the hysteria which led a frightened town into wrecking the lives of its children*, provides a comprehensive account of the Lawrence Affair. More recently, former Attorney General Kimberly B. Cheney's *A Lawyer's Life to Live: A Memoir* (2021) adds additional information to Davis's account from the perspective of a participant. While details of the Lawrence matter will not be repeated here, relevant aspects of it from these works will be referred to because of their impact on the ensuing Router Bit Affair and trooper's death.

place just 35 miles apart from each other in the state's three-county Northeast Kingdom (NEK), a governor-appointed board of inquiry delved into the Irasburg Affair (Orleans County) in 1968, followed by a special commission examining the Router Bit Affair in St. Johnsbury (Caledonia County) in 1979. In between, other legislative and executive branch investigations, including one for the Lawrence Affair unfolding in northwest Vermont, accompanied by those from outside of government conducted by contractors, also took place. They included:

1975—Performance Audit of the Department of Public Safety, by a legislative committee;

1976—Report to Governor Thomas P. Salmon by The Special Committee to Review All Vermont Criminal Convictions Involving Evidence Produced by Former Law Enforcement Officer Paul Lawrence and to Recommend in Which Cases Pardons Should be Granted, by a citizen panel;

1977—A Study of Services and Practices of the Vermont Department of Public Safety, by an independent management consulting firm;

1979—A Report of an Investigation of the Practices, Procedures and Personnel within the Department of Public Safety, by the Vermont Attorney General;

1980—Report of Interim Commissioner Warren M. Cone, Department of Public Safety to Governor Richard A. Snelling;

1980—Report of the Committee to Inquire into the Organization, Structure and Administrative and Management Policies of the Department of Public Safety, by a legislative committee;

1980—Investigation into the Activities of the Vermont State Police by the Office of the Attorney General;

1981—Report to the Commissioner Department of Public Safety, by a private law firm.

Hidden within the volumes of work recorded in these inquiries lie the first insinuations made by the Irasburg board attributing racist inclinations, ineptitude and vindictive behavior to the VSP. Like a looming specter, that assessment formed a strong, unspoken reality simmering in the background affecting the following studies as each built on the other. As a result, for over half a century, an unquestioning, accepting public has consumed a steady diet assigning racial prejudice and neglect to the department because that first inquiry has gone unchallenged. Admittedly, the racial bias attributed by the board to a white man towards a Black family in Irasburg leading to his firing a shotgun into their home in July 1968 did exist.[†] However, it took on a life of its own thereafter when others frustrated at the time it took to investigate the case perceived its tentacles penetrating into the ranks of the VSP, rendering it guilty by association.

The weaponization of the historical record began with Irasburg, serving as the genesis for future "affairs." A contemporary vibrant, and frenzied, press, aided by vociferous self-interests from the clergy and politicians cherry-picking through the facts, succeeded so well exploiting the racist allegations that a decade later in 1979 commentators still referred to the VSP's "mishandling of the case." The insinuation persisted and on its twentieth anniversary the public once again heard of the department's purported "shameful handling" of the investigation.[5] In 2011, a respected journalist and editor of *Vermont Life* magazine said it again, reiterating unproven allegations that the VSP had more interest in investigating the Black victim

---

† **DISCLAIMER:** Publicly available archival records describe that none of the individuals charged with offenses resolved by no contest pleas during the Irasburg and Router Bit affairs have been found guilty of a crime or in violation of a department regulation. Those dispositions do not constitute either an admission or finding of guilt and none of the information contained herein infers, directly or indirectly, otherwise.

of the violence than in pursuing the white culprits involved.[6] This opinion persists, demonstrated by a Burlington newspaper alleging again that police "mishandled the investigation" and another that the prosecution of the white perpetrator "was far less thorough" than a subsequent adultery case brought against the Black victim.[7]

Consistently, these serious allegations, oft-times citing inaccurate accounts of what actually happened, fail to acknowledge that the VSP vigorously interviewed more than 220 witnesses (Appendix A) and quickly solved the shooting case. It required more than 2,000 officer hours to do so, while spending a mere eight hours, or an estimated .003% of their time, on the secondary adultery matter.[8]

Noteworthy Vermont historians mimicked the media's dire assessments in their authoritative texts, comfortably reciting a board of inquiry's finding the VSP was essentially racist. If not explicitly, then implicitly, their entries winked, repeating those characterizations because they did not consult the actual records that could have otherwise informed their opinions. Had they tempered their criticism by considering the observations of incoming Gov. Davis's secretary of civil and military affairs, former Attorney General Frederick M. Reed (1958–1960), soon after the release of the devastating Irasburg report, perhaps a much different, more accurate and fairer conclusion could have resulted. Reed immediately recognized the report's deficiencies and cautioned Davis to distance himself from them because they "leave something to be desired, both in form and substance."[9]

Despite others in high positions sharing Reed's assessment, the knee-jerk reactions to perceived police misconduct persists to present day, exemplified by the Vermont Human Rights Commission charged with addressing race-related complaints. In the same manner that the Irasburg hearings faulted the VSP a half-century ago without affording it traditional due process protections allowing it to defend against allegations of racism in the ranks that Reed also noted, the commission's rules allow it to impose significant embarrassment to a purported wrongdoer without similar guarantees. They allow the public disclosure of secret information but without affording a defendant an opportunity to lodge a meaningful defense beforehand or access to an appeal process thereafter that imposes a challenge to disprove disputed allegations.[10] As Reed characterized about the

Irasburg matter, such blatantly unfair deficiencies "condemned (the VSP) publicly without any of the processes normally available to either side in a legal controversy." The impossible recall of the sound of a ringing racist bell continues to present an unfair situation to any party falling victim to the unilateral application of rules painting their actions in an untested manner that raises the possibility of politically-correct motivations lurking in the shadows.

Neither had the historians, media or pundits assessing the VSP's conduct during the Irasburg Affair ever considered the "seat of the pants" methods the quasi-legal Irasburg board employed. The resulting "loopholes and contradictions" of its work left even its proponents admitting the deficiencies and flawed conclusions it reached. The fact that a state legislative committee determined the national racial unrest at the time constituted an existential threat to Vermont's own public safety and its effects on the VSP also escaped their attention. Nor did they appreciate the rapid changes in law and previously accepted procedures that the VSP worked under that could have provided them a deeper understanding of the challenges police routinely faced: *Mapp v. Ohio* (1961, evidence); *Gideon v. Wainwright* (1963, right to counsel); *Escobedo v. Illinois* (1964, right to counsel); *Miranda v. Arizona* (1966, right to counsel); and, *Terry v. Ohio* (1968, stop and frisk). Finally, they never acknowledged the human toll that working for the VSP extracted from its officers. It stood in virtually last place position in the U.S. and Canada for pay and benefits (remaining there for many years thereafter), requiring its troopers to work an excessive number of hours a week above what other state workers did, and without overtime; including during the Irasburg investigation when all days off and vacations were canceled.

Leading off with Vermont's dean of historians, Samuel Hand, followed by others, including the Vermont Historical Society, their representations lack these important perspectives to support their observations. Their unfamiliarity with police work has cast what the records demonstrate was a robust investigation of a straight-forward crime into something unproven and accomplished only by innuendo: a reprehensible display of racial prejudice practiced by the VSP.[11] It is a legacy that persists to recent times in the myopic view of many assessing the difficulties police face, straining to interpret innocent actions as somehow racist.

The time has come to reconsider the Irasburg board of inquiry's work as something more akin to what a close examination reveals it to be: a shallow, politically-driven historical curiosity assigning undeserved blame to the VSP that continues to warp the perceptions of a current generation. There are often two, and sometimes more, sides to a story and the absence of a modicum of a compassionate, respectful perspective from the VSP's side, silenced until now, that does not abide the standard narrative is necessary to provide much needed balance.

Notwithstanding the traumatizing effects of the Irasburg Affair, the condemnation an increasingly insular VSP high command received a decade later during the Router Bit Affair when it retreated defensively into a "fortress mentality" after 1968 seems to have legitimacy; but still deserves re-examination. Revisiting the voluminous primary records from each of these matters offers up a more complete picture than the one usually painted by historians and pundits demonstrating the presence of much nuance escaping recognition. Concerns arise on both occasions with an examination of the public (Irasburg and Lawrence) and secret (Router Bit) proceedings that cast a different light on what should have been fair processes rendering fair outcomes.

A quasi-military police force is beholden to many masters. Laws created by legislators allow it to exist, to fund its operations, to establish the limits of its authority, to create an internal chain of command, and to assure its integrity when it stumbles. Within the VSP, evolving and adjusting to the fallout from Irasburg after 1968, to run afoul of its political overseers during the next decade meant hazarding one's career. It posed a conundrum for its members, forced to silently swallow their fate dished up in a political environment leaving little room for independent thinking or opportunity to defend themselves as they evolved into convenient scape-goats.

Because of their visibility and high stakes, each of these occasions attracted a privileged coterie of Vermont's political and judicial elite sitting in judgment. They included governors, attorney generals, campaign managers, and their ambitious aides seeking future high position that their participation could make possible. Politics and a dizzying number of conflicts of interest existed among them threatening life-changing, career-ending consequences for anyone breaking rank. Protective of their reputations and position, this tight-bound, male-dominated, Ivy League-educated group held their cards close to their chests. Notably, none of them ever experienced the practical difficulties associated with the demands of everyday law enforcement as they nonetheless blindly abided the devastating findings of the Irasburg board of inquiry.

In their insulated positions and collective lack of perspective, the VSP's taskmasters came to taint the public's understanding of what actually happened in the larger events. Vermonters drew their conclusions from what they could witness during the open hearings and the assessments provided by the media. But, was it accurate? Were the public's perceptions of the VSP misled because of what areas those sitting in judgment allowed a light to shine into? Or was the department denied a full airing because facts were withheld or slanted, records tampered with, investigations curtailed or the applicable law the police worked under not considered? And, what were the personal relationships these highly placed men shared behind the scenes that could offer the prospect of backroom deals the public was not privy to?

The consequences of these investigations loomed huge for the VSP as it evolved internally over the course of the decade when these men sat in judgement of it. As a result, it went from an easy-going, permissive organization into one attempting to delicately tread the difficult legal landscape after 1968. That pivotal year saw the assassinations of national leaders (Robert F. Kennedy and Martin Luther King), racial tensions and rioting in cities around the country and student unrest on college campuses. At home in the NEK, Orleans County received unwanted national attention that spring, singled out as a "hunger" county because of widespread poverty and malnutrition among its inhabitants. Unwilling to abide by warnings from within his administration to immediately address the problem head on, Gov. Philip H. Hoff turned elsewhere to, instead, interject Vermont into the national race problem. He joined with New York City Mayor John Lindsay to institute the Vermont-New York Cooperative Youth Project bringing hundreds of inner-city Black youths into a rural environment that many residents disliked and/or resisted. Only days before the ensuing Irasburg violence further discord threatened public safety when rogue out-of-state motorcycle gangs rioted in Grafton and a National Guard soldier was shot at in Brattleboro. There had never been a summer in Vermont like 1968 for the VSP as it sought to handle the challenges these events imposed while fighting off, for the first time in its history, allegations that racism infused its ranks.

None of the three "affairs" taking place between 1968 and 1979 individually brought on the radical changes awaiting the VSP beginning in 1980. However, in their collective effects during that decade the department entered into a new-found world that none of its Depression-era founders could have ever envisioned; that is, until Irasburg exploded.

ON SOURCES

The two official accounts of the Irasburg and Router Bit affairs summarily recite their respective panels' interpretations of the evidence presented during their work and rests in the custody of the Vermont State Archives and Records Administration. The 753 pages of testimony from 33 witnesses and 187 exhibits (including many multi-page investigative reports) provided during the 5 days of public hearings in the Irasburg matter were substantially reduced to a 30-page pamphlet entitled *Findings and Recommendations of Board of Inquiry Investigating the so-called Irasburg Affair.*[12] A single transcript copy of those proceedings exists today only because VSP Commissioner Erwin A. Alexander personally paid $550 for it in order to defend himself against charges lodged against him by Hoff; who also peevishly withheld permission for a court reporter to prepare it unless Alexander asked and paid for it. The Router Bit matter conducted out of the public's eye involved that panel's consideration of some 10,000 pages of investigations and sworn testimony encapsulated into its 105-page summary "Report of the Keyser Commission Regarding Certain Alleged Irregularities in the Vermont Department of Public Safety."[13]

Together, these two documents present the official viewpoints of what occurred with each receiving a different reception by the press and public upon their release. Whereas the Irasburg report, the first of its kind in state history, recited its findings in ways that found general acceptance and formed public opinion approving its condemnation of the VSP, the latter did not. Times had changed during the decade that separated the two reports and the cautious, hands-off treatment the Keyser Commission afforded the VSP surprised many expecting something similar to the Irasburg findings. The reason for their differences reflects the substantial changes taking place within the political landscape, the tumultuous upheavals occurring inside the VSP itself, and the sensitive aspects that racism and suicide presented.

Lastly, the archives also retain the papers of elected officials serving at the time: governors Deane Davis and Richard Snelling and Attorney General John Easton providing much needed additional context. In toto, they shed substantial light regarding the racist allegations the VSP received beginning in 1968 that set off the course of future conduct of high-ranking officers retreating into the "Kingdom of Redstone" and becoming outliers in state government in the next decade.

To understand this time period more fully requires assessing other events taking place. The Vermont Historical Society retains some papers concerning the VSP's formative years and those of Attorney General James L. Oakes and the Board of Inquiry's young law clerk, M. Jerome Diamond. While the ambitious 50-page outline of events Diamond prepared for the board steers closely to the facts, it also subtly infers the presence of racial bias by VSP investigators that may have begun with Oakes's personal recitation of events he provided beforehand.[14] The VHS files also contain information regarding the so-called "Young Turks," a group of junior, hyperactive Republican and Democratic legislators in the early 1960s that had a strong impact in the political arena for years.[15] This group included Hoff, together with others associated with the Irasburg Affair who formed important, strong bonds advancing their respective careers and the course of state politics.

Pursuing Hoff's papers for more particulars, housed at the University of Vermont's Silver Special Collections, presents its own challenges. Immediately at the end of his term as governor in 1969, just days after the Irasburg board of inquiry rendered its report, he "went so far" Vermont State Archivist Tanya Marshall writes, as to send his purportedly "non-executive" papers to the university rather than follow standard protocol forwarding them to the Secretary of State's office for storage.[16] In his rush to place them into a separate repository away from prying eyes, Hoff appears to have included at least some of his executive papers. That February, after his successor, Deane Davis, assumed office and apparently without access to duplicating resources, Hoff sent him copies of clearly executive letters concerning the Irasburg matter asking that he make copies and return them to him admitting that "the originals of these letters are in the files at the University of Vermont."[17]

Hoff accomplished his goal to limit access to his records so well that few substantive materials relating to him exist in the state archives. While Marshall writes that Hoff further restricted the use of his papers transferred to the university requiring his written approval for release during his lifetime, Curator of Manuscripts and University Archivist Christopher Burns adds additional insight. He reports that the restriction only came about in 1973 after Hoff signed a deed of gift agreement.[18] The lapse in time between the university's receipt of the papers in 1969 and the 1973 agreement prompts a question of what and who may have purged those official documents in the interim? Did they contain more information about the Irasburg matter that could cast a different light on the case and alter the accepted understanding of it?

Surprisingly, even shockingly, the VSP has retained no records about this tumultuous period in its history. When the author sought information regarding members of its high command concerning the trooper's suicide during the Router Bit Affair that generated thousands of pages of investigative reports, the department could provide only a single, redacted 4-page report. It also declined to supply a communication from an interim commissioner of public safety to the governor citing, in the legal-speak words of the records custodian, "the common law executive privilege."[19]

The department's inability and/or refusal to provide additional information indicates that the files generated during any of the "affairs" simply does not exist. That condition began literally from the moment Cpl. Howard Gould killed himself as a result of the router bit matter. When his widow sought access to her husband's personnel records during a lawsuit she filed in 1981, a department attorney sheepishly admitted they had been "destroyed inadvertently in 1979" immediately following his death.[20] A second inquiry by the author for information made to the Montpelier Police Department where Gould's suicide took place at Vermont's state house produced a similar response that it had no such information. It could supply only a single green and white-striped "Master Index" card providing little information beyond assigning case number 79-06164 to an event cryptically coded "4216" involving the officer.[21]

In the end, the VSP's leaders only temporarily succeeded in gaining their sought-after isolation at Redstone after Irasburg and before the Router Bit Affair unraveled before them. But they did so at the cost of causing such confusion within the ranks that an innocent, honorable trooper could not stand the strain that led him to commit suicide at the very location where the politicians did their work.

The tragedy of his act and the symbolism of its locale is heartbreaking.

ACKNOWLEDGMENTS

BEYOND THE COLD, STARK SURVIVING RECORDS of the "affairs" themselves, the emotions of surviving participants remain so raw a half-century later that only a few agreed to revisit this dark and difficult period in their lives. When contacted by telephone, one important witness threatened to sue the author if s/he was identified (they are) before curtly advising that the real story of the Irasburg Affair had never been told, never would be told and hung up. A NEK newspaper still publishing today and caught up in the matter similarly refused to respond to the author's repeated inquiries after learning about the topic of discussion. Some agreed to speak about the Irasburg and the Router Bit matters, but with varying degrees of enthusiasm ranging from open willingness to reluctance to no interest whatsoever declining to return phone calls or respond to emails. Within the VSP itself, some asked "why bother," while others professed only a vague recollection of things, forgetting completely with the passage of time that a state trooper took his life in the process.

However, his family did not forget and they remember his passing as though it happened yesterday. To them, I express my deep appreciation for the helpful information and insights they shared, and permission to publish the special images used herein. They include his wife Charlene, now living outside of Vermont, her brothers, former state troopers Albert and Donald Ravenna, and her son, Jason, a Vermont deputy sheriff who escorted the author to the location behind the statehouse where his father took his life. Each recalled him in the tenderest of terms, describing his honesty and extreme devotion to the state police that, with his family, he considered the sum and substance of his existence. Reading between the lines of the impersonal archival records confirms their belief and it is a privilege to tell his particular story in a way that has not been done before.

Attempting to recreate the interplay between some of the participants posed a further challenge. For insights into the politics of the era and the media's reporting on it, the author extends his great appreciation for the help extended by Stephen C. Terry, who also provided a foreword for this project. A reporter in the 1960s for the *Rutland Herald* working closely on the 1968 campaign trail with various candidates (later becoming the paper's managing editor and Sen. George Aiken's legislative assistant), Terry had one-of-a-kind access to many of the people described herein. His willingness to share intimate details on several points have made this story richer than it might have otherwise been.

The author also expresses his appreciation for the interest, guidance and encouragement provided by a distinguished group of experts willing to revisit this period. These include: former Vermont Attorney General Kimberly B. Cheney; former University of Vermont Professor of United States and Canadian History (and authority on the Black experience) and current Professor of History at the University of Calgary, Harvey Amani Whitfield; attorney, legal historian and author Paul S. Gillies also providing a foreword; former VSP patrol commander and current Professor of Criminal Justice Michael J. Carpenter; and, educator-historian-author H. Nicholas Muller III.

Finally, much thanks goes out to Richard Watts, director of the University of Vermont's Center for Research on Vermont, and student interns in his charge, who provided needed access to archival materials during the 2020 COVID-19 lockdown. Enola Mercer and Luke Vidic searched out a number of important files providing fresh details about events that have been neglected until now. Enola's careful perusal of papers relating to the Youth Project and Luke's examination of the Hoff papers, where detailed information concerning the VSP and military interactions during the Grafton riots rests (and an eccentric Virginia inventor trying to convince the VSP he could stop cars from nine miles away with a special radio frequency) made the work very enjoyable. Program Coordinator Emily Anderson and student Calista Hanna also provided their expertise formatting, laying out the manuscript and designing the cover for the book that Nanci Austin-

Bradley at the State Archives contributed to by providing many other interesting documents and images under her care.

A heartfelt thank you to each.

Dramatis Personae

Irasburg Affair

Aiken, George D.—Vermont governor (1937–1941); U.S. senator

Albright, Roger—member, Vermont Council of Churches, Commission on Human Rights

Alexander, Erwin A.—VSP commissioner (1965–1970)

Angell, Philip A.—Orange County State's Attorney

Baton, Maxwell L.—attorney for Larry Conley

Blum, Richard C.—assistant attorney general

Bottum, Edward J.—clergy intern

Bouffard, Paul—Catholic priest

Brown, Kyle T.—attorney for state troopers

Chilton, Billy J.—VSP criminal investigator, Montpelier

Christowe, Stoyan—state senator, Windham County

Collins, Benjamin M.—secretary of civil and military affairs, Hoff administration

Collins, Donald—warden, Vermont Fish and Game

Collins, Dorothy M.—member, Irasburg Board of Inquiry

Conley, Howard—father of Larry Conley

Conley, Larry G.—Irasburg gunman

Cram, Roger—VSP trooper, Derby

Daley, John J.—lieutenant governor, Hoff administration

Davis, Deane C.—governor (1969–1973)

Davis, Glenn E.—VSP executive officer, Montpelier

Dean, Harold—VSP director of enforcement, Montpelier

Diamond, M. Jerome—law clerk, Irasburg Board of Inquiry; attorney general (1975–1981)

Edson, Merritt A.—VSP commissioner (1947-1951)

Eldredge, Robert A.—attorney for VSP

Emerson, Lee—governor (1951–1955), attorney for Bernadette Roy

Foote, Ralph A.—lieutenant governor, counsel to Irasburg Board of Inquiry

Gibson, Ernest W. Jr.—Vermont governor (1947–1950); federal judge; chairman of Irasburg Board of Inquiry

Gibson, Orville "Hoot"—deceased farmer

Goodnow, Dana O.—VSP detective, Drug Abuse Unit

Green, William—VSP station commander, Derby

Hayes, Lloyd T.—editor, *Newport Daily Express*

Hebard, Emory—representative, House of Representatives

Hoff, Philip H.—governor (1963–1969)

Hogan, James—VSP trooper, Derby

Hovey, Don—reporter, *Caledonian Record*

Hunt, Franz A.—publisher, *Newport Daily Express*

Iverson, Robert H.—VSP lieutenant, records division, Montpelier

Jeffords, James M.—law clerk to Judge Gibson, attorney general and U.S. senator

Johnson, Brenda—David Johnson's daughter

Johnson, David Henry Lee, Sr.—Family patriarch

Johnson, David—son of David Johnson Sr.

Johnson (aka Small), George—son of David Johnson Sr.

Johnson, Ophelia—wife of David Johnson Sr.

Lawrence, Barbara A.—friend of David Johnson Sr.

LeClair, Earl—father of Richard LeClair

LeClair, Richard E.—driver of vehicle in Irasburg

L'Ecuyer, Gregory—attorney general investigator

Lessard, Jean G.—VSP trooper, Montpelier

Lindsay, John—mayor, New York City

Lium, Sten—state's attorney, Caledonia and Essex counties

MacDonald, Bruce—VSP trooper, Montpelier

Mahady, Frank—assistant attorney general

Marshall, Lane F.—VSP trooper, Derby

Mitchell, Robert W.—owner-publisher, *Rutland Herald*

Newell, Gordon G.—clergyman

Oakes, James L.—attorney general (1967–1969)

Pearson, Leonard—Caledonia County State's Attorney

Potvin, Clement F.—VSP troop commander, St. Johnsbury

Rachlin, Robert D.—attorney for David Johnson Sr.

Reed, Frederick M.—secretary of civil and military affairs, Davis administration

Rexford, Paul R.—attorney for Barbara Lawrence

Roy, Bernadette—passenger in Richard LeClair's car

Shanks, John B.—VSP detective, St. Johnsbury

Skinner, Ruth—state police dispatcher

Springer, Lewis E.—state court judge

Sorri, Fred—reporter, *Monterey Peninsula Herald*

Terry, Stephen C.—chief, Vermont Press Bureau and reporter, *Rutland Herald*

Wade, Laurence A.—VSP detective, Derby

Washburn, Lawrence—VSP detective, St. Johnsbury

Wibecan, Kenneth—columnist, *Brattleboro Reformer*

Wick, Hilton A.—member, Irasburg Board of Inquiry

Router Bit Affair

Adams, Gordon—VSP corporal

Bardelli, John F.—investigator, Connecticut State Police

Baumann, William H.—VSP commissioner (1951–1965; 1977)

Bouffard, Dennis—VSP trooper, St. Johnsbury

Cain, Francis J.—member, Keyser Commission

Charron, Nelson "Ticker" Lee—defendant

Cheney, Kimberly B.—attorney general (1973–1975)

Cherington, Joel—commissioner, labor and industry

Collett, Nancy—psychiatrist, Vermont State Hospital

Cone, Warren M.—VSP commissioner (1979–1980)

Corcoran, Edward W.—VSP commissioner (1970–1977)

Costello, Thomas—representative, House of Representatives

Davis, Hamilton E.—author

Farmer, Edward—VSP corporal

Field, Robert E.—VSP station commander, St. Johnsbury

Fish, Edward R.—VSP station commander, Middlesex

Gensburg, Robert A.—prosecutor, Lawrence Affair

Gibson, Charles E. Jr.—member, Keyser Commission

Gilbert, William—aide to Governor Snelling

Gould, Charlene—wife of Howard Gould

Gould, Howard Gary—VSP corporal, St. Johnsbury

Gould, Jason—son of Howard Gould

Gray, Dale O.—Caledonia County State's Attorney

Guillot, Laurent C.—investigator, Connecticut State Police

Heffernan, John P.—VSP field force commander, Montpelier

Hudson, Paul—assistant attorney general

Keyser, F. Ray Sr.—chairman, Keyser Commission

Kostelnik, Carol—VSP trooper, St. Johnsbury

Kurrle, Robert J.—VSP counsel, David Reed hearing

Lauzon, Michael—Hardwick chief of police

Lawrence, Paul D.—VSP trooper-defendant

Lay, Nelson R.—VSP troop commander, St. Johnsbury

Lynch, Francis E.—VSP commissioner (1977–1979)

McGee, P. Scott—Lamoille County State's Attorney

McKenzie, Gregory—deputy attorney general

Merriam, Stanley T.—VSP corporal

Meyer, William L.—professor, UVM

Mills, Gordon—member, Keyser Commission

Morse, Gerald—senator, Caledonia County

Ohradan, Martin A.—investigator, Connecticut State Police

Palmisano, Joseph—VSP counsel, David Reed hearing

Patch, George O.—VSP support services, Montpelier

Philbrook, Paul R.—VSP commissioner (1980–1984)

Plante, Peter P.—member, Keyser Commission

Putter, David—assistant attorney general

Ramey, Milford W.—VSP criminal investigations, Montpelier

Ravenna, Albert J.—VSP, attorney general investigator; Howard Gould's brother-in-law

Ravenna, Donald—VSP officer; Howard Gould's brother-in-law

Reed, Cornelius—VSP corporal

Reed, David A.—VSP detective, St. Johnsbury

Ryan, James H.—VSP executive officer, Montpelier

Salmon, Thomas P.—governor (1973–1977)

Snelling, Richard A.—governor (1977–1985; 1991)

Spear, Richard A.—VSP criminal investigations, Montpelier

Truex, Thomas—VSP trooper, St. Johnsbury

Valsangiacomo Jr., Oreste V.—attorney for David Reed

Woodruff, William—psychiatrist

Part I

NIGHT-RIDERS

We were working 15 and 18 hours a day. You've got to understand this, everybody was dead tired at the end of the day. We felt we should proceed very carefully, that is just exactly what we did.

Testimony of Vermont State Police Criminal Investigator Cpl. John B. Shanks before the Irasburg Board of Inquiry, Nov. 7, 1968.

Chapter 1

REVOLUTION

THE HEAT AND HUMIDITY OF THURSDAY, July 18, 1968 had begun to relent by the early hours of the next day in the quintessential northern Vermont town of Irasburg. The rumbling exhaust of a powerful late model Oldsmobile and two shotgun blasts coming from within aimed at the front of a home occupied by a Black family recently arrived from California shattered that peaceful tranquility—for longer than anyone would know. When the perpetrators looped back to view the occupants' reaction to their attack and fire more shots, the family's patriarch waited in the dark to unload his 9mm Luger pistol, returning fire but without effect. Days later, a VSP officer guarding the home discovered the man *in flagrante delicto* with a white woman introducing further complexity into an already bewildering set of facts because their adulterous affair presented police with yet another violation of state law. Like a flash fire, allegations of racism soon infused the VSP's extensive investigation into the shooting that allowed an ambitious publicity-seeking attorney general, struggling in the midst of a primary race for governor, to interject himself into the mix.

The late-night incident precipitating these events had antecedents that went back as early as Vermont statehood nearly two centuries before, the slow recognition of a need for statewide policing leading to the formation of the VSP in 1947 and the growing concern of "race riots" set off in Newark in 1967 spreading to other American cities with the recent King and Kennedy assassinations reinforcing notions it could ultimately touch Vermont. The violence in Irasburg also exposed the undermanned, overworked, and uncoordinated condition within Vermont's law enforcement community. Because of the attorney general's effort to intrude into the investigation, it also upset the pre-existing cordial relationships between police and locally elected prosecuting attorneys that awaited correction after his term in office expired allowing them to return to normalcy. The violence further shattered the confident pretentions of the Montpelier political elite exposing them to the potential anger of Vermont's growing progressive population threatening their hold on or path to power. They needed to assuage the press and deflect political backlash from the extraordinary set of facts and, of course, lay the burden on a sacrificial lamb; a role the VSP conveniently assumed.

The incident in the early hours of July 19, 1968 and its aftermath has become known as the "Irasburg Affair." In more than a half century, it has not received either full nor satisfactory investigation or explanation. It still hangs like a gathering storm over the state and Vermonters understanding of themselves.

Out-of-State Influences

To appreciate the magnitude of the changes and challenges a fiscally strapped, over-worked, undermanned and underpaid VSP faced in 1968 requires understanding some of its history. Vermont has the distinction of being virtually the last state in the nation to create a law enforcement agency with state-wide authority in 1947; Kentucky did so in 1948, followed by Alaska and Hawaii in 1959. Why the Green Mountain State delayed for such a long period after other states already embraced the need for such a capability (Texas began the process in 1835) lies in the state's strong adherence to tradition and reluctance to change, reinforced by a parsimonious, rural dominated government. That abiding trait effectively undercut its ability to adapt to the modernity other parts of the country already accepted as inevitable over the course of the past century. In many ways, the characteristics of this mountainous, isolated population that continued to identify closely with a century-old idyllic notion of the inherent strengths of the common man exemplified by Andrew Jackson in the 1830s only increased and hardened with time that made turning from the past an abhorrent thought. In the mid-nineteenth century, the arrival of the railroad forced Vermonters out of their comfortable complacency and into a world offering new prospects to increase their well-being. While they took selective advantage of what it promised at the time, in the next decades they slide back to their traditional ways, living in relative isolation in comparison to the vibrancy experienced in distant metropolitan centers. With the more recent intrusive effects of the automobile and other innovations in the early twentieth century, Vermonters once again confronted the notion of accommodating new forms of technology into their midst.

Transportation and the increased ability to communicate with those outside the Green Mountains made access to the state easier for anyone seeking to escape life in coastal cities. They came in droves and while the number of vehicles registered in Vermont in the 1920s increased from 31,000 to 90,000, fully 40% of those on its highways that decade came from other states, exceeding 50% during the summer months.[22] In 1965, Gov. Hoff warned of more changes coming to the state because of the rapidly developing highway system. "Population expansion and attendant problems of urbanization," he said, "make the open space and untouched beauty of Vermont the envy of countless thousands. It would be naïve to think that this population explosion will not have a tremendous impact upon our state," warranting the addition of 42 new troopers to the VSP.[23] VSP Commissioner Alexander agreed such an increase was needed because of the state's atrocious accident rate killing a staggering 80 people in the first half of 1965. Still under construction at the time, he argued that the 70 miles of existing interstate highway required the additional troopers to patrol and conduct equipment checks. Unrepentant in acknowledging the no-nonsense attitude the department took in dealing with the motoring public, he said that "Every day is a crack-down" to enforce the law.[24] By 1968, the number of vehicles registered in Vermont climbed to 208,737 (up from 199,706 in 1967), some involved in an eye-popping 12,557 accidents taking place in the preceding two years investigated by the VSP. Fatal accidents increased to such an extent that Vermont's roads were considered more dangerous than anywhere else in the United States.[25]

The effectiveness of the VSP in dealing with motor vehicle-related problems presented an important obstacle in solving the shooting taking place in Irasburg in 1968. It is traced directly to the woeful inability of the Department of Motor Vehicles (DMV) to respond in a timely manner to police requests for information concerning potential vehicles used in the attack. Described by its commissioner that year as operating in the "horse and buggy days" when it came to retrieving vehicle information held in its files, the DMV's inability to assist police with timely information caused days of delay in that investigation. That kind of inability, one senior VSP officer reported, routinely "severely hampered" other investigations to such a degree that even when information was provided it proved "useless in cases where swift apprehension" was necessary.[26]

While the VSP operated principally as a motor vehicle enforcement agency until the late 1960s, with the opening of the interstate beginning in mid-decade new challenges arrived in the form of different types of crimes committed by more sophisticated individuals. They exploited the access to the Green Mountains afforded by beckoning super highways cutting across the landscape from Brattleboro near the Massachusetts border in the southeast corner of the state to Derby on the forty-fifth parallel at the Canadian border (I-91) and from White River Junction midway on the Connecticut River at the New Hampshire border cutting northwest to Burlington on the east shore of Lake Champlain (I-89). The phenomenon of out-of-state illegal influences arriving in Vermont had long existed due to the strong attraction of those seeking seclusion in the Green Mountains. It first appeared centuries ago during the Revolutionary War when deserting soldiers from George Washington's army arrived in droves and then in the early 1900s when addicts seeking to escape stringent laws elsewhere and looking for easy access to drugs flocked into one of the last unregulated states, marking it as a safe place for lawbreakers. By 1947, the state gained such a reputation for its derelict law enforcement ways that Rutland's chief of police called it a "sanctuary from the law in the mountain regions." "Vermont is like an isolated island," he said, "surrounded by areas with state police departments" able to address the problem in their own jurisdictions.[27]

In 1949, Vermont Sen. George Aiken further recognized the problems of isolation causing outside industry to withhold entering into remote areas because of its deficient road system. Unable to counter the influences of monied outsiders, Vermonters watched them helplessly exploit their natural resources and take advantage of the state's paucity of laws curbing it. During a conference in Lyndonville (a short 30 miles from where the Irasburg violence occurred), Aiken noted the challenges local communities faced, falling victim to those outside forces situated in what he called, for the first time, the "Northeast Kingdom." The lack of transportation and power, he said, extending to that part of the state where it took two days to reach from metropolitan centers required much change before it could move forward.[28]

Perhaps a bit of snappy branding that Aiken picked up elsewhere, the NEK moniker encapsulated the differences experienced in its three counties of Caledonia, Essex and Orleans distinguishing them from the rest of the state because of their marked poverty, level of education and kinds of weather.[29] Each of these challenges persisted for the local population in the following years, reflected in census records where, statewide, between 1960 and 1970, the Vermont population increased from 389,881 to 444,330. After Aiken spoke, the number of inhabitants of Orleans County counted at 21,190 in 1950 (already on the descent from 21,718 in 1940) dropped further to 20,143 by 1960, recovering a miniscule ten individuals by 1970 to 20,153. In Irasburg, the population decreased from 852 in 1940 to 711 in 1950 where it remained in 1960, increasing to 775 by 1970.[30] For whatever increase the state experienced as a whole during these years, the NEK stagnated for decades.

RACE

Vermont's checkered experience with race relations exploding in Irasburg began at its creation as the first state (1791) to qualifiedly outlaw slavery in its revolutionary-era Constitution of 1777. Recent scholarship belies any notion that the population actually abandoned the practice then because it lingered on in the next decades. While census figures for minorities in general, and the Black population specifically, reveal each category maintained smaller numbers in Vermont when compared to other states, a fact that continues to the present day, they have had a disproportionate and positive impact on the state's culture. In Vermont, the few instances of overt racism attacking the physical well-being of minorities taking place in the past nonetheless provide little solace within the population at its possibility. Various programs have come and gone, but one in particular has persisted to current times demonstrating the enduring goodwill of the state's people. The roots of the Fresh Air Fund began in New York City in 1869 in an effort to bring thousands of inner-city children into a rural environment for brief periods during the summer.[31] Beginning in 1877, Vermonters provided them opportunities to see and experience life from a different perspective away from the slums and crime that the metropolitan centers offered. In Vermont's NEK, the presence of these children and young adults generated a range of interest and community involvement ranging from open-armed welcome to the shattering events in Irasburg.

Why Irasburg became the scene of Vermont's coming of age on the issue of race demands a study beyond the scope of this book. Harper Lee's well-received *To Kill a Mockingbird* (1960), and film of the same name starring Gregory Peck (1962), provided a needed basis for contemporary discussion on the topic. It was a moment when Vermonters advocated for their children's exposure to racial issues in the easily-understood context of a white attorney advocating on the behalf of a Black client charged with raping a white woman.[32] Individual perceptions thereafter regarding the specific presence of "racism" and "racial prejudice" within the state intruded into the thought processes of its inhabitants, but without definition. The newspapers they read did not generally try to define the terms they used, apparently believing, much like U.S. Supreme Court Justice Potter Stewart's pragmatic observation in 1964 regarding pornography, that "I know it when I see it," that did not require deeper introspection of racism's characteristics.[33]

The Vermont legislature itself struggled in the summer of 1968 to specifically define racial terms when called on to guide the state's place in the national debates about race and race relations (Appendix B). When the Irasburg board of inquiry rendered its findings in December that included references to race, only its lone female member ventured to express her personal feelings about the extent of suspected racism and prejudice in the state (Appendix F). Conversely, many others denied its existence making sweeping, conclusive statements muddying our understanding of Vermonters' mindsets at the time.

Excluding overt racism's intention to harm a minority community that requires no definition, others have nonetheless sought to comment and render their opinions about it in the context of what happened in Irasburg. However, they have not recognized, or failed to sufficiently differentiate, between the degree of prejudices admittedly existing within that small community and those purportedly held by the VSP providing law enforcement in a rural situation. Irasburg did not have an established police department manned by local resident-officers familiar with the community. The closest it came to any type of immediate enforcement rested with an elected constable or distant deputy sheriff who may or may not be trained or available when called upon. As a result, the VSP, already charged with statewide responsibilities and focused on the motor vehicle problem, became the default law enforcement agency as it strained to satisfy a diverse population under difficult logistical and financial constraints.

Circumstantially, condemning a strapped VSP for its purported racial prejudice in 1968 becomes problematic when considering that within its ranks, with the possible exception of a couple of men, virtually none of its officers exhibited any interest in making race an issue in their work when providing protection was their mandate. VSP Commissioner Alexander exemplified this mindset of racial tolerance during the Irasburg hearings. Born in 1904 and raised just ten miles away from the town in Glover, he recalled in his teenage years the importance of the Fresh Air Fund to the area, witnessing the presence of colored children arriving for the past "40, 50 years." "I can remember," he said, "back when I was 14, 15 years old, my mother had two" of the children at their home.[34]

Before Alexander moved away from Glover in 1928 to begin his law enforcement career as an inspector with the Vermont DMV (established in 1918), he certainly witnessed the presence of racist advocates coming into the state. The Ku Klux Klan never established a solid following in Vermont, but between 1922 and 1924 it succeeded in making inroads into several communities working out of its Rochester, New Hampshire offices. Springfield established the first state chapter, followed by others, including St. Johnsbury in the summer of 1924.[35] The year before, field representatives of the popular Fresh Air Fund traveled throughout the state to pave the way for the arrival of 1,500 children from New York City that summer.[36] In July 1924 as the Klan moved in, the effort repeated when a city organizer came to St. Johnsbury to prepare for 200 children to arrive in the community.[37] Whether in response to that work or not is not known, but that July "for the second time in two months" a local newspaper reported, "the big illuminated cross of the Ku Klux Kan with the three letters blazing behind it lit up the sky" in St. Johnsbury.[38] Unintimidated at such a display of bigotry, many of the residents continued to open their homes to the Fresh Air children.[39] Soon after, an estimated 200 Citizens of the Invisible Empire "gathered in a large meadow on the Johnson farm at St. Johnsbury Center to hear the Rev. Mr. Merrill" as he "explained at length the ideals and aims of the organization."[40] More crosses burned in Burlington, Montpelier, Barre, Plainfield and East Clarendon while along the Canadian border in Newport another appeared on a hilltop announcing the Klan's presence.[41] That September, 2,000 of its members from Maine, New Hampshire and Vermont gathered again in St. Johnsbury, this time in full regalia, arriving en masse in 300 cars.[42]

The unsavory burst of such activity did not last as the organization's presence declined in the next years, last seen in Montpelier in 1927 when hooded Klansmen paraded in the town.[43] Notwithstanding the Klan's absence, feelings of resentment existed among some of the local population because of the favorable treatment the Fresh Air Fund youngsters received. "We have done splendidly for these children who so much needed our help," one St. Johnsbury man said about them, "but let us not forget to do as much for our own."[44] That feeling continued in the next decades becoming a strong indicator of the mindset of some among the region's populace by the time of the Irasburg Affair.

When the KKK formed in the 1920s, the state's Black population constituted a seemingly unthreatening, miniscule number of individuals. While the census for 1920 shows a statewide population of 352,428 individuals, only 572 are identified as Negro. In the NEK, the combined population of the three counties numbered 57,039, including a mere eight people of color. None of them lived in Irasburg's Orleans County, a single, 19-year-old man worked in a saw mill in Essex County and seven others engaged in occupations in Caledonia County as a horse trainer in Danville and laborers at a Ryegate mill. Only one childless couple from Massachusetts lived in St. Johnsbury, Warren and Cora Freeman, where he worked as an upholsterer.[45]

By 1960, the state's Black population decreased to 519 individuals, 206 of them living in rural communities of less than 1,000 inhabitants, a characteristic of many in the NEK. The combined population of the three counties also fell by more than 10,000 individuals over the past decades to 49,012, where a total of 42 identified as Negro lived: 9 in Orleans (none in Irasburg), 7 in Essex and 26 in Caledonia.[46] While the subtle prejudice they and those of the Jewish and Catholic faiths experienced during the 1950s and 1960s did not become physically harmful, it nonetheless existed. As historian Sam Hand said of these years, "Vermonters had their prejudices."[47] It presented itself in quiet ways that did not upset the population as a whole, but instead weighed down on its victims. However, that began to change in the next few years as the social and political landscape quaked, prompted by the progressive policies of the state's first Democratic governor since 1853.

YOUNG TURKS

Philip H. Hoff constituted a force unto himself, bent on challenging and calling for change to what he considered a staid, status quo instilled by century-old Republican policies. A handsome, charismatic, driven Cornell Law School educated attorney, Hoff arrived in Vermont in 1951 soon after his graduation to pursue a job offer in Burlington. By the end of the decade, he had embarked on his way to upend Vermont's comfortable, hundred-year political order. After an unsuccessful foray into local politics as a budding alderman, in 1960 he was elected into the 246-member Republican-dominated House of Representatives as the city's sole representative, seated alongside a minority of 49 other Democrats. His gregarious ways led him to associate with other progressive freshman Democrat and Republican solons whose ages averaged two decades less than their 59-year-old peers.[48]

They called themselves the "Young Turks," recalling the efforts of students and politicians working to modernize the Ottoman Empire at the turn of the century.[49] A dozen men from both parties participated, including Republicans who later appeared during the course of the VSP "affairs": Richard W. Mallary from Fairlee (Router Bit); senior advisor, 62-year-old Stoyan Christowe from Dover (Irasburg); and, though not routinely identified as a Young Turk because of his position as a senator from Windham County, Harvard-educated and future attorney general James L. Oakes (Irasburg). Not directly involved with the problems involving the VSP, others of their members included Republican Ernest W. Gibson III of Brattleboro who served as chairman of the Vermont Public Service Board when his father, federal judge Ernest W. Gibson Jr., oversaw the Irasburg Board of Inquiry; he subsequently served as a justice of the Supreme Court. The early promise presented by this group became so apparent in 1961 that one newspaper singled them out for "special mention." They "represented the most cohesive, ultimately persuasive and forward-thinking group in an otherwise disorganized House," it wrote. "It may be predicted," it continued, they would "be the nucleus of leadership in the House in 1963 and from there who knows?"[50] They exercised their strength immediately, calling for an investigation into the state highway department placing freshman senator and member Oakes at its head as chairman.[51]

A decade later, senior member Christowe provided a succinct note for posterity tying all of the Young Turks' together. He reveled in his association with them all when its members, including Hoff and other legislative newcomers to the ranks, conferred on him the title of "Grandfather Turk." Expressing his thanks, and writing with a sense of both seriousness and levity, the Macedonia native told his friends that:

The new title I shall bear with pride and dignity and I shall pray to Allah and His Prophet Mohammed for the blessing, vigor and wellbeing of the present and future generations of Young Turks, Old Turks, and Grandfather Turks, until the time comes when I, the original Old Turk of the 1961–62 Session, become canonized and sanctified as the progenitor of our noble tribe.[52]

Much changed in the next decades when that noble tribe met in reunion in 1988 to hear their leader Hoff decry the condition the state had fallen into. He complained about the Burlington traffic and observed that "it is hard to find open land on (the) drive from Burlington to Woodstock—a lot of scrub and brush." Becoming more serious, he pivoted to reminisce about their earlier time together, remarking that "We were exponents of change" and asked his audience "How do you feel now—does the state need change?"[53]

The explosive change of the 1960s that Hoff and his fellow Turks sponsored ("A Revolution in Government," the Vermont Historical Society's *Freedom and Unity* proclaimed) began soon after his election as governor in 1962.[54] The hotly contested election saw Hoff squeak out a win over Republican Gov. F. Ray Keyser Jr. (the son of the state supreme court justice presiding over the inquiry into the Router Bit Affair in 1979) by 1,348 votes out of 121,389 cast.[55] In the NEK's three Republican stronghold counties, Keyser garnered a combined 7,607 votes to Hoff's 6,404. In Irasburg, the vote split evenly with the governor receiving 103 votes to Hoff's 100.[56] Campaigning on a platform of change, Hoff was greatly surprised to witness the accuracy of his calls after arriving at his office following his inauguration (Keyser never invited him in to discuss the transition beforehand). Devoid of any papers because his predecessor removed them, Hoff learned quickly that state government proceeded more on momentum that it did on planning.[57] It lacked clear policy direction and had little appreciation for necessary fiscal planning or how to envision and execute plans for the future. As the next years demonstrated, Hoff intended to address each of those deficiencies.

While Hoff faced myriad challenges on multiple fronts to modernize the current state of affairs for Vermonters at large, he maintained great compassion for its minorities. Not immune to the presence of prejudice, years earlier between 1958 and 1961 he successfully prevailed in a court case that drew much attention representing the efforts of foster parents in Rutland to obtain a birth certificate for a bi-racial child in their custody. Despite such issues, he believed Vermonters in general did not harbor prejudice. "Vermont has no significant racial problems," he said in 1965, attributing its absence to "Vermonters always believing in the equality of man and the dignity of the individual."[58]

However, a respected Black physiologist at UVM's medical school disagreed. Dr. H. Lawrence McCrorey, a future member of the board of directors of Hoff's initiative to bring Black children to Vermont, understood the problem from the perspective of a tiny minority community in a white state. "There is no question that a basic attitude of racism exists here," he said. When asked to define racism, he explained that it "is an attitude of innate inferiority of the Black man. And this, of course, can be manifest in several ways—in actual maneuvers designed to block the Black man's attainment of basic human goals, i.e. jobs, housing, schools, etc. Or in subtle ways like racist remarks, and the failure to include Black history in the schools, or the public support given to the teaching of incorrect American history, and so on."[59] The white director of the Brandon Methodist Youth Fellowship also agreed that racism existed in Vermont. "Of course!," he said, "Anyone who thinks otherwise is either a dreamer or a fool." When asked to define it, he replied in characteristically Vermont fashion, likening it "to a cesspool used infrequently. It develops a crust which cuts off the odor making it doubly treacherous to the unwary."[60] Racism's subtle characteristics did exist and after the national Civil Rights Act of 1964 became law, Hoff began to push for changes in the state's fair-housing policies and created the Governor's Commission on the Status of Women.[61] Vermonters also took separate actions to counter the racial confrontations taking place in the South when some departed between 1965 and 1967 to participate in the "Vermont in Mississippi" project seeking to strengthen Black leadership.

At the same time, the momentum for change nationally fomented by Black people rioting in 1967 in Newark and Detroit (where 43 died and 1,400 buildings burned) had significant consequences in Vermont.[62] A commission chaired by Illinois Gov. Otto Kerner, with New York City mayor John Lindsay as its vice chairman, studied the mayhem and wrote a telling report identifying its roots. Its undeniable conclusion seared an impression into Hoff's mind when he read that America was "moving toward two societies, one Black and one white—separate and unequal," blaming white racism for the problem. It also made an impression in Vermont where one newspaper editor opined months before the Irasburg violence that "The race problem is far removed from us here in Vermont, but rural America has the obligation to make a contribution to the problem." The town of Randolph, he said, and many other Vermont towns, "would be a truly American community if it had a better balance of population and the nation would benefit, by welcoming Negro families who would contribute to the life of our communities, and the work that needs doing in all of them." The Vermont Development Department and local Chambers of Commerce needed to coordinate with other agencies, he said, to see what could be done to involve the state in finding job opportunities for Black Americans.[63]

The Kerner report also advocated for generous provisions for that part of the population in the form of costly programs and guaranteed incomes, irrespective of an individual's willingness or ability to contribute. Laying such burdens on a society resentful of such favoritism generated little acceptance. In March 1968, national journalist and Pulitzer Prize winner William S. White wrote in a Vermont newspaper that proceeding in this manner constituted "an invitation to deprived or simply angry people to seek their remedy in yet more violence. This is the melancholy reality of it."[64] Other experts agreed, including a Detroit psychiatrist and law professor closely studying the rioting the year before on the behalf of the National Institutes of Mental Health. Tired of the "etiquette of social science research today," he dismissed the Kerner Commission's underlying premise that racism existed. Instead, he said that those responsible for the rioting generally made "a good income and they were rather confident about themselves and their future." The disturbances did not result because of hopelessness and despair, he continued, but, rather, as an expression of the kinds of trouble society should expect when "the closer the distance becomes between the lower and middle class, the more militant and aggressive and assertive the lower class becomes."[65]

THE VERMONT YOUTH PROJECT IN "HUNGER COUNTY"

The divergence in opinion flooding the nation on whether racism, poverty and despair prompted inner city rioting, or any of the other countering points of view, had legitimacy constituted secondary issues to Hoff. He thought the issue boiled down to public safety prompting him to position Vermont, a "tranquil island in a sea of civil strife," to enter into the fray.[66] "I was shocked," he said of the Kerner Commission report, "because in anyone's terms it was the most scathing indictment of white society I have ever read." He called the racial situation in the country a "national disgrace," believing that "We as Vermonters and Americans simply must do something about this national disgrace. It is a problem which threatens to destroy our nation."[67] Similarly, on another occasion he wrote, "We know that the seeds of the conditions which have led to explosions in the cities exist in Vermont. As Americans and Vermonters, we have a responsibility for the safety and welfare of this country's citizens."[68] His principal assistant, Secretary of Civil and Military Affairs Benjamin M. Collins, emphasized that viewpoint expressing Vermont's need to intervene in some fashion on the basis of public safety to quell the rioting. "We are responding to the threat of civil disorder," he said, "and not the need for human dignity and social justice."[69] A resolution passed by Vermont's Legislative Council on April 11, 1968, reinforced Hoff's direction and called for a study committee to determine the state's role in "the struggle for Negro equality."[70]

The ensuing brain-child of the Hoff-Collins initiative took the form of the Vermont-New York Cooperative Youth Project, an ambitious supplement to the already existing Fresh Air Fund in place for over a century. At this particular moment in fashioning Vermont's response to race relations, their plan did not break new ground. In 1944,

Rev. Alvah "Ritchie" Low, originally from Aberdeen, Scotland, of the United Church of Johnson instituted a similar effort. He too felt the need to accelerate the state's role in race relations after spending time in Harlem speaking with Black lawyers, doctors, soldiers and others about their problems. "Race relations," he said, "is one of the touchiest subjects facing this country today and the time has come for the church to give expression to its talk and resolutions. The time has come when goodwill must be more aggressive. Sermons are not enough. Trouble is just around the corner if we don't do more to give the colored people of the nation equal opportunity with the white man."[71]

Low's concerns for their plight led him to work with well-known Black leader Rev. Adam Clayton Powell at the Abyssinian Baptist Church in New York City. Together, they created the program to bring children from Harlem under the auspices of Powell's church to Vermont in the summer to spend time in rural settings.[72] More than 80 Black children first arrived in 1944, and then in the next years, coming to 20 communities spread out across northern Vermont, including Irasburg, Newport, Derby Line, Troy, Westfield and Lowell.[73] The program drew such acclaim that *Time* and *Newsweek* magazines wrote stories about them and officials in Connecticut and New Hampshire copied the "Ritchie Low Program." A robust social gadfly penning his many "Just Between Ourselves" columns for Vermont newspapers, Low went on to write "The Vermont Plan for Racial Tolerance." He became an important voice in race relations and traveled throughout New England spreading the word before his early death in 1949 at age 50.

Two decades later, and apparently unaware of Low's pathbreaking work, Vermont officials felt the need to do something as soon as possible. At Hoff's direction, Collins coordinated with Mayor Lindsay to bring some 600 Black and Hispanic teenagers from the city's ghettos to Vermont during the summer of 1968. Because they believed it necessary to have a similar number of white Vermonters attend, their plan included a recruiting process to gain their support and participation from around the state. Housing the many young people meant using the dormitories at the state's three colleges (Castleton, Johnson and Lyndon), the University of Vermont and the Job Corps Camp site in Ripton. Costs for the project bringing them and their counselors together for three two-week periods was estimated at $300,000. Hoff and Collins established a private non-profit corporation called the Youth Project of Vermont, Inc., with both serving as officers (Hoff became its president concurrent with his duties as governor) and on its executive committee, to receive and distribute the necessary money. The two men poured their energy into the project devoting substantial time throughout the spring and summer communicating with a variety of private and institutional donors for support. "I hope," Hoff told one contributor in May, "to demonstrate that Vermont's commitment is continuous and not a function of my being in office."[74]

The chronology of Vermont's frenzied efforts to institute Hoff's goals explains the mismanagement plaguing those trying to make it a reality in such a short time. No pre-planning with an eye towards its future effects occurred beforehand that eventually caused the project to falter and die in just two years. Not until Hoff's and Collin's arrangements with Lindsay had gotten well under way, the legislature's Equal Opportunity Study Committee conducted its first meeting on May 27 at the State House to pursue its April 11 mandate to convene.[75] The rushed atmosphere surrounding its work (conducted on a "crash basis," Collins said) forced it to admit that Hoff's project was "organized on short order with very little advance preparation."[76] Hurrying in their work, 15 people attended the meeting, representing eclectic interests from the legislative and executive departments, education, law, industry, the media, religion and (its sole Black member) the head of the Burlington chapter of the NAACP.

While the legislature charged the committee with "defining the role of Vermont in the field of race relations," even the most basic parameters of its work remained unanswered. As its chairman reminded its members, the "question of a definition of what the mission of the committee might be" remained open. Nobody could identify specifically the extent of their authority believing that, generally, their goal was to provide policy directives that would "probably" be long-term. Essentially adrift in their venture, identifying appropriate terms when referring to the races as "Black," "black," "White," "white," "Yellow," "Red," and "Brown" in different contexts challenged the committee in deciding when such terminology should be used (Appendix B). The appropriate use of the word "ghetto" also entered into their discussions indicating further consternation in how to communicate with others about their work. Despite their good intentions, a questionnaire sent out by the committee to the Black community seeking its input omitting the word "Negro" offended a substantial number of people.[77] On all levels, the appropriate use of language addressing sensitive race-related issues threatened to provoke the ire of many.

Other views diverged as the committee's members reflecting their varied constituencies disagreed whether racism even existed in Vermont while some acknowledged its presence. Over the course of several hours, they discussed: the need for legislation to deal with discrimination; the costs associated with running Hoff's youth project; whether to make $10 weekly payments to each of the participants; the use of state facilities to house the teenagers; and staffing. While a legislator forcibly interjected at one point that "morals can be legislated and attitudes can be changed by legislation," Hoff's fellow Grandfather Turk, Stoyan Christowe, seems to have disagreed, proposing a more radical observation on race relations. "Sometimes revolution is forced," he said, "upon people by circumstances" referring to his own experience in Macedonia with the Turks. His pragmatic observation acknowledged that despite all the planning one might wish for to institute Hoff's goals, the momentum for change had already shifted out of their hands and into the emotions of the populace. Irasburg soon confirmed the accuracy of his prediction. At the end of their meeting, the most the committee could offer was its support and a hope it all worked out well (Appendix C).

Politically, Deane Davis campaigning in the Republican primary for governor, expressed his own reservations about Hoff's and Collin's frenzied planning for such a large project. However, he chose to support it because of Hoff's nationally-recognized commitment of the state to serve as a laboratory for racial change that he did not want to see fail. While the press rapped Davis for his reported disinterest in the Black plight because he publicly clashed with Hoff ("I just don't believe there is any great amount of white racism in Vermont," he said), his record supporting various projects on their behalf belies that allegation.[78] Extant records of Hoff's non-profit corporation reveal further that he personally contributed $200 to it in 1968.[79]

The press also weighed in on the youth project in ways causing significant concern among the participating teenagers that summer viewing it as biased. "Vermont teenagers and their parents," one summary of the project relates, "led the denunciation of the mass media as the single greatest culprit in fanning the flames of fear and misunderstanding. Many expressed great anger at the way they perceived the press slanting and distorting their programs."[80] Their perception of biased, uninformed reporting continued throughout the summer and fall as the Irasburg Affair unfolded. It subjected many other people to the same unfair treatment the students reported, and with lasting consequences.

With his fractured plan in place, Hoff announced it to the public. He also proclaimed May as "Vermont Response Month" calling on Vermonters to read the Kerner report and "to look into their hearts and minds" for guidance to lead the way for the rest of the country. Mayor Lindsay immediately lavished praise on Hoff's efforts, taking "enormous pride in giving this project my full support." He, too, looked forward to the results of the experiences of his city's youth in the Green Mountains hoping "to develop a new generation of citizens who are neither separated by ignorance of each other as individuals, crippled by racial hatred and discrimination, nor immobilized in mutual progress by regional prejudices and fear."[81] The Vermont Council of Churches Board of Trustees also threw its weight behind the effort. Calling on the state's various congregations, that body sought their cooperation seeking ways to "establish better understanding of our common humanity with all mankind under the Fatherhood of God."[82] The message was warmly received in Irasburg where one local clergyman soon charged to the forefront in a personal battle fighting racism.

Placing these young adults around northern Vermont meant utilizing locations in the NEK and surrounding communities where more challenging living conditions existed than in the rest of the state. In 1968, 23.1% percent of Vermont's population lived in poverty (compared to .007% in California and 13.8% in New York), reflected in Orleans County where one in four suffered from want of adequate food.[83] Local residents also experienced the recent embarrassing revelation from the National Committee on Hunger and Malnutrition that they lived in one of the nation's 300 so-called "hunger" counties.[84]

In Orleans County alone, 241 families and their 1,030 members relied on Vermont's decidedly deficient food stamp program for support. "How can there not be (malnutrition)," one area official explained to a shocked public on hearing the news, "when you have people with weekly incomes of $60 (minimum wage in 1968: $1.40 an hour) and seven or eight children to feed?"[85] On hearing the news, State Director of the Office of Economic Opportunity Thomas C. Davis (son of campaigning gubernatorial candidate Deane Davis) ordered officials around the state to scour their files for evidence of instances affirming the national committee's assessment. Quickly finding proof of malnutrition and rickets in victims in the NEK, Davis alerted Hoff the bad news appeared true. He also admitted that it was "a long existing problem which only recently has been highlighted."[86]

A shaken Hoff, heavily focused on his youth project, ordered an inquiry into the situation, headed by Lt. Gov. John Daley leading a 7-car convoy of officials on a "Poverty Tour" across the NEK on June 4, 1968. Despite their want and hunger, residents unashamedly opened their doors to show them how they lived. "We saw and heard of situations," Daley said, "that were—I just could not describe them to you—things that I had been told existed but I had never really believed it. There were children living in such squalor that it was difficult to eat your lunch."[87]

The experience left Daley and several members of his team "visibly shaken," according to Department of Mental Health Commissioner Jonathan P. A. Leopold reporting back to Hoff.[88] It incapacitated him to such an extent that when he headed a community meeting that evening he performed poorly, Leopold said, "apparently severely upset by the observations he had made on the tour." Standing in front of Newport's crowded Municipal Hall ("filled nearly to capacity" with some 400 attendees), Daley and his team listened to area residents explain the stresses in their lives. A transcript of the hearing and Leopold's moving account details a list of challenges the poor faced: the inadequate food stamp program; the inability of the poor to pay for hot school lunches for their children; the need to increase the minimum wage to $2.00; high property taxes consuming inadequate social security benefits; not buying food in order to pay expensive hospital bills; their inability to obtain adequate paying work because of a lack of training; and, children leaving school to support their families.

The head of the local poverty agency, Community Action for the Northeast Kingdom, wrote to Daley after his departure detailing the things they saw that day having such an effect on him. They included the "dire need of indoor plumbing, running water, hot water systems, bathing facilities, central heating, sound roofing and numerous other home repairs."[89] Obtaining personal financing for these improvements from the federal Farmers Home Administration proved out of the question, he related. Many of the families they saw on their tour had already been refused its assistance because they could not demonstrate an ability to repay the loans "or simply because the family has a reputation which is considered 'unacceptable' to the FHA administrator."

Regardless of their education, employment or personal hardships that one woman at the meeting said was widespread in many county families, another explained simply that those impoverished residents only wanted "decency and acceptance in their community." While one legislator witnessed vehement dislike during the tour for their intrusions ("When I talk to these people, I sense an iron curtain going up. They get very, very mad. They don't want to know what I have seen. The reaction has been almost vicious"[90]), the meeting ended in a peaceful manner where "quietness and orderliness" prevailed. "The statements made by many of the deprived," Leopold wrote, "were simple, eloquent and extremely moving while they were talking about the two most basic needs of man—food and shelter." "I am impressed," he told Hoff, "with the gravity of the situation and the absolute necessity for finding means to resolve the problem."

The solution seemed beyond the communities' ability to obtain when faced with a large population forlorn at any prospect of assistance bringing in industry, creating paying jobs able to satisfy even their basic needs and increasing educational opportunities in order to maintain stability attracting the young to remain. Orleans school teacher Howard Frank Mosher, the author of the acclaimed *A Stranger in the Kingdom* based on the approaching Irasburg Affair, emphasized the need to improve education. "Our impoverished rural children," he said, "desperately need the early vocational training, remedial reading classes, and health and psychological services that better schools could provide. The deprivation of poor people in the Northeast Kingdom is outrageous, but that of their children is intolerable."[91]

The NEK's reputation as a place where poverty and lack of education reigned and in Orleans County where its inhabitants suffered from hunger and malnutrition presented only a part of the problem. That same month, 120 union and government officials from around New England met at Stratton Mountain to advance their shared economic concerns and to hear about the conditions in Vermont. Admitting his own "state of shock" from his recent visit to the NEK, Economic Opportunity Director Davis called for action to address "a very, very bad rural poverty situation in the state." "What we saw there," he told the assembly, "was very, very bad. It was unbelievable that somehow we could allow such a thing to happen to people of this state."[92] On another day, the conference members attended a picnic at Dorset's Emerald Lake where over 400 poverty-stricken Vermonters and their children from the southern part of the state were bused in to share a cookout and tell their stories. One child from the many identified as skinny, with bad teeth and wearing ragged clothing drew laughter when he went up to a Black union member and rubbed his arm "to see if the color would come off." The event astounded the out-of-staters witnessing the ravenous group wolf down hotdogs and hamburgers before boarding the buses to return home. After they left, the union people talked among themselves and expressed their outrage at what they witnessed.[93]

When the conference ended, one Waterbury, Connecticut union member, who was Black, and with tears in his eyes, told a Vermont official about his impressions of that day. "How can people legislate against people like this and deny them the bare necessities of life? God help us all. They're happy today, but tomorrow they have to go back into the blackness of their lives. We've got to do more, we've got to do more."[94] Over the next two weeks a reporter traveled the back roads of Bennington and Rutland counties and wrote a devastating eight-part series of articles describing what he saw.[95] He encountered so many compelling instances of poverty that his reporting presented a devastating indictment of the state's condition in the south repeating the same dire situation officials witnessed in the NEK.

The situation appalled and incited Vermont's Commissioner of the Department of Administration, William F. Kearns Jr. On June 10 he pled with Hoff to immediately launch "a complete war on poverty," headed by "a Supreme Commander to mobilize and direct the war." "Poverty is not a problem of welfare," he said, "Poverty is not a problem of education. Poverty is not a problem of health. Poverty is not a problem of jobs. Poverty is not a problem of housing. Poverty is all of these and more." To begin to remedy it Kearns called for action and that "All of the resources, men and money, of the state government should be directed against the war on poverty as a first and over-riding priority." Avoiding any reference to Hoff's pending youth project and its costs, Kearns tactfully said that "By licking the problem of poverty and its attendant conditions, the future allocation of resources would be much more effectively used than they can be, or have been, in the present situation."[96]

Two days later, Lt. Gov. Daley leading Hoff's Committee on Hunger in Orleans County released its 10-page list of problems it identified during its NEK tour proposing solutions for him to consider, followed by its one-on-one meeting with him.[97] Then, on June 14 another of Hoff's high-level committees, this one headed by Commissioner Kearns calling separately for immediate action on the poverty issue, provided him with an additional list of fifteen important challenges state agencies faced in providing for the common weal.[98]

Overwhelmed at the many demands made on him in this last term as governor and unable to focus on any one of them despite his promise to tackle poverty head on, Hoff did nothing. His inaction, together with the state's inability to provide necessary funding for the many deficient programs his administration identified, later led a frustrated Daley to reconsider his support for the youth project conducted at the expense of Vermonters. "It is my opinion," he said, "that our concern should be directed at taking care of deprived children in Vermont. When we have completed that task, and when we have no more deprived children in the state, we should then look beyond our borders and do all we can to help others."[99]

Rutland Herald reporter Stephen Terry witnessed first-hand Hoff's scattered and unfocused actions during this time period and was present when he ordered Benjamin Collins to coordinate with Lindsay on the youth project. "Hoff was so involved in national matters," Terry recalled, "as well as his always deep concern over racism that he virtually all but abandoned his state responsibilities. He was also into heavy drinking which didn't help either. So, I am not totally surprised that he didn't react to the Daley report and focus on underlying poverty in Vermont and the Kingdom. In fact, Hoff could be unpredictable. He would focus on some subjects and then abandon others."[100]

At the same time, other problems hounded Hoff's efforts to bring Black teenagers to Vermont. During the spring and summer of 1968 after he announced his plans Vermonters fearful at the prospect of losing their jobs to Black new comers read repeated newspaper accounts of push back. "Vermont White Racism Block to Summer Plan," the *Rutland Herald* headlined about the youth project, together with another announcing that "Youth Program Official Finds Racism, Bigotry in Vermont."[101] When the State Library board of trustees sought support from the Marshfield community to change the name of "N-----head Pond and related feature names in Vermont," it entered its "strong local opinion" in opposition. The U.S. Department of the Interior refused to accept their decision and told the board that from then on federal "mapping agencies have been instructed to delete these names from future publications."[102] Other displays of racism and bigotry occurred around the state and by the end of May a *Rutland Herald* editorial stated plainly that "It is about time to admit, without equivocating, that Vermont is a white racist state."[103] Another article, labeled "Racism in Politics Hit," reported further that the U.S. Commission on Civil Rights called on politicians themselves to look inward at their own racist attitudes and to include Black people in the workings of the parties.[104]

Stresses related to race cut across Vermont society and politicians knew that their survival, despite their personal feelings, meant, at least, some form of public recognition of the problem. In his own rush to interject the state into the fray to fulfill his personal vision and institute the youth project, Hoff later conceded his actions doing so precipitated much of the resulting hard feelings. Admitting that "it destroyed me politically," he said that "If I were to do it again, I would make a greater effort to inform the citizens of Vermont just what was involved."[105] Unrepentant and self-assured in his progressive viewpoints embracing liberal policies, Hoff experienced further loss in his 1970 run for the U.S. Senate. After suffering a smashing defeat by his Republican opponent, he admitted again that "Once you get beyond your constituents, you're going to get out of there. And that's what happened to me."[106]

Hoff's lack of planning and persistent positioning himself too far ahead of the voters posed significant problems in 1968 for those Vermonters uninterested in embracing his goals that contributed to a particular mindset igniting the Irasburg violence. His impatience in prioritizing his pet project ahead of the state's glaring poverty and hunger problem clamoring for his attention, expecting Vermonters to ignore the crying need for food and shelter, to instead embrace the arrival of hundreds of Black teenagers made little sense to many.

Rather than solving the public safety problem Hoff said existed, he threatened one.

Chapter 2

POLICING CHALLENGES

ADAPTING

THE VSP RESPONSE TO THE CHALLENGES Hoff precipitated and its conduct in the Irasburg Affair marks a defining moment in its institutional history. The events unfolding during the summer of 1968 saw it transition from an agency primed to deal with the mayhem caused by motor vehicles to one coping with the fallout wrought by a redundant youth project impacting the Irasburg community in a hunger county, preceded only days before by the violence caused by out-of-state motorcycle gangs in Grafton. Their combined effects had a profound impact on a traumatized VSP command staff causing it to defensively retreat inward, guiding the department down a darkening path in the next years.

Before reaching that turning point, a deeper examination of the department and its history explains just how divisive 1968 was. As one of the nation's latecomers embracing the need for a police force with state-wide authority, Vermont's past reveals its hidebound treatment of law enforcement's needs. It struggled early on because of limited resources as it sought to abide legislative mandates imposed on untrained and ill-equipped agencies to do things beyond their reach. Elected town constables and county sheriffs constituted the state's only law enforcement mechanism since its founding in a situation that continued for the next century and a half. In the interim, county prosecutors (state's attorneys) and attorney generals (created in 1904) charged with enforcing the violations those officers investigated recognized the difficulties they experienced when faced with complex offenses. Irregular salaries for police from cash-strapped towns and municipalities and payment for their services on an ad hoc basis meant that statutory fees and simple good will dependent upon hoped-for rewards decided whether or not to investigate a matter. Private and public detectives from outside of Vermont, mainly Boston's Wood-Morgan Detective Agency and members of that city's police department, came to Vermont on special occasions when called in by the attorney general or governor. When not involved, the overall capacity and structure devoted to detecting and investigating lesser crimes by Vermonters remained woefully deficient.

That condition began to change in 1934 when the attorney general recommended to the legislature "the creation of an efficient system of State Police" as other states had already created that resulted in two committee studies in the next two years.[107] Their forward thinking and pragmatic members rendered a telling exposé describing the threat that creative criminals using motor vehicles, with access to deadly firepower (machineguns), posed to rural Vermonters. The state's inhabitants received protection from questionably trained, elected sheriffs, and their politically-appointed deputies, and sparse numbers of police chiefs. Both committees called for an overhaul of the disjointed, piecemeal practices, derisively terming it an "ancient system" that included, among several others, various agencies with enforcement responsibilities (motor vehicles, fish and game, fire, identification, and attorney general) to transition into a single entity able to deliver the protections that those living outside of Vermont already received. No valid reason could explain why those residing in the metropolitan centers should have an advantage over them because, one committee wrote in telling fashion, "Rural people are entitled to organized police protection as much as those who dwell in cities."[108] The effort met a resounding defeat in 1937 by a vote of 170–19 in the House of Representatives because of costs associated with its implementation. The legislature also favorably answered the vociferous calls in the press that a state-wide enforcement capability would threaten the ability of sheriffs to collect fees.[109] Fourteen sheriffs and their 300 deputies, more than 250 constables, and police chiefs in 12 communities around Vermont could breathe a sigh of relief that such an entity would not threaten their comfortable ways. This condition persisted throughout the World War II years before jolting them out of their complacency.

Created in 1947, the VSP (a part of the Department of Public Safety) represented a reactive response to a sad incident. The manner of its formation is characteristic of the way that many of the state's past legislative directives were instituted, resisting proactive measures in the face of obvious need until necessity forced change. It occurred because of a tragedy in Bennington in December 1946 when 18-year-old Bennington College sophomore Paula Jean Weldon failed to return from a hike.[110] The confusion over how to conduct the search for her entangled the county sheriff's department, the Vermont Highway Patrol (VSP's predecessor), FBI and police from New York and Connecticut putting on embarrassing public display the state's inability to respond to an emergency.

Weldon's disappearance propelled a previously resistant establishment to move forward and create a department of public safety. Gov. Ernest W. Gibson Jr., later in charge of the Irasburg Board of Inquiry, proposed the new agency and in January 1947 during his inaugural address briefly mentioned it when he sought legislative approval. Deeming it a "desperately needed" measure, he envisioned the existing motor vehicle department being rolled up into the VSP with expanded authority to investigate crimes. He also noted the increased stature the state could command because of its officers. "Garbed in a distinctive uniform," he said, and "traveling in a distinctive automobile will not only be helpful in preventing crime and in protecting property damage in rural areas, but can be a great advertising medium for our state."[111] The measure passed by a vote of 146–77 in the House of Representatives and 23–6 in the Senate that Gibson signed into law on May 18, 1947. Why it took so long to implement such a measure, one so obvious to other states, can be attributed in large part to a fierce independent streak, a characteristic made obvious to one researcher of the VSP in the 1990s when he interviewed a legislator opposing a proposal that could benefit Vermont law enforcement. "I voted against that bill," he said, "because I figured that Ethan Allen would have voted against it if he was here!"[112] The solon's telling and flippant candor admitting his unwillingness to assist police is enlightening, but not wholly unsurprising in light of the reputation the VSP gained beforehand during the 1968–1979 time period encompassing the Irasburg, Lawrence and Router Bit affairs.

Following its formation, the VSP experienced a relatively scandal-free, two-decade honeymoon period before Irasburg. Its relatively unremarkable formative years saw the agency grow at a modest pace in response to the dynamic growth the state witnessed, the evolving nature of crime and the expectations of Vermonters to be free from it. Between its creation and 1968, manpower increased from an initial 50 officers (working a minimum of 70 hours a week) to 102 men in 1960 (working 54 hours) and, finally, 166 (working 45 hours).[113]

By 1968, it became clear that increasing demands on the department exceeded its ability to respond, leading officials to conduct a study to identify where to concentrate limited resources. Their report, a 17-page document entitled *A Crime Control Program for the Vermont State Police*, recited only the work it did on offenses reported to the VSP and no other state law enforcement agencies.[114] The department's inability to prepare a more comprehensive report accompanied by timely data able to assist it and other agencies reflects the inadequacies that Vermont police experienced in delivering law enforcement services in the 1960s. As with the deficiencies experienced by the DMV to provide information to the Irasburg investigators about possible suspect vehicles, the fault lay with the absence of a centralized data collection capability; two deficiencies other states had either already overcome or were far into the process of correcting.‡ In 1966, VSP Commissioner Alexander explained to Hoff that he could not provide him with information he needed on his department because of "the extreme difficulty experienced in obtaining the necessary information

‡   A similar problem occurred in 2021 when Gov. Phil Scott blamed Vermont's Department of Labor's antiquated "50-year-old mainframe" computer system for allowing massive program fraud involving some 90% of claims made to it. https://vtdigger.org/2021/04/30/labor-department-suspends-online-claims-system-to-curb-surge-of-fraud/

and statistics required to conduct a proper analysis."[115] Months later, the chief of statistics for the DMV and VSP reiterated that "There is a definite need for a system of collecting, processing, filing, and analyzing of criminal offenses known to all law enforcement agencies in the state. The collection of this data would result in a clear picture of the crime trends in the state and measure the results of investigative activity to solve crimes."[116] Without the ability to assess the true nature of Vermont's crime problem, police struggled in a piecemeal fashion to understand the challenges before them and plan for the future, or to solve offenses in a timely manner.

Issuing on Aug. 1, 1968 while in the throes of the Irasburg investigation, the VSP's report opened, "Vermont's crime record, following the national pattern, has shown a sharply worsening trend." Major crimes investigated by the department increased 131.9% since 1958, while minor crimes grew 169.9%. Overall, the number of investigations exploded from 2,691 in 1958 to 6,841 in 1968, headed by offenses related to larceny and breaking and entering; the latter demanding long hours to investigate. Additionally, those constituting murder, rape and assault also caused great concern. "Such crimes," the report said, "with their overwhelming impact on human lives, outrage the citizenry, as other, more numerous offenses do not, and the time and effort required for their investigation are far greater than their numbers tend to suggest." Further, "Faced with this rapidly growing crime problem and the prospect that it will continue to become worse each year as the population grows, as improved highways make transportation of persons and goods faster and easier into and through Vermont, and as activities (such as pari-mutuel racing) formerly not seen in the state are introduced," the department warned it "feels strongly that now is the time to take decisive steps to increase the effectiveness of the State Police in fighting crime."

Abiding by the predictions of other officials of rapid, approaching growth in the next years, the VSP also recognized the important role it played allowing it to happen. "This Department has a very real and heavy responsibility in connection with this expansion for developing a program which will provide the necessary protection of lives and property. Assurance of adequate law enforcement and police protection will most certainly have considerable bearing on Vermont's desirability as a place to locate industries and as a place in which people will desire to live and work." Reading those words reveals the VSP's understanding that its function in government was to provide the requisite underlying safety necessary for the state to advance in standing and not to impede that progress by engaging in petty racist behavior.

However, that laudable feeling did not extend entirely throughout Vermont's law enforcement community. Perhaps the most notorious practitioner offsetting the goals expressed by the VSP was Addison County State's Attorney Ezra Dike, an opinionated official and Bristol store owner who had little tolerance for Black people. Tired of the "punks" and "hippies" responsible for area crime, he singled out Blacks for particular attention. "You know," he said, "you can say all you want to about the Ku Klux Klan, but this country was a damn sight better when they were riding high." Attacking the court system for its role in advancing civil rights, calling them "civil wrongs," he said that "The biggest trouble today is the recent Supreme Court decisions. Because of them, a few damn stinking n-----s and hippies are padded. The other 90% of us are stomped on." "Now, I don't care if any n----- comes in my store," he said, "He can come in here if he wants any time. He can come in here and buy what he wants and get the hell out. I ain't waiting on a damn n-----." When Dike learned of the matters unfolding in Irasburg, he called it "a damn left-wing attempt to discredit the state police."[117] Such clearly racist statements from an official occupying the highest law enforcement function in the county was soon reflected fifteen miles away in Ripton where Black youth project teenagers assembled only to experience a hostile reception from the community.

CRIME AND VIGILANTES

Dealing with issues related to the looming societal problems outside of Vermont, such as race, that could influence the relocation of others into the state able to assist its economic growth was not reflected in the VSP's report for 1968. Instead, it recited the overwhelming number of complaints it received concerning the property-related offenses of burglary (1,198 in 1968) and larceny (1,029). These two crimes drew not only the attention of the VSP, but a frustrated public threatening to institute vigilante measures to deal with it if the police could not. The specter of a return of vigilantism scared the state's political leaders in 1968 recognizing its potential presence during the Irasburg violence. This more recent display recalled an incident a decade earlier involving the death of Newbury farmer Orville "Hoot" Gibson in 1957. Already disliked, Gibson reportedly beat an elderly hired hand for spilling milk drawing great anger from local residents. Gibson went missing that New Year's Eve, discovered three months later on the bank of the nearby Connecticut River, trussed up and drowned. Allegations characterized by future Gov. Deane Davis's secretary of civil and military affairs, Attorney General Frederick Reed, called it a "vigilante slaying" involving two local men seeking retribution against Gibson for the assault. However, charges prosecuted by Reed against one of them resulted in his acquittal (the case against the second man was later dismissed) leaving the question of vigilantes' involvement or if it was a suicide an open matter that lasts to this day. It soon turned political when members of the community expressed their great displeasure at the trial's outcome. Nine local residents demanded that the governor bring in the FBI to investigate. If he did not, they planned to petition the U.S. Senate to investigate "Vermont's political organizations, our judiciary and our law enforcement organizations."[118]

The raw emotion that Gibson's unsolved death generated remained in the next years and on its tenth anniversary in 1967 a newspaper recounted the inaction of other attorney generals to solve it. Listing off their names to their further embarrassment, they included Charles J. Adams, Charles E Gibson Jr., John P. Connarn and current attorney general James Oakes who, it wrote, "is not known now to have done anything about the case so far."[119] Months later, another paper exhorted Oakes "to retain an active interest" in the Gibson case, insinuating a threat to his political future that became all too real by the time of the Irasburg violence.[120] As Oakes explained to the Irasburg board of inquiry in November 1968, defensively justifying his intrusion into the ongoing VSP investigation, he said he perceived this more recent violence as indicative of the continued presence of vigilantes in the state. "I did not want, during my term as Attorney General," he said with particular emphasis, "to have another vigilante case go unsolved and I was determined, come hell or high water, that we were going to discover the person who committed this particular crime."[121] Oakes's fault lay not with the urgency of the Irasburg investigation that the VSP agreed with, but in his highly unusual intrusion into it contrary to established protocol that only complicated and strained the relationships between their agencies.

Other examples of vigilantes threatening public safety in far-off cities was also evident. Vermonters read FBI Director J. Edgar Hoover's assessment of the problem in an article headed "Emergence of Vigilantism Threatens U. S. Society" just a month before the Irasburg violence. He offered little hope for the immediate future warning of the approaching "long, hot summer" that could descend into "an unprecedented holocaust of racial conflict."[122] Vigilante groups formed in Chicago and Newark as "anti-riot" civilian forces assuming such names as PRE-ARM (People's Rights Enforced Against Riots and Murder) driving through Black and Hispanic neighborhoods stopping and searching cars.[123] The National Rifle Association also intervened admonishing its 800,000 members to arm and present themselves as "a potential community stabilizer."[124] As Hoff planned his youth project in Vermont, an anonymous critic warned him what could happen as a result with a bit of doggerel aping the NRA's recommendation:

> Hoff wants to bring n-----s to the North Country
> and wants them to live with you and me.
> But as any casual observer will see,
> No n-----s will be living near his family.
> So Hoff claims Vermont responsibility,
> For riots that happen down country.
> But he and Lindsay overlook one trifle,
> Every Vermont farmer owns a 30-30 rifle.[125]

Other examples of Vermonters threatening to assemble in vigilante style between 1967 and 1968 also existed. On one occasion, unidentified individuals entered into a remote "hippie" village in Marshfield, where N-----head Pond was situated, to dynamite some of their huts. When they did not move out, a headline announced its near-total destruction, "Burned by Vigilantes" setting five of their six huts on fire that brought in VSP arson investigators.[126] Burlington car dealers tired of nighttime vandalism and thefts of vehicles parked in their lots threated to form a vigilante force of their own if police could not provide protection.[127] Residents living along Lake Champlain faced so many instances of "roughnecks" invading their property they formed their own "patrol by boat, at night" to ward them off.[128] One owner of a small island near Isle La Motte expressed additional concerns about the lawlessness on the lake. "Prior to 1930, vandals had stripped the Island of its seven cottages or buildings," he wrote, carrying off their contents without facing punishment. More recently a large group of "60 to 80 ruffians and desperados—mostly from Canada" arrived to wreak their havoc tearing off no trespassing signs, cutting down trees, harassing a young caretaker couple, and leaving "broken bottles, tin cans, food scraps, rubbish and filth" in their wake. "The indecency, lewdness and immorality of these infidels and despoilers is astounding and indescribable," he said. Commiserating with his plight, all Gov. Davis's secretary Frederick Reed could offer in the aftermath of the Irasburg Affair was that his complaint "poses a real problem to Vermont." "The Governor has great sympathy," he responded, "with land owners who are faced with problems such as yours and would like to have far more police available, but at the present time we are badly understaffed throughout the state."[129]

Threats of additional violence existed on the Massachusetts border in Pownal where yearly influxes of large numbers of hippies began arriving in 1967 to take over abandoned buildings once occupied by migrant negro agricultural workers. Locals and others from far off drove by to harass them working in their gardens and ogle as they bathed naked in a nearby stream prompting local officials to seek assistance from the governor's office. Reed intervened once again and directed the VSP to investigate and then meet with him to "discuss what possible moves can be made, not only in Pownal, but in other areas where these hippie colonies are being established to the end that we might find some way to clean them out."[130] Other examples of potential lawlessness because of a scarce police presence occurred when so many valuable dogs were stolen around the state. As one newspaper claimed, "It used to be a hanging affair to steal a man's horse. It should also be one for those who steal pet dogs. If authorities can't take care of the obnoxious characters running this racket maybe some vigilante action is called for."[131]

Reflected in the VSP crime report of 1968, complaints of burglaries of remote, seasonal homes and camps posed significant problems. One of Hoff's and Oakes's admirers wrote to each earlier strongly addressing the issue. Describing a litany of dozens of burglaries in Roxbury (including the 130 committed by one man) and 1,400 parolees roaming the roads, he lamented that Vermont was home to an "evil cult" of criminals. The unacceptable number of break-ins demanded, he said, that they support the state's police more aggressively. They deserved it, he wrote, because "the Vermont law enforcement officers I have met on every level and without exception, have impressed me as dedicated men. They display a devotion to duty that the public should deeply value; and they should be encouraged, not discouraged, by the state's administration."[132]

In Bradford, officials described the volume of burglaries as "the No. 1 law enforcement problem in this area" warning against the "formation of vigilante groups."[133] The situation led one NEK landowner victimized by a burglary to contact Gov. Davis pleading for help providing a telling characterization of the kinds of challenges that law enforcement faced in this particular rural environment at the time of the Irasburg violence. "There are among the local youth," he wrote, "hot-rod hippies, some of whom have been in trouble with the courts more than once. They are well-known to the local residents but taking affirmative action is avoided for fear of greater reprisals such as burning down a barn or store. From what I gather those youths have no fear of the law. Their families employ a former governor now practicing law in Barton (Lee E. Emerson, who played a role in the Irasburg Affair); and whether or not the prestige of their lawyer is the reason, the judge in Newport repeatedly lets them off with a 'slap on the wrist.' This, in turn, discourages the state troopers who, in my opinion, are by and large a fine group of men; but there are just not enough troopers to adequately patrol this region."[134]

In southern Vermont's Windham County, another twist to the burglary problem presented itself. The huge influx of commuting out-of-staters prompted adventurous developers working in an atmosphere devoid of zoning laws to construct more than 4,000 new homes, with an additional 5,000 projected by 1974. The savvy businessmen quietly purchased small acreages adjoining one another to combine them into large, single tracts sometimes exceeding 500 acres. Vermont officials had no appreciation of their intentions until 1969 when the tax department, much to its surprise, uncovered at least sixty-eight transfers of large tracts to the private developers. The largest, 27,000 acres in the Camel's Hump area, was followed by 4,000 acres in the southern Vermont town of Readsboro.[135] Land values rocketed upwards forcing the owner of a 55-acre woodlot in Guilford paying $24 a year in taxes beforehand to pay $585 by 1967.[136]

Predictably, the unattended new homes brought numerous complaints of more burglaries and loss of property. The chairman of the regional planning commission complained that a lack of police presence to stop it threatened a return of vigilantism in the form of "local citizen law enforcement." That year a single individual drove round the county's back roads and in two neighboring counties committing a staggering fifty-one burglaries before his capture. A VSP supervisor understood the frustrations citizens expressed at a community meeting, but warned that vigilantes were not the answer. Admitting that he had too few men to cover the seventeen towns under his command, with troopers working eighteen-to-twenty-hour days, he solicited the public to understand their lack of resources and instead be on alert to "spot alien cars" and report them.[137]

The inability of the VSP to provide a sufficient number of troopers to counter the troublesome burglaries was exacerbated by the public's anger at the huge number of ski thefts. They represented 43.6% of all larcenies in 1968 taking place at the state's increasingly popular ski resorts, a phenomenon linked directly with the ready access provided by the new interstate highway system. Prompted by the department's handling of Orville Gibson's death in 1958, the next year a Criminal Investigation Division (CID) formed. It relieved uniformed troopers from conducting investigations into major crimes, allowing them to continue with traffic enforcement and resolving minor offenses. Initially successful, the division of labor between them blurred when the burglaries and thefts increased so much that by 1968 overwhelmed detectives were forced to rely again on uniformed troopers for assistance. Diverted from those other responsibilities, the overall performance of the department reflected in the number of crimes cleared by arrests fell appreciably. In 1959, 21% of major crimes were solved by arrest, whereas by 1968 it fell to 17.1%.[138] As demonstrated by the difficulties the VSP faced during the Irasburg Affair that year, teamwork between the uniformed and plain clothes officers tested its ability to rise above those disappointing numbers.

The public presence of the VSP in 1968 is reflected through the work of its 124 uniformed officers and 22 plainclothes detectives; while authorized to employ 194 officers that year, the department apparently could not attract enough applicants. Because of time off, vacations, sick leave, etc., on an average day 78 troopers and 14 detectives worked, spread out over a 24-hour period. The decision to deploy personnel in certain tasks coincided with the increase in accidents taking place most noticeably between Thursday and Sunday that meant uniformed troopers' days off occurred most often between Monday and Wednesday. Reflecting the unique way that Vermont distributed its manpower, the uniformed officers worked a minimum of forty-five hours a week on either of two shifts, each nine-and-one-half-hours long from 8 a.m. to 5:30 p.m. and 5 p.m. to 2:30 a.m. Within each of the five troop areas, only a single officer remained on duty between midnight and 8 a.m.[139] They received no pay for overtime work, or when called in to attend court proceedings, and frequently saw work days extend beyond the end of their shifts.

The demands made on troopers proved so onerous in December 1965 that the department faced, according to Commissioner Alexander, "mass resignations that appeared imminent" unless a reduction in work hours took place.[140] An experimental work schedule with less hours was implemented for the next several months, but abandoned when the department returned to the status quo. No concessions came the troopers' way when Hoff's planners disagreed with Alexander that they should receive favorable treatment for their sacrifices and be afforded the same benefits other state employees experienced working a lesser number of hours. Accepting the loss, Alexander warned Hoff that because "this department has no monopoly on skilled people," in the future prospective recruits would move on to seek positions in private industry.

The heavy work load placed on troopers in 1968 included investigating an estimated 9,000 accidents a year, issuing 30,000 defective equipment tickets and between 14,000 and 15,000 other tickets, and responding to between 8,000 and 9,000 criminal complaints.[141] Calls issued for an increase of 43 more uniformed officers to handle routine enforcement and an additional 26 to deal with the increased responsibilities the recently opened interstate highway system imposed.[142] Detectives working mainly during the daylight hours, unless called out at other times, also experienced great demands for their services. Demonstrating the great care they took in investigating the troublesome number of ski thefts alone required at least three detectives. Because skis did not bear individual serial numbers identifying them, they needed to establish a clear connection between the initial theft and the thief's arrest. "In most instances," the department's 1968 report stated, "it is necessary to be at hand at the moment the crime takes place and to be able to follow the movements of the thief to the point where it can be absolutely proved that he is the culprit."[143] Despite the allocation of manpower to the effort, the department admitted that "in most instances, it is nearly impossible to apprehend" the responsible individuals.[144]

Arrests could not be made on suspicion alone, but only on clear evidence that a crime had been committed and that the person arrested did it. As Commissioner Alexander succinctly described to the Irasburg board of inquiry the two principal responsibilities of law enforcement, "It is our policy to investigate thoroughly all charges of criminal conduct and report the facts learned to the proper prosecuting authority."[145] Whether an investigation concerned a burglary, the theft of skis or someone firing a shotgun into a house, each deserved a thorough investigation before passing it on to the local state's attorney for prosecution. However, these basic instructions on accepted criminal procedure throughout the country and in Vermont seems to have fallen on deaf ears in the turmoil of the Irasburg Affair when the board condemned the VSP for following these established practices.

To overcome the manpower shortage problem in 1968, the department called for an additional seven detectives with authorization to place them in Bethel, Brattleboro, Middlebury, Rutland and St. Albans, naming a polygraph operator for the southern part of the state to assist with the more than 300 examinations it conducted annually, an additional fire investigator and to find some way to relieve the stresses caused by having two detectives assigned to the recently opened pari-mutuel race track in Pownal to ward off infiltration by organized crime.[146] The turnover rate within the department increased during these years before falling, perhaps reflecting the stresses on its members during and after the Irasburg Affair (when it carried seventeen vacant trooper positions just three months before): 4.6% in 1967, 7.3% in 1968, and 12.4% in 1969.[147]

Complicating the call for additional manpower, in January 1968 the department faced a firestorm of trouble when allegations of troopers having to comply with issuing a set quota of tickets each month arose. Caledonia County State's Attorney Sten Lium (appointed by Hoff in 1965 to replace outgoing attorney Robert D. Rachlin who was involved in the Irasburg matter), and persistent VSP gadfly in the next years, lodged the complaint in open court that immediately placed the department's command staff on the defensive. Fiercely protective of the low-paid, hard-working troopers he worked with, the 31-year-old New Hampshire native bearing Harvard credentials (B.A., J.D. and an M.B.A.), marked him as perhaps the most intelligent and formidable opponent the department higher-ups faced in these and following years, ready to attack the inequities that officers suffered under. Lium was also unafraid to defend them from challenges lodged from outside the department allowing officers the time needed to institute their own organization able to advocate on their behalf, later known as the Vermont Troopers Association.

Other state's attorneys agreed with Lium's assessment concerning the quota mandate, including some who said it interfered with the investigation of serious felonies that drew further condemnation from Hoff. A recent legislatively-imposed requirement that the department establish criteria for officers to meet in order to receive favorable performance evaluations able to increase their pay precipitated the problem. According to troopers communicating quietly with Lium and other state's attorneys, they told them that their VSP superiors imposed the requirement that they write 13 tickets a month in order to receive a positive rating. Neither Commissioner Alexander or the department's executive officer, Maj. Glenn E. Davis, denied that a quota actually existed, but challenged the prosecutors "or anyone else (who) knows of a better way to reduce lawlessness on the highway, and accidents, without a strong enforcement program to meet with them at any time for their recommendations."[148]

Lium's allegations and the defiance it generated from the VSP high command caused such consternation within the legislature that a representative introduced a bill calling for a first-of-its-kind investigation into the department's operations.[149] While the proposal evolved to include a study of all the state's law enforcement agencies, Lium maintained his steady aim on the VSP supervisors. Immediately after the Irasburg board issued its findings in December 1968 castigating the department, he produced his own paper describing the problems caused by the policies of high-ranking officers and the quota debacle. Entitled *The Vermont Department of Public Safety, 1947–1968: The Birth, Flourishing, and Degeneration of an Institutionalized Ideal,* the 21-page document summarized the department's history to recent times identifying for the first time the existence of a separate "Kingdom of Redstone" ruled by a select few wielding unlimited authority over troopers from their headquarters.[150] Concerning the quota allegation, he recounted a conversation between Maj. Davis and Capt. Harold Dean with the editor of St. Johnsbury's *Caledonian Record* that the newspaperman repeated to him. They were there, he reported, "to keep these accusations out of that paper." When asked whether arrests for minor traffic offenses "would lead to public resentment," Dean became "visibly agitated," Lium wrote. Reportedly pounding his fist "in his hand or on the table," he said "We're an army at war with the civilians, and they know it!" His emotional response repeats Commissioner Alexander's frustrations in 1965 with the department's inability to lower the staggering accident rate (more than 12,000 between 1967 and 1968) and dozens of fatalities that he said called for a "crack down." Observing Dean's outburst, Lium wrote, that Davis "sat right there and said nothing." The quota debacle, together with a litany of other complaints, led the prosecutor to call for the dismissal of the VSP high command, including Alexander. As for the self-aggrandizing and empire building that Davis and Dean pursued, Lium said they should be "neutralized."[151]

Notwithstanding the prosecutor's disdain for the VSP commanders, they survived the quota incident and went on to summarize in their report for the year the challenges the department faced with its current level of manpower. In conclusion, they warned that "It is evident that both major and minor crime is sharply increasing in Vermont, and that the greatest increases are in those types of crimes generally considered the work of habitual or professional criminals. It is also clear that present forces, both uniformed troopers and plain clothed detectives, are inadequate to permit sufficiently thorough investigations of these offenses." That prescient caution soon played out immediately as the VSP moved on to conduct the Irasburg investigation.

POLICE TRAINING

As the national problems with rioting in metropolitan centers unfolded that urban police countered in a haphazard, often violent fashion, in 1967 Vermont police came to understand their own inability to deal with it. In March, Attorney General Oakes and other police officials gathered in Montpelier to endorse a proposal to create a state Law Enforcement Training Council (LETC) to provide instruction to newly-hired local officers; an effort implicitly excluding the VSP. A factor driving their decision concerned the lack of consistent, uniform training available to police in basic law enforcement procedures. After a county sheriff pointed out that "Demonstrators in California are trained more than police officers. They are better equipped and better trained than we are as policemen," VSP Maj. Davis agreed. However, he warned, "We are completely familiar with them, and our intelligence reports tell us that they could be in Vermont overnight."[152]

In addition to preparing for the potential arrival of out-of-state agitators, the department also kept a close eye on other organizations. In 1967, it concluded that because of the increasing mobility of offenders, "crimes are no longer being committed by the local individual but in most cases by an individual(s) from quite some distance away." These included "organized groups from all the New England States, Western New York State, California and Canada (committing) crimes in the State of Vermont."[153] Other domestic groups with concerning interests, some notably racist, already drew further attention from Vermont's law enforcement community because of extremist right-wing philosophies. As identified in the files of Hoff's secretary, Benjamin Collins, they included: Freedom, Inc. (Wardsboro); Green Mountain Patriots (Shaftsbury); Green Mountain Rifleman (Bethel); The National Committee for Economic Freedom (Burlington); The Neighborhood Group (St. Johnsbury); "Neill Letters of Contrary Opinion" (Saxtons River); Vermont Freedom Forum (location unidentified); and Young Americans for Freedom (Woodstock).[154]

With the fear that outsiders bearing ulterior motives could arrive in Vermont, together with the suspect local extremists threatening dire problems, Davis and many others rallied behind the training proposal; an effort that half of all other states already embraced. While uniformly endorsed at its start, it later caused substantial problems for the VSP in the 1970s because it granted the attorney general substantial authority to administer it thereby threatening VSP dominance in training matters. Those fault lines became even more apparent when the two agencies clashed during the Irasburg investigation the next year. Thereafter, the discord only increased and interfered with VSP relationships with other local police agencies and its counties' state's attorneys. It became so bad that the two governors following Hoff considered removing the independent authority the VSP enjoyed and to place it under the control of an overarching "super agency" responsible for a number of public safety measures. The festering ill will that training caused remained until change finally occurred in the 1980s. It came about only after the suicide of a state trooper pulled into the Router Bit Affair of 1979 because of the explosive distrust existing between the governor and the VSP caused, in part, by training coinciding with the aftermath of the Irasburg Affair.

How did police training, a seemingly straightforward and uncontentious governmental oversight function, become such a divisive issue? Vermont's geography played an important role in creating the discord where, in a rural, mountainous environment, the VSP stationed officers out over a large area allowing only infrequent contact between them, instilling in each a need to rely on their own instincts because of far-off backup. Municipal and county officers did not face such a challenge because their close proximity allowed them to associate and interact with each other on a more routine basis. To achieve a similar outcome and establish its own sense of identity after its creation in 1947, the VSP instituted a training process intended to "build esprit de corps" binding its members together.[155] Police training played an essential role allowing that to happen, but was executed in haphazard fashion when past experience provided little example to follow because of Vermont's rural condition.

In 1937, when a legislative committee doubted that the state's county sheriffs employed at least "a man of sufficient aptitude and training" able to conduct investigations, it discovered that only one or two of them required deputies to attend schooling "once a week for two or three months."[156] The next year, southern Vermont police recognized the need for more intense training and created the Windham County Peace Officers' Association (1938–1973). The organization welcomed the participation of town constables, municipal police officers and county sheriffs. Unable to obtain government support to pay for it, the financial burden fell on the officers themselves. They volunteered both their time and money to attend and obtain a certificate allowing them to participate in advanced training. In 1947, as many as 61 men attended the initial courses to listen to FBI agents from the Albany division share their expertise.[157] That same year in Montpelier, those officers chosen as the first members of the VSP, with their salaries, uniforms, and equipment all paid for by the state, gathered to attend a separate course of training. Over the course of six weeks, the FBI instructors appeared again to assist the fledgling agency in getting its law enforcement bearings as quickly as possible. That early association persisted as the VSP continued to rely on training provided by federal agents in the next years while, at the same time, maintaining a persistent tight grip over its own curriculum distinguishing them from what local authorities received. As a result, the process of police training unfolded in, what one government agency called in marked understatement, an "unregulated and somewhat disjointed manner."[158]

In 1965, Commissioner Alexander admitted the challenges his department faced with training because it did not receive adequate funds to establish a separate division devoted to it. "Training has been a hit or miss proposition," he said, and that Vermont was the only New

England state without such a division in its table of organization able to address it. Notably, between the date of the department's formation in 1947 and 1964, only eight recruit classes received instruction lasting between one week and four months.[159] Neither did it have adequate facilities available to conduct training, restricted to using the Norwich University campus for just the summer months because students occupied it for the rest of the year. Despite the need for clarity and leadership in training of VSP officers that Alexander called for, Hoff's planners' parsimonious response simply told him to find the money he needed from his current budget.[160]

The law creating the VSP in 1947 required it to establish a training school for its members and also mandated that "it shall be available to local governments within the State."[161] While that obligation was fulfilled in a haphazard manner providing in-service training to local officers after receiving in-house instruction provided by their own agencies, it did not mean that the VSP had to permit them to attend initial training alongside troopers. Municipalities resented such slights and, threatened at the prospect that the new agency could alter their traditional functions, retaliated in petty fashion to limit the authority of troopers within their communities. A general understanding arose between them that because the VSP was intended as a rural-oriented department it could not come into towns with established police departments unless invited.[162] However, because law breakers did not recognize such formalities, it made the VSP's compliance impossible which only provoked additional reason for local authorities to resent their intrusions.

By 1967 the discord between the state and local police agencies reached such an intolerable level that Attorney General Oakes publicly derided their ongoing mutual attacks. Speaking publicly, he admonished them all and said that "It is time to lay aside the negative cut the other fellow's throat attitude of some, and the defensive over-protective everything we do is right attitude of others." Most police officials, he said, did their best "despite a history of being underpaid, undertrained and inadequately supported by a public, which has only recently become aware of the harm resulting from weak law enforcement;" probably referring to the examples set by out-of-state agencies responding to the urban rioting.[163] Another legislator agreed with Oakes's assessment warning that there was "little or no cooperation between state police, sheriffs' departments and local police."[164] When the legislature met to consider funding an investigation into the difficulties between agencies, a debate between Oakes and Alexander ensued. Whereas Oakes wanted the money for his LETC, Alexander sought the purchase of an additional eight cruisers to increase the mobility of his overworked troopers. Oakes ended up receiving half of the money as the remainder went into the statewide study of policing leaving Alexander the loser.

Oakes hoped that placing police training under the authority of a single agency could alleviate some of the ill feelings between police and the Vermont legislature took the first tentative steps to make it happen. Its initial effort adopted the proposal he and others endorsed, authorizing the creation of the LETC, effective July 1, 1968. It was charged with setting minimum standards and providing training for local officers separate from that conducted by the VSP. While initially placed under Oakes' authority where he could control its course, and purse strings, in 1971 the function transferred to the DPS that assumed administrative and fiscal oversight of its operations. Until that happened, an increasingly uneasy relationship existed between Oakes and the VSP that became evident during the Irasburg investigation. In his ongoing campaign for governor at the time, Oakes made many announcements in support of the state's law enforcement community, but which he seems to have known only superficially. In December 1967, he wrote to Alexander seeking something his office should have already had in its files, specifically "a list of all law enforcement agencies in the state with names of the chiefs of police."[165] Alexander duly complied and two weeks later provided him with the list and an estimate that the number of officers in them numbered approximately 250. For his further edification, Alexander told him there were 38 wardens working for the Department of Fish and Game.[166] Oakes's inability to identify specifically the constituency he advocated for, some two years into his term of office, indicates a surprising unfamiliarity with everyday policing that became even more apparent during the Irasburg Affair.

From a political perspective, Oakes unabashedly made it a point to let others know the power he wielded. Proud in his role as attorney general ("swinging his Harvardian knowledge and bearing around," one detractor said), he told the public he occupied a position as important as the lieutenant governor's allowing him to reap the same rewards as the second highest paid elected officer in the state.[167] He gained both supporters from within the legal community and opponents from outside suspicious of his motivations. The several glowing letters in Sen. Aiken's files supporting Oakes when he sought a federal judgeship in 1969 are off-set by those describing a man pursuing ulterior interests. "A Marxist Liberal," "selfish," "how will it make me look best," a "crusading liberal," Gov. Hoff's "buddy" and his final rejection by voters in his bid for governor in 1968 all disqualified him from judicial office they said.[168] Regardless, he bore his authority openly, calling himself "a proven winner" when on the campaign trail.

Oakes also explained to a public audience that while locally elected county state's attorneys handled their cases on that level, as attorney general he had "supervisory powers and indeed, does initially investigate homicides and certain felonies."[169] Unspoken in any of Oakes's pronouncements on the subject, but which he admitted during the Irasburg hearings, was his lack of authority to intrude into the investigative functions falling within the VSP's prerogative. Neither did his muddled expressions ever identify the decision-making process he used to make clear to state's attorneys and local police in which cases he planned to exercise his authority or the way in which he intended to oversee and coordinate their work. By his conduct, Oakes exploited for the first time a grey area in established police-prosecutor relations, invoking his authority when the opportunity fit his subjective interpretation of need while at the same time reserving to himself the ability to withhold it when circumstances became difficult, or embarrassing. When the Irasburg board of inquiry considered his particular relationship with the VSP in this regard, it chose to fault the latter claiming that "Commissioner Alexander and others of high rank, did not consider they should coordinate all their investigative activities with those of the Attorney General's office."[170] Notwithstanding, that finding deserves re-examination in light of the available evidence concerning Oakes's overall conduct and motivations behind it.

As Oakes worked on the LETC, the training of VSP officers proceeded throughout 1967 and 1968 in a manner consistent with "the national trend towards maintenance of law and order." Two recruit schools took place in 1967 and 1968 where new officers received "395 hours of classroom instruction and practical work, and 180 hours of supervised study and notebook preparation." Topics covered included firearms, motor vehicle laws, accident investigation, first aid, criminal law investigation and arrest, evidence, and truck weighing.[171] The department also recognized the seismic changes wrought by recent U. S. Supreme Court rulings affecting traditional enforcement methods. Beginning in 1966, immediately after decisions such as *Miranda v. Arizona* affecting the rights of suspects, the VSP instituted training that included "Civil Rights and Constitutional Guarantees" that became a part of future recruit classes.[172] The additional training received favorable responses from the troopers asking that more of it be made available. On a parallel course, for local officers Oakes assumed the responsibility to train them before the LETC conducted its first courses in May 1968. He instituted four two-day seminars conducted in Rutland, Burlington, Springfield and Barre in the fall of 1967, entitled "Techniques in Felony Investigations." They were conducted by FBI agents and members of the VSP laboratory covering evidence collection and analysis, interviewing, interrogation and prosecutions. It does not appear that Oakes arranged for those officers to receive the same kinds of training the VSP did concerning the changes that the Supreme Court ordered be implemented.

Because of the creative instincts and sophistication of out-of-state criminals arriving in the state, the VSP came to understand that many of its "former practices and techniques of investigation are now found to be unusable and ineffective."[173] This included a need for additional training beyond civil rights in other areas of criminal procedure. It became apparent in November 1967 when Barre police refused to arrest a suspect requiring the presence of the VSP and FBI to untangle. Confusion over what the Supreme Court intended in some of its recent decisions caused the conundrum forcing local police to withhold taking action in the case for fear of making a false arrest.[174] Even Vermont high school students understood the challenging problems police faced making it an issue for debating teams to argue the pros and cons of Congress establishing uniform criminal investigation procedures.[175] The caution by Vermont police to take action in Barre because of the unsettled state of criminal procedure in order to avoid liability provides an important lesson. It sheds needed light into what happened during the course of the careful investigation conducted by the VSP in Irasburg, also working to avoid criticism and liability, that Oakes intruded into and then so heavily disparaged to the board of inquiry adopting his view.

Until that rupture occurred, and concealing the growing distance between himself and the VSP, during his run for governor Oakes called for a "Three-P Plan" for all police agencies in the state concerning more pay, more prestige and more public support.[176] With state troopers making only $111 a week in 1968 and local officers leaving their departments because of inadequate salaries, the economics of staying in police work remained difficult. VSP officers continued to experience such significant disadvantage in the next years that by 1975 their pay increased to a mere $140 a week ranking them 50th among the 50 states and 11 Canadian provinces.[177] Issues surrounding salary, benefits and ability to maintain a quality of lifestyle dogged the VSP for years. "How come," one concerned citizen wrote with emphasis to Gov. Davis's secretary Frederick Reed in 1969, "the governor cannot get sufficient funds to pay enough STATE POLICE an appropriate salary? Why can't the governor get the necessary funds?"[178]

During the Irasburg board's hearings in November 1968, a rumor reached it that VSP leadership required troopers to provide personal funds to pay for the department's representation before it. When called to shed light on the allegation, third-in-command Capt. Dean tried to correct its misapprehension and explain the historical problems the state police faced in getting their needs recognized and dealt with. "Over a period of the past two years and perhaps even longer," he told the board, "members of the Department have felt that there was a need for a State Police Association." Some form of an independent organization was required because, Dean explained, "State police are a little unique in Vermont in that they, as far as salaries (and) benefits, these come directly from the legislature and not from the Personnel Division." Whereas other states' police forces relied on specialized government departments charged with administering their benefits, Vermont did not because the legislature insisted on maintaining tight control over its purse strings. Other Vermont state employees had the benefit of their own employees' association to represent their needs and while it tried to negotiate on the behalf of troopers (many were members), the officers believed it deficient because of their unique situation. Gov. Hoff also recognized the lack of protections afforded to VSP officers because of the department's unique structure. It "is a semi-military organization," he said, "which makes it touchy. You can't apply the same standards to it as you can other classified state employees."[179]

Just as the Irasburg investigation concluded, VSP command personnel recognized the hardships they and their men faced, made worse by the adverse, inaccurate reporting by the press and unfounded racist allegations made against them that they could not defend against. To address the overall lack of support they experienced, the troopers' superiors discussed how to provide an effective voice for them all. Dean explained further to the board that they formed a committee to establish articles of association, retain an attorney to write them and file the necessary corporate papers with the state. Membership was open to all officers (nobody was required to join) who paid a graduated membership fee ranging from $10 for commissioned officers, $7 for non-commissioned officers and $3 for troopers. The funds they provided could then be used, as Commissioner Alexander explained, to provide financial assistance to any officer and his family as a result of injury in the line of duty, to employ attorneys when "sued as a result of their activity in the performance of their employment," and to "assist any officer who, through illness or misfortune requires additional money to provide for his family."[180]

Regardless of whatever merit lay behind the planned organization's intentions, and without citing any information to the contrary contained in the hundreds of pages of testimony and exhibits, the Irasburg board saw no need for it. Calling it a "somewhat nebulous organization set up for the protection of the State Police," the board questioned the legality of forming any new organization representing their needs when there was already a state employees association. Refusing to credit Dean's and Alexander's reasonable explanations and avoiding the uncomfortable fact that state police were under the direct control of the legislature, the board called on Oakes's office or a legislative committee to "investigate this activity of the State Police leadership" and to determine the legality and justification for it.[181] Ultimately, its recommendation backfired and the nascent organization the officers described evolved into the Vermont Troopers Association that exists to this day.

A final concern of great importance consumed the attention of VSP investigators in 1968. The specter that drugs presented elsewhere caused a sudden, virtually overnight impact in Vermont between 1967 and 1968 with the arrival of mobile dealers from elsewhere. "The influx of tourists, itinerant workers and out-of-state students," the department's Drug Abuse Control Program (also issued on Aug. 1, 1968 as the Irasburg investigation unfolded) said, "accompanied by drifters and individuals bent on making a profit through the peddling of illicit drugs and influencing others to participate," including members of organized crime, constituted the problem. Whereas a negligible number of drug investigations occurred in 1966 (resulting in zero convictions), they increased to 180 in 1967 and then 535 by 1970. VSP planners noted that in just the preceding few months "it has become shockingly apparent that even Vermont has been infiltrated, and the illicit possession, manufacture, buying and selling of drugs is becoming more and more widespread, especially among our young people." They also expressed concerns of how the consumption of drugs affected the rise in criminal activity because of "personality changes" experienced by users, posing "a threat to the Vermont way of life."[182]

As the drug problem settled in, the VSP became the only official voice expressing a forward-thinking approach to deal with it that no one else wanted to touch. In fiscal year 1968, one of its investigators devoted 11% of his time providing information to 41 different groups and speaking before more than 2,500 individuals. The department needed additional help, but could not generate sufficient interest from any other state agency to engage with the problem. Within the governor's and attorney general's offices in 1969, the refusal of the departments of health and education to assist caused great frustration. There was, according to Attorney General James Jeffords complaining to Gov. Davis, a "lack of direction and coordination" as well as a persistent refusal by the Health Department to assist with regulations that it kept passing back to the DPS as its responsibility. Disinterest in dealing with the problem was so bad that officials relegated it to the Governor's Committee on Youth. "I cannot emphasize how disappointed I am that we cannot start taking more direct steps sooner," Jeffords wrote, hoping that "this situation can be altered."[183] Only three detectives from the newly-constituted Drug Abuse Unit within the VSP's CID investigated a range of those offenses at the time, including one savvy officer playing an important role in the Irasburg investigation. Until Vermont adopted a realistic strategy to deal with the burgeoning drug and manpower problems, just these few officers constituted the state's only frontline defense as its resources stretched to a breaking point.

The VSP in the late 1960s bore immense responsibilities, shouldered by a stressed cadre of officers working crushing hours and receiving low pay, to protect the interests of Vermonters, their way of life and the bucolic visions that envious outsiders had of them. Significant economic consequences threatened their wellbeing if the department did not provide the measures necessary to ensure the safety of those inside its borders able to attract outside investors. National unrest elsewhere in the mid-1960s meant that the department remain agile and able to pivot to address the new forms of crime arriving in the state while complying with its overall public safety mandate. It was also a time when parsimonious politicians prioritized policies and programs to foster better relations with those outside the Green Mountains in hopes of alleviating the racial discord that cities experienced, but often to the disadvantage of their leading law enforcement agency.

The hundreds of pages of transcripts, exhibits and police reports contained in the Irasburg board of inquiry's files provides no indication that it ever considered these immense pressures and stresses on the VSP. Aside from the calls of a few religious leaders alleging the department was racist that the media exploited, there is no evidence in the records of its presence, that it ever abandoned its many public safety responsibilities or engaged in the oft-reported charge of "racial prejudice" they said existed. The board's adoption of the calls of others that the department failed in its investigation of the event presents significant questions because the evidence indicates a strong finding to the contrary. Looking at the facts, rather than those unsubstantiated, biased inferences and innuendo, sheds needed light on this difficult period in Vermont history and our understanding of the Irasburg Affair.

Chapter 3

Before the Blasts

Easing into Controversy

From what perspective should the events of the summer of 1968 taking place in "hunger" Orleans County's Irasburg community be described? Several are possible: victim, accused, clergy, community or media. And what were the underlying political and/or economic motivations of each interest and their impact on a population pulled into the affair where many simply sought to lead their lives in peace apart from the national race debate? Notwithstanding the results of the board of inquiry viewing the evidence that now calls for reconsideration, only a VSP point of view remains, silenced for the past half century.

Following his graduation from the University of Tennessee Law School in 1968, and while awaiting admission to the Vermont bar in December, recently arrived 26-year-old Chicago native M. Jerome Diamond began work as Judge Gibson's law clerk only days before the board of inquiry convened.[184] During his judicial career, Gibson chose 18 men as his clerks utilizing the criteria of whether they planned to remain in Vermont afterwards in order to "enable the state to benefit from whatever job experience they gained in the job."[185] He apparently saw such promise in Diamond that for his first task he assigned him the responsibility of examining the Irasburg investigation to guide the board's work.

When it completed its hearings in November and before releasing its final report to the public the next month, Gibson summoned Vermont Press Bureau chief Stephen Terry to meet him for lunch. Without disclosing its final decision, Gibson sought to assure Terry, and thereby the larger press corps incessantly pursing the story, that the case had been "really well investigated." He came to that conclusion, he said, singling out Diamond's exemplary work and that he was satisfied with the result.[186] This previously unknown aspect about Diamond's participation and the strong reliance Gibson placed on him provides additional insights into aspects of the board's conduct and the quality of its findings. It demonstrates just how much credibility, or lack thereof, it placed on the testimony and evidence it received from witnesses as filtered through the lens of his clerk.

In his preparation of an outline of events for Gibson before the hearings began, Diamond made an inadvertent, and prescient, observation that affirms the omission of a VSP perspective is missing from the story. Because he lacked any law enforcement experience, Diamond seems to have struggled to understand and reconcile the mass of information contained in the VSP investigators' reports he read. His unfamiliarity with how criminal investigations were conducted further appears to have left him perplexed at why police did not immediately arrest an early suspect right after the shooting took place leaving him to assert it instead "went in every other direction."[187] Diamond's observation also indicates he had a hand in drafting the board's ultimate findings where it repeated a second time that the police investigation "went in many other directions."[188] Those findings likewise faulted the VSP for not moving "as rapidly as they might have" to arrest the perpetrator because it turned its attention instead to a second criminal offense (adultery) involving the Black victim occurring during the shooting investigation.[189]

As a result of its own lack of investigative experience and understanding of the responsibilities expected of law enforcement authorities in assembling evidence before making an arrest, the board's seeming incorporation of Diamond's misdirected attitude insinuating inaction, delay and neglect substantiating a finding of VSP racial bias towards the Black victim infused its findings. Tellingly, they are the ones that the incoming Gov. Deane Davis administration sought to distance itself from. It believed that they "leave something to be desired" and which Attorney General Oakes and his principal deputy also said contained many "loopholes and contradictions" warranting further investigation; both observations further undercutting the quality of the board's work that continues to falter to this day when closely examined.[§]

Why did the VSP's investigators proceed "in every other direction," as Diamond complained, instead of arresting the first person they became suspicious of for the shooting incident? How could its inquiry of the secondary adultery matter constitute bias, or racial prejudice, when an objective examination of the facts shows that police were doing what it is police do: investigate crimes? The events in Irasburg presented a firestorm of criticism from outsiders questioning the VSP's conduct at a time when the quality of another noteworthy investigation faced its own scrutiny. U.S. Supreme Court Chief Justice Earl Warren's inquiry into President Kennedy's assassination became public just four years earlier and faced much ridicule for its finding that Lee Harvey Oswald worked alone.[190] Recognizing the approaching intense scrutiny that a Vermont public would place on perhaps the most important investigation the VSP conducted in its two decades of existence describes why it sought to avoid that kind of derision. Instead, the evidence shows it proceeded in a methodical manner to fulfill its obligation to solve a complex, often conflicting, set of facts requiring some 20 officers working 2,256 man-hours driving 20,943 miles to interview more than 200 witnesses and costing the state over $13,000 to unravel.[191] By conducting such an exhaustive investigation into two crimes brought to its attention in close order, the VSP's comprehensive response seems to answer Diamond's uninformed questioning of its work.

The Irasburg Affair swirled around the interactions of two men who did not know one another, one white and one Black. Twenty-

---

§   Noteworthy findings by the Board of Inquiry inconsistent with the primary sources in its possession are noted in the order they arose during the course of the VSP investigation.

one-year-old Larry Gene Conley and 39-year-old David Lee Henry Johnson Sr. crossed paths shortly after midnight on Friday, July 19, 1968 when Conley fired a shotgun into the front of the Irasburg home occupied by the recently-arrived Johnson and his family. Conley's family lived on property a short distance away from Irasburg in Glover that his father, Howard, owned. Their land bordered on acreage previously occupied by VSP Commissioner Alexander during his childhood, but who denied knowing its current occupants after he left the area in 1928. Howard was a local schoolboard member and businessman who ran the Howard Auto Sales business in Newport, the Green Mountain Fence Company in Glover and a fence-installation business in New Jersey. While the extant records provide little information about Larry Conley personally, a brief letter written to Gov. Hoff by an unidentified correspondent who apparently knew him characterized him as "a decent kind of boy."[192]

As Howard protested before the board of inquiry, his family was not racist pointing to the presence of Black workers from New Jersey staying at his home that he said was not unusual. "We hired all colored people," he explained, and that they routinely came to Vermont to pick up and take back materials for his business, using his place to eat and sleep.[193] The family, including Larry, routinely interacted with them during their visits and Howard noted that he never understood his son to have ill feelings towards them.

Born a short distance from Glover in Barton, Conley's background is consistent with the characterization of his being "a decent kind of boy" as someone who departed the community in 1966 to begin a three-year enlistment in the Army. He worked hard and advanced rapidly in rank in the next two years, receiving glowing reviews from superiors and promotion to sergeant. Before coming home on leave from Fort Dix in New Jersey that summer, he was enroute from a prior assignment in Korea heading to his next duty station in Germany where his enlistment would expire in April 1969. The records do not specifically relate what kind of problem he had before his stay in Vermont, but the attorney representing him at court proceedings during the Irasburg Affair said that he experienced a "nervous breakdown" while at Fort Dix.[194] Just days after Johnson's home was fired into and while police conducted their investigation, on July 23 the five-foot, eleven-inch, 170-pound Conley suffered a significant shoulder injury. While assisting others trying to rope a loose bull, he was pulled violently into a fence post that left him wearing a sling in the next days.[195]

David Johnson, also a former member of the U. S. Army, posed a different kind of challenge to the investigation because of the many conflicts he presented. The findings of the Irasburg board never addressed the legitimate concerns the VSP faced in verifying Johnson's identity, his military service and other aspects of his life choosing instead to characterize those routine investigatory practices as racist. However, that assessment is severely undercut by an astute observation made by the board's sole female member that has never received attention. Writing separately from its final report, Dorothy Collins noted that in her opinion, one that did not find its way into the board's findings, "The apparent lack of stability in the emerging personality of the Rev. Mr. Johnson tended to confuse the (case) for officers and public alike." (Appendix F).

The VSP shared Collins's assessment of Johnson's shady past because his credibility marked an important aspect of its investigation in bringing charges against a potential suspect in the future. As the star witness-participant in an exchange of gunfire during his encounter with Conley and who provided information implicating other California-based suspects, Johnson's truthfulness struck at the core of any potential prosecution. His association with a white woman who came to Vermont with him and his family prompted him to report to authorities the ill feelings within her clan that did not approve of their inter-racial relationship. Other impressions Johnson made with members of the Irasburg community looking out for his best interests also caused them to question his background. They included his friend, a local clergyman, who subsequently experienced a change of heart sharing his own disillusionment with Johnson to a Newport radio audience after the shooting. "If only David would tell the truth," he said, "if only he had not deceived people about his coming from royalty, his claim to having two degrees from Villanova, and his pretense to be working on a doctorate, if only he had just been himself, perhaps this would never have happened."[196] Those observations proved only a part of other questionable aspects concerning Johnson troubling police.

"Shotgun Blasts Shatter Negro Minister's Home," the *Burlington Free Press* screamed in its July 20 headline when it and other newspapers reported the event. Nothing of this magnitude involving race relations had ever occurred in Vermont before, so the rush was on among the state's newspapers to be the first to report on it with as much emphasis as possible. According the journalist Stephen Terry, a great deal of concern existed among the several editors spreading the word fearing that they could be scooped by a national publication at some point (*Life* magazine did report on it in April 1969). This only increased the pressure among them to pre-empt any outside media giant from commandeering the story and to draw as much attention to their coverage as quickly as possible. This could also increase circulation and thereby their employers' profits. The resulting coverage created a feeding frenzy often providing inflammatory and inaccurate reporting tainting the public's understanding of what actually happened. Concurrently, *Rutland Herald* publisher Robert W. Mitchell cautioned on July 20 that "Every effort must be made by officials, from Gov. Hoff on down, by the news media and the citizenry to demand full particulars before leaping to reckless conclusions."[197] His prescient warning had little effect as the media vigorously pursued any angle it could find regardless of truth; precisely the kinds of complaints that the youth project participants complained of in its reporting of their activities.

Leading off with their stories after July 20, the press drew particular attention to David Johnson's race and clergy status. The media repeatedly provided glowing descriptions of him in ways that soon drew suspicion from others. Johnson provided the press with a rich accounting of his military background saying that he left the army two years earlier after a 25-year career, including service during the Korean War, with the rank of master sergeant. He was also reportedly a member of the noted all-Black 555th Parachute Infantry and the 101st Screaming Eagle Airborne Division with 200 parachute jumps under his belt and had received ordination as a Baptist minister several years previously.[198]

The violence of the incident aside, these initial reports about Johnson's background made a member of Attorney General James Oakes's staff uneasy, prompting him to notify VSP officials to convey his suspicions. Contrary to the board of inquiry's singling out and condemning the VSP for initiating the ensuing investigation into Johnson's background as being racist, it was, in fact, the attorney general's office itself prompting the effort. It constitutes an important, unchallenged and telling aspect of the Irasburg matter that the board never acknowledged casting further concerns about the quality of its work. It further explains, in part, why Diamond's dismissive complaint that the VSP investigation "went in every other direction" remains inaccurate.

Assistant Attorney General Richard C. Blum working from his Burlington office acted as Oakes's head of consumer affairs, responsible for representing the state during racially-related housing complaints before the Vermont Commission on Human Rights. In a first-of-its-kind case in Vermont, in 1968 Blum gained notoriety when he brought suit against a Shaftsbury couple for refusing to sell publicly-offered land to an out-of-state Black veterinarian willing to pay the full asking price. Blum was the only person dealing with these kinds of cases and Johnson contacted him in early July soon after his arrival in Vermont. He sought Blum's assistance to obtain the refund of a deposit he made for the purchase of an Irasburg home that he bought sight unseen through the mail, but was dissatisfied with. After the shotgun blasts into the second home he and his family moved into, Johnson traveled to Burlington to meet with Blum again in order to convey his belief of who might be responsible for the act. "Rev. Johnson," the VSP's Capt. Dean reported after Blum conveyed to him about his relationship with the white woman (Barbara Lawrence) accompanying him to Vermont, "feels that Barbara's brother, who lives in California, along with other members of the family, are incensed because of the relationship between Barbara and himself and may be responsible for the shooting."[199]

During Johnson's conversation with Blum, his military service also came up and he showed the attorney his military identification card. What the prosecutor saw caused him concern because it appeared that the date of birth "had been altered or appeared to be altered" prompting him to report this and the potential California connection to Dean. As the officer recounted, it led the two men to suspect "there was a possibility that Mr. Johnson, Rev. Johnson, might not even be Mr. Johnson" because "there had been no positive identification made at this point." The two discussed how to verify his identity using fingerprints and Dean agreed that the VSP would handle the task.[200]

The VSP found itself in a delicate position in making inquiries about Johnson because of the racial aspects of the case. Lt. Robert H. Iverson, in charge of the department's Identification, Records and Criminal Investigations office handling routine background investigations, oversaw the effort. As he explained to the board of inquiry, Johnson's report of someone else wanting to harm him prompted further questions about the case that placed his truthfulness into question; the potential race-related motivations of the person shooting into his house was not the issue, but his credibility to sustain a later conviction of that person was. To answer those questions, simply conducting a background investigation could help to resolve any concerns. As a result, Iverson wrote to a Florida police department where Johnson reportedly had a connection asking for assistance, explaining the reason for his inquiry. "Up until the time Rev. Johnson moved to Vermont," he explained, "we had, at least in the open, no known offenses involving so-called racism or alleged violation of civil liberties." However, he said, since that time "we have had any number of allegations against officials including the State Police accusing these officials of so-called racism, etc." Iverson ended his request asking that it remain confidential because "this whole investigation is somewhat touchy as we are dealing with a Negro who allegedly is claiming discrimination."[201]

It did not take long for police to begin to piece together information on Johnson, born in 1929 in Coatesville, Pennsylvania, inconsistent with the portrayal he offered to the press, an Irasburg clergyman befriending him, and from what he offered during sworn testimony to the board of inquiry. On the last occasion, he recounted a lengthy story about his military service appearing in none of the official records that either the police or board ever received. It included his alleged enlistment in the army at age 12, service during World War II and receipt of many distinguished awards and medals he described in detail.[202] He provided no written proof to substantiate his claims and very little of it could be verified by the military. Instead, its records revealed only that he served in the Army after the war ended between 1946 and 1947 and then the Air Force from 1948 to 1954. Contrary to his statements to the press, an Army public information officer wrote that "There is nothing in his record, to indicate that he was ever assigned to either the 555th Parachute Infantry or the 101st Airborne Division. Further, there is nothing in his record to indicate that he was parachute qualified."[203] Even the board of inquiry could not accept Johnson's account, finding that "although he claims additional service, we have been unable to determine what he claims is so."[204]

As the nation's central repository of fingerprints, the first entry in the FBI's files concerning Johnson occurred in July 1944 when he applied for a civilian job with the Army's Provost Marshal's Office. Additional entries followed, describing various inquiries from police and sheriffs' departments in Philadelphia and San Bernardino and Rialto, California between 1946 and 1962.[205] Some entries appear as routine pre-employment inquiries made for positions identified as "laborer" (for the Army) and "trackman" (Pennsylvania (Railroad) Police). Another shows his involvement in criminal activity recounting an arrest by St. Petersburg, Florida police in January 1952 for assault with a deadly weapon, reduced to carrying a concealed weapon with a sentence of thirty-days and a $50 fine. On May 24, 1954, Johnson was arrested again by St. Petersburg police, this time for being absent without leave from Lockbourne Air Force Base in Ohio.[206]

As the country watched what happened in Irasburg after the shooting, an interested local press made its own inquiries about Johnson, including newspaper editor Lloyd T. Hayes of the *Newport Daily Express*. Hayes wrote to Fred Sorri, a reporter at the *Monterey Peninsula Herald* in California that covered the Seaside community Johnson came from to see if they had any information on him. They did indeed, and in response Sorri provided a devastating account of Johnson's past describing a litany of events attributed to him. Moved to do so "in the interest of better journalism," Sorri cautioned Hayes to be wary of what Johnson said and "to take a new look at what may be a hoax" because it appeared that the Vermont press may "have been taken by a con artist."[207]

Sorri also expressed his displeasure at Johnson's disparaging reports of his flight from Seaside because of racial unrest. He strongly refuted his allegations and called it a "successfully integrated community" where a quarter of its 24,000 residents were Black, including many occupying responsible government positions. Recent scholarship recites similar findings that in the 1960s Seaside constituted a successful post-WW II boom town where Black and other minority servicemen and their families flocked to take advantage of its vibrant growth and economic opportunities.[208] One local leader in the civil rights movement, and former army officer and Tuskegee Airman, described the kinds of challenges they faced gaining acceptance into the community in 1968. "Our population is one of the most cosmopolitan in in the state," he said, "we have a tremendous variety of racial, ethnic and cultural strains, all of which have been woven into our way of life. Our challenge is to see that this new way of life is the truly American way of life in which each man is accepted on his own merit or rejected on his own shortcoming not because of his color or his accent, or by the name he calls his God."[209]

Individual merit and a willingness to participate to make the community better marked the successful individual of color in the vibrant, accepting Seaside community. Johnson's description of why he left the city does not jibe with the perceptions of others living there and it appears he did so not because of unrest, but the kinds of rejection he received from his peers that the civil rights leader identified.

In his inquiries with the local police department and members of the clergy, reporter Sorri learned additional information about why Johnson may have chosen to leave town in 1968. His sources had little favorable to say about him, describing him as "a smooth talker and a teller of tall tales," Sorri wrote. Police said he first came to their attention several years earlier reporting "how guns were being stolen at Fort Ord (the local military installation) and sold to the Minute Men," that resulted in an FBI investigation going nowhere. "He seems to enjoy fabricating stories about himself," Sorri explained, and described that while Johnson was never arrested, police also suspected him of "procuring girls for soldiers at neighboring Fort Ord."

Telephone inquiries by VSP Chief Criminal Investigator Billy J. Chilton to the Monterey County Sheriff's Department provided no further information, but verifying Sorri's allegations from the Seaside Police Department (SPD) did.[210] An officer from that agency told Chilton, according to his notes, that Johnson was an "old friend, knew him well" from his past run ins with police. The most recent occurred on June 27, 1968 the officer said, shortly before Johnson arrived in Vermont. It is not clear what the reason was, but seems a civil-related problem concerning "mortgage furniture." The police department had four file cards of entries relating to Johnson beginning in January 1964 when he volunteered to assist police "in undercover capacity claiming to have been a Lieutenant Colonel in the Army." While he was never arrested during his time in Seaside, Johnson was also suspected, Chilton wrote, "of organizing girls for prostitution, hanging around Fort Ord, gambling and pimping. Doesn't pay bills and receives welfare assistance" and moving "from apartment to apartment without paying rent." In sum, Chilton recorded that Johnson was "considered to be all around undesirable worthless liar counterfeit, etc." Strangely, his official report incorporated in its entirety as an exhibit into the board of inquiry's proceedings appears to have sections pertaining to Johnson's involvement with California police cleanly cut out. It is the only one of the board's 187 exhibits that appears altered while in its possession.

When a second VSP investigator traveled to the SPD, he found more information concerning Johnson's embellished background. After he became involved in a domestic disturbance in October 1964, he reportedly told officers "he was with the Air Force Intelligence and gave his rank as Lt. Colonel," despite his departure from the military a decade earlier. However, when he presented police with an identification card, it showed his rank as airman. On another occasion (probably in the early 1950s) when military police encountered Johnson, he tried to pass himself off as an Air Force sergeant that resulted in his discharge. The female officer at the SPD providing the information also told the VSP officer that she was a neighbor of Johnson's and related her interactions with him. She described a bizarre story of their first meeting taking place in Vancouver, British Columbia while she and her husband were on their honeymoon. Johnson approached her, she said, "and told her that he knew her and knew what she drove for a vehicle, and that she was a policewoman in Seaside, California." This surprised her, the officer wrote, "as she had never, to her knowledge, seen or knew of Johnson previously to this." Despite their becoming neighbors in Seaside, the officer never knew of him "holding any steady employment." The last time she saw him, Johnson said he was headed for Vermont to speculate on property.[211]

Johnson, repeatedly referred to as a minister and "reverend" throughout the Irasburg Affair reporting and during the board of inquiry's proceedings, wore a distinguishing cassock-style shirt with a white clerical collar and a gold medallion hanging from his neck. The trappings earned him great deference during the hearings where the word "reverend" appears repeatedly before his name in the transcript. It also appeared in the many media and other accounts that the Vermont public consumed up to recent times providing him with a label daring anyone to question his credentials.

Consistent with his recitation of his unverified military service, the legitimacy of Johnson's ordination as a minister remains clouded. He told the board that he "entered the clergy shortly after 1950" when he studied under two military chaplains and "took two, four-year courses in Theology." He further explained he had only recently been ordained "under the Monterey Baptist Association" in proceedings conducted on Jan. 13, 1968 at the Ocean View Baptist Church in Seaside; documented prominently as Exhibit Number One during the board's proceedings.[212]

However, when local reporter Sorri sought information about the event from the pastor recommending him for the position to the church hierarchy other facts spilled out. "I called Johnson's pastor," Sorri wrote to editor Hayes, "and asked him if it were true that he recommended to the Baptist (Negro) Council that Johnson be ordained and he said it was, but that it was against his will." When Sorri asked why, the pastor told him "He (Johnson) caused a carousement in my church. He told the officers I was holding him back because I would not recommend he be ordained. He said he could get somewhere if he was ordained. So, against my will, I recommended it after my officers told me to go ahead and let him go." Sorri then contacted and inquired of the official responsible for approving Johnson's ordination and learned that "he did so only at the recommendation" provided him by the pastor. While Johnson testified that when he left Seaside he worked as an "Assistant Pastor," no proof of his employment was ever shown. Rather, as he also explained, "I worked for Montgomery Ward during the day; I ran the R.B.A. Janitorial Service at night, plus I had a small janitorial business of my own that I cleaned homes," while his wife worked "as a cocktail waitress for the N.C.O. Club at Fort Ord."[213]

When Orleans County Catholic priest Father Paul Bouffard tried to explain to the board of inquiry what Johnson told him about his ordination, he was prohibited from testifying. Beforehand, he said that after Johnson's arrival in Vermont and first meeting him that he provided him with literature describing the process. He "had this ritual that was used," Bouffard testified, "apparently in California, for this particular group of Baptists, that he belongs to, of ordination ceremony and I found it rather novel, so I looked through it." It was apparently so novel that when VSP investigator Chilton inquired of church officials if Johnson was listed in the Baptist Year Book, his name did not appear.[214] When attorney Robert A. Eldredge representing the VSP inquired of Bouffard if he had done anything himself to confirm "whether or not Mr. Johnson is a member of the Baptists," board attorney Lt. Gov. Ralph A. Foote immediately called out to its chairman, "Governor Gibson," to object. While the proceedings were supposedly "informal" and non-adversarial, Foote said he was also "interested in protecting people." His interruption provided the board with winking insight that any further inquiry into the legitimacy of Johnson's ordination process could be harmful to him and should be prohibited. Gibson understood what Foote implied and stopped Eldredge cold telling him "I think you are out of order." Despite Foote's "protective" efforts on Johnson's behalf, Bouffard was able to convey a response to another of Eldredge's questions of whether he had knowledge of any "prejudice or racism on the part of any members of the Department of Public Safety." "No," he said, he did not.[215]

COMING TO VERMONT

Before leaving Seaside, California and his shady past behind, David Johnson resided there with his thirty-five-year-old wife, Ophelia, seventeen-year-old daughter Brenda and her four-year-old daughter Yvette and two sons, seventeen-year-old George Small and fifteen-year-old David Lee Jr. While records established their marriage occurred on Aug. 27, 1951 in Elkton, Maryland, it also appears Johnson maintained a second intimate relationship with another woman when they lived in St. Petersburg, Florida. At the time of his arrest in that city in 1952 for assault with a deadly weapon, Johnson identified a Juanita Small as his common-law wife residing in the same home with him and Ophelia calling her "his legal wife."[216] His marriage with Ophelia continued thereafter and following their move to Seaside at an unknown time, sometime around 1967 he became involved with another woman who had significant involvement with the Irasburg matter.

At eighteen years of age, Barbara Ann Lawrence (nee Northam) married Arthur D. Lawrence in 1963, an army soldier seven years her senior stationed at Ft. Ord. The two experienced periodic separations because of his service obligations and in 1967 he received posting to Vietnam, leaving her alone with their two children, two-year-old Tessa and one-year-old David. She met next door neighbor Johnson at some point before her husband left. The two became intimate for the next several months as their relationship intensified and they prepared to move to Vermont together in July 1968. Barbara said she fell in love with Johnson and that the two discussed marriage. As she explained to VSP investigators, she found him a better sexual companion than her husband and that she and Johnson engaged in it "possibly more" than forty to fifty times during their time together in California. Barbara admitted the extra-marital affair to Arthur before he left for Vietnam and, apparently recognizing he could not restrain his young wife in his absence and the difficulties presented by a white woman associating closely with a Black man, even in enlightened Seaside, told her "To be careful." He also instituted divorce proceedings against her alleging "mental cruelty" as the basis, Barbara said, "so there wouldn't be any dirt in the courtroom." The uncontested divorce waited a year before becoming final in March 1969, meaning that Barbara remained married in the eyes of the law until then.

Barbara further explained her relationship with Johnson that she proceeded under with the understanding that Ophelia, living under the same roof with him for the past seventeen years, was actually his common-law wife. "One time we were having an argument," she told investigators, "and he lost his temper and he said 'Well, what makes you think that Ophelia and I are married, we were never married.'" On another occasion when she was present, Johnson challenged Ophelia directly saying that "You'll find a lot of people that don't know too much about me, because you can ask people if they know if you're my wife and she can be sitting right there and we aren't even married." From Barbara's perspective, ignoring her instincts to the contrary, she thought Johnson may have been lying about his legal relationship with Ophelia "just to keep me on."[217] When investigators inquired if she knew anything about Johnson "being a reverend or is he a reverend," she could only respond that "I understand that he is, I've seen his license, but I wasn't there at the (Jan. 13, 1968) ordination. Just he and his wife were." None of this information was ever considered by the board of inquiry in its subsequent condemnation of the VSP for its investigation into the close relationship between Johnson and Lawrence after an officer discovered them committing the felony crime of adultery.

Although it does not appear he shared his reasons with Lawrence why he wanted to come to Vermont, Johnson alleged it was because of the racial problems in California. In an account that left Seaside residents bewildered as reporter Sorri related, he told the board of inquiry "I felt that it would be better to try to raise children in peace and quiet than to have to carry razors, knives or guns to school every day, which on several occasions the authorities caught the children at various schools in Seaside and the immediate area, doing so."[218] He saw an advertisement in a real estate publication for a home in Irasburg that he arranged to purchase, sight unseen, that later required the help of Assistant Attorney General Blum to obtain a refund of the $900 deposit he paid. The circumstances are not clear, but before arriving Johnson registered by mail two recently purchased new vehicles with the Vermont DMV in March and June that later prompted questions by the VSP because of a tax-related issue. He also received specially-created vanity registration plates with his initials, DLHJ on one, and another bearing, for an unknown reason, BJJ.

The main reason the shotgun blasts fired into Johnson's home after his arrival recast Irasburg from a sleepy, impoverished community into a hotbed of racism is traceable to one man. While he possessed unquestionable heartfelt and well-meaning intentions, the rapid hysteria he stirred up because of his unbridled hatred for racism ultimately came to compromise his own moral compass. His allegations of its presence in the community where it had never been raised before spread like wildfire to deeply affect how his and following generations viewed the town and the VSP, the agency most directly harmed by what he said.

The Rev. Gordon G. Newell (1918–2007), a native Vermonter born in Northfield, received his education at the Montpelier Seminary during his formative years. After graduation, he attended the Irving School of Drama in New York City, the Bangor Theological Seminary and Tufts University. He became a traveling minister, going principally between Maine and Massachusetts before returning to Vermont in 1966, where he took up residency in Irasburg. He became the first minister at the newly formed Cross Mountain Parish in February 1967 and worked at the community's former congregational church, now called the United Church of Christ.[219] While he appears well-received in his professional life, Newell's troubled financial condition followed closely behind, leading him to seek relief from over $17,000 of debt in bankruptcy proceedings initiated in Burlington in December 1967.[220]

Newell first became aware of the impending arrival of a Black family in Irasburg in early July 1968 when his church organist, "Mrs. Twombley," passed the word to him. In the close-knit community, Twombley found out about it from the real estate agent Johnson communicated with to purchase a home. Newell immediately began preparing his congregation for the newcomers expressing hope during sermons that should any member of a minority come to town they receive Christian kindness in turn.[221] Newell greeted the Johnson and Lawrence families upon their arrival on July 4 and struck up a close relationship with them over the course of several meetings at the second home they moved into. Johnson and Newell seem to have hit it off initially as the new arrival shared that he hoped to set up "a religious retreat in Irasburg," as "a place where people in the religious communities could come for a convention (in) small groups."[222] Other community members unfamiliar with the backgrounds of the two families also came to the house welcoming them and bringing food to share.

Some also expressed discomfort at Johnson's lack of employment and living arrangements with Lawrence. "It makes me so damn mad," one woman wrote about the family and the hunger situation in Orleans County, "to see people sit on their rears and have so many things that myself and my family can't have because we're paying so many taxes so these folks can sit around. This poverty deal in Orleans County makes me so angry I could scream. If someone needs just a little help to put him on his feet or help him over a rough period, they can't get it but if they're willing to sit around and not work at all, they can get all the help they want apparently."[223]

One of Gov. Hoff's correspondents complimenting him for his youth project provided him with additional accounts of area people unhappy with their arrival. "Well, Hoff brought the n-----s to Vermont," one "very kindly old gentleman" from Montpelier said, "now let him live with them. The people in the South know how to handle the n-----s; we don't want them up here." Her husband became so upset with the bigotry he heard in St. Johnsbury, she said, "that he has had to walk out of a restaurant or else punch some of these people right in the mouth."[224] Similar sentiments arose during the investigation after the shooting when a VSP officer speaking with witnesses was told that a man "made a threat that he would shoot any negroes who came around." At the same time, another said "he would shoot a cop before shooting a negro."[225]

When Newell's church held its annual fair on July 17 in this "hunger county" town, members of the Orleans County Farm Bureau Women attended to distribute nourishing free milk to the crowd and to ward off the effects of the current heat wave.[226] Johnson's two sons, David and George, and their sister Brenda also appeared. The presence of the three Black teenagers at a popular white-attended traditional community function, where its members took advantage of the many rides for children, to view and purchase "fancy work, plants, knick-knacks," attend a rummage sale and consume tables full of food, presented a novel opportunity for some. Locals twenty-year-old Patricia Poitras and her sister both attended and danced with the two boys when the music played. They were probably just as struck by their appearance as a fifteen-year-old Vermont girl attending the youth project at the same time a short distance away at Lyndon State College. Writing to Hoff after the session she attended ended, she described that "this was my first contact with Negroes. I soon found out these kids were as much human as I was."[227]

But the enthusiastic teenager was not married and Patricia was, with her husband away at the time working in Barre. The uninhibited welcome she and her sister extended to the two young men appears to have drawn the ire of some. As one woman recalled witnessing their dancing, "People weren't ready for that in Irasburg. All that's the kind of thing that makes people raise their eyebrows, you know."[228] Concerned at what the display of friendship between the races could mean for someone resentful of the girls' actions, police later contacted Patricia asking her about what happened. It was all innocent fun she said and that she "saw nothing wrong with it at the time, but that since the shooting she has wondered what people might have thought of it."[229]

Captivated by the appearance of a Black family arriving with a white woman and her children and only hours after the shotgun blasts taking place two days later, Rev. Newell immediately took to the airwaves to express his disgust at whoever committed such a deed. Strident at first, he told his radio audience that "We will not retreat, we will not compromise, we will not sit idly by. We will speak loudly and clearly. We will <u>act</u> until every white citizen in this state is moved to a new kind of morality that will restore the Johnsons to their rightful place of dignity and happiness in the State of Vermont, so help us God." However, by the end of the month after Newell interacted further with Johnson and learned more of his background, his approval of the man, as one newspaper wrote, "has backed off a little." Johnson was not as he first appeared and Newell now understood that, included within the story of his twisted past, his purported religious education presented difficulties. He found it differed significantly from the standards of the established American Baptist Church requiring a college degree followed by three years of seminary before ordination. However, the more recent forms of "Progressive" branches of the church ("many, many, many" of them existed, Newell said) only required that a person "go to Bible school for a month or six months, then a local church confers ordination."[230] Beyond the piece of paper that Johnson provided professing his ordination that the board of inquiry prohibited any questioning about, none of the circumstances behind it were ever investigated to show that Newell's suspicions were incorrect. Whether Johnson belonged to some alternative branch or sect that Newell referred to, or received his ordination through a "novel" ceremony that Rev. Bouffard was barred from talking about, remains an unanswered question.

By September, Newell faced a dilemma because of his initial strong support for Johnson after his arrival in July followed by revelations concerning his suspect credentials. Publicly, he made forceful statements on Johnson's behalf after the adultery case broke saying that "I don't care what moral law he breaks, I don't give a damn what people say or what the church says. I will stand by this man."[231] However, in private he faced the cold reality before him. When he met with other religious leaders quizzing him about events in Irasburg after the shooting, he told them an embellished, but false, tale that someone threw a dead racoon on Johnson's porch with a note attached reading "You will be next."

A VSP officer contacted Newell after his allegation appeared in the media to inquire where he got his information. He first told him that Johnson reported it to him, but when the officer advised that he denied having done so ("This is Newell's story," Johnson said), he changed course and said that someone else had told him. Arguing that Johnson must have known about the incident nonetheless, Newell turned to attack him for the falsity, saying that "he had caught him in some untruths before and perhaps he was not telling the truth at this time." The officer persisted with his questioning until Newell, described by then as "quite flustered" and "repentant," recognized his difficult situation and inquired "if he should ask the news media to print a retraction" of his remarks.[232] He was told "to do as he felt best" and later admitted making the outrageous report that soon severed his relationship with Johnson.[233] His false allegation also intensified the suspicions of discerning observers in and out of the state awakening to question his initial outburst alleging racism in the community and the state police.

However well-intended Newell's initial involvement with Johnson was, he represents the kinds of challenges the VSP faced in unraveling what happened in Irasburg. The investigators' tasks only became more difficult when reputable men of the cloth appeared willing to mislead them and engage in deceit when questioned.

GRAFTON

Life in Vermont in July 1968 exemplified the accuracy of two adages: a Dickensian "best of times and worst of times," but also an intrusive "long, hot summer" that FBI Director Hoover feared. Locally, state officials predicted in June that "the most profitable summer tourist season in the state's history" approached, confirmed by the highway department's observation of a five percent increase in vehicle traffic.[234] In the southern Vermont community of Guilford where Attorney General Oakes lived, out-of-state visits increased 25% above 1967 levels while in Middlebury, on the first day it opened, the community welcome center counted 37 cars bringing 102 visitors from 14 states to its doorstep.[235]

At the same time, the stories of poverty and hunger around the state roiled, made worse by another unwelcomed event. "Motorcycle Gangs Bring Out Police, National Guard Unit," the *Rutland Herald* announced on July 15 just days before Irasburg exploded describing the mayhem taking place over the past two days in the southern Vermont town of Grafton. Three years earlier, after rioting at a motorcycle rally in Laconia, New Hampshire, and upon Hoff's order, the VSP coordinated closely with the state's Army National Guard and New Hampshire State Police to thwart a repeat of it in Grafton where similar rallies had taken place since 1958 at a local farm. Extensive preparation between the agencies resulted in comprehensive plans created by the VSP and National Guard coordinating their responsibilities.[236] Whereas the VSP "Operations Plan" proposed the disbursement of 54 of its officers, in this Vietnam-era the National Guard prepared a more ominous "Confidential" document under the guise of "Task Force GRAFTON." It identified the "Enemy Forces" it planned to deploy 125 riot-controlled troops (carrying their rifles and bayonets, but without ammunition) against as "undetermined numbers of unruly civilian personnel" in order to maintain control. Fortunately, the pre-planning was not needed, but remained in place for succeeding rallies in Grafton in 1966 and 1967 where continued fear of violence persisted until things changed significantly in 1968.

Some 6,000 motorcyclists and 11,000 spectators, including members of the Hells Angels, the Devil's Disciples, the Apostles, the Comancheros and the Slum Lords descended on the town to attend the tenth annual motorcycle scrambles. Trouble soon followed with gangs ranging through the village destroying its swimming pool, tearing up fences and leaving the place in shambles. How is it possible, one local couple wrote to Gov. Hoff (on the same day Irasburg exploded) about the mayhem, to "see how some of these misfits can bait our police, take over the town, drive into buildings, move out furniture, leave filth and rubbish all over?" Forced to retreat to the safety of their homes to avoid the carnage, they resented the ruffians' freedom to "bait our officers who were outnumbered 20 to 30 to 1, their sitting and riding in the middle of main street so all traffic is stopped" and "their fanning out and forcing cars off the state highways, encircling a car in traffic, hitting it from all sides and forcing it to do their will; and their chasing women with small children in their car, their swarming from the sidewalks into a line of traffic, climbing on a car and stomping it into a shambles roof, fenders, hood."

"Our police officers," they said, "need their hands untied so they can do the job they want to do and we want them to do. Let's back up our own and give them some laws to work with so law and order can be enforced and a real deterrent."[237]

The reports do not describe the apparent breakdown in the planning the VSP and National Guard envisioned that allowed the problem to escalate to the extent it did. Perhaps the distance separating Grafton from their staging area fifteen miles away in Bellows Falls contributed to a delayed response. Ever observant of any VSP stumbles, Caledonia County State's Attorney Sten Lium attributed it instead to a lack of "decisiveness" on the part of its command staff, identified as "one or two men lacking the will to act."[238] Or, perhaps a more pragmatic answer lay with the prospect of what unleashing 125 rifle-bayonet wielding riot-fighting soldiers as the nation's cities did into a rural Vermont community entered into their deliberations.

After the violence, the commander of the National Guard troops took no offense to his men not being called in and said that their mere presence in the area "had a pacifying effect" keeping it to a lower level than it would have otherwise been.[239] Regardless, at one point a sniper stationed on a bridge over Interstate 91 opened fire on a National Guard truck striking it, but not injuring either of the two occupants. Despite the presence of police and soldiers, numerous knifings and "chainings" took place, a man was "bound with wire which was sealed by melting a glass beer bottle over the wire" and another seriously hurt when thrown into a camp fire. Thirty-two individuals received medical aid at two local hospitals, a motorcyclist died when he drove off a road and 12 motorcycles were stolen. In total, the response cost the state some $10,000 for law enforcement (50 VSP troopers and 45 local officers), backed up by New Hampshire's 50 troopers, local police, deputy sheriffs and 3 canines standing by across the Connecticut River ready to assist.[240]

In the midst of campaigning for governor, Attorney General Oakes went to Grafton from his Guilford home after receiving a telephone call from an elderly woman asking "if he couldn't do something about the ruckus." Shocked at what he found, Oakes called the event "an outrage to the people of Vermont" and immediately placed 29-year-old Assistant Attorney General Frank Mahady in charge of an investigation into why event organizers failed to arrange for adequate law enforcement coverage.[241] Mahady's inquiry resulted in a seven-page report to Hoff that did not discuss the availability of the National Guard or why it was not deployed in an effective manner. Instead, it called on the legislature recommending statutory changes to deal with permitting these kinds of events. Despite the mayhem, he singled out a welcomed feature deserving special recognition. "One encouraging aspect of the weekend was the close cooperation between the Bellows Falls municipal police and the Vermont State Police," he wrote, "Such cooperation among law enforcement agencies is laudable and should be encouraged."[242] His assessment repeated what Hoff already expected of VSP Commissioner Alexander when he selected him from a field of eighteen applicants to name him to the post in 1965. He came with glowing endorsements from other police departments recognizing his cooperative nature. As Alexander told the press at the time, their relationships were "very good. They do anything for us, and we do anything for them."[243]

Alexander also played an important part in the summer of 1968 in the larger field of regional law enforcement cooperation in his role as chairman of the New England State Police Administrators' Conference (NESPAC). As one of its six members, Vermont obligated itself to provide aid to other New England state police agencies during emergencies with the understanding it could receive similar assistance when needed. While his department handled the Irasburg matter, in August Alexander acted on NESPAC's behalf requesting United States Attorney General Ramsey Clark to provide the organization with over $1,000,000 in grant funds to purchase a wide array of military-style equipment needed to respond to increased instances of "police emergencies." He envisioned enough materiel to equip a 1,000-man force out of the 2,300 state police officers working in New England able to move quickly throughout the six states "for the control of riot and civil disturbances."[244] Shortly afterwards, Clark approved a separate request from Hoff for funds to allow Vermont to implement a program of its own directed towards "the prevention, detection and control of riots and other violent civil disorders."[245] Together, the various projects demonstrate the VSP's involvement with important cooperative efforts in and out of Vermont to quell problems such as the Grafton rioting. The issue of cooperation between law enforcement agencies became a significant factor during the Irasburg hearings when the board characterized the VSP as obstructionist for refusing to cooperate with Oakes. It is an assessment that none of the evidence before it can substantiate. Neither can it be reconciled with Alexander's own character and the professional example he set dealing with significant issues requiring such cooperation throughout New England during very difficult times.

When Hoff stewed over the Irasburg Affair in the fall of 1968, and contrary to Mahady's glowing report of cooperation between police agencies, he recited the VSP's performance in Grafton as the reason why he tried, but ultimately failed, to fire Alexander.[246] Sensitive to a fault over the ways that law enforcement conducted its work and its potential effects on public perceptions, particularly with his youth project at stake, Hoff sought to maintain a tight grip on its ability to intrude into people's lives. A year earlier he interceded into law enforcement operations to prohibit the VSP from photographing people attending large gatherings. Despite Alexander's explanation that the Secret Service requested the VSP photograph potential troublemakers in crowds greeting President Lyndon Johnson's arrival in Burlington in 1966, Hoff thought police holding cameras visible to the public "a very bad practice." "To me it smacks a threat," he said, "and I see very little justification for it." However, he did recognize the problems that the Grafton event posed and allowed the department to take photographs, but only if "real difficulty develops."[247] What and when that "real difficulty" arose remained a subjective interpretation and may have been one of the kinds of missteps Hoff thought Alexander's officers committed in allowing the mayhem to grow to the level it did.

After Hoff left office, Alexander sought permission from Gov. Davis to resume photographing large crowds without receiving approval from his office beforehand. While Davis disagreed with Hoff's general prohibition, he apparently wanted the practice continued and told Alexander that if he had questions to "please feel free to contact me." The intervention of politicians exercising their personal interpretations of appropriate police procedure interfering with commonly accepted practices provides additional information about the kinds of micromanagement the VSP experienced in this time period. It further explains why the Irasburg board of inquiry believed it possessed a similar ability to interpose its interpretations of what constituted correct procedure when, as Alexander noted, it simply lacked the necessary knowledge and experience to guide it to such a result.

As the Grafton problem festered, the Fresh Air Fund and Hoff's Youth Project continued in full swing with hundreds of inner-city youths arriving and spread out across the state at educational institutions and private camps: Camp Marycrest in Grand Isle, Skyacres Girl Scout Camp in Washington and Camp Wihakowi in Northfield.[248] The same day the motorcyclists arrived in Grafton on July 13 and as the poverty stories began to appear, an incident involving Larry Conley, still on leave from the military, unfolded at the NEK's Crystal Lake State Park in Barton, a short distance from his Glover home.

Eighty-nine Black and white teenagers attending the program at Lyndon State College spent the day swimming and lounging on the beach under the supervision of their counselors. The experiences of this particular group associating together in a rural setting differed markedly from those attending a camp on the other side of the state in Ripton near Middlebury. There, counselors reported the community "was essentially hostile" to their presence, whereas they experienced little outside pressure in Lyndon because they housed themselves in the school's dormitories away from population centers. They participated in various programs involving writing, journalism, filmmaking and radio, creating various programs broadcast to the public via local commercial stations. While isolated in the college environment, their presence was certainly known by both well-wishers and those resentful at their presence.

It also appears that their young counselors, inexperienced, untrained and rushed into their roles by Hoff's frenzied push to make the program happen, advocated for them to intermingle in a permissive manner that some found objectionable, particularly when conducted in public. As an assessment of the Lyndon attendees' experience records of the kind of supervision they received, "Interracial dating was encouraged and widespread."[249]

The familiarity between one Black female counselor and a Vermont teenager became so intense that upon the boy's return home in Bennington, he posed a problem to his parents. "Since his return," his mother complained to youth project officials, "any effort of discipline on our part was met by open hostility and rebellion on his part, finally resulting in his running away from home and returning to Lyndon."[250] The counselor then concealed his presence for days before his discovery and being sent home. Such conduct eventually forced officials to acknowledge the lack of direction the program provided leading them to recommend "that participant screening be strengthened (and) staff orientation be intensified."[251]

The closeness that the Black and white teenagers shared in this unique environment seems to have drawn the attention of Conley and a couple of his friends upon their arrival at the park late that morning. Park caretaker Percy Wells, present at the time, later told police that "there had been no trouble with white boys at all," but that "a negro was after one of the female lifeguards and he spoke to the fellow to cut it out, which he did."[252] However, the lifeguards and counselors told another story.

Over a 20-minute period a reportedly drunken Conley unleashed a torrent of profanity at the boys in the group, calling them "sons of bitches of n-----s" and "fucking n-----s," and that he wanted to "show them not to come up to this part of the country." A female lifeguard witnessing his tirade told Conley to stop and he and his friends soon departed.[253] While none of this information was ever conveyed to police at the time, the board of inquiry pointedly disparaged the VSP for not uncovering it during its investigation of the shooting. From the board's perspective, the department stumbled because it "had not seen fit to check with any of these counsellors as to whether or not there had been any racial incidents involved in this program."[254] In light of all the work the VSP was consumed with in the Grafton mayhem and pursing voluminous numbers of leads in the Irasburg matter taking place days later, the board's condemnation of the department bears little reason.

Other reports concerning the Black community also appeared in newspapers that made some wary at their presence. In April, a forceful advocate of the Black Power movement spoke before a Vermont audience at Windham College (composed of "mainly white and students in a white racist school," he said) warning of the coming unrest in the cities. In an article entitled "Negro Guerillas NOW, Says Militant," he refused to provide further details to the attendees, explaining that such information was "off limits." However, he told them enough to understand that Blacks were already arming and training in the ghettos to strike out at the white population. When asked what whites could do to help the negro cause, he told them, "If you're serious, if you're true radicals and want to do something, do what John Brown did. And in case you don't know what he did, he had a gun."[255]

Weeks later, the *Brattleboro Reformer* newspaper announced the appointment of Kenneth Wibecan, a 37-year-old, less confrontational Black man from New York City, to write a weekly "Negro Viewpoint Column."[256] Experienced in book publishing in the city, Wibecan went on to write a series of insightful columns presenting the Black experience in the Green Mountains challenging white perceptions of what it meant. Not roundly appreciated, and similar to what David Johnson faced in Irasburg a month later, in March 1969 Wibecan's West Brattleboro home was fired into with a pistol by an unknown assailant in a case that was never solved. Other subtle instances of racism presented themselves before Irasburg exploded, but not as obvious as those taking place in Barton. On July 17, a Black New York City program director working on the youth project faced blatant disrespect from a ticket agent at the Burlington airport refusing to either acknowledge his presence or respond to his inquiry about lost luggage. Angry at his experience, the man wrote to the *Burlington Free Press* to report his unfavorable impression at this clear display of racism.[257]

Chapter 4

SHOTGUN

MIDNIGHT BLASTS

UNDERDOG ATTORNEY GENERAL OAKES was locked in the political battle of his life the summer of 1968 seeking the Republican nomination for governor. A strong supporter of Hoff's Youth Project, he warned that racism, poverty and ignorance constituted "the handmaidens of violence."[258] Yet, like Hoff, he never truly acknowledged the extent of such problems existing in his own backyard such as the presence of hunger and poverty in Orleans County or engaged in discussions aimed at resolving it around the state. When Oakes attended a second poverty tour in southern Vermont in August with other candidates, the accompanying press noted that his campaigning efforts remained paramount as he spent much of the time shaking hands instead of inquiring about the needs of the poor.[259]

On July 10, Oakes opened an office in Montpelier to carry his messaging forward and increase his presence in the northern part of the state where, according to one newspaper, "he will spend more time during this phase of the campaign."[260] Concurrently, in Brattleboro columnist Wibecan lamented the struggles Black soldiers faced returning from Vietnam. "Is it humanly reasonable," he asked, "to take a Black man—spend a year teaching him how to kill—send him into the mud and slime of Vietnam to practice his skill—then return him to America—face him with unbearable living conditions—tell him to be non-violent—and also tell him 'Don't worry boy, these things take time'—and expect him to obey?"[261]

The potential for overt racially-related conflict in northern Vermont that Wibecan implicitly warned about festered, but did not manifest itself that week when Oakes faced tough questioning on the campaign trail from white union members in Barre. Uninterested in his economic plans for the state, they asked instead about more heartfelt concerns, quizzing him about his stance on gun control. In this time following Robert Kennedy's assassination on June 6, governors throughout New England advocated for more control over firearms. They directed their attorney generals to draft laws adopting the stringent Massachusetts model requiring both their registration and that owners carry identification cards.[262] Oakes said he favored the move, but drew sparse support from his audience.[263] Little did he know, the issues surrounding racism, poverty, ignorance and firearms would soon rise to the surface in Irasburg.

Donald Collins of Glover worked the past eleven years as a state fish and game warden covering the Barton area in Orleans County. He was familiar with Larry Conley's father because he repaired small engines for him in his spare time. He had little involvement with Larry before he left to join the army in 1966, but it all changed on July 16. Just three days after harassing the colored teenagers at the state park and the day before Patricia Poitras and her sister danced with David Johnson's two Black sons, Conley had another idea. Collins had agreed to travel to Derby to look at a boat engine for his father to see if he could repair a bent crankshaft. Larry picked him up for the twenty-mile trip and, as they drove, he asked the officer what "he thought the troopers would do if they caught anyone harassing that bunch in Irasburg." When he testified before the board of inquiry Collins specified further that Conley inquired "what I thought would happen if anyone went over into Irasburg and bothered the colored family." He also told him that "he wouldn't mind harassing them if he could find someone to go along with him."[264] As a law enforcement officer, Collins knew exactly what would happen, providing him with a response encapsulating his view of what "the overall opinion of the enforcement in the State of Vermont would be." "I told him," Collins said, "I wouldn't do it; that the State Police would have to enforce the law if anybody went over and did a harassment of them."[265]

Uncovering the story of what happened afterwards required extensive work by the VSP and a grant of immunity to one of Conley's friends laying the whole thing out.¶ Nineteen-year-old Richard Earl LeClair, from Barton, explained that he and Conley ran into each other at a local garage around 2 p.m. on July 18, two days after the latter's conversation with Warden Collins and a week after he returned home on furlough. LeClair was waiting for a friend to take him to St. Johnsbury to pick up his car from a repair shop, a loud, high performance 1968 Oldsmobile 442 two-door sedan, jade-green in color with a white top, bearing Vermont tags 161847 that became notorious in the next hours and days. The two talked about Conley's absence from the area and his duties in the military before he offered to take LeClair to pick up his car. The two drove around the area in Conley's 1965 Rambler for a while, stopping at a local market where he purchased a four-pack container of Budweiser beer, each sixteen ounces, the first of many they consumed in the next hours. They briefly visited the park beach where Conley harassed the youth project young adults a few days before and then drove to St. Johnsbury drinking all of the beer during the trip.

The two arrived at the St. Johnsbury garage just as it was closing at 5 p. m. where they separated, driving their own cars back towards home. Midway through the trip, Conley stopped at a market in West Burke where he purchased two more four-packs of beer and then pulled off the road into a turnoff on the outskirts of town. The two sat and reminisced for the next hour and a half consuming all of the beer. After arriving back in Barton, they left Conley's car at a local gas station where he got into LeClair's car and the two drove to

---

¶ The following summary is derived from the confession of Conley's friend, Richard E. LeClair, dated July 31, 1968 (Board exhibit 27) and the change of plea colloquy taking place on Aug. 22, 1968 (exhibit 122) when Conley appeared before District Court Judge Lewis E. Springer Jr. and listened to Assistant Attorney General Frank Mahady and his attorney, Maxwell Baton, describe for the court the events taking place. Additional information comes from other witness statements and sworn testimony from the board of inquiry's files.

LeClair's house to get gasoline stored in a tank located there. They then returned to the same local market where Conley purchased beer earlier to buy another four-pack. The two returned to the park where they waterskied and met nineteen-year-old Bernadette Roy, visiting with her and staying until around 10 p. m. The three then drove to the local home of Roy's sister and her brother-in-law, Roger LaRocque, where they watched television until the news ended around 11:30. By this time, LeClair estimated that he and Conley had consumed a large quantity of alcohol: sixteen of the sixteen-ounce cans of beer.[266]

LaRocque did not know what the three had in mind when they left his place assuming the two men were taking Roy to her home in Newport.[267] When they departed the house, the three got into LeClair's car and Roy sat between them. As they drove off, Conley said "Let's go over to my house and pick up my shotgun," explaining to Roy that he wanted it "for hole (mole?) shooting." LeClair drove the couple of miles to Conley's father's home in Glover and parked in his door yard. "Larry got out of the car," he said, "went into the house and came back with a shotgun and put it on the rear seat of my car. He got in and put four shotgun shells on the dash of my car."

As the three headed back north leaving Barton on Rte. 5, Conley said "Let's go to Irasburg and scare the n-----s." They had little to fear of any police interfering when the VSP staffing regime for night shifts provided for, at most, two or three troopers covering the three-county NEK. Nobody in the car objected and LeClair soon turned west onto Rte. 58 for a few miles before arriving in Irasburg "a little after midnight." He was already familiar with the small town, with houses clustered around a village green and others nearby, because of his employment driving a milk truck in the area. Conley asked him "Which house do the Negroes live in?" and, after passing the green and intersecting with Rte. 14 heading north through two gentle turns, he pointed it out. It was on the right, set back about 100 feet from the roadway, lit by a single porch light. A street light on a pole in front of the house also shown down on the road that, together with whatever light came from neighboring homes, constituted the only illumination of the area.

Called the "Phillips house," Johnson was in the process of purchasing it from a couple, paying $150 a month in rent for seven months and the balance covered by a mortgage, after the sale of the neighboring first house was cancelled and the attorney general's office assisted in getting his deposit returned. The structure still stands, a large three-story Victorian building (painted yellow at the time) with, as Ophelia Johnson described, "13 or 14, maybe more" rooms and no electricity on the top floor or telephone.[268] With the exception of sons George and David asleep in a second-floor bedroom, the rest of the family and Barbara Lawrence was awake and seated in the dimly lit living room facing the roadway with the window shades down and the front door open on this warm evening. LeClair explained that as they neared the house Conley told him to slow down, retrieved the shotgun from the rear seat and loaded two shells into it. As LeClair proceeded at ten to fifteen miles an hour, Conley pointed the gun out the passenger window and fired both rounds towards the house striking a living room window.

Johnson was in a downstairs bathroom at that moment when he said he "heard a noise of glass breaking" that "sounded like a firecracker." "I then heard a second shot," he told police, "and then my daughter yelled and said someone was shooting at our house." He rushed out into the hallway and shouted upstairs to George "5 or 6 times" to get his German Luger pistol from his bedroom and bring it down. He purchased the Model 1937 9mm weapon, serial number 2400, in Marina, California just two months before coming to Vermont and George knew where he kept it.[269] Impatient at the time it took for him to respond, Johnson dashed up the stairs where he met him midway to receive the pistol. His other son, David Jr., also came part way downstairs, but he told him to go back into his bedroom and hide.

Johnson then chambered a round of the Winchester 115-grain jacketed ammunition from the pistol's magazine and continued up and into his bedroom. From there he could look out to the roadway through a set of opened windows to see, in the available light, what he described as a red vehicle with a white top resembling a Pontiac GTO or Chevrolet Malibu stopped on the side of the road. Unhesitant in his next moves, Johnson knelt down near the window and fired off three rounds in the vehicle's direction, none finding their mark.

Apparently unaware that anyone was in the unlit living room or that Johnson was returning fire over the sound of his loud car, LeClair quickly accelerated northwards. As they rode, the three occupants discussed their next move and Conley said, "Let's go back and see if we woke anybody up." They went about a mile northward to the Lowell Corner turnoff where LeClair circled back. Conley then crawled into the back seat with the shotgun, loaded it again and rolled down the left rear passenger window. During the five minutes all that took, Johnson ran downstairs to the living room and told everybody to get down on the floor or hide behind furniture. When Ophelia announced "here comes the car again," Johnson ejected the clip from the Luger that left one round in the chamber, and inserted a new one with several more.

Standing near the darkened doorway, he watched as the vehicle slowed down and approached on the wrong side of the road nearest to the house. This time Conley let off, Johnson recalled, three more rounds towards the house. After the vehicle passed by completely, he went out onto the porch and fired off all of his rounds directed towards its taillights; in total, he said he shot "approximately nine times."

LeClair remembered hearing only three shots, but nonetheless accelerated rapidly, squealing his tires, and headed back towards the Irasburg green as Conley called out "That fellow really means business." While none of Johnson's rounds struck the car, one did hit neighbor Elwood Kennison's house. After Kennison summoned police during the ensuing investigation, they found that it "entered the dining room through the north wall, struck the floor, ricocheted off the floor, continued across the room, struck the wainscoting on the south wall of the living room and bounced back near the north wall where it was found approximately 3' westerly of the entrance hole."[270] A laboratory analysis confirmed that it came from Johnson's Luger.

As soon as LeClair's taillights disappeared, Johnson told son George to go to neighbor Harold Snider's house and ask him to call the police while the family gathered on the front porch. Directly across the street, Ruth Skinner, an off-duty state police dispatcher, was also awakened by what she described as the sound of firecrackers. After the second set of shots, she went downstairs and saw the Johnson house lit up and George rushing by headed towards Snider's house.

"What's up," she asked him, and he told her they had been shot at and she said she would call the state police.[271] George continued on to the Snider's house where he woke up the household banging on the front door, gaining their help as well and calling the VSP for him.[272] Skinner's home soon became a base of operations for police where a radio scanner was installed in her kitchen to facilitate communications between officers working on the case and their offices. The presence of troopers could also be closely monitored by the media thereafter because the VSP did not possess the kind of technology allowing it to share confidential communications via the air waves.[273] Their every move was closely monitored in the next days by an intensely interested press and public watching their investigation unfold.

CASE NO. 273620

Thirty-five miles away at Troop B (Baker office, radio call sign KCC-588) headquarters in St. Johnsbury, a dispatcher received Skinner's call just minutes after midnight. She immediately radioed the information to Corporal James Hogan, assigned to the Derby substation responsible for handling the Irasburg area; a total of ten troopers worked out of that office, under the command of Sgt. William Green. The number of officers on duty the night of July 18–19 is not known, but the situation changed quickly in the hours after Skinner's call when everybody from Green on down in rank had their days off and vacations cancelled for the next two weeks to work the crushing hours the investigation demanded of them.

Hogan, only a few miles away from Irasburg in Orleans when he got the call, could not respond because he was in the middle of quelling a breach of peace complaint.[274] Instead, he directed the dispatcher to assign the matter to Trooper First Class Lane F. Marshall in Derby who just returned to his cruiser at 12:16 a.m. from a matter he handled at the local hospital.[275] Marshall's father, Lt. Everett Marshall, commanded the Troop A station in Colchester at the time and witnessed his son's swearing in ceremony into the VSP a year earlier in April 1967.[276] After ten weeks of training at Norwich University that summer, the 23-year-old Marshall graduated together with 28 other troopers. They included Jean G. Lessard who soon played a significant role in the case and Paul D. Lawrence responsible for the convulsions the state's law enforcement community experienced during the "affair" bearing his name in 1973–74.[277] The well-liked and respected Marshall later went on to attain the department's most senior position as director of state police.

It took Marshall eighteen minutes to get to Johnson's house, arriving there at 12:34 a.m. where he met him in front of the residence. Before he could begin to interview him, Marshall recounted Johnson shouting out, pointing "to a vehicle which was going by in a southerly direction and exclaimed, 'There goes the car.'" Marshall quickly stopped the vehicle and found it was owned and operated by Rev. Gordon Newell's son-in-law, but was not involved with the shooting.[278] What kind of car the man drove and whether it matched LeClair's jade-green colored vehicle is not described, but could have provided insights into the accuracy of Johnson's white-over-red description. The timing of the man's presence appears fortuitous as Newell recalls he first learned of the incident hours later, around 4:30 a.m., when Brenda called him.[279]

The initial account that Johnson provided to Marshall demonstrates the vagaries surrounding eyewitness testimony. Albeit the person making the report is presumably trying to be as truthful as they can, there are still concerns about accuracy when an event is recalled under stress, particularly in an exchange of gunfire situation. "Mr. Johnson," Marshall recorded, "advised that 3 or possibly 4 subjects had driven by the house in a northerly direction on Rte. #14 and fired, he believed, 2 shots at the house. The vehicle being a red and white late model car, continued north 3 to 4 hundred yards, and turned around and returned, firing 3 more shots at the house on the return trip. The vehicle then stopped, evidently to survey the damage."

Overall, Johnson's account was accurate, but it took a full-blown investigation of many days to uncover aspects of it proving otherwise. In particular, his report, repeated by others, that the car's color was white over red sent investigators in many directions before finding out its actual white over green configuration several days later. As one investigator explained during the board of inquiry's proceedings, "we were rather suspicious (about the vehicle's colors) right from the start;

we were not completely sold that this was a red and white one" and that other colors had to be checked out as well.[280] Assistant Attorney General Mahady who later participated in the investigation agreed with the confusion police faced and said that when he finally saw LeClair's car under nighttime lighting conditions that its green color appeared red.

After Johnson provided Marshall with his account, the officer inspected the immediate area and found two 12-guage shotgun shells, approximately eight to ten feet apart, on the north side of the road nearest the home that he took into custody. He then radioed his dispatcher for assistance from another trooper (presumably the outpost officer assigned to the area), only to learn he was not on duty. He further requested the dispatcher to contact the Newport Police Department to alert them to the incident and to watch for vehicles meeting Johnson's description.

"I then proceeded south," Marshall wrote, "on Rte. 14, checking all pull outs, side roads and driveways between Irasburg and Albany (seven miles away) and could find no vehicle to match the description given by Rev. Johnson. The village of Irasburg and surrounding area was also checked, with negative results." When Marshall returned to the home, Johnson told him "I would have all kinds of help, and that he would be in the Governor's Office in the morning." With nothing more he could do in the middle of the night, the officer returned to his Derby office where he "left word of the incident for Sgt. Green and Cpl. Wade, who took over the case."

Later that day, Johnson typed out a "Letter of Appreciation" on Marshall's behalf and sent it to Attorney General Oakes asking him to forward it on to the proper authorities. "State Trooper Lane Marshall," he wrote, "did everything humanly possible without hesitation to apprehend 3 men in an automobile, knowing they were armed and he was out numbered."[281] When he testified before the board of inquiry, Johnson repeated his admiration for Marshall and said he "acted above and beyond the call of his duty without hesitation of regard of his life. My family and Mrs. Lawrence also thought likewise."[282] Uncertain in how to respond to Johnson's glowing assessment of Marshall because of the attorney general's own interest in the case, Oakes's deputy Jonathan Brownell cautioned him that "I would feel under all the circumstances the less said by this office the better." Oakes agreed and wrote back to Johnson omitting any reference to Marshall's name or the work conducted by the VSP drawing particular attention to the importance of his own office. "Please be assured," he wrote, "that I, and every member of my staff, will continue our unremitting efforts to bring the perpetrator of this deed to account."[283] The tensions between Oakes and the VSP were increasing beyond their ongoing training differences and on this occasion he seems ready to avoid acknowledging in any way the efforts of police to investigate Johnson's situation.

By the time Marshall was dispatched to Irasburg, LeClair, Conley and Roy were already miles away racing along back roads. Right after Johnson fired his full clip at them, LeClair recalled that "I accelerated and drove out of town, turned left by the park and then took the Creek Road (proceeding south on the east side of the green) and turned left at the Four Corners (heading east on Kingdom Road), went to the road that leads from Barton to W. Glover (Barton Road), turned left and came (via East Albany and Roaring Brook roads) to Barton." Once they reached the town and stopped at Conley's car left behind at the gas station, he got out and put the shotgun into it. He then followed LeClair to his house where he parked the Oldsmobile "in the yard between the house and garage" and he and Roy got into Conley's Rambler. The three then drove the eighteen miles from Barton to Derby Center "by way of Willoughby Lake," taking more back roads before arriving at Jay's Snack Bar. After they "had lunch," the men took Roy to her home in nearby Newport and returned to Barton. There, Conley dropped LeClair off at his home between 2 and 2:30 a.m. and left.

On Saturday, July 20, the two men met again at Conley's home and read about their escapades in the newspaper. "What the heck did we do that for?," Conley said, "That wasn't very smart." He also confided to LeClair he "wouldn't have to worry about the shotgun as no one would ever find it." Later that day the two huddled together "on our story and agreed to stick to one story when the police came and questioned us." That story included omitting any reference to Bernadette Roy's presence that evening. She soon facilitated that process by leaving Vermont a couple of days later to live with an uncle in San Marcos, California placing her well out of the way of investigators. The ruse worked so well that her participation that night did not become known until weeks later when LeClair finally disclosed her presence.[284]

LeClair's account of what happened must be considered with other evidence indicating another perspective. Conley never pled guilty to any offense, instead agreeing to enter a no contest plea because of other information contradicting and/or mitigating LeClair's statement. According to Conley's attorney, Max Baton, this included that as many as six witnesses saw him at Jay's Snack Bar during the time LeClair said they were in Irasburg; two waitresses testified before the board of inquiry to verify Conley's presence at that time. Another inconsistency concerned the type of gasoline that LeClair says they got at his father's house that Baton contended would not have worked in LeClair's high-performance car. Baton also disputed Johnson's account of the many shots he fired at the car over the distance of an estimated sixty feet without hitting it once. Finally, the fact that the government granted LeClair immunity in exchange for his cooperation against Conley signaled to Baton he had every reason to be untruthful in his account without any fear of being penalized. "The only purpose," of making these points to the court, Baton said, "is to indicate there were things about the State's case that might not make it so open and shut as a recital of various witnesses and what they would say."[285] None of this information seems to have made an impression on the board of inquiry, concluding that Conley fired the shotgun into Johnson's home from a vehicle driven by LeClair.[286] It also found that Baton's conduct with regard to his involvement with one of the waitresses at Jay's Snack Bar counseling her not to talk to a VSP investigator was "most questionable" and "in the nature of an obstruction of justice."[287]

In Irasburg, before the morning of July 19 was over and as police assembled, Johnson's friend, the Rev. Newell threw gasoline on what was only a smoldering fire at the time. He came to their house around 5 a.m. after Brenda called to notify him of the shooting and spent the next few hours with the family as his outrage grew at observing the shattered windows. Prompted by Johnson's report to Trooper Marshall right after the shooting that he planned to contact the governor's office, and without the benefit of a police investigation confirming or refuting his belief, Newell immediately cast in his mind the event was racially motivated and could not restrain himself further. He left around 8 a.m. and went back to his church to prepare an incendiary indictment against whoever was responsible setting the tone for what was about to unfold (Appendix D). Quickly gaining access to a radio audience courtesy of station WIKE in Newport later that morning, he read a strident recorded one-page statement that "was to be quoted across our nation" conveying his anger. "We will not retreat," against this injustice committed against a colored minister and his family he said, "until every white citizen in this state is moved to a new kind of morality, so help us God." "It was quite obvious," he forcibly told the press, that "someone was out to get" the Negro minister.[288] He also notified other state religious leaders and called the governor's office to rally their support. Rev. Roger Albright, the executive minister of the Vermont Council of Churches and chairman of the Vermont Commission on Human Rights, also expressed his distress. He called the shooting a "contemptible terror tactic," providing "tragic evidence of the troubled society in which we live. Surely we don't need more than this to be convinced that the racist disease has infected even the small towns of Vermont."[289]

Politicians and citizens alike jumped into the fray expressing their divergent views of what happened exposing the fissure of area and state attitudes before an investigation had taken place. Politically ambitious local representative, Republican Emory Hebard, a resident and real estate agent in Conley's Glover hometown, said that "There was a lot of talk in Irasburg for the past two weeks. People were unhappy that a Negro family moved into the town." Assigning blame for the shooting, he said that "The governor and his people are determined to stir up Vermont and created problems and certainly earned this one;" an apparent reference to Hoff's youth project that he later argued disingenuously he supported.[290] Hebard's dislike for the governor and his liberal policies irked many Vermonters who viewed him as obstructionist to his progressive agenda. One correspondent wrote to Hoff after the shooting that "if there is any bigger bigot than Mr. Hebard, then I would like to know who it is," suggesting that "it would be wise to look into his background a little further." He also proposed that Hoff place undercover officers in Irasburg "who have no qualms about shooting down night riders" and to "catch Mr. Hebard's night riders." Thankful for his concern, Hoff wrote back that "Mr. Hebard must live with his conscience, such as it is, while you and I try to live with ours."[291]

A woman from southern Vermont also wrote to Hoff describing Hebard as "incendiary" and that if "Hebard & Co. have anything to do with it, I don't think the perpetrators will be very severely dealt with," counting Hebard among them. In this time shortly after Robert Kennedy's assassination and saying that she thought Hoff had the same "sensitive, fearless quality" Kennedy possessed, she also feared for his life. "Please," she pleaded, "have a police guard about you at all times," otherwise "A 'knoble' (sic) woodchuck (Vermont Redneck) may well decide to 'do you in' in order, perhaps to rid Vermont of 'them n-----s' or for whatever reason his or her warped mind might dream up." Hoff thanked her also for her suggestion that he have a body guard, but said that "if I am unable to travel throughout the State of Vermont without police protection, then I am of no value as a governor either to myself or to the people of this state."[292]

Other Vermonters readied themselves to take action. Another woman wrote to Hoff and said that people were on the lookout for "a red & white Pontiac" and that "my husband is going to get deputized & we are both going to watch all cars of that make."[293] Someone else told Hoff to offer a substantial $5,000 reward because a lesser amount would not generate sufficient interest for anyone with information to come forward. Another said "I am outraged," and told Hoff that the treatment Johnson received "completely negates any and all of the youth programs that were held at Lyndon State College, University of Vermont, Castleton & Ripton. Also the Poverty Program for Orleans County." A Committee of Concerned Students and Faculty at UVM also weighed in asking Hoff to investigate what it perceived as "the possible lack of police and judicial integrity." When an allegation arose that a VSP officer involved in the investigation was racist, another correspondent unloaded. "I don't think Vermont has a place for him. Why don't you send him to the South where he could club negroes in the street to his enjoyment and pleasure like the rest of the law enforcement there."[294]

Proud of his alarm alerting the public to racism's presence, and before he became disillusioned with Johnson in the next days, the literally bankrupt Rev. Newell later contended that his actions at this pivotal moment also made him a victim. He complained it was so because of the ire he felt from the VSP and attorney general's office at his vocal advocacy on Johnson's behalf as the investigation unfolded. He became defensive about what he had done and turned to attack the VSP itself because of the time it took to conduct its investigation. In his mind, his call to action and its response constituted the necessary "Prologue" to the entire story, announcing that "The curtain now rises on Act I."[295]

In this toxic environment infused with unproven allegations of racism and a governor protective of his youth project and reputation, and with political and religious leaders watching closely, VSP personnel knew full well from the very beginning that any of their missteps would not be missed. Newell's unsubstantiated, inflammatory allegation that racism lay behind the shooting poisoned its ensuing investigation guaranteeing it would become one of the most difficult and consequential moments in Vermont's race-related history.

INVESTIGATION

The story of how the shooting in Irasburg was solved is contained in over two dozen VSP reports, a couple of memoranda prepared by attorney general personnel and several court documents. Their many pages reveal a frenzied investigation conducted over a short period of time involving at least twenty VSP officers. They contacted and interviewed a staggering number of not less than 220 named witnesses, several of them multiple times, crossing and recrossing the countryside driving over 20,000 miles tracking them down. When located, they asked questions, corroborated their statements by talking with others, conferred among themselves to identify additional people that should be contacted and discussed how to approach them when inconsistencies arose. Their careful efforts portended the same exhaustive investigative process that Connecticut State Police officers used in their extensive investigation of the VSP during the Router Bit Affair a decade later.

Attorney General Oakes, still campaigning for governor, and his staff expressed their great frustration at the VSP's inability to quickly convey to them the results of their interviews in written form soon after they took place. They also raised questions inferring VSP negligence in its investigation because many of the finalized reports were dated weeks after the shooting. However, there is a simple explanation for the process the department used traceable to the economics of the times when it clamored to the legislature, and waited, for more support in the field. As Commissioner Alexander explained to the board of inquiry the challenges the process put on officers, "Ordinarily, if possible, a man will complete his reports during his duty tour." However, he continued, "in this case here the men were working practically around the clock, they were getting together frequently to check on what had been done by what officer and they were making notes all the time and stating what they had found out and they had no chance to make them up and bring them up to date."[296]

The delay in preparing reports only increased because of the logistical challenges they faced. Initially after their interviews, and when they had the time in this rushed environment, investigators documented their work by either writing down or tape recording it that then went to a single secretary-typist-dispatcher at the Derby office. Then, "as soon as she finds time," one investigator further explained to the board, "she types them, then they go to the sergeant, then on to the lieutenant then on down through (the chain of command)."[297] It was admittedly a tedious process, but if the department had sufficient resources and ability to streamline it Oakes could have had access to the information quicker than what he experienced. In the press of time and lack of resources, the delays were not intentional or neglectful, but Oakes and the board of inquiry inferred otherwise.

As Rev. Newell prepared his radio address to his intended national audience the morning of July 19 alerting it to racism's presence in Irasburg, Cpl. Laurence Wade arrived at his Derby office to find a note from Trooper Marshall about the events taking place a few hours before. He learned for the first time about the shots fired into Johnson's home, his finding two shotgun shells beside the road and his unsuccessful search of the area for the white over red high-performance vehicle. He also learned that Johnson "would be in Governor Hoff's office the first thing in the morning to get this matter straightened out."[298]

The 12-year veteran, who became a detective just the year before, immediately contacted his superior, Lt. Clement F. Potvin, at Troop B headquarters in St. Johnsbury. Potvin's authority extended over the entire three-county NEK area and the northern part of Orange County. Twenty-nine officers worked under his command as he brought his 19 years of experience to bear overseeing Wade in the detective division and Sgt. Green and his uniformed troopers working in the Derby office. The two conferred briefly, agreeing to meet at Johnson's home as soon as possible. Before leaving Derby, Wade instructed the St. Johnsbury dispatcher to contact all area body shops in the event someone came in with a vehicle bearing a bullet hole. He also told the dispatcher to contact a local garage to see if it had recently sold a vehicle matching the description of the one that Johnson provided.

Wade and Potvin met in Irasburg by 9:15 a.m., but only after Potvin mistakenly went to Newell's house. Apparently, Marshall first heard his name when he spoke with Johnson and then passed that information on to Wade who then advised Potvin during their call. Potvin probably interrupted Newell as he prepared his radio address, but who agreed to escort him to the Johnson house.[299] After speaking with each other, Potvin and Wade agreed that the lieutenant would take charge of the investigation for now. Among the many other officers participating, Wade's counterpart in the St. Johnsbury office, criminal investigator Cpl. John B. Shanks, also worked closely with them. These three men constituted the principal investigators overseeing the work in the field, assisted by officers from other stations and headquarters personnel in Montpelier.

While Newell subjectively cast the shooting event in racist terms, without such proof Marshall, Wade and Potvin all described it objectively based on the facts before them. Marshall and Wade called it a "Shooting," while Potvin and Shanks assigned the appropriate legal term "Breach of Peace," to it, with Potvin adding "By Shooting at a Dwelling House in Township of Irasburg." Months later after the sensation it caused around the state with allegations of racism swirling, in neighboring Caledonia County State's Attorney Lium characterized it in similar fashion, calling it a "serious act of vandalism."[300]

Unable to immediately identify a motive, Marshall recorded it as "Unknown." Similarly, Wade wrote that "No knowledgeable answer could be given at this time for the motive or cause of this shooting." Subject to a review of the evidence by the county prosecutor making the appropriate charging decision, regardless of what police called it, a person commits a breach of peace when they make a punishable disturbance of some kind. Even if the prosecutor wanted to charge an offense based on racist intentions, Vermont had no law against it forcing him to find some other statute, such as breach of peace, that fit the crime. Faced with little evidence to the contrary, police proceeded in their investigation to try and identify who was involved with this disturbance and to then present their findings to the prosecutor handling the case from then on.

Because of the sensitive nature of what they faced and the audience of onlookers following their every move, the VSP proceeded cautiously to gather evidence. As detective Shanks explained to the Irasburg board in response to a question posed by its counsel, Lt. Gov. Foote:

> There were a lot of strong suspicions in my mind, all through the case, and there were so many people that were coming forward with information and so many things to be checked out, it was almost impossible to, as far as I was concerned—we were working 15 and 18 hours a day. You've got to understand this, Mr. Foote, everybody was dead tired at the end of the day, we felt this was something that we should do and as I say, there were so many things that had to be checked out that you just couldn't let go until the next day and we didn't want to jump to any conclusions, at least as far as I was concerned, so therefore, I tried to be just as careful as I possibly could, in checking out all the leads I was involved in, before jumping to any conclusions.[301]

The investigation began with Potvin and Wade interviewing Johnson at length to expand on what he told Marshall earlier. The officers then conferred with the department's director of enforcement in Montpelier, Capt. Dean, with more than two decades of experience. Dean assumed overall responsibility for the investigation for the first three days until July 21 after Larry Conley's involvement became apparent. Substantial additional work took place to conclusively tie the case together and prove he did it, but in the time after July 21 Dean was sufficiently satisfied of the progress that he returned responsibility to Potvin. After they spoke on July 19, the officers agreed that their most immediate need required assigning troopers to remain on Johnson's property on a 24-hour basis that Dean coordinated with other stations around the state to provide.

Around 3 p.m. that afternoon, Wade arranged with Dean to expand their investigation to locate the vehicle involved. The white over red color combination that Johnson and his son George recalled seeing, together with a neighbor's observation it was white over some dark color, initially guided the direction of their work. Dean agreed to contact the DMV and all car dealers in the St. Johnsbury and Newport area to examine their files to try and find a vehicle meeting their description. It soon became apparent that the witnesses' well-intended eyewitness accounts of the vehicle's color could not be easily verified, demonstrated by Wade's experiments using other vehicles with different color combinations. "We had run other cars through underneath the lights in that area," Wade explained to the Irasburg board, "and found out you could come up with different colors, we really weren't sure, except on two-tone cars."[302]

The only color investigators could rely on concerned its white top, which meant utilizing the DMV's records where information on the more than 208,000 vehicles registered in the state existed. Compared to other states, Vermont lagged significantly far behind in many areas relating to law enforcement and the DMV was no different. The absence of a centralized computerized data base for criminal records, deficient numbers of troopers and support staff, a radio communications system in desperate need of modernization and recent calls for more cruisers in this rural environment constituted only a few of the most glaring problems the VSP faced.

The DMV experienced the same kinds of challenges because of its own antiquated recordkeeping system, demonstrated by the lengthy five days it took to provide investigators with the information Dean requested.[303] In defending his agency to assuage the concerns of Attorney General Oakes when he experienced the same kind of delay to his own request two days after Dean's, DMV Commission James Malloy wrote that "We do not have computerized facilities to extricate the information requested by you." To accomplish the task, he said, meant arranging with their contractor, R. L. Polk Company in Detroit, to retrieve the information from its data center in Cincinnati, Ohio. "The computer base," Malloy explained, "worked into the night extracting the information requested by you from the source material. Early the next day the prepared material was sent to this department via air mail and we received same on the third day from your inquiry. It was immediately hand carried to your office." Malloy never explained the two-day delay between Dean's and Oakes's requests, instead concluding that "To sum up the operation, the information was delivered to your office within 3 days of the inquiry."[304] Oakes responded that, while he appreciated the DMV's assistance, "it should not take that long to get this type of information" from the state's own facilities. It "should be forthcoming in a matter of minutes," he said, "as for example a list of all 1968 General Motors cars that have high performance engines or certain models in a given town or county."[305] These kinds of infrastructure problems in Vermont state government persistently threatened the quality of the VSP's work in this and other criminal investigations into the future.

Whether the five-day delay materially hindered the Irasburg investigation remains unclear because the VSP did not rely solely on the DMV as it pursued its work in other ways. A round-the-clock security detail of two troopers at a time sitting on Johnson's porch or in their cruisers and patrolling the area, with the presence of investigators asking questions and examining the premises, brought much activity to the household. Their interactions with the family were cordial and friendly, Johnson said. "They came in," he testified, "we talked, drank coffee, had coffee and doughnuts or whatever the people had brought over that was available for the officers or anyone else that came and this is just like right in the line of duty." Johnson's daughter Brenda recalled her conversations with two of the guarding officers as they sat on the porch in the middle of the night. "I talked to them about their job," she said, "and we talked about accidents that they had seen and I asked them about classes and, well, they told me they had gone to classes, seen films, which they had to do on occasion when some accidents took place and said they were pretty gruesome things. We talked about the policemen in California. I told them how they carried shot guns in their car with two officers to a car, so far as I know only one officer assigned to a patrol car here in Vermont."[306]

In the hours after Wade and Potvin initially conferred, investigators began their probe accumulating information from nearby, moving around the town looking for anyone that might know about the midnight disturbance. Little actual physical evidence existed beyond the two shotgun shells Marshall recovered and the shattered glass windows on the front of the house. While the board of inquiry faulted the VSP ("made no effort," it wrote) for not photographing or making casts of tire marks along the roadside, the experienced Wade explained why. Pragmatically, he said that "We observed some marks which would show that a car was on the shoulder of the highway, but nothing that would be identified, no particular tread or nothing. Plus the fact there was a lot of other cars in the area at the time of my arrival" made it impossible to say when the indistinguishable marks were laid down rendering any effort making casts pointless.[307]

While Potvin interviewed the residents of houses near Johnson's, Wade and Cpl. Lawrence Washburn spent the rest of the daylight hours trying to find those attending the fair at Newell's church two days earlier. Potvin spoke with nearby children and adults who heard the midnight commotion, but they could provide no information of value. Concerned that the shooting occurred in retaliation for the white women dancing with Black teenagers, Wade and Washburn looked for those witnesses. They made some progress, speaking with the Johnson children about what happened and identifying a number of people requiring them to travel to Newport to track them down. The two generated additional leads that sent other investigators to Barre to make further inquiries. Meanwhile, Trooper Marshall and Cpl. Hogan spent the day traveling between Troy, Albany, South Albany, West Glover, Barton, Brownington and Orleans chasing down more leads provided to them by other investigators and dispatchers in the Derby and St. Johnsbury offices receiving information from the public.[308] As Capt. Dean recalled, they received "more reports of cars than you could shake a stick at."[309] Despite the many interviews they conducted, none could identify anyone with a racial bias against the family or who might have fired the shots from a white-over-red high performance vehicle.

As their work continued into the night, around 11 p.m. Rev. Newell contacted Potvin and asked him to come to his home because he had information about the shooting. He also conveyed that it concerned the involvement of three individuals that, for the first time, included the name of Larry Conley. Potvin then met with Wade and Washburn in the Irasburg area to give them their names and directed them to begin conducting background checks while he went to Newell's home. There, he met with twenty-two-year-old Bruce Brown, accompanied by his wife, to report a conversation he had earlier that morning with Larry's brother, Bruce Conley. Brown could provide little information, telling him only that Bruce said Larry and two other men he named committed the shooting and nothing more. Despite the brevity of the information, Potvin found him credible enough that he met with Wade and Washburn and told them to find the three men and interview them. He also asked Brown to try and find out more information from Bruce Conley, only to learn two days later that Brown retracted his earlier statement tying Larry Conley and one of the men together.[310]

Unaware of the misleading parts of Brown's statement, Wade and Washburn located the two men he identified and spoke with them between 1 and 3 a.m. on July 20, but each provided believable alibis removing them from suspicion. At 3:30 a.m., they arrived at Howard Conley's Glover home to speak with Larry. It proved a consequential interview that subsequently had substantial impact on how the board of inquiry viewed the actions of police in the next weeks. Notably, because of the huge volume of interviews police conducted in rushed fashion, with the exception of only a couple, none of the more than 220 contacts they had with potential witnesses were reduced to formal, written statements sworn to by the individual before rushing off to conduct the next one. This further frustrated the board that found their absence, particularly Conley's on this occasion, a major failure of their investigative process, but which also lacks an appreciation for the hurried stresses police faced.

Howard Conley agreed to allow the officers to speak with Larry and, after the two signed an "interrogation form" acknowledging they read him his rights, the interview began. Conley described his movements between July 18 and 19 when he met with his friend Richard LeClair, their driving around, spending time at Crystal Lake and arriving at Roger LaRocque's home late on the 18th. Omitting any reference to Bernadette Roy's presence, he said they stayed there until 11:30 p.m. when they left and returned to the lake for a period before driving to Jay's Snack Bar in Derby. There, they ran into a friend, Roger Fortin, around 1 a.m., and his girlfriend, a waitress described a "a shapely girl with dark hair, a short skirt and bulging breasts." After a period, the two left Derby arriving back in Barton between 2 and 2:30 a.m. where they parted. "Conley advised," when Wade inquired about the shooting incident, "that he did not go into Irasburg at all on Thursday evening and knew absolutely nothing" about it. Conley also reported that he owned a single-shot 12-gauge shotgun that sat in his car outside as his father interjected it was used to shoot pigeons at the Barton Fairgrounds. They agreed that Wade could take the weapon and conduct whatever tests he wanted with it, which he did.[311]

At this point, 24 hours after the shooting, Conley had become only a potential suspect in a case drawing substantial outside interest. His alibi remained unchecked as his shotgun underwent testing to see if it fired the two shells that Marshall recovered from the roadside; it did not. There was insufficient evidence at the time to tie him to the shooting, and certainly none on which to base an arrest. However, the Irasburg board concluded otherwise and mischaracterized Wade's impressions of Conley and how police viewed his participation at that particular moment. Writing incorrectly in its findings that the officer's report identified Conley as "a prime suspect," in fact, it did not and Wade later specifically rejected such a characterization in his testimony, saying he was only a "suspect" at the time.[312] Washburn responded similarly and said he viewed Conley in a neutral way subject to further investigation because he had no "actual suspicion" of his involvement, but, instead "reason to believe that he might have" been.[313]

Capt. Dean agreed with their assessment, but also admitted that "I suppose in our zeal, we moved a little bit too fast (in conducting the interview) as far as Conley was concerned. We really weren't prepared to interrogate him effectively and efficiently." Explaining to the board the process leading up to the arrest of an offender, he said that "The investigating officers very often are satisfied that they are on the right track and that they have the suspect, but this doesn't necessarily mean that they have evidence enough to arrest him or convict him or get a warrant and this was the case as far as the Conley matters were concerned. At this point, I believe that almost every officer involved in this investigation, was satisfied that Conley was involved, but we certainly didn't have enough evidence to make an arrest, or prove it."[314] Even Assistant Attorney General Frank Mahady agreed there was insufficient evidence to arrest and charge Conley at this early stage of the investigation.[315]

There was much more work for police to do and, despite the board's inferences that their ensuing inquiries into the background of other witnesses, including David Johnson, was unwarranted, the investigators pushed on.

THE ATTORNEY GENERAL INTERVENES

As officers scrambled to identify and meet with witnesses and gather evidence, and Rev. Newell took to the airwaves to pronounce the presence of violent racism in Irasburg, Attorney General Oakes moved to interject himself into the situation. Only days earlier, he appeared in Grafton to inquire into the aftermath of the motorcycle mayhem and appoint Mahady to begin a more thorough examination. Born in Springfield, Illinois in 1924, James L. Oakes received bachelor's and law degrees from Harvard where he served as editor of its law review before becoming clerk to Second Circuit Court of Appeals Judge Harrie B. Chase. At the end of his clerkship, Oakes practiced law in San Francisco before moving to Brattleboro in 1950 to resume that work. Politically ambitious, he won a Vermont senate seat in 1960 as a Republican and went to Montpelier as one of Gov. Hoff's Young Turks.

In 1965, he participated in the civil rights movement as Hoff's personal representative, traveling to Alabama where he attended the famous Selma to Montgomery march.

In 1966 Oakes ran and won election to serve as Attorney General, sworn in in January 1967. In 1968, Hoff, in his third term losing luster and with his popularity further damaged by the divisive roll-out of his youth project, announced he would run for the U.S. Senate. The prospects for a Republican to replace Hoff looked favorable, and Oakes jumped into the party's primary running against Deane C. Davis, a native of Washington County and well-respected lawyer who eventually ascended to the roles of president and chairman of the National Life Insurance Company. Davis had over the course of a long career established a reputation as a competent, Vermont-born leader who espoused traditional Vermont Republican virtues.

During his campaigning Oakes sought a means to blunt Davis's sustained attacks he was soft on crime and neglectful of the needs of Vermonters in the northern part of the state. In turn, he argued in favor of gun control and opened an office in Montpelier to increase his presence and stabilize his faltering electioneering against his stronger opponent. On July 19, the press reported that Oakes planned in the next days to come to St. Johnsbury and Lyndon State College to meet with attendees at the Vermont-New York Youth Project.[316] Through such efforts he hoped to elevate his public persona in the NEK and, perhaps, shed the mantle that Davis bestowed on him of being "a warmed-over" version of Democrat Gov. Hoff.[317]

Oakes first learned of the shooting in Irasburg when he heard it on the radio around 5:30 p.m. on July 19. He recalled that he soon spoke with either second-in-command Maj. Glenn Davis or Capt. Dean by telephone to express his intention, as he testified, "to exercise some jurisdiction in the case" and come to the Johnson residence. Oakes did not tell police what he meant by "some jurisdiction" and, as Dean and Commissioner Alexander testified, he never told them he planned to take over the investigation. Oakes acknowledged his limited authority in that capacity and admitted to the board of inquiry that he had "no jurisdiction over the Department of Public Safety, directly" because it "is a branch of the Governor's Office." Rather, his oversight authority allowed his office, as one with concurrent jurisdiction with the county states' attorneys, to supervise their prosecutions of serious cases. Even on those occasions difficulties arose defining the appropriate role for his office's involvement as Oakes sheepishly admitted that his "supervisory jurisdiction is somewhat difficult to set forth."[318]

While Oakes found it difficult to explain his role in criminal investigations, the state's law enforcement agencies and county state's attorneys did not, with each authority already participating in a longstanding protocol that worked well for them. Police investigated cases and sent them to the prosecutor for action and, if needed, he requested assistance from the attorney general. Without specific authority to intercede in the VSP's work and when there was no pending prosecution by the Orleans County State's Attorney Leonard Pearson for him to supervise, Oakes participation in the next days rested more on "professional courtesy" between agencies than it did on any lawful requirement they coordinate their efforts. Oakes severely tested that relationship during this most controversial investigation conducted by the VSP since the Orville Gibson affair a decade earlier (which the press reminded Oakes he had not solved during his tenure), one it understood on July 19 as a breach of peace disturbance. As Commissioner Alexander and Chief Criminal Investigator Chilton told the board, neither of them could ever recall investigating such a case where the office of the attorney general became involved. Alexander said that never in his forty-one years of experience had an attorney general ever sought to intervene. "I had always understood," he testified, "that the Attorney General's Office, primarily (sic) to help the State's Attorneys and to assist in trying cases and so forth and not as an investigative officer." Notwithstanding, Oakes entered to challenge that longstanding tradition, the first attorney general to do so. Tellingly, immediately after James Jeffords assumed Oakes's position in January 1969, he recognized and moved to remedy the gray area of responsibility that Oakes created. He promised not to interfere with the VSP's investigative responsibilities and thereby sought to remove the strained relationships between the agencies that arose during his predecessor's time in office.

The differences in their respective responsibilities seems only to have arisen at this precipitous moment as the elections approached. It only accelerated as Hoff sought to save his tarnished youth project, despite evidence of Vermonters' hunger and malnutrition in Orleans County, by finding a scapegoat for the troubles in both Grafton and Irasburg. In the field, Oakes's presence immediately took on political undertones causing Potvin in charge of the VSP's investigation to question if he meant to use the occasion as a way to advance his campaign for governor. Regardless of the law, established police-prosecutor protocols and unique circumstances of the times, the Irasburg board consistently viewed Oakes favorably as an entitled co-equal partner in all respects and readily faulted the VSP for any perceived failure by it to recognize that position.

Oakes first arrived in Irasburg the day after his call to the VSP, accompanied by his wife and daughter, a volunteer counselor working with the youth project. He found Alexander and Dean also present and observed a handful of troopers engaged in work. Oakes introduced himself to Johnson and the two talked about what happened. Concerned at the absence of a telephone at the house, Oakes made a call to the telephone company to arrange for its installation, despite an ongoing strike by its workers. As he explained, he believed that having a telephone at the residence could both "save the state money" by avoiding to have a 24-hour police guard and to "make the Johnson's more secure."[319] Oakes also spoke with Alexander and Dean to receive an overview of what the investigation had uncovered so far. Around mid-day, Alexander accompanied Oakes and his wife in their car, traveling to a restaurant in Barton for lunch, where they discussed the case.[320] Meanwhile, Johnson left and drove to Newport to purchase "a supply of 9mm ammunition."[321]

As the Irasburg board probed the relationship between Oakes and the VSP, a point of substantial controversy arose as to when the department notified him of Conley's name as a suspect; a person interviewed only a few hours beforehand and whose alibi still needed checking. The board reasoned that had the police immediately concentrated their efforts on Conley that, together with the attorney general, they could have solved the case quickly. This would have then avoided, it insinuated, any further inquiries into the backgrounds of other witnesses that uncovered the embarrassing information about Johnson. While Alexander and Dean testified that they provided Oakes with Conley's name as a potential suspect during their first meeting,

Oakes waffled. He seemed to say that they had not, but also that he could not remember because they just "talked in generalities about various leads." His vacillation also appears in his personal, handwritten notes headed "Re Conley," where he acknowledged more affirmatively his name could have indeed come up: "Talk general—recall no names—if (Conley) mentioned was 1 of several & not prime."[322]

Oakes also briefly recorded the additional work police faced as they discussed whether the incident was "related to (Newell's church) dance" that the VSP thought most likely. He also noted his own theory that the culprit could have been Johnson's next-door neighbor; a thought prompting him to assign his northern investigator, Gregory L'Ecuyer, to look into. Alexander presented his personal view saying that he thought it involved "Some boys in the area who had gotten beered up," which Oakes recorded "turned out to be true." Dean provided him with additional information concerning Johnson's own feelings about the "possibility of someone in his background coming on from California in an effort to do him harm" that the attorney general agreed thought possible.[323] Despite knowing of Conley's existence, investigators had much more work to do to prove or disprove his involvement as they sorted through the various theories.

Compared to the detailed reports of police citing names, dates, times, locations and results of interviews, Oakes did not recall any of the events based on his own contemporaneously prepared notes. The ones he relied on for his testimony to the board were prepared months afterwards in preparation for its hearings that reveal his confusion over when he learned about certain pieces of evidence. As he testified to the board, "There are several of the dates that I have in there that are slightly off." When Oakes submitted his account of events to Judge Gibson beforehand, he acknowledged in an accompanying letter the limits of his ability to recall their timing. To do so, he said he had to rely on his deputies for assistance "in case my own memory has lapsed." Some of his confusion may also be attributed to his assistant, Frank Mahady, whose own chronology of his actions prepared months later did not always coincide with the police reports reciting correct information. As with Oakes, neither Mahady or L'Ecuyer prepared reports contemporaneously detailing their actions. Notwithstanding this inability to substantiate Oakes's claim inferring police did not tell him about Conley, the Irasburg board nonetheless positively credited his account to his advantage. In doing so, it fell into the same trap Oakes did in confusing the chronology of events dismissing any contention that the VSP notified Oakes of Conley's name on July 20, finding instead that they waited five days, until July 25, to do so.[324] The evidence indicates otherwise.

Announcing to the public that Oakes "called off his gubernatorial campaign" when he traveled to Irasburg, the press conveyed his angry impressions about what happened on the heels of the recent Grafton mayhem. "This is another outrageous act of violence—another outrageous shooting following the shots fired last weekend on a National Guard truck in Bellows Falls. We are simply not going to have this type of thing in Vermont. We will leave no stone unturned to solve it. Vermont is not going to become a haven for marauders."[325] Neither was it to be a home for vigilantes such as those he believed responsible for the death of Orville Gibson in 1957 that the press hounded him and his predecessors about for failing to solve. That was, he said, the reason why he decided to become involved with the Irasburg matter.

With that kind of publicity circulating and while Alexander, Dean and Oakes conferred, VSP investigators scrambled to conduct their initial inquiries and then assemble at their Derby office at 3 p.m. on July 20 to share information. A general "troop meeting" was conducted, one officer wrote, that included all sworn personnel in the three NEK counties "summarizing the developments of the case at this time."[326] Wade recalled further that their meetings took place as frequently as twice a day during the investigation, accompanied by many others that officers had in their cars out in the field. Potvin told Wade "on several occasions" he personally kept the attorney general's office up to date on what was happening.[327] Cpl. Shanks sought to further explain to the Irasburg board the number of other meetings they attended and their interaction with Oakes's office that delayed Conley's arrest for the shooting. "We discussed these things among the officers that were involved many, many times," he said. "We discussed them with (Assistant Attorney General) Mr. Mahady. I can remember at least 25 conferences with him, if not once, asking his opinions and so forth and he gave us the benefit of his experience and the experience of his office which we certainly appreciated. And, I thought that in doing these things, that we tried to approach them very, very carefully and possibly this is the reason why we didn't jump right down on Conley at this time."[328]

Nonetheless, Oakes's overall ire at his relationship with the VSP appears related to a delayed formal meeting between the two agencies to share information that did not occur until July 25 because VSP investigators were so busy.[329] Additionally, Oakes experienced substantial pressure in the week after the shooting coordinating his busy political campaign. Between 75 and 80 young adults spread out over the state pushing his progressive Republican platform that required his appearance at numerous locations to counter Hoff's prediction of a Davis primary win.[330] On the day of the Irasburg violence, he was in Burlington campaigning before quickly turning his attention to the NEK in the next week. He appointed a campaign chairman for Caledonia County and appeared in Lyndonville and St. Johnsbury advocating on the behalf of the state's colleges and for the region to become an economic showplace for northern Vermont and New Hampshire. He then turned his attention to march in a Brattleboro parade with Grandfather Turk Stoyan Christowe, traveled throughout Rutland County and made plans for an aggressive schedule in other southern counties. Perhaps piqued at his lack of understanding of the progress that the VSP was making in Irasburg, he took a subtle jab at their work while campaigning, singling out the recent Supreme Court decisions concerning police procedure. "The net effect of court decisions," he said, "stressing individual rights will be the upgrading of the quality of police investigature (sic) work."[331]

While the press continued to identify Oakes as heading the Irasburg investigation, in actuality he maintained distance from the VSP and never specifically told its officers he intended to assume command of it. As Commissioner Alexander told Hoff, if Oakes had requested access to his department's information on a daily basis it would have been provided. But, he said, "since no such request was made it was proper for us to assume that the Attorney General was satisfied with the information given to him. If he was not, all he had to do was to say so."[332]

By the end of the day on July 20, Potvin learned that Fish and Game Warden Donald Collins had information about Conley and arranged to meet him. Collins reported the trip he made with Conley when he inquired what police would do if he harassed the Black teenagers at Crystal Lake and his response that he should not do it. Collins also said that the day before he visited the Conley home and saw a shotgun partially covered by a blanket or jacket resting on the back seat of his mother's car. He described it as a 12-guage, with a walnut stock that appeared in good condition. Potvin took Collins to Irasburg to show him the shotgun that Conley handed over earlier, but Collins said he did not believe it matched the one he saw and which a laboratory analysis confirmed was not involved.[333]

On Sunday, July 21, Oakes returned to the Johnson home and met again with VSP personnel. Nothing of note occurred and he departed at some point to issue a press release requesting the public to contact his office with leads.[334] Interjecting himself directly into a parallel investigative process rather than asking people to contact the VSP directly was highly unusual and demonstrates further Oakes's willingness to test the lines of responsibility between the two offices. It also upset the established protocol existing between police and local prosecutors guiding their respective lines of authority to this time. His move to begin a second investigation is also understandable in the context of his flailing political campaign seeking traction against a strong opponent. While he interjected himself into the Grafton inquiry without causing problems, it proved both a cumbersome and confusing process in Irasburg when his office tried to pass on scrambled information to the VSP that he learned as a result.

Shortly after 5 p.m. that afternoon, Trooper Roger Cram interviewed Conley's friend, Richard LeClair, at his Barton home. While Conley identified him to police the day before during the interview at his father's home, it appears that the volume of leads and availability of manpower delayed a meeting with him any sooner. During their discussion, LeClair repeated their agreed upon version of events placing the two of them at Jay's Snack Bar in Derby at the time of the shooting and omitting any reference to Bernadette Roy's participation. "LeClair seemed to know what he was talking about,"

Cram wrote, "almost as if he had rehearsed the story."[335] It turned out he did.

At 9:30 p.m. that day, Cpl. Washburn met with the two individuals that Conley identified the day before, Roger Fortin, distinguishable because one of his legs was missing, and his buxom girlfriend Dianne Belanger, as the people who saw him at the drive-in around 1 a.m. on July 19. An experienced investigator, Washburn handled many aspects of the decade-old Orville Gibson case and discovered his body floating in the Connecticut River months after his disappearance. He knew how to interview witnesses and quickly uncovered the evidence seriously damaging Conley's alibi when the two denied his statement. It could not be true, they said, because neither of them could have seen him as Dianne was not working and Roger was not there at the time.[336] Their account notwithstanding, during the Irasburg hearing two other women working at the snack bar that night testified they distinctly remembered seeing Conley present at the time. The discrepancies presented by these, and other, accounts provide insight into the kinds of challenges police faced in distinguishing between credible and questionable statements as they sought to carefully untangle the story behind the shooting.

At 11:30 p.m., Det. Wade met with his superior, Chief Criminal Investigator Billy Chilton to turn over the shotgun he retrieved from the Conley residence and asked him to take it to the department laboratory in Montpelier for ballistics tests. The investigation also revealed by this time a number of inconsistencies in some of the things that their star witness Johnson presented in his involvement with the Irasburg community and Rev. Newell. There was also the outstanding issue of whether someone from his past, particularly resentful at his association with Barbara Lawrence, meant to harm him. "We had to investigate all avenues," Wade testified, "because we had nothing concrete on any particular (individual)." Seeking answers, Wade also requested that Chilton "run background investigations" on both Johnson and Lawrence.[337]

Conducting inquiries into witnesses' and suspects' past conduct is a routine practice of police because it often provides additional information able to resolve inconsistencies, support or mitigate representations of their involvement and provide other leads to solve crimes. Both Chilton and Lt. Robert Iverson sought to explain this basic, important part of police work to the Irasburg board.

"In a mysterious case of this nature," Chilton said, "it is customary to conduct a background to establish motive. In this case, it could have been jealousy, revenge, monetary," as well as related to "racial prejudice."

"In every criminal investigation," department counsel Eldredge inquired of Iverson, "is it routine that a background check be made such as in a case of this, where you are attempting to discover someone in the background that might have hated Mr. Johnson enough to shoot at him?"

"Yes, sir," he responded.

When asked, "Then, what you did in this case was the usual and ordinary thing?" Iverson replied in the same manner.[338] Regardless, board chairman Gibson took umbrage at Chilton's inquiries of California witnesses without having gone through the Vermont attorney general's office working, in turn, with the California attorney general to obtain the information. Chilton responded that in his experience he never consulted with the attorney general in the past while conducting routine background investigations and saw no reason why to do it in this case. Dissatisfied with Chilton's response, Gibson reminded him that he "had a lot to do with creating" the VSP in what seems an accusatory tone insinuating that Chilton intentionally sought to sidestep Oakes in the process.[339]

Notwithstanding these routine efforts by police to close any loopholes in this critically important case, Oakes slammed this aspect of the investigative process. Apparently unaware that his own deputy, Frank Mahady, did not believe enough proof existed to arrest and charge Conley at the time, he specifically identified officers Chilton, Iverson, Wade and Cpl. Dana Goodnow as the ones responsible for the delay their ongoing investigation caused.[340] Compounding the misplaced blame, the Irasburg board also accused the VSP of delaying the investigation because of its background work. It contended that it should have ended immediately after Cram interviewed the two witnesses in Derby indicating that Conley's account was untrue.[341] Based on this particular finding, the historiography of the Irasburg Affair for the past half-century has assumed a life of its own characterizing the time the investigators took to make these routine background inquiries to close loopholes as, instead, their pursuit of a Black victim rather than arresting the culprits responsible for the shooting.

Aside from the police, members of the public also wanted immediate answers. One angry Vermonter, resentful at the reputation that religious leaders assigned to Vermonters as racist, delineated some of the questions he had about the pending investigation. "How many pellets have been recovered" from the Johnson residence window frames, he asked, and "How many witnesses other than members of the Johnson family actually saw shots being fired from a car allegedly belonging to night riders?" It would also be interesting, he said, "to know more about the background of the recently arrived reverend: his education, military service, source of finance and his Vermont sponsors." Finding answers to these and other questions could, he ended, redeem "the good name of Vermonters" and be spared the "ugly insinuations (spread) in the future by professional crusaders."[342]

After meeting with Chilton, Wade traveled to the Johnson residence to check on troopers Jean Lessard and Bruce MacDonald, the two officers standing watch, arriving there around 1:30 a.m., July 22. Even at this late hour, members of the Irasburg community remained restless and Wade overheard several individuals engaged in intense conversations with some of the Johnson family. Their discussions concerned the interactions of their children with the Johnson children dancing together at Newell's fair. "It was felt by this officer," Wade noted, that two of the people "were asking quite a few questions of the Johnsons, which were not necessary, except to perhaps find out how much the police actually knew about the shooting."[343]

As complicated as the investigation was proving to be, nobody expected the bizarre event about to unfold just hours after Wade left the premises.

Chapter 5

ADULTERY

"A PERSON WHO COMMITS ADULTERY SHALL BE IMPRISONED IN THE STATE PRISON NOT MORE THAN FIVE YEARS OR FINED NOT MORE THAN $1,000, OR BOTH." VSA 13 § 201 (1947), REPEALED 1981.

DURING THE 15-YEAR PERIOD between 1953 and 1968, excluding those handled by local police departments, the VSP investigated 102 cases of adultery (also called the Blanket Act) resulting in charges filed against offenders. Eighty-three instances of the felony crime resulted in convictions statewide, seven of them taking place in the Orleans Municipal Court with jurisdiction over Irasburg. Lt. Potvin, now in charge of the shooting case in that community, was the investigating officer in four of the nine cases handled in that particular court (two of them apparently did not result in convictions). Before assuming his current rank, between 1963 and 1968 he approved of another two of the ten adultery cases filed by the VSP around the state; all resulting in convictions.[344] Now, in addition to his pressing responsibilities concerning the shooting, Potvin faced yet another instance of adultery, this time involving Johnson and Lawrence taking place directly under the noses of his troopers.

The two recently-arrived California residents came from a part of the country where adultery did not constitute a criminal offense. Instead, as Lawrence's Pacific Grove attorney explained to Orleans County State's Attorney Pearson concerning the adultery case he eventually brought against her, a "younger generation" viewed it as "more of a popular hobby." Cautioning Pearson about the prosecution of his client, the attorney also advised him that since the matter "has received a large amount of publicity in the San Francisco and Monterey County press" and was not a criminal offense in California, that others could view any actions taken against her and Johnson as "a Vermont political matter and of racial prejudice." He also teased Pearson (wrongly) that he could not prove Johnson was a married man at the time of the alleged offense and that "our local colored population is offering long odds that you will not be able to do so."[345]

If the attorney's jab was accurate, what did the local Black community understand about Johnson's relationship with Ophelia? Did it confirm Lawrence's belief that he and Ophelia were not married? Fraught with difficulty that no other prosecution for adultery in Vermont history presented because of its racial overtones, the VSP and Pearson entered into a minefield of challenges to resolve this felony offense, one backed up by a history of enforcement.

Barbara Lawrence's admission that she and Johnson engaged in sex dozens of times in California, a seeming "hobby" for them, exploded into view just a few hours after Wade observed members of the community quizzing the Johnsons about the case. Between 5:00 and 5:30 a.m., on July 22, with two officers stationed nearby, dressed in a nightie and wearing panties and a bathrobe, she left her second-floor bedroom and came downstairs to the living room. A light was normally on, but apparently switched off as the dawn light began to filter in making things distinguishable. She saw Johnson, perhaps tending to the coffee pot he kept going to fuel the 24-hour guards outside, and the two sat together on a couch.

"We were necking, or petting," she later told police, and she removed her panties while "he just pulled his pants down" and the two "started having sexual relations." During the next few minutes, she admitted that Johnson "did place his penis inside my sexual organ" until they heard a noise.

Trooper First Class Jean Lessard, a classmate of Lane Marshall's, joined the VSP just the year before and was stationed at Troop K in Montpelier when he received the assignment to guard Johnson's residence. Six officers from other stations worked the 24-hour duty, two assigned to each eight-hour shift. Lessard and Trooper Bruce MacDonald, also from Troop K, drew the late shift from midnight to 8 a.m. and worked together spending time stationing themselves on the front porch, sitting in their cars or walking around the property. Shortly after their shift began, a light rain fell leaving the unprepared officers cold in their short-sleeved summer uniforms. A request to their dispatcher to have someone bring them coats brought another trooper to the house, arriving with them around 2 a.m. The three officers then went into the unattended living room where they shared the coffee that Johnson kept available for them whenever they wanted it. Lessard and MacDonald had been in the room a couple of times on past evenings at Johnson's invitation to partake and things were no different on this occasion.

Hours later, the two officers sat in their cruiser, parked in the driveway 20 to 30 feet away from the house. MacDonald recalled that Lessard said he was going to get more coffee and offered to bring some to him, but he declined. Leaving MacDonald alone for the next few minutes, Lessard walked around the horseshoe shaped driveway, and along the side of the house smoking a cigarette before climbing the front steps onto the porch leading to the living room.

"I saw an arm in the opening," Lawrence recalled from her position lying on the couch, as Lessard stopped in the doorway and went no further. He sensed movement to his right and saw Johnson between her legs and "getting off" as he sank down to the floor on his knees at the side of the couch. Looking further, he saw Lawrence on her back wearing a bathrobe with "the lower half of her body" exposed and that Johnson had what appeared to be a nightie in his hands.

Johnson swung an arm towards Lessard, waving for him to leave and in a "hoarse whisper" told him to "get out, get out" as Lawrence began "whimpering or crying."

Lessard quickly apologized and said, "Oh, excuse me. I didn't know I was interrupting" and left the doorway. He retreated to the lawn where Johnson followed telling him he "would get me my coffee."

Lessard declined, apologized again for the intrusion and returned to the cruiser where MacDonald sat. When he got in, MacDonald recalled he appeared "disturbed, embarrassed, or something" and asked him to move the car to another part of the driveway. He did so and Lessard shared with him what he just witnessed. In the meantime, Lawrence recalled that she "waited in the kitchen for approximately five minutes, then I went upstairs."[346] As soon as their shift ended at 8 a.m. and their replacements arrived, the two officers drove to the Derby office where Lessard told Sgt. Green about the encounter. Green told him to prepare a statement, which he then provided to Wade who arrived by 9 a.m. after his long day before and that ended just a few hours earlier.

The ill-timed tryst between the two Californians presented a wholly unexpected intrusion into the ongoing shooting investigation. While Lessard never observed the two actually engaged in sex, he had sufficient reason to believe they had. As he testified, when he opened the door "They were separating" and "either had started with it, were in the act of it or had concluded it." Lessard's observations constituted, at least, a reasonable suspicion approaching a higher level of probable cause sufficient for the state's attorney to institute felony charges against the two for adultery.

When that later happened, the VSP faced a firestorm of skepticism questioning how Lessard's account could possibly happen, belittling him personally and the department specifically for what many considered the harassment of a Black man. Adultery was never prosecuted in the recent past, their detractors said, ignoring the many cases in which it was. Notwithstanding, additional reason for suspicion for the authorities' actions existed because of the Supreme Court's recent decision in *Loving v. Virginia*, 388 U.S. 1 (1967) overturing laws banning interracial marriage because they violated constitutional safeguards. The toxicity of those few moments in Johnson's living room only elevated tensions to a higher level than ever before.

None of the hundreds of pages of transcripts and reports in the Irasburg matter recite the prevailing legal standard of proof required to prove adultery. Nor do they acknowledge the challenge this particular offense presented to the VSP when an officer witnessed the commission of a felony in his presence; a first-of-its-kind occurrence in recorded Vermont jurisprudence. As the Vermont Supreme Court determined years earlier in the controlling case concerning adultery, "When it is proved that the parties were found in bed together under circumstances affording presumption of an intention to commit the act as charged then the requirement of the statute is met." *State of Vermont v. Myrtie Bell Woods*, 107 Vt. 354, 357 (1935); reiterated and approved in *State of Vermont v. Martha Vadney*, 108 Vt. 299, 302 (1936) holding that proof of intent is not required. Similarly, in a civil context alleging alienation of affections, the court ruled that adultery "may be proven by circumstantial evidence" and that it "must be such as will lead the guarded discretion of a reasonable and just man to the conclusion that the act was committed." *Parker v. Hoefer*, 118 Vt. 1, 11 (1953).

Evidence that adultery occurred did not, as one defense attorney contended, require Lessard to actually "see (Johnson's) organ in her organ."[347] Instead, as the supreme court ruled, bare circumstantial evidence was sufficient to show it happened. However, it was a less desirable situation than one where more conclusive evidence existed able to convince a jury beyond a reasonable doubt, the highest level of proof required to sustain a criminal conviction. Under close scrutiny by the clergy and press in their investigation of the shooting, and contrary to the retrospective opinion of the Irasburg board that circumstantial evidence was sufficient to arrest Larry Conley in the shooting case, the VSP pushed on to meet the higher level of proof required at trial. Success required nothing less as it now faced the dual, explosive challenge of dealing with the Black victim of violence participating in a separate felony offense with a white woman.

Both the shooting and adultery cases needed only one thing to meet the higher standard of proof required to obtain a conviction and break each of them wide open: an actual eyewitness-participant willing to testify against the principal offender. Chilton and Wade launched into their work to accomplish the task upon receiving word from Lessard of the most recent crime he witnessed. The two already agreed the prior evening to look into Johnson's and Lawrence's past because of his conflicting stories and the possibility that someone from California committed the shooting and this new crime only affirmed that reasoning.

Aware that they came from Seaside, Chilton contacted the local police to make his initial inquiries with a high-ranking officer. The information spilled out conveying the unsavory entries in the department's files suspecting Johnson "of organizing girls for prostitution, hanging around Fort Ord, gambling and pimping," not paying bills and receiving welfare assistance. Wade looked elsewhere and contacted the Irasburg post office, requesting it to record the names and addresses of letters coming from and going to the Johnson household.

The next day, Wade learned that one of Johnson's sons wrote to an address in St. Petersburg, Florida that he passed on to Chilton for further inquiry.[348] As a result, additional information came out concerning Johnson's arrests in the 1950s for assault and being AWOL from the military. The press and clergy, echoed by the Irasburg board, interpreted these efforts to collect evidence as racially motivated because of their timing coming so soon after the discovery of him and Lawrence caught *in flagrante delicto*. However, the primary sources reveal they proceeded in a methodical, timely manner in the same way that police routinely conducted their work, which included contacting Attorney General Oakes to advise him of this latest development.

Late that afternoon Capt. Dean contacted Oakes to let him know about the situation. He testified inaccurately during the Irasburg proceedings that he did so on July 24 when other evidence showed it actually happened on the same day it occurred on July 22.

As the VSP radio records reveal, at 5:25 p.m. on that day, Dean requested the St. Johnsbury dispatcher to contact Oakes to ascertain a telephone number where he could be reached because he needed to talk to him; the request was repeated at 5:26 p.m. after an apparent miscommunication about the number provided to Dean. While Oakes said he could not remember receiving the call in his ensuing disparagement of the VSP, Dean, and his wife overhearing the conversation, said otherwise. Dorothy Dean was present when her husband made the call that afternoon and heard him tell "the Attorney General of the incident of the adultery occurring early that morning by and between Johnson and Lawrence."

Additionally, she heard her husband explain to Oakes, then heavily engaged in campaigning, "that his purpose in calling was that the Attorney General was running for Governor and that it was (his) feeling that the Attorney General should want to know the information as to the adultery before sticking his neck out."[349]

When asked about his conversation with Dean, Oakes did not deny it occurred. Instead, he avoided its uncomfortable undertones, waffling that "I have no recollection of that telephone call. It is quite possible that it was made, but I have no recollection of it. It certainly sounds that it would be. My answer, if he reported these facts (about the adultery) to me, that so far as I could see, they have no relevance or bearing on the investigation of the shooting incident. So that I simply have no recollection of it." His lack of any recollection about the call is consistent with his inability to recall his earlier encounter with Alexander and Dean at the Johnson residence when they told him that Larry Conley's name came up in the shooting case.

Oakes never confirmed the additional information from Dean that he wanted to warn him about the adultery allegation to avoid embarrassment on the campaign trial because he was not asked about that part of their conversation. Acknowledging that a high-ranking VSP officer sought to bring him up to date about the new charges to warn and protect him from making misstatements to the public during a tough campaign appear as aspects of the Irasburg Affair that Oakes apparently did not care to have known. As their conversation ended, the two agreed to delay any action on the adultery matter because the two cases were not connected and Dean "assured (Oakes) that our investigation would continue as it has in the past."[350]

The next days demonstrate the kinds of problems that the experienced police investigators faced conducting their many interviews and chasing down leads when a politically charged gubernatorial candidate, frustrated at the time it took, sought to intervene. Approving of Oakes's intervention into the shooting case, the Irasburg board said it was only solved because of him. The reason for its harsh reasoning? Because after discovery of the adultery offense on July 22, it wrote, "most of the activities of the members of the State Police were directed towards digging up anything that could be dug up about Rev. Johnson."[351]

The evidence points elsewhere.

On July 22, the VSP did consider Conley as a suspect (but not the "prime suspect" as the board repeatedly characterized him) providing a questionable alibi, discounted by two witnesses, concerning his presence at a Derby snack bar at the time of the shooting. Richard LeClair admitted he accompanied Conley that night, but mentioned nothing about the two witnesses. Nor did either man identify the missing Bernadette Roy as their companion. Both accounts left police still searching for clues to prove or disprove them one way or the other. And who were the other one or two occupants of the car that Johnson said were present. Nobody had any information able to answer that question. On July 23, the laboratory analysis of Conley's shotgun revealed it did not fire the two shells Marshall recovered at the scene. On that day, Potvin and Detective Dana Goodnow recovered one of the 9 mm bullets Johnson fired embedded in his neighbor's kitchen wall. Was the whole thing staged, some in the community asked, and did Johnson himself actually fire off both the shotgun and pistol shots?

Searching for answers, Goodnow and Shanks traveled to Nashua, New Hampshire to speak with a Conley relative while other troopers fanned out trying to find the white-topped red vehicle that Johnson described and waited for the DMV to provide them with a list of possible matches. There were so many troopers working on the case that Potvin remained available in the three-county Troop B area to handle routine calls making it impossible for him to travel to Montpelier to meet with an impatient Oakes demanding answers. In Brattleboro, columnist Wibecan penned a piece entitled "Welcome to Vermont," consoling Johnson and his family that "you are not alone." "The rest of us Black people in Vermont," he said, "may not have had shotgun pellets flying through our living rooms yet, but we have become aware of the subtle white racism that exists here as well as everywhere else in America."[352] The tension could be cut with a knife.

Five days after the shooting, on July 24, the DMV finally provided authorities with a list of possible vehicles to guide them in locating and speaking with their owners. Nothing indicates that any of the DMV's information actually led investigators to LeClair's white-over-green car or to any other vehicle that might have been involved; questions only answered through dogged gumshoe detective work. Unwilling to wait for the results of their inquiries and to receive additional updates on the investigation, Oakes decided to become more aggressively involved.

He assigned the 29-year-old Mahady and investigator L'Ecuyer (both lacking law enforcement experience) to work on the case full time. Two investigative channels now worked in parallel in an environment where, Mahady alleged because of his frustration at the time it took for police to type out their reports, there existed "a definite lack of any central gathering point for information—a lack of coordination."[353] His unfamiliarity with the deficiencies in support services that the VSP experienced in preparing reports and uninformed impressions about their mutual interaction differs markedly from what other officers witnessed. They easily recalled that their meetings took place sometimes two times a day to share information as Det. Shanks's recited his personal involvement with Mahady on some two dozen occasions.

When Oakes learned that eight of the vehicles identified by the DMV were registered in the Barton area and might fit the description of the suspect vehicle, he refused to wait any longer for the VSP to conduct its work. Instead, with his assistants, he went on an amateurish foray into the countryside without telling the VSP looking for a blue Chevrolet Camaro to ascertain the accuracy of a rumor the owner had changed his tires to avoid detection. The car's registered owner, Gary Marcotte, had already been spoken to by VSP investigators who dismissed his participation because of a verified alibi. Regardless, Oakes still pursued the lead that he marked with a star next to Marcotte's name in his personal notes listing the vehicles identified by the DMV.

"And so," Oakes testified to the Irasburg board, "the three of us drove up to this fellow's house to see if we could get a look at the car and to see if the tires were changed, specifically. We couldn't tell this. We drove back by it and we still couldn't tell about the tires, but we did see this 1968 blue Camaro with white stripes around the front of it and we then proceeded to set our sights—this fellow became our Number One suspect."

Number One suspect? Now, regardless of the work the VSP did discounting the owner's involvement, Vermont's campaigning attorney general turned investigator single-handedly targeted the owner of a blue car with white stripes that did not fit Johnson's description as the leading culprit for the shooting. Oakes's suspicions about the owner fell apart as the three men spent the next three days "checking out his story" only to find that "he turned out not to be the person." As a favor to Oakes, it appears that the board of inquiry simply chose not to wade into resolving that bizarre scenario and just ignored it.

Another of Oakes's theories that Johnson's neighbor might be responsible for the shooting sent L'Ecuyer on a two-day quest to debunk. Despite Potvin's insistence to Oakes that another individual he thought responsible had a strong alibi removing him from the suspect list, it took Mahady and L'Ecuyer another two days to come to the same conclusion. It also appears that Mahady and L'Ecuyer confronted Rev. Newell about his relationship with Johnson. "One day two investigators ~~from the Attorney General's office~~," his notes describe with the stricken words, "came to my home and asked if it were customary for a reputable clergyman to give out information from the pulpit that a colored family might move to town based purely on some rumors that had been whispered about?" As with the apparent excision of Johnson's police record from a VSP investigator's report while in the board's possession, this alteration of a second exhibit with stricken words seems to indicate an effort to distance Oakes's office from the comedic aspects of his second investigation.

Oakes himself also spoke directly with two "confidential informants" calling him in response to his request that anyone from the public with information to contact his office. He believed one of them provided "quite accurate" information, identifying him as "Don Hovey of the *Caledonian Record* (newspaper) whose sister is the town clerk of Barton, with offices next to Gov. Emerson."[354] Mahady had a much different impression from his boss after he spoke with Hovey and said he "was playing games with us."[355] Oakes did pass on the substance of the public's reports he received to the VSP, but they went nowhere, causing further problems because of their inaccuracies and inconsistencies. While the board of inquiry concluded with admiration that Oakes's intervention ultimately solved the case, the evidence indicates it only added an unnecessary layer of confusion and delay.

While Oakes wavered from one suspect to another in his enthusiasm to solve the crime, the VSP continued in dogged fashion to chase down leads and share their results with his two assistants. Despite their collective suspicion that Larry Conley was involved,

Mahady continued to agree with officers that insufficient evidence existed at the time warranting his arrest.

Based on information that Goodnow and Shanks gained in Nashua from Conley's relative, additional inquiries sent them to a Barton garage to speak with young men loitering about. Rumors that an automatic shotgun was used in the shooting sent investigators down more rabbit holes searching for non-existent proof. Additional interviews followed that, by the end of the week, pointed more directly at Conley as the responsible person. While investigators sought additional information to confirm their suspicions, on Saturday, July 27, Oakes summoned Mahady to his home and directed him to focus his efforts on Conley. From this point on, Oakes separated himself to pursue his campaign for governor, relieving the VSP's concerns for the moment that politics intruded into the investigative process allowing the two agencies more freedom to interact with each other.

FINGERPRINTS AND A CONFESSION

As Capt. Dean promised Oakes when he advised him on July 22 about the adultery matter that the VSP investigation into the shooting case "would continue as it has in the past," other officers continued to look into Johnson's report that someone from California might have responsibility. While Oakes later tried to distance himself from this part of the investigation, it was one of his own attorneys, the head of his consumer affairs division, responsible for sending it in this direction. On July 26, Assistant Attorney General Richard Blum shared his concerns about Johnson with Dean apparently without Oakes's knowledge. The two discussed Johnson's belief that someone from Barbara Lawrence's family could be responsible and that his military identification appeared altered. To establish his identity, they decided that the VSP would obtain his fingerprints to answer their questions.

Dean had summoned Wade to their Montpelier headquarters earlier that day to confer with him about the case. They decided to assign undercover officers to enter into bars in Newport, Orleans and Barton to make further inquiries, notifying two of them to begin that evening.[356] Around midday after his conversation with Blum, Dean ordered Chief Investigator Chilton to go to Irasburg to question Johnson about the information he provided to Blum, to fingerprint him and to speak further with Barbara Lawrence. Chilton proceeded immediately to the Johnson residence, arriving there around 2 p.m., where recently promoted Detective Corporal Dana Goodnow joined him. Goodnow, a savvy 12-year veteran officer currently living in southern Vermont and recently assigned to the Narcotics and Drug Abuse Unit, was called in to assist because of his familiarity with NEK criminal suspects from past assignments.

Goodnow previously accompanied Potvin when the two recovered the bullet from Johnson's neighbor's house and traveled with Shanks on their trip to Nashua to interview one of Conley's relatives. The rush of events in the next few hours provided a high level of drama for both Chilton and Goodnow as each dealt with Johnson and Lawrence in separate events that, without considering their context, provided significant ammunition for those unfamiliar with what actually happened to try and disparage the VSP. However, looked at chronologically, utilizing the testimony from each of the participants, the events reveal the unique challenges that police faced in trying to unravel both the shooting and adultery allegations as claims of racism swirled around them.

The two officers found Johnson at his home, sitting on his porch with members of his family, and Lawrence elsewhere on the property. Johnson already knew, because of Oakes's investigator L'Ecuyer's presence and who already spoke with Blum, that police wanted to take his fingerprints. He greeted the officers indicating his readiness to have them taken as they invited him to have a seat in the cruiser to talk and where Chilton sat behind the wheel. Johnson sat in the front passenger seat while Goodnow sat behind them.

At one point, Johnson told the officers about other places where his fingerprints might be located, embellished with more lies about his background. "I can tell you where you can contact the Sheriff's Department in San Bernardino," he said, "where I was a part-time sheriff" or "the Hall of Justice in San Bernardino where I was a licensed detective, and a licensed special officer."[357] Johnson's questionable comments about his fingerprints continued later when he swore under oath to the Irasburg board they were also taken during his time in the military when "I was cleared for Top Secret and Crypto(graphy), which is the highest clearance you can get in the service." None of it could ever be verified.

When they began questioning Johnson, Chilton said they wanted to clarify some discrepancies that had come up. Their interactions were cordial and unalarming as he queried about the color of the car involved in the shooting and a tax-related issue that seemed inaccurate on paperwork he filed with the DMV to obtain his license plates. Chilton then switched direction and asked about Johnson's four-year-old "granddaughter" who was actually his daughter's child. Johnson explained the confusion with the paperwork and that he called the child his granddaughter to avoid embarrassing his 17-year-old daughter who had made a mistake becoming pregnant at a young age. Considering Chilton's inquiries into Johnson's credibility in a markedly different light and interjecting its impressions of how police should conduct their inquiries and routine background investigations, the Irasburg board deemed that "none" of them had "any bearing on this case, and none of which was any of his business."[358]

The questioning continued as Chilton inquired of Johnson about his ordination into the clergy, marriage to Ophelia and military background. Johnson answered each of his questions and told them about his military experience, including conflicting information that in 1948 he served both in the Navy Reserves and in the Army as a paratrooper making 45 parachute jumps. He also told them, Goodnow recorded, "emphatically that he was never arrested and has no record of any kind." None of this information proved accurate. At one point, Chilton suggested to Johnson, maintaining the validity of his ordination, that firing on the car speeding away from his house the night of the shooting was inappropriate conduct coming from a minister and that he should have "turned the other cheek."

Johnson disagreed and told him, "Have you heard the part about the Lord helps them that helps themselves." Listening to Johnson from the backseat, Goodnow thought his attitude and response peculiar and "very out of place at this time."

When Chilton switched and asked him about someone resentful at Lawrence's relationship with him coming from California to commit the shooting, the tension began to increase. What Johnson thought was a meeting to take his fingerprints now moved into a sensitive subject he did not want to discuss. Chilton already knew of Trooper Lessard's report that he saw the two of them together the morning of July 22, and when he inquired further about his relationship with her, he exploded. "Man, give me a break," Johnson shouted, "What are you trying to accuse me of?"

Chilton responded with words that others later interpreted as bearing a racist connotation when it appears, as he and Goodnow explained, they constituted an emphasis, saying "Boy, I'd like to give you a break.".

Johnson opened the door, shouted words to the effect of "I want you to know I am a man, not a boy," and called several times for Lawrence to come to the car as he stormed towards the house. As Chilton testified, he was "shouting and screaming," "very upset and alarmed, disturbed, and violent," and said he was going to call the governor's office and have their jobs. He charged up onto the porch where one of his sons stood and told him "to bring the pistol inside and the clip" and went in. Fearing for their own safety, Chilton and Goodnow got out of the car with their weapons drawn and directed a nearby trooper to move his cruiser and place it between them and the house.

After two to three minutes Johnson came out holding the pistol, but his demeanor, Chilton said, was a "complete switch. He was very calm, cooperative, pleasant." Potvin arrived by this time and spoke with Chilton before asking Johnson if he would cooperate with the fingerprinting. He agreed and Chilton removed the necessary equipment from the back of his car, placing it briefly on the trunk lid in a move that later drew harsh public criticism. As Johnson and others contended, Chilton intended to embarrass him in public by taking his fingerprints in the driveway where passing cars could see them. Chilton disagreed as he understood they would take them in the living room, where they soon moved. Attorney General investigator L'Ecuyer witnessed the uneventful process and examined Johnson's papers while Chilton worked. Chilton left when he finished, but later faced allegations of racism from Johnson in the next days, apparently because his use of the word "boy" when speaking with him. Defending himself when questioned by the press, Chilton said simply that Johnson is "trying to find everything he can to cry discrimination."[359]

As Chilton dealt with Johnson, Goodnow began to interview Barbara Lawrence about the shooting, seated in the cruiser and witnessed by another officer. Upset at what was happening with her father, Johnson's daughter Brenda loudly harangued Goodnow and the other troopers present in a "very obscene and violent" manner," Goodnow testified, that included referring "to our ancestry a little bit." Goodnow and Chilton agreed that the environment was not conducive to a quiet conversation and, with Lawrence's consent, Goodnow and the other officer left with her to travel to their Derby office to continue their interview.

Significant questions later arose during the Irasburg hearings concerning the legality of Goodnow's conversations with Johnson and Lawrence. Were they investigating the shooting case or, instead, pursuing the adultery case against Johnson? When board counsel, Lt. Gov. Foote, confronted Goodnow alleging he was investigating Johnson on the adultery charge and should have warned him of his rights not to make incriminating statements during their interview in the car, Goodnow shot back.

First, he said, he had no intention of using whatever Johnson said against him in court proceedings and therefore advising him of his rights was inapplicable.

Second, he told Foote that the process they used complied with the recent changes in police procedure imposed by the "Supreme Court, and has nothing to do with my private ideas. I think you are aware of that."

Foote continued to spar with him and insist that Johnson should have been warned when Chilton inquired about his relationship with Lawrence, drawing another sharp response from Goodnow.

"Well, first off, you are assuming that I, when Mr. Chilton said this question that I should have jumped up and told him not to answer? Is that what you're saying? That I should advise him not to answer?"

Unable to engage further on this point with a clearly knowledgeable and capable detective, the court reporter noted simply in the transcript that Foote provided "No oral response." The issue of when police must advise people of their right not to make incriminating statements continued as Goodnow moved on to interview Lawrence.

Their meeting at the Derby office also included, during the course of the next couple of hours, Wade, Green, Hogan and Det. Robert Pellon. Each of the officers testifying before the board of inquiry provided consistent accounts of how it progressed, accompanied by the vagaries of modern technology dogging them. Lawrence quickly began to speak, Goodnow related, "she started talking and admitting to the shooting thing immediately; there was no delay or no anything like that." Fifteen minutes into her account, Lawrence inadvertently altered its course throwing another twist to an already tangled set of circumstances.

It happened as Goodnow pursued Johnson's allegation about a possible California connection responsible for the shooting. Notwithstanding that unanswered question among the many others infesting the case, the Irasburg board strongly dismissed the VSP's justification for such an inquiry as "unbelievable" because it "already had their prime suspect," Larry Conley.[360] However, that contention must be tempered because, instead, police viewed Conley only as a potential suspect at the time and their responsibility as expansive to sort out the evidence to see if that, or some other explanation such as someone coming from California, was true.

"I had my theory," Goodnow said, "some of the other fellows had their theory, what was involved. Some of the other officers were of the opinion we had the wrong car; we were looking for the wrong color car." "Trooper Hogan was there and myself," he said, "and we were checking with her relative to the possibility of obtaining more evidence from her that maybe someone she knew, possibly her husband, had committed this shooting. I had talked to her about the fact that he, being in Fort Belvoir, Virginia; he could have made it home here on a four-day pass and that he could have done the shooting."

When she said she had no reason to believe he was involved, the suspicious Goodnow continued to probe asking if there "may be some reason that she is holding back, that maybe her husband did have a reason to do this shooting." Lawrence then responded without understanding the ramification of what she was about to say. "Well, I don't believe it is," she said, "because he knew about the affair we were having in California."

Goodnow immediately appreciated the implications of her admission and halted the interview. The experienced officer understood fully the seriousness of what Lawrence just said because of his personal involvement investigating four instances of adultery in the past and assisting other officers on four other occasions with their own work. Cpl. Green witnessing the interview had also conducted several other investigations into the crime. Contrary to the allegations made by politicians, clergy and the media that adultery was a trivial crime unworthy of investigation in these more enlightened times and was rarely prosecuted, the judiciary, and thus the VSP, viewed the felony offense differently; evidenced by the 102 cases prosecuted in Vermont over the past 15 years. As Goodnow explained further, the cases he participated in were conducted specifically because the county courts in Orange and Windsor counties where he worked ordered them to take place.[361]

When questioned during the Irasburg hearings why he proceeded to inquire further about the adultery case when the shooting case still remained, Goodnow said he was obligated to. "Because I had some grounds of probable cause there," he explained, "I just felt that it was my duty that a crime had allegedly or possibility that a crime had allegedly happened, at this time and not by carrying it further and inquiring and investigating at this time, that I would be derelict of my duty."

Recognizing the need to pursue his duty in yet another instance of suspected adultery, Goodnow advised Lawrence "that this information that she had just given me and any information in regards to the affair or the adultery charge, could be used in a court against her." At 5:28 p.m., he provided her with a form describing her so-called Miranda rights (to remain silent and to the presence of counsel) that she acknowledged and signed, telling Goodnow "she wished to get this thing straightened out and get it off her mind." The chronology of their exchange confused the board of inquiry in its findings that added to its overall unfavorable impression of the VSP. Rather than credit the testimony of the principal interviewing officer, and the others attending, of how their discussion unfolded, it found that Goodnow should have notified her of her rights as soon as they sat down in the Derby office.

The board seems further confused about tape recordings made by two recorders that began well into their conversation leading it to believe that what occurred beforehand was intentionally omitted.[362] "The tape recording does not indicate," it wrote in its findings, "until well along in the interview and *not on a timely basis* (emphasis added) that she was warned of any of her so-called Miranda rights."[363] Goodnow's testimony answered these questions, explaining that the issue of Lawrence's rights only arose when she brought up the new crime well after the interview began and that that was when he started to record her responses to questioning. "I had a small hand tape recorder," he said, "I placed in the ash tray in the desk next to her and I told her 'You are going to have to speak loudly, I don't know whether it works good.' I had just been issued it two weeks before and never had access to that before. I believe it was Detective Pellon, when he came in, he advised me that the tape recorder I had, wasn't going to pick up the conversation, so this is where we took this other (recorder) and started that. We did have some difficulty starting that, in getting it to operate or function properly."

Lawrence's story quickly spilled out as she told the officers about her strained relationship with her husband, the months-long affair with Johnson, their many trysts and discussions about his divorcing Ophelia and marrying her, their coming to Vermont and admitting to engaging in intercourse with him on July 22 when Trooper Lessard interrupted them. Hogan recalled her "relaxed state" answering their questions "freely and elaborat(ing) on a lot of them." Goodnow wrote out a two-page account about what happened that she signed, witnessed by himself, Pellon and Wade. Despite the evidence before it, when her admission was discussed before the board of inquiry, Judge Gibson interjected and called it an "alleged confession," conveying his skepticism about its legality.

Lawrence's concerns for the well-being of her children remaining behind at the Johnson residence prompted additional exchanges with the officers. "She was very apprehensive," Goodnow said, "about returning to the Johnson residence, she was afraid that she was going to get in difficulties with Mr. Johnson," fearing "bodily harm for, either her, or possibly her children." She wanted to return, but asked the officers not to mention her confession to Johnson and, if they did not, "that she felt that she may be somewhat safe."

Chapter 6

THE CASE BREAKS

ANOTHER CONFESSION

THE DAY AFTER Chilton and Goodnow completed their work with Johnson and Lawrence, on Saturday, July 27, Det. Wade continued to pursue the potential California connection. He also contacted military authorities in Ft. Belvoir, Virginia where Lawrence's husband, Arthur, was stationed to inquire of his whereabouts between July 18 and 19. The reason is not clear why, but Wade also asked "that a check be made to ascertain if Mr. Lawrence was a minister."[364] The records do not indicate that Wade ever received a response.

Wade and Shanks then returned to the Texaco gasoline station in Barton that Shanks went to earlier based on the information they learned in Nashua to speak again with its proprietor, 20-year-old Roy Babcock. Babcock leased the station rent-free from the LeClair estate for the past six months and is where several young men, including Richard LeClair, were seen frequenting. Babcock expressed little interest in talking, but after the persistent Shanks returned several times in the next couple of days he agreed to provide some information because of the favorable treatment he received from police in a past encounter. The most he was willing to tell Shanks was that the vehicle involved in the shooting was "a 1968 Oldsmobile Sport Coup, white top and possibly reddish brown or dark colored bottom."[365] A background check of Babcock revealed his lease arrangement with the LeClair family explaining why he refused to provide any further information implicating Richard.

Inquiring further, Shanks learned that LeClair drove a 1968 Oldsmobile with a white top and green bottom; information that did not fit Johnson's white over red description. When confronted during the Irasburg hearings why police did not immediately turn and focus on LeClair at that time, Shanks tried to explain the concerns police had resolving the conflicting reports about the car's color.

"The thing that was throwing us all off," he said, "was the car. This is why we still had so many other facets to investigate that we couldn't just drop everything because every bit of information that I had obtained was a red bottomed car and we could not associate a red-bottomed car with any of these people that were involved or had anybody seen them, other than a red bottomed car, and so this here is one of the reasons why, as I say, I think my own mind, as I recall it now, that this whole case, that even though I felt that there was a possible connection, the thing that was bothering me was the fact that this red car, and we had checked out so many other leads we were sure of the right ones, then it turned out to be wrong and we felt we should proceed very carefully, that is just exactly what we did."

On Monday, July 29, Potvin met with Green, Shanks and Cpl. James Lilley to go over the evidence. Larry Conley's and Richard LeClair's names kept coming up and they agreed that because their stories about their whereabouts on the evening of July 18–19 seemed suspicious, they should be re-interviewed, give written statements and offer them the opportunity to take a polygraph exam.[366] Mahady and L'Ecuyer also appeared to receive a briefing and provide assistance. At some point around this time, Potvin told Mahady about the information Game Warden Collins provided concerning his encounter with Larry Conley when he asked what police would do if he harassed the negroes at Crystal Lake.

The men agreed to break into two teams as Potvin and the two attorney general representatives went to see LeClair while Shanks and Lilley visited Conley. The second team's attempt to re-interview

Conley at his father's home did not go well. According to Shanks, Howard Conley "stated that his son would not speak to us anymore and if we thought his son was guilty, to get a warrant and arrest him, as he planned to contact an attorney to get legal advice."

Potvin's team had better, albeit minimal, luck. For the second time after his first interview with Trooper Cram on July 21 who thought his account rehearsed, Richard LeClair, in the presence of his father, recounted his involvement with Conley the night of July 18. He maintained once again that the two were at the Derby snack bar at the time of the shooting and nowhere near Irasburg. While "his story was not without minor inconsistencies," Potvin wrote, "he did not make any incriminating statement."

LeClair's white-over-green 1968 Oldsmobile was also inspected and no evidence of Johnson's return gunfire found. The veteran officer, however, did believe that LeClair participated with Conley in the shooting, but because "there as little or no physical evidence to place them at the scene, some other method of obtaining the facts had to be found."

On July 30 the case broke open. While the officers huddled again to compare notes from the day before, Mahady and L'Ecuyer returned to the snack bar to re-interview Conley's alibi witnesses, Fortin and Belanger. Shanks and Green spent the day tracking down five more witnesses who provided additional information that took them hours to determine it had nothing to do with the investigation. Late that evening, suspicious of LeClair's demeanor from their meeting the day before, Potvin returned with L'Ecuyer to his house to probe further. The young man continued to provide little additional information, but also indicated that he could be of more help if he received immunity for his involvement.

While they talked, detectives Shanks and Lilley waited outside in their darkened car, just down the street from the house. The two watched as Howard Conley "drove up the street with his wife and was about to turn to go to the LeClair residence when he saw our car and then turned left instead, and turned around and went down into Barton Village."[367] After their meeting with LeClair and hearing that Conley's father appeared intent to contact him making their connection clearer than ever, Potvin and L'Ecuyer conferred with

Mahady. The three agreed they still had, in the prosecutor's words, reached an "impasse" in the case and that the immunity LeClair sought should be seriously considered. Mahady recounted that he spoke with Oakes three times before convincing him that the lack of evidence in the case required they give favorable consideration to LeClair in order to charge Conley.

The next morning Mahady obtained three search warrants for Howard Conley's residence, his auto sales business and LeClair's home. Teams executed the Conley warrants during the day, but uncovered no evidence related to the shooting offense; a shotgun found in a closet proved unconnected.

By late afternoon, Mahady recalled, "It was apparent to me, at this point, that we were working against time and that time was definitely on the side of the perpetrators of this crime, and that a successful prosecution could be conducted only if young LeClair would cooperate and be truthful with us." He went to the LeClair house with Potvin and confronted the father and son telling them they strongly suspected the boy's involvement. Mahady spoke separately with his father and assured him Richard would not be prosecuted if he cooperated because it was imperative to proceed and charge Conley.

For the next two hours, between 5 and 7 p.m., Richard retracted parts of the story he told before and explained further his involvement with Conley on July 18 and 19. He told them about running into Conley at the Barton gas station and how they spent time traveling to St. Johnsbury, Crystal Lake, Irasburg and Derby before returning home in the early morning hours. He also told them about all of the beer they consumed in the time leading up to Conley's firing his shotgun out the window of his car. However, his account was not complete because he continued to omit any reference to the presence Bernadette Roy seated between the two of them.

Shanks arrived at the LeClair residence where he took 36 photographs of Richard's car (only the one published herein exists) before Mahady and L'Ecuyer drove it to Johnson's home to see if he could identify it. Despite its green lower portion, Mahady admitted that in the night light "the bottom of the car can look very red. It looked red to me," and Johnson agreed it was the vehicle he saw the night of the shooting.

The investigators and Mahady returned to the St. Johnsbury office where they prepared the necessary paperwork for Conley's arrest warrant. Potvin and Mahady also discussed the pending adultery case against Johnson and Lawrence and the two agreed that, as Mahady testified, it "would be withheld until the Conley shooting case was concluded."

At this moment Mahady, working on the behalf of Oakes then embroiled in the middle of a desperate campaign for governor and impatient for a significant break in the case, faced a huge problem. In the ensuing ten days since the shooting, after police carefully considered the physical evidence and spoke with more than 200 witnesses, exactly what could Conley be charged with? There was no evidence of any intention to physically harm anyone in the Johnson house. Instead, there was only information showing that, as Commissioner Alexander recounted, two "beered up" young men who went out on a midnight joyride to harass the Black occupants of a house in Irasburg. Similarly, as Potvin concluded in his report detailing his involvement in the case, "No definite motive could be established and it appears that the participants could have been under the influence of intoxicants at the time of the offense as by the statement of Richard LeClair, he and Larry Conley consumed 16 (16 ounce) cans of beer between them on the afternoon and evening of the offense." Despite Oakes's strong desire to root out and institute charges against those involved with vigilantism seeking to intentionally inflict bodily harm on Black people, the lack of any facts to support such a scenario forced Mahady to confront reality. Instead, his duty called on him to assess the situation objectively in its entirety, without emotion as police had, and pursue the most appropriate violation of state law that fit the facts before him.

On July 19, 1968, Mahady alleged in court paperwork, Larry Conley "did, then and there, disturb and break the public peace by tumultuous and offensive carriage, by firing guns, and by the destruction of property, to wit: windows at the residence of one David Johnson of Irasburg, and by assaulting another person, to wit, one David Johnson," all in violation of 13 V.S.A. 1021(1).[368] The facts simply did not demonstrate any intention to murder or seriously harm Johnson, but, in essence, to harass him by engaging in a breach of peace, a felony offense carrying a potential five year sentence and

$1,000 fine. Because the VSP also worked with Orleans County State's Attorney Leonard Pearson during the investigation, Potvin suggested that Mahady invite him to join in signing the warrant application. When Mahady called Pearson, he agreed to participate, but said he did not have a driver's license and asked if a trooper could pick him up. Mahady denied the request because, he said, there were no officers available and that "well, this is only a courtesy call anyway."[369]

With no evidence to indicate otherwise, the Irasburg board took the extraordinary step slamming Pearson for not appearing and said he "refused" to sign the paperwork.[370]

That did not happen.

Instead, the circumstances show that Oakes's push to get the case finished as soon as possible because of his ongoing campaigning did not include coordinating his work with this particular locally elected official threatening to share the limelight in resolving this notorious case. His interference into the case and Pearson's benching ran counter to established protocol that routinely saw police and state's attorneys working together in cases occurring in their counties.

The voters did not forget his slight in September.

With LeClair's confession in hand and Johnson's assessment that his car appeared to be the one involved, Mahady obtained an arrest warrant for Conley the next morning, Aug. 1. He recalled that in their moments together before Conley's arrest, Potvin confided to him that "he was afraid that there was some leak to the Conley family in his Newport office and he expressed considerable concern about it and said that when this is all over, 'I am going to find out about it.'"[371]

Meanwhile, Oakes started the day at 6 a.m., shaking the hands of workers arriving at the American Optical Co. in Brattleboro, followed by an appearance at the local Holstein-Friesian Association to do the same thing before departing for Newport to appear at Conley's arraignment. Vermont Press Bureau Chief Stephen Terry accompanied Oakes on the 165-mile trip and recalls that Oakes was very circumspect and spoke little during their time together. He did, however, convey his great interest to be present in court and that he believed substantial evidence existed to charge Conley.[372] Meanwhile, Potvin and Shanks, accompanied by Mahady, arrested Conley at his father's Glover home at 11 a.m. and took him to the courthouse.

For reasons never disclosed, the sheriff receiving custody of Conley, also a good friend of his family, took the extraordinary move of allowing him to go free before his arraignment to have lunch with his father. Conley returned and court convened at noon with him seated next to his attorney, the former Orleans County state's attorney Maxwell L. Baton.[373] Conley entered his not guilty plea to the charge and Mahady, with Oakes seated at his side, argued to Judge Lewis E. Springer that the seriousness of the case should require Conley to post a $5,000 bail. Calling the request "shocking," Baton said that "Even looking on the blackest side of it, it is absurd to think that this was done for the intent of killing." After inquiring about Conley's ability to post bail and receiving assurances from the sheriff that his family was held in high esteem in the community, Springer agreed to his release on posting $2,000 bail.[374]

Potvin prepared a press release before the hearing that he provided to the media after Alexander read and approved it in the moments before it began. The brief statement announced Conley's arrest and ended with the observation that "Commissioner E. A. Alexander feels that the case has no racial overtones and was not caused by racial prejudice. Today's events according to the Commissioner did much to remove the stigma which he believes had unfairly been attached to the State of Vermont as a whole and to the Northeast Kingdom in particular."[375] Alexander's statement differed little from those made on other occasions when he termed the shooting as "a prank" committed by "a crackpot" or boys all "beered up."[376]

However, his most recent characterization of the case as being devoid of racial overtones piqued Gov. Hoff's special assistant, Arthur Ristau. He and Hoff also prepared a release of their own (dated the day before and apparently in anticipation of Conley's arrest) alerting the public not to prejudge the case as the state sought to "secure justice as well as to assure the protection of constitutional rights of the individuals involved."[**] Ristau contacted Maj. Davis to read its language to him

---

[**] Written on Hoff's behalf, it read: "I would like to compliment our Department of Public Safety and the Attorney General's Office for the skill and dispatch with which this investigation has been conducted. This has been an extremely sensitive situation and I'm pleased that both agencies, working together, were able to conduct their activities mindful of the welfare of the people of the community and the obvious delicacy of the circumstances. There has been an arraignment

ahead of the arrest and before Alexander's pronouncement, believing the two were in agreement. It irked the administration, Ristau wrote to Lt. Gov. Foote representing the Irasburg board during the hearings, to have two different official statements on such a notorious case where Alexander's interpretation of events "lent a slightly different perspective to the role of our State Police."[377] The fact that Hoff's representative was communicating directly with the board's prosecutor during the extraordinary hearings about "the role of our State Police" in Irasburg reveals another troubling aspect to the story. Ristau's letter conveys directly to the board Gov. Hoff's displeasure at Alexander's efforts to minimize the race allegations to correct the misperceptions of racism in his department that could interfere with his plans to make it the cause for the whole sad affair. It further reveals the carefree, easy way that officials kept in touch with each other behind the scenes when they should have maintained distance between them to avoid any inferences of undue influence or intrusion into the board's work. The media also noted the differences between the two press releases that seemed to only feed further rumors.[378]

During the Irasburg hearings, Potvin was questioned why he made the statement that there was no evidence of "racial overtones" because Conley told Warden Collins he wanted to harass the Black people at Crystal Lake, expressing the same sentiment to LeClair before they drove to Irasburg. "I think it would be fair to say," he responded, "that there were indications that it did (exist), but we hoped that it did not." Alexander explained that he approved the release based on the information available to him at the time and that he "felt it was proper." "I knew pretty much what had been discovered," by the time of Conley's arraignment he said, "although at that time, I hadn't seen all the reports. A lot of the reports weren't even written up at that time." He said the clergy and press was responsible for characterizing the case in racial terms giving it "a different slant, entirely" from what the facts demonstrated. He also repeated that "I felt, and I feel now that I was right, that this was simply a case of some young fellows

in this investigation but I would urge all Vermonters not to prejudge the case. It is our firm intention to secure justice as well as to assure the protection of constitutional rights of the individuals involved."

getting beered up and it happened to be Mr. Johnson that got picked on. If (he) hadn't been there, it would have been someone else."

Conley may have had "racial prejudice," Alexander said, but "as a whole, I don't think there was."[379]

He later explained to Hoff that "it would have been an irresponsible untruth to have said that the (DPS) had established a racial prejudice against the Rev. Johnson and his family as the motivation for the incident."[380] The good intentions of Potvin and Alexander to remove the stigma of racism in the NEK and to qualify the VSP's understanding of the facts could not withstand Hoff's great ire at the department as a whole. Its performance during the Grafton motorcycle mayhem two weeks earlier that he believed deficient and now the misstatements about Conley's motives only provided additional firepower to a governor intent on firing Alexander.

After Conley's arraignment, Potvin, Oakes, Mahady and others gathered at Frank's Restaurant for lunch. During their conversation, Potvin handed Oakes a copy of a letter he received from Lloyd Hayes at the *Newport Daily Express* written to him by the California newspaper reporter containing unfavorable information about the principal witness in the case, David Johnson. Uninterested, Oakes told the board of inquiry that "He showed it to me and I handed it back to him, because, in my mind, it was irrelevant." He also said that Chilton's inquiries into Johnson's background during the investigation did not involve him. "Our office had nothing to do with (it)" he related, "it didn't concern us in any respect whatsoever, because we were trying to find out what the shooting case involved and not what Mr. Johnson's background consisted of."

Why Vermont's attorney general overseeing the prosecution of the most important case in his career involving one of the most explosive matters to ever face the state did not want to know about information, whether favorable or unfavorable, pertaining to the credibility of his star witness remains a mystery. The news from California and results of Chilton's inquiries constituted critical pieces of information that could be used to question Johnson's account of what happened. It could have also led to additional information that police did not know about. Conley's experienced and aggressive attorney would relish the opportunity to cross-examine him at trial based on the many falsehoods uncovered. Additionally, a prepared prosecutor would want to know of them beforehand to try and mitigate their effect during direct examination. Rather than acknowledge these trial realities, Oakes and the Irasburg board simply deemed the information irrelevant, salacious ("slurs and innuendo," Chairman Gibson said) and inadmissible.

The presence and effects of the press during the VSP investigation also arose during the Irasburg hearings. Potvin's suspicion that his office leaked information to it was never proven and was an allegation that Alexander specifically rejected after an investigation of his own. Additionally, the board's insinuation that the department solicited the press to conduct some of its investigatory responsibilities was never demonstrated.[381] While Alexander said he did speak with the media to learn what they had found out, he never asked it to do any work on his behalf. "We receive and evaluate information from many sources," he told Hoff, "and the tips and bits of information which law enforcement agencies receive in this manner are often essential to the successful investigation of incidents of criminal activity. To characterize the receipt of information relating to the background of the Reverend Johnson from a newspaper as 'unprofessional and improper' is wholly unwarranted and presumably results from the ignorance of those making the characterization of the manner in which law enforcement agencies throughout the country receive and evaluate information relating to criminal activity which they have under investigation."[382] Nonetheless, the board of inquiry's double standard condemning Alexander for speaking with the press meant it never examined the circumstances of Attorney General Oakes's own relationship with Don Hovey, the *Caledonian Record* reporter. Hovey personally provided Oakes with information that he deemed "quite accurate," leading him to direct Assistant Attorney General Mahady to chase down, but who later discredited Hovey's account.[383]

The information that the California press generated about Johnson did prompt Potvin at some point after Conley's arrest to try and lessen the tension surrounding the racial aspects of the case. He had several conversations with Rev. Newell and his associate, Edward J. Bottum, "a plump, bespectacled" student at the Andover-Newton

Theological School in Massachusetts working with Newell during the summer, about some of the information that police gathered.[384]

The reason Potvin did so does not appear in the records, but indicates his intention to convey to the clergy in a confidential manner some of the complications that Johnson's background posed in order to lessen community concerns they were acting in a racist manner. Potvin rationalized that he could share such information with those outside of law enforcement because the two men were ministers (Bottum was not yet ordained) "charged with teaching and enforcing the law of God. Police officers are charged with enforcing the law of Man. I felt that they are a cut above the ordinary person, and some things are discussed with ministers that aren't discussed with the ordinary man on the street."[385]

Potvin shared the information from California with them, as well as the recent episode when Johnson and Lawrence were discovered together in a compromising position. The news from California shocked Newell, he said, leaving him "confused, bewildered, stunned" because it "contained information that would stagger any man."[386]

Potvin also confided some of his personal feelings about the situation that made him uncomfortable. He "voluntarily admitted that he might be a little racially prejudiced," Bottum testified, "although he felt he had handled the case impartially." Newell explained he was not concerned about Potvin's bias and believed he was "very much interested in putting the community on guard against what he considered to be a threat."

"Prejudice," he said, exists in everyone "in one way or another and I do not believe that the state police that I talked with are racists and I interpret that as being persons who are out to get a particular race or group."

"Racism," he said, "is a vicious thing, whereas prejudice may be something about which people do nothing but talk," before repeating that he never witnessed any racism on the part of any member of the state police.[387]

The conversations between the three men ranged further as Potvin told them that "Vermont was a pretty good state as it is now and he was a little concerned what would happen if a lot of colored people came."

When Bottum told him that the Johnsons might go to Minnesota, Potvin responded, "The sooner the better as far as I am concerned." He told them of his pragmatic concerns about the costs the state incurred for the investigation and that "state troopers had to cancel their leaves on weekends in order to guard the house and he was just pretty disgusted with the whole thing." Johnson's relationship with Lawrence also provoked Potvin when they discussed the adultery matter. "You know," Bottum recounted his words, "it is the epitome for a colored man to have intercourse with a white woman. You know there are some white women who think that it is great to have intercourse with a colored person."

When asked what he meant, the officer responded "Have you ever seen a colored man in the shower?"

When Bottum met Potvin at his office for another discussion, the lieutenant unloaded. "He said," Bottum testified:

> If he ever got into a situation like this with a colored man again he would handle the case a lot differently. I asked him what he meant by that—again I cannot remember his exact words—but something to the effect that he would be less helpful and tougher. He also said that he was keeping a file of all the information on Rev. Johnson so that if Rev. Johnson should leave Vermont, there would probably be inquiries about him and he would have all the information on hand to reply to these inquiries.

Bottum also expressed his concern at Potvin's plans to pursue the adultery matter:

> I requested Lt. Potvin, even pleaded with him, I would be given permission to go and confront Reverend Johnson with the facts and then if there was any truth to this adultery thing, Barbara should leave and this could all be cleared up. Nothing would happen in the future. Reverend Johnson's career would not be ruined, it would not harm his family and so I requested that

he please let me go and confront Reverend Johnson with the facts. But he would not permit me to do this. He said I could give a general statement but not to get the police involved, something to that effect. This I just couldn't understand—why he was doing this. It made me quite frustrated and angry at him when it seemed to me we might be able to accomplish the same thing by confronting Reverend Johnson, by letting Barbara leave for California; but for some reason he seemed set on arresting Mr. Johnson and Barbara and I asked him what good could be accomplished by this and he couldn't give any answer. He said it was in violation of the law and I said, what about the children and then he made a derogatory remark about Reverend Johnson's son George and his relationship with a white girl.

He said police had seen him with this white girl, and I can't remember exactly what it was, but to the effect that they suspected that there may be something going on there. So I asked him what good could be accomplished by this and he just said it (adultery) was a violation of the law and he seemed to have no regard to the feelings of Reverend Johnson and his family. So, this made me very angry at one point and I said 'Dammit, they are human beings you know.' This is how angry I felt at his attitude towards the Johnsons. This is the first time I ever swore at a police officer. I don't swear very often. I was just that mad.[388]

When he later learned of Potvin's statements, Commissioner Alexander issued him a verbal reprimand. Notwithstanding Potvin's feelings, his relationship with Newell continued as the minister provided the police with additional, unspecified information about Johnson that investigators deemed of importance to their inquiries. Potvin was not alone in his impressions about Blacks in Vermont. Mahady recorded another statement made by an unnamed trooper when he drew up the charges against Conley. "One state police officer," he wrote, "informed me that I had charged young Conley with the wrong crime. When I asked him what he meant by this, the officer told me that Conley should have been charged 'with shooting coon out of season.'"[389]

The publicity after Conley entered his not guilty plea to Mahady's breach of peace charge generated a new twist to the story. The prosecutor soon received calls from Potvin and an attorney representing Richard LeClair immediately afterwards with the news that a third person accompanied him and Conley the evening of July 18–19. For the first time, Bernadette Roy's name entered into the investigation, now represented by former governor Lee Emerson running interference on her behalf with the authorities. Currently living with a relative in California where she fled soon after the shooting, Emerson arranged for her to return to Vermont to meet with Mahady. While Mahady rightfully claimed that he obtained the first interview with Roy taking place on Aug. 22, and despite Oakes's repeated announcements that the case was only solved because his office interviewed the critical witnesses, his interaction with Roy is the only instance in which his office obtained relevant information outside of what the VSP learned through its own work. None of the records substantiate Oakes's claims that his office solved the case and show that whatever witness interviews Mahady and L'Ecuyer conducted took place days after VSP investigators already spoke with them.

Conley's attorney demanded that his client receive a speedy trial and Judge Springer agreed, ordering it to begin just two weeks later, at 9:30 a.m. on Aug. 14.[390] The news rattled both the participants and public as other events quickly unfolded in an atmosphere rife with rumor. On Aug. 2, Conley and LeClair met on two occasions to discuss their fate. LeClair's father, Earl, told his son that he heard that Conley's case could be settled if he paid a $750 fine and Richard carried the news to him at his father's business.

"Larry said he would (pay it) in a minute," Richard recounted, "if it wouldn't be spread over the newspapers. He said he had that much money in the bank and would draw it out the next day. We talked about it being a good idea to settle the case as it would save a lot of trouble on everybody's part." Howard Conley then appeared and the three of them drove "to a hayfield near the cemetery" to talk. Larry told his father about paying the money to resolve the case, but Howard countered he thought he had located six witnesses at the Derby snack bar able to testify that he was there at the time of the shooting.[391] Det. Shanks unsuccessfully sought to verify this alibi information that the Irasburg board rejected in its findings.

LeClair's next encounter with Conley took place at the LeClair home later that day in the presence of LeClair's father when they discussed Bernadette Roy's participation. "The next day after Larry Conley was arrested," Earl LeClair said, "Larry came to the house at supper time and told me he would like to see Richard and me." The three went outside to talk in LeClair's garage where Conley asked Richard "if he ratted on him." Earl told him that they had consulted with an attorney and that it was probably he who told police about Roy. Conley explained that he had not told his attorney about Roy because of the agreement the two men had to keep her out of it.

"That was the most foolish thing I have ever done," Conley said recalling what happened that night in Irasburg.

When their conversation was interrupted by a telephone call from Bernadette's father, Gerry Roy, saying he was coming over to talk with Earl, Conley said "I'm going. I can't face Gerry."[392] Meanwhile, at the Johnson residence the next day, during the late afternoon hours a car with four men in it drove by harassing him. "You fucking n-----," one of them shouted before the car turned around and drove past a second time. This time, another occupant pointed his hand at him and yelled "Bang, bang." Despite a rapid response and investigation by a trooper, the incident went unsolved.[393]

More Arrests

Theology student Edward Bottum's understandable feelings that the adultery case should be resolved without charges filed against Johnson and Lawrence faded away on Aug. 9 when the duty that police had to enforce the law Det. Goodnow described presented itself. The prior agreement between Oakes and Potvin that the matter wait until the shooting case finished met a sudden end because of circumstances unseen by either man.

On Aug. 8, Lawrence prepared a handwritten statement concerning her relationship with Johnson retracting everything she confessed to VSP investigators in Derby on July 26.

"There was no sexual relationship," she wrote, "between Rev. Johnson and I. The only reason (her first statement) was given to the state police was I thought that even if I said nothing had happened between us meaning Rev. Johnson and I, sexually, they would not have taken my word."

"I was nervous," she continued, "and upset and was not given a chance to think clearly of what I was saying or signing."[394] Lawrence and Ophelia Johnson signed the document.

The circumstances surrounding the preparation of a document completely denying her first statement are shrouded in mystery. Police had no knowledge of it and only learned about it months later when the press reported it's existence during the Irasburg hearings. A criminal law practitioner will recognize that the language utilized in the statement bears earmarks that an attorney prepared it. Testimony from Johnson's lawyer, St. Johnsbury attorney Robert Rachlin, revealed he provided a copy of it to the board of inquiry at some point after first receiving it from Johnson on Aug. 10 "on the occasion of our first interview . . . at the Newport Airport."[395] Further, it does not appear that Lawrence's counsel, Paul R. Rexford of Newport, was involved in its preparation when she admitted her involvement with Johnson on Aug. 12. Notwithstanding whoever prepared it, if the VSP had been advised of her retraction on Aug. 8 when she signed it the bizarre events taking place the next day might not have occurred.

In the fierce competition between Vermont newspapers and the national media seeking information about the Irasburg matter, local editor Lloyd Hayes of the *Newport Daily Express* newspaper (circulation between 4,000 and 5,000) also took an active role. He communicated with his counterparts in California about Johnson and wrote a blazing editorial after his arrest with Lawrence for adultery on Aug. 9, entitled "Johnson Jottings," surrounding the circumstances of a Black family appearing in Irasburg that many interpreted as racist; it was one of many media efforts that police believed only made their work more difficult.

According to Rev. Newell, Hayes's opinion piece marked an important turning point in the public's perception of the shooting event. "Now," he wrote, "the Irasburg Incident was changed to the Irasburg Affair. It no longer belonged to Irasburg, the State Police, the Northeast Kingdom. It was now national news, sordid, sensational, and full to the brim with racial prejudice." It also presented the prospect, in Newell's mind at least, that the state police fed confidential information to the press causing him to raise the issue of racism within its ranks. Without any proof and accomplished only through the use of innuendo, he challenged the VSP that "at long last the racists had accomplished their dark work" in dirtying up David Johnson.[396]

Hayes also ran a travel agency at his newspaper office and on the morning of Aug. 9 it received a call from "a young man" at the local airport asking, perhaps curious because of his recent notoriety, why Johnson was trying to purchase tickets for California. Already suspicious that he and Lawrence committed adultery, Hayes became concerned "that it looked like someone was trying to leave the state" to avoid the law and he called State's Attorney Pearson and Potvin to see if either of them had any information about it. Pearson explained that when he received Hayes's call between 10 and 10:30 that morning while at court, he knew nothing about the case, probably because of the agreement between police and Oakes to keep it quiet for the time being. Hayes was also concerned that someone could escape prosecution for an offense he believed serious and pressed Pearson to pursue the adultery case.

Potvin also had no knowledge about either Johnson or Lawrence trying to leave the state, but also became concerned. He called Cpl. Green, then assisting Pearson at the Newport courthouse handling pre-trial conferences pending on the court's docket. Potvin directed him to get the necessary information about Johnson and Lawrence from the Derby office and give it to Pearson for him to determine whether it should be prosecuted and arrest warrants issued. Green directed Trooper Marshall to retrieve the statements made by Lessard and Lawrence and Johnson's marriage certificate and bring them to the courthouse. After reading the documents and satisfied they made a case for adultery, around noon Pearson provided the officers with the arrest warrants. He later explained that he "was faced with a situation where action in the matter was imperative"in order to preserve both his pending adultery case and to assist the attorney general in preserving the testimony he needed in the shooting matter.[397]

Potvin immediately contacted Assistant Attorney General Mahady and advised him of what was taking place.[398] While Mahady admitted that he received Potvin's notification, there is no evidence he either objected to what was happening or that he advised Attorney General Oakes of the situation.[399]

According to the *Daily Express,* Johnson made reservations the day before for Lawrence and her children to return to Seaside, California on a 1:45 p.m. flight out of Newport. When they arrived to pick up the tickets some confusion arose over their inability to pay for them. The four then left indicating they planned to get the money wired from California.[400]

However, in a curious portion of the board of inquiry's report, it determined otherwise. "Mr. Johnson testified," it said, "that Mrs. Lawrence had become upset after the shooting incident and that she desired to return to California, that he had a credit card with United Airlines, that he had checked at the Newport Airport and these people informed him that they had no connections with United Airlines."[401]

A review of the 38 pages of Johnson's testimony provides no such information either directly or indirectly about any report of Lawrence's return to California or problems they encountered at the airport. Johnson never "testified" about going to the airport at all because it was never a topic of discussion.

There is also no information in the board's documents describing what happened after they left the airport. However, displaying another instance asserting allegations without attributing them to witness testimony or evidence, it again filled in the blanks. "Knowing that Mrs. Lawrence's husband was still in the Army at Fort Belvoir, Virginia," it wrote, "Rev. Johnson determined to take Mrs. Lawrence to Fort Devens, Massachusetts, and request the Army to see that she secured passage to California."[402] Where that unverified information came from is another in an increasing string of unexplained mysteries contained in the board's findings.

While Green worked to obtain the arrest warrants, Potvin sought out Johnson in order to be ready to arrest him when Green reported back. He observed him around 12:30 p.m. driving his white 1968 Pontiac Firebird bearing its distinctive "BJJ" license plate with Lawrence as passenger, headed south on Rte. 5 in the Lyndonville area. He lost sight of them at one point causing shift supervisor Cpl. Hogan, after learning the warrants were issued, to warn area cars to be on the lookout for them.

It is not known what they did for the intervening three-and-one-half hours, but at 4 p.m. troopers Claude Hebert and Alan Dunklee observed Johnson driving his car ninety miles away in the Bethel area. It is also unknown why at any point during this lengthy time neither Mahady or Oakes ever sought to consult with Pearson about the pending arrests directly affecting their star witness in the shooting case. Johnson and Lawrence were taken into custody without incident as a search of his person found two pocket knives.

While the board of inquiry wrote that police arrested the two "at gunpoint," there is, again, no evidence in the record to substantiate the claim.[403] They were driven to the VSP's Montpelier office where officers read them their rights to remain silent and access to an attorney, as well as the two warrants, providing copies to each.

By 7 p.m., Johnson and Lawrence were back in Newport where they were fingerprinted and photographed before making separate appearances before Judge Springer an hour later to impose a $1,000 bail requirement on each. Neither of them could post that amount of money, nor pay for attorneys leading Springer to appoint Rexford to represent Lawrence while the ACLU stepped in arranging for Rachlin to handle Johnson's defense.

Rev. Newell and his associate, Edward Bottum, also attended the hearing and spent the rest of the night with them and Johnson's family at the Newport jail in the sheriff's custody. Unfamiliar with the unusual circumstances surrounding the arrests, Newell continued to insinuate that race prompted the work of police. "I can't help but wonder," he told the press, "if this were a white man under similar circumstances if pressures of this type would have been brought to bear. Whether Johnson is guilty or not guilty, I wonder if he will find any dignity in the state of Vermont from now on. It is all rather strange to me."[404]

Newell also provided a telling account of the time he shared with the Johnson family that night and the words that passed between them:

We were more than a little distraught and our exchange of words were guarded, almost unreal as we faced together the reality that urged itself upon our troubled minds. Finally I said: 'If only David would tell the truth—if only he had not deceived people about his coming from royalty, his claim to having two degrees from Villanova, and his pretense to be working on a doctorate—if only he had just been himself, perhaps this never would have happened.' Brenda, David's 17-yr old daughter was furious with my lack of understanding. She eyed me cautiously, suspiciously and then said: 'You know very well if my father had come here as a mere laboring man he would never have been accepted.'

I knew I had said the wrong thing; that, truthfully I do not understand the mind of the Negro family that are struggling desperately and against tremendous odds, to establish themselves as human beings. I added more fuel to the fire (and this further verifies my ignorance) by saying: 'You're wrong, Brenda, had you father come to us as an honest laboring man instead of as a fake professional man, he would have much more support than he now has.'

Mrs. Johnson, strong, stalwart, poised said simply: 'I just want to be accepted as I am. Can you accept me just as I am, Rev. Newell?' I could, and I do.[405]

News of the arrests prompted two responses from state officials. Described in the press as "greatly disturbed," (compared to journalist Stephen Terry's description of his being "ballistic and turning his ire on the VSP" convinced it was racist[406]) about the charges against Johnson, Hoff spoke about the "Irasburg incident," avoiding any reference to an "affair." "I had a talk with my wife the day he was charged with adultery. It's curious, but I can't remember a prosecution for adultery since we've lived here." Questioned further about his thoughts, he declined to speak saying

"I'm in a touchy situation, I don't think the governor should get involved in prosecution of criminal law." At the same time, the state's Human Rights Commission headed by Rev. Albright took up the circumstances surrounding Johnson's aborted purchase of the first home in Irasburg. A bank reportedly turned him down for a loan to finance the purchase of the second home and the Commission deemed it necessary to inquire further into why that happened.[407]

The ordeal traumatized Barbara Lawrence, separated from her children as she sat incarcerated wanting desperately to return to California as soon as possible. Apparently unaware of his client's retraction of her confession to police on Aug. 8, Rexford worked quickly with State's Attorney Pearson to resolve the case, agreeing to a period of probation and a $125 fine. While the record provides no evidence to directly support the contention, another factor driving a quick ending, Rexford said, concerned Barbara's fear that her "life was endangered by the Johnson family."[408] The parties appeared before Springer the afternoon of Aug. 12 where Lawrence entered a no contest plea to the charge of adultery. Surprisingly, Rexford never saw either her waiver of rights or confession that she gave to detectives on July 26 before the hearing. Wade also attended and supplied copies of each to Judge Springer and Rexford.

It is required in criminal proceedings that when a defendant enters a plea pursuant to an agreement between the parties for the prosecutor to provide the court with a recitation of the facts supporting the offense charged before accepting it. Sometimes the facts are best conveyed by investigating officers with the most knowledge of what occurred and Springer specifically asked Rexford if he was "willing to stand on an informal statement by the prosecuting officer and the State Police Officers in regard to the facts?"

Rexford agreed and Wade provided a summary of what took place.[409]

Assistant Attorney General Mahady also attended the hearing as an observer during a break from participating in depositions taking place in the Larry Conley matter in the same courthouse that day. For whatever reason, Wade's routine participation in the Lawrence hearing greatly disturbed him and, for no apparent reason other than to, perhaps, disparage the VSP and Pearson, he made a startling claim during the board of inquiry's hearings. It ran entirely contrary to a transcript of the Lawrence hearing describing what Judge Springer and the attorneys agreed to.

"I sat in the back of the courtroom," Mahady told the board, "I did not participate in any way in the proceedings and the most disturbing thing which occurred on that particular day; it disturbed me quite a bit, as a member of the bar. The hearing, as far as the State was concerned, was run, for all intents and purposes, by a detective of the Vermont State Police, Detective Wade. Mr. Pearson, the State's Attorney was present, but it was obvious to me that Mr. Pearson was not conducting the hearing on the part of the state, that Mr. Wade was. I found this quite disturbing."[410] While Pearson made only a few statements, the transcript reveals nothing unusual or out of the ordinary from what occurs during any routine change of plea hearing that justifies Mahady's statement. It appears as another of the curious aspects surrounding the Irasburg proceedings.

Lawrence's hearing concluded as the parties anticipated. Springer imposed a suspended sentence of not less than six or more than twelve months and a fine of $125 that, together with costs, totaled $161.20. The money arrived quickly from California, wired to the court by Lawrence's mother and she and her children departed Vermont soon after. In the interim, Johnson posted bail, met with Rachlin and awaited the outcome of his case, also prosecuted by Pearson.

When he heard of Lawrence's change of plea, Johnson expressed shock and anger. Alleging she was "paid off" to do so, he told the press, "Now isn't this a dilly. This is like being sold out behind your back. Who is buying out who? See what friendship will do to you. Isn't there anyone you can trust?"[411] The disposition of the case caused similar concern within the ranks of the clergy when Rev. Newell's friend, Rev. Albright, head of the Vermont Council of Churches, publicly lodged an outlandish allegation that the state paid her fine and transportation costs in exchange for her plea. Rexford objected immediately to Albright's uninformed intrusion calling it a "very untrue and very ill-advised statement."[412] At the same time, the breach of peace case against Larry Conley in which Johnson was expected to testify as the prosecution's star witness ground on under the control of Oakes's office.

The local and national press closely followed all aspects of the three cases and understood that Oakes participated in each, repeatedly identifying him as leading the shooting inquiry; although even he admitted to the board of inquiry it was the VSP. Franz A. Hunt, the publisher of the *Newport Daily Express* where editor Hayes worked, provided additional information about his interactions with Oakes and the public's attitude towards the various events. On one occasion on the campaign trail, Oakes ran into Hunt presenting him with a copy of the letter he received from the Monterey newspaper carrying derogatory information about Johnson. When he sought to question Oakes about it, Hunt said that he "brushed it aside as though there was nothing to it." The more recent charges concerning Johnson's participation in adultery prompted Hunt to hound Oakes asking what he was going to do about it. It seemed odd to Hunt that Oakes "jumped in with both feet" in the shooting case, but "then cooled off and forgot all about" the adultery matter.[413]

On Aug. 16, Hunt followed up and wrote Oakes a letter causing him great consternation and anger. His letter is telling because it conveys the heartfelt feelings of many in the community he routinely associated with confiding their concerns to him. "We are very much interested in the adultery case," he wrote to Oakes, "involving the so-called Rev. Johnson of Irasburg. We as well as a large segment of the population in this area want to see this case vigorously prosecuted." The adultery charge, he said, "is not the first time Johnson has been in trouble and the family doesn't seem to be very welcome here now. If the man was sincere in his statement that he had come here to start a new life, we would feel entirely different. But his actions since coming to Irasburg indicates he is pursuing the same course as he did in California. Briefly, we are interested in helping those who want to try to help themselves. But this is not the case here." Hunt spoke previously with State's Attorney Pearson before writing to Oakes requesting him to provide Pearson with assistance in prosecuting Johnson, now represented by two additional highly capable attorneys from Middlebury working with Rachlin. Vermont did not have fulltime county state's attorneys at the time and the role was held by local lawyers willing to assume the responsibility on a parttime basis while working in their own practices. With Pearson facing a juggernaut of legal talent, Hunt told Oakes that "You, of course, know very well the ability of the local State's Attorney, and his need for assistance in this case," before requesting that he advise him "that you have assigned him some needed assistance."[414]

The following day, Pearson wrote a brief, three-line letter to Oakes ("Dear Jim," he opened) asking his office to provide him with help with Johnson's trial, scheduled to begin on Sept. 4.[415] The entanglement of the Conley and Johnson cases caused great concern for candidate Oakes in responding, then only days before the Republican primary, contending that Pearson's actions were "extremely irritating." Contrary to Mahady's admission that he knew of the plan to arrest Johnson and Lawrence hours before it happened, Oakes faulted Pearson's failure to consult with his office beforehand that he called "unwise."[416] The evidence refutes any insinuation that Oakes was not aware of what Pearson and the VSP planned in arresting Johnson and Lawrence and shows that neither he or Mahady sought to intervene when they could have.

Writing back in a formal, albeit terse, manner to "Mr. Pearson," Oakes maintained his distance, brushing him off the same way he did with Hunt when approached with the information from California about Johnson. "Where a State's Attorney needs assistance because of crowded dockets or inexperience," he wrote, "our office attempts to help where possible. The Attorney General's Office has never, however, to my knowledge, participated in a prosecution for adultery, apparently leaving such matters to the local State's Attorney's usually wise discretion." His decision also rested, he said, on his belief that the prosecution "is apparently the first of its kind for many years in your county" and that the case was not "initiated on the complaint of any aggrieved spouse."[417]

Oakes's displeasure may be understandable from the viewpoint of someone desperately campaigning for governor, but fails to acknowledge the extraordinary situation Pearson faced with the unexpected evidence that one or more of those involved with a felony offense planned to leave the state. Neither did Oakes ever acknowledge the unique facts underlying the adultery charge itself, a crime he admitted fell under the auspices of the state's attorney. The reason he questioned Pearson's actions in the first place concerned the history of adultery cases in Vermont, usually pursued in civil court by spouses harmed because of the other's infidelity. However, the actions of Johnson and Lawrence were unlike those matters Oakes referred to and constituted a highly unusual criminal case where a police officer sworn to uphold the law witnessed a felony offense taking place in his presence. Oakes's distaste for such prosecutions also fails to acknowledge the seriousness that Vermonters felt about adultery evidenced by newspaperman Hunt's concerns on the behalf of his community and the more than 100 cases investigated and prosecuted in the state's courts for the past 15 years.

Convinced at his position ("so that there will be no misunderstanding as to the relationship between your office and mine in this matter") Oakes provided the press with a copy of the letter he wrote to Pearson. It quickly drew the ire of the *Burlington Free Press* questioning what the gubernatorial candidate was up to in an editorial headed "Oakes' Behavior Strange." Calling itself "nonplused," the newspaper took issue with Oakes refusal to assist Pearson "which clearly prejudice" his case against Johnson.

His declination to assist was "irregular on several counts" and decried his prejudging of the case that, in turn, conveyed to the public it was unjust before addressing the law criminalizing adultery itself. While other states "have wiped such laws from the books," in Vermont "it is still there to be applied when a prosecutor feels it should be applied and it remains the duty of the courts to decide whether it is properly applied." This "should be the attitude of Vermont's chief law enforcement officer," but, the editorial concluded, "it looks very much as if he is playing politics with this case."[418]

Why had Oakes, who repeatedly and vigorously represented to the public and the board of inquiry that his office possessed the ability to oversee and intervene in cases that state's attorneys handled and did not do so on this occasion appears consistent with the newspaper's view. With the Republican primary only three weeks away, getting entangled in a messy adultery case involving members of two races did not mix well with another one more compelling one involving the shot-gunning of a Black family's home in the middle of the night.

Seeking to put the matter to rest, Oakes responded to publisher Hunt's letter days later refusing to become involved in the matter, but not before taking a swipe at both he and the state's attorney. "I should suppose," he wrote, "that the only reason Mr. Pearson needs assistance, he feels, is that the case has received an extraordinary amount of publicity" referring to Hunt's recent reporting of Johnson's arrest with accompanying photographs of him entering and leaving jail. "This must be the first case of its kind which has warranted such complete coverage!," he said.[419]

A flurry of activity ensued as the cases against Conley and Johnson progressed. Mahady coordinated with Gov. Emerson for a member of the attorney general's office to travel to California to arrange for the return of his client, Bernadette Roy, in the Conley matter. Roy finally arrived back in Vermont around Aug. 21 when she was immediately contacted by the sheriff who, in an extraordinary move, interviewed her on the behalf of the Conley family. She met with Emerson and Mahady the following day and provided information consistent with Richard LeClair's account of what she did with him and Conley on the night of July 18–19. Her presence in the state and willingness to testify against Conley turned the tide in his case and brought him and the attorneys before Judge Springer later in the day to enter a plea of no contest and avoid the trial set for Aug. 26.

Mahady explained to Springer that his office viewed Conley's case "very seriously." But, the charge of a breach of peace brought against him, punishable by not more than five years imprisonment and a fine of $1,000, seemed odd to outside observers. "Attorneys for other states are surprised at our (law)," he said, but one he defended because it addressed intrusions into the lives of people peacefully occupying their property. This was not a case providing for an increased penalty because the occupants were of another race, but, rather, one where a community's peace was violated by Conley's firing a shotgun that damaged Johnson's home. Race may have motivated Conley as Mahady described his conduct that night, but it seems to have constituted a lesser concern in resolving the matter in the context of whether or not Springer accepted or rejected his no contest plea.

Because of his age, lack of a criminal record and exemplary military service, Springer accepted the agreement of the attorneys that Conley not receive the most serious sentence possible and explained his reasoning. "I want you to know," he said, "that four years, or however long it has been, you have served in the Army, and your good record you have had before that, have been substantially negated by what you did on the night of July 19, as far as I am concerned. I understand that young fellows sometimes do things under the influence of beer that they might not do on more sober reflection, but that is no excuse in the eyes of the law. I know too many have thought of this as a lark, but you should also have given thought to the fact that the security of every citizen of the United States is one of the things you have been serving in the Army for. I think you should realize that there will be a substantial blot on your record no matter what your service may be from now on in the eyes of the law-abiding members of the community and the state of Vermont."[420]

Springer was also influenced by the state's giving immunity to LeClair in resolving the case, which, he said, "has a substantial impact as far as my thinking on this matter is concerned." Before imposing sentence, he observed further that "Even though that house was lighted up and you could see there was nobody behind the windows, nevertheless you could not have known but what somebody would walk across one of them at the time you shot, and somebody could have been severely injured, even though you thought you were firing at a vacant window. This is not the sort of chance a person should have to take in his own home."

The penalty for his conduct meant a suspended sentence of not less than 6 or more than 18 months imprisonment and a fine of $500.

Johnson's case remained on Springer's docket and on Aug. 22 prosecutor Pearson sensed a looming problem with it. He trusted Lawrence's promise to return to Vermont from California to testify, but became so uneasy he sought a court order compelling her to do so. Springer issued it on Aug. 24 and by the end of the month Pearson received a blistering response from her California attorney. "It is not her intent," he advised, "nor has it been ordered by competent authority that she return to Vermont. If any attempt is made to return her it will be resisted in the courts here."[421]

Unfazed, Pearson coordinated with California prosecutors to institute proceedings for her return, scheduled to begin in a Monterey County courtroom on Sept. 6. Vermont authorities scrambled to meet the deadline and on the evening of Sept. 5 Pearson, Potvin, Hogan and Wade met to chart their course of action.

Another individual also attended their meeting and who provides further insight into the credibility of the board's findings. Orange County State's Attorney Philip A. Angell Jr.'s involvement mystified the board contending his presence as something "we do not understand."[422] It also inferred his participation in a scam to defraud state government of funds used to send him and Wade to California for the Lawrence hearing. Further impugning his integrity, it challenged Angell unjustifiably to "come forward and say, 'Here's what happened.'"[423]

As the records before the board amply demonstrate, Angell's participation in the case is made abundantly clear that he did so for honorable, unchallengeable reasons. They further show that: he personally met board member Hilton Wick during one of its recesses and fully answered his questions that Wick memorialized on paper on behalf of its other two members; he assisted police in dealing with the state's Byzantine financial processes imposed on them when they needed funds to conduct out-of-state investigations; he sat through days of the board's hearings waiting to tell his story; and, that Chairman Gibson refused to allow him to do so. Unsurprisingly, and with marked restraint after the hearings concluded when the fallout from the board's wandering, deficient findings impugned him, Angell lodged his own complaint against it, arguing it lacked "objectivity."[424]

Angell's role was not suspicious or untoward, and no scam existed to defraud the government by either himself or the VSP; facts the board never acknowledged. Mystified at how the board concluded the monetary question posed such a problem, Angell said that if only it had consulted the documents he supplied to it the answers could be found.[425]

As a fellow state's attorney in a neighboring county, Angell became upset with Oakes's refusal to assist Pearson with the Johnson case and volunteered his services to help out. His personal displeasure with Oakes's involvement with other state's attorneys existed beforehand because he experienced the same kind of refusal in some of his own cases. Angell appeared openly in court proceedings alongside Pearson during pre-trial hearings in Johnson's case when neither his attorneys or Judge Springer ever questioned his presence or lodged any complaint about his participation. Regarding his involvement with the VSP, he explained to board member Wick that he thought Pearson instituted the charge against Johnson and pursued it because "the State Police would lose face." Regardless of Pearson's decision, Angell said he did not think "the prosecution was based on racial prejudice" and that police had sufficient reason to believe "a crime had been committed and (that) once this evidence was in the hands of the State's Attorney it was the duty of the State's Attorney to prosecute."[426]

Wick's memorandum also records Angell's explanation of what happened when the prosecutors and police decided that he and Wade should go to California to assist in the court proceedings concerning Lawrence's return. To fund their trip, his memo reads, "they called Captain Dean of the State Police to get permission to spend money to do this and he indicated he would have to call them back after discussing the matter with someone else. He called them back in Newport shortly thereafter and indicated they could go. However, none of them had sufficient money, so late the same evening they went to the Passumpsic Bank office in Newport after contacting a bank officer and signed a note for $1,500. They received some cash but mostly Travelers Checks. The signers on the note were Pearson, Angell and Wade."

Wade's letter to Oakes during the hearings provides additional information available to the board that describes their financial problem late that evening. After Dean told the men they would have to guarantee the loan for the time being, he explained that the next morning a check would be sent from the state to the bank to cover it. The bank representative agreed to the arrangement and provided the money and travelers checks after the three signed the note.[427] The men could have avoided the troublesome process had Oakes agreed to assist them beforehand, but as Pearson testified, his office "refused to help in any way, shape or manner."

As Wade and Dean explained further to the board, relying on the use of personal funds to investigate crimes and receiving reimbursement later was a standard practice for the VSP. Gov. Hoff agreed with former Commissioner William Baumann years earlier to waive any requirement that the department obtain permission from his office for travel expenses incurred by investigators working on cases out of state.[428] Just weeks before the officers' need to travel to California arose, Hoff again recognized the VSP's situation and approved the state's Department of Administration delegation of authority to VSP Commissioner Alexander to approve and spend up to $9,000 in state funds for "out-of-state travel (by) your agency personnel."[429]

Ignoring the documents before him, Chairman Gibson confronted Dean during questioning in an uncomfortable public exchange revealing further his unfamiliarity with the process. It replicated the same kind of unfamiliarity Gibson exhibited when conducting out-of-state background investigations that he thought required the involvement of attorney generals from each state. "Isn't it the law, Captain Dean," he said, "that you've got to go through the Governor's Office and put a voucher in there (for out of state travel)?" When Dean told him "No, sir," Gibson shot back "I think it is."

Dean then reminded Gibson of the long-standing practices the VSP worked under in such cases. "Starting from your time as governor (upon the VSP's creation in 1947), the Department of Public Safety has been unique in being granted a blanket authorization for out-of-state travel in matters of criminal interest, not only to bring back prisoners, but to develop evidence and we have in our files, I believe, copies of those. They are available here today."[430] Gibson avoided further questioning of the prepared officer, or accepting the additional evidence he offered in support of his testimony. The board's later failure to acknowledge and omit from its findings the authority that Hoff granted the VSP on two prior occasions and Wade's detailed explanation of how the monies were repaid as contained in its own exhibits, and Angell's recitation to Wick of what happened, presents significant concern whether Gibson appreciated the many other nuances surrounding the Irasburg Affair.

Angell and Wade arrived in California where, after several days of delays, they attended the superior court hearing in Salinas on Sept. 10 to determine if Lawrence should be compelled to return to Vermont. Both men testified about the adultery prosecution against Johnson and the need for Lawrence's testimony. However, the court refused to intercede, finding that Lawrence would suffer undue hardship if she had to leave her two small children behind. Angell and Wade immediately called Pearson and Potvin in Vermont to advise they had lost their principal witness and headed home, arriving at noon on Sept. 11. After a brief meeting, Wade and Green agreed with Pearson and Angell that nothing more could be done and that the case against Johnson must be dismissed. Pearson appeared before Judge Springer later that afternoon for a brief ten-minute hearing witnessed by an audience of forty people. He moved to dismiss the case and Springer agreed to do so "with prejudice," meaning it could not be re-instituted at a later time. In light of the great tension many experienced, Springer added lightheartedly, "That's not racial prejudice, either."[431]

Hoff wasted no time after learning of Pearson's dismissal, vowing "a full-scale investigation" into all aspects of "the Irasburg incident." "The people of the state are entitled to know what this is all about. And they are going to know," he promised. He wanted a three-person board to probe "into every single aspect" of what happened in the NEK since the Johnson family's arrival and for "the chips to fall where they may." Reportedly "privately critical of the role the state police played," Hoff carefully told the public that "I am not blaming a soul" in what the press understood as an effort "to ward off any charges of a witch hunt."[432] Meanwhile, his youth project proceeded, continually drawing his attention and concern at what the events in Irasburg meant for its future.

More Violence

In what should have been a moment of celebration at the removal of a cloud from over Johnson's head only ended in more trouble. Many people gathered at his home to revel in the events of the day and where he and Rev. Newell stood in the kitchen talking with him around 10:30 p.m.

At one point, 17-year-old Brian Crowe, described by Newell as a "fair-haired, clean-cut youth," walked into the room and stood looking at Johnson. Newell was so shocked by what happened next that he later wrote down their conversation. "Is there something I can do for you, son?," Johnson asked. Turning his head to look at Newell instead, he replied, "No, there is nothing you can do for me." Newell then extended his hand in friendship to shake his, but the boy pulled back, apparently, Newell thought, "as if uncertain what kind of man I was." Becoming agitated, Johnson then "struck out" and said "This is my friend, Rev. Newell. Why do you draw away from him? He is my honored guest and my friend. You will treat him with respect, or leave."

Newell continued to report the exchange of words as follows:

> "Please, David," I pleaded, "the boy meant no harm."
>
> "This is not a boy," David exploded. "He is a man and he must take on the stature of manliness."
>
> "Then let him leave," I urged, "and let's forget it."
>
> "NO," said David, "he cannot leave now. What are you here for, man?"
>
> "I came as a friend," came the quick reply.
>
> "Then why do you insult my friend, Rev. Newell? Is it because you know he has helped me, has stood by me?"
>
> "Please, David," I urged, "Let's forget it."
>
> "No!" I will not forget it. What do you want, Man?"
>
> The young man eyed him for a long moment and then said: "I have known goddam Negroes like you before."

By now Johnson's 17-year-old son George entered the room to witness their conversation. As soon as he heard Crowe's comment, "he fell upon" him, Newell wrote, "and struck blow upon blow to his face that soon flowed with scarlet blood, no different in color than the blood that runs through" his own veins. The confrontation continued.

"In the meantime," Newell recounted, "the Rev. David Johnson had left the room. He soon reappeared with his German Lugar. He pulled back the jack and pointed the gun at the young man who had called him a goddam Negro. I stepped in front of David Johnson. 'Fire if you must, David,' I pleaded. 'Fire if you must,'" before he handed the weapon to an onlooker. The mayhem, so incongruous with the celebration taking place elsewhere in the house, led Newell to observe what Johnson wrought from his actions. "The Rev. David Johnson," he wrote, "had that day won his place in the sun. But the sun which rises, also sets, and he all but lost, or perhaps better, he nearly lost all that night in a victory that, for a Negro among whites is shallow, partial and in the end quite empty."[433]

The violence at Johnson's house capped a stressful week in Irasburg where the press said "a hurricane of racial unrest" swirled. Rumors of "large-scale vigilante action" headed by area committees, threats of people descending on Johnson's home to inflict harm, Newell's receipt of numerous threats, and a newspaper vehicle tailed by a car "decorated by Confederate flags" presented a toxic environment indicating that violence was not far off.[434] Johnson's attorney, Robert Rachlin, wasted no time when he heard about it. He immediately arranged that a telegram be sent to Commissioner Alexander stating: "Urgently request presence of suitable number of state police in vicinity of Johnson residence in Irasburg on account of persistent reports of vigilante committee directed against Johnson coupled with recent disturbance at his home."[435] At the attorney general's office, Mahady also wrote to Hoff seeking his assistance to assign troopers to guard Johnson's home, advising further "that we are beginning an investigation into these alleged committees."[436]

Police arrested six men for events taking place on two separate occasions near the Johnson home: four for driving past the house shouting "n-----, n-----," threatening to burn down his home and two others for making threats.[437]

During the trial of one of the defendants in early November, just days before the Irasburg hearings convened, evidence that Johnson either precipitated one of the confrontations or responded to it by firing his pistol in a threatening manner was omitted because Mahady vehemently objected to its introduction keeping it from the jury. The problem he faced as the prosecutor concerned defense counsel's inquiry of Johnson testifying on the state's behalf about his actions.

When questioned specifically what he did in response to the shouting, he said "I just sat on my porch and looked at them." When asked again "You did nothing?" he replied, "No sir."[438] Johnson's response, according to the memorandum Mahady wrote for the board of inquiry, seems to have provoked a startled response from a court officer. "On at least one occasion," he wrote, the officer "made gasping noises" at hearing Johnson's account.

Mahady interpreted her interruption as meaning that she thought his testimony was "inconsistent with that of a previous state witness." Later, the officer "saw fit to yell to me," he continued, within the hearing of everyone in the courtroom, "that I had failed to call one of the witnesses which I had under subpoena."

It apparently concerned someone who could provide testimony contrary to Johnson's statement that he had done nothing in response to the shouting. Mahady's careful choice of words in his memo also advised the board that Det. Wade was called to testify on the behalf of the defense about "the inconsistent statements that a state witness had allegedly made to him." What Mahady carefully omitted was the identity of the witness Wade spoke with and that Johnson was that person.[439]

Mahady's objection to Wade's testimony may have successfully kept information undercutting Johnson's credibility from the jury, but it did not remain silent forever. In an interview of two witnesses about the confrontation conducted by a reporter in 1988 on the 20th anniversary of the Irasburg Affair the missing information about Johnson's firing his pistol was revealed.

His neighbor across the street, Ruth Skinner, did not have a favorable impression of him. "One day I seen him come out his front steps, go to that shed there, get his German Luger, shoot it in the air, then call the police and say he was shot at. The state troopers came racing up from Newport. I said, 'That coon's at it again. You guys sure are stupid.'" However, the second witness, Bertha Sheltra, whose family befriended the Johnson family after their arrival, said Skinner's interpretation of the events was "all wrong." Instead, she said, Johnson fired the shots because he "was scared for his family, but he wasn't trying to hurt anyone else." Johnson's actions bewildered many and Skinner's husband delivered a parting warning to the reporter at the conclusion of her interview with his wife. "Anybody like him come around here acting uppity like that again," he said, "is apt to get the same thing."[440]

While the jury was never allowed to hear about Johnson firing his gun that could have undermined his account that he only sat on his porch and did nothing, it quickly found the defendant in the case not guilty.[441] Just a few days after testifying at that trial, Johnson appeared before the board of inquiry to provide more sworn information about the events taking place on the evening of July 18–19 when he admittedly fired his gun numerous times. He was never questioned about the other incident and, despite knowing about it, the board never made any inquiries of its own that could have undermined Johnson's credibility.

Mahady's promise to investigate the allegations of vigilante committees in northern Vermont ended as quickly as it began, timed with the conclusion of Attorney General Oakes's political career. With three troopers on a twenty-four-hour watch stationed at Johnson's house once again ("until this thing cools off," Commissioner Alexander said), on Sept. 9 Oakes announced that Mahady's investigation "is just about over." He also confidently awaited the results of his primary race for governor taking place the next day.

But on Sept. 11, when Johnson's adultery case was dismissed, an admittedly "shocked" Oakes suffered a major defeat, described variously in the press as a "trouncing" and "smashing victory" for his opponent, Deane Davis.[442] Whereas Oakes campaigned on a progressive agenda dealing with poverty, natural resources and education, Davis struck a more pragmatic chord with the electorate calling for fiscal restraint and addressing rising property taxes; the kinds of things that Hoff's Poverty Tour identified months earlier.[443] Statewide, Davis crushed Oakes by a three to two margin, garnering over 36,719 votes compared to Oakes's 21,791.[444] In the NEK where he tried to make an impression directing the Irasburg investigation, Oakes experienced an embarrassing thrashing. In Orleans County, where he belittled State's Attorney Pearson, only 701 voters supported him, while 2,486 went for Davis. In the two other counties, Oakes received 1,051 in his favor and Davis earned 2,386 in Caledonia, while in Essex 201 voted for him and 386 for Davis. Hoff lamented the loss his fellow Young Turk suffered, voicing his "wonder about the Republican Party" and asking if "they represent the people or the establishment."[445]

Oakes actually had little reason for concern about the setback. Help was on the way in the form of the father of one of his fellow Young Turks, the chairman of Hoff's soon-to-be established board of inquiry, including a sympathetic second board member, paving his way to a lifetime appointment as a federal court judge.

Chapter 7

AFTERMATH

CONFLICTS OF INTEREST

ASSEMBLING AND ASSIGNING AN APPROPRIATE MANDATE to the administrative body Hoff wanted with his board of inquiry, essentially a hybrid adjudicative body, posed a significant challenge. Could a governor order it be done and, if so, how much authority could it lawfully exercise? The Vermont Constitution did not recognize such an entity and its existence could only be permitted if its language inferred the chief executive's ability to delegate powers otherwise permitted to the judiciary to another body. In addition, Hoff wanted whatever entity he created to possess the power to compel the testimony of witnesses and the production of evidence by subpoena. In early September he turned to Oakes for an opinion and who agreed that while he could create the board, it could not utilize subpoenas.[446] The absence of authority to compel witnesses to appear posed additional problems for the Irasburg hearings, and the validity of the conclusions it reached, because several of those "invited" to provide critical testimony simply did not show up.

Legality about the board's existence notwithstanding, other factors affecting its legitimacy, credibility and the way it conducted its work presented further problems that none of its creators appreciated. However, former attorney general Frederick M. Reed, and incoming Gov. Davis's secretary of civil and military affairs in January, did and issued him a warning about its problems. The board's *Findings and Recommendations* had issued just weeks earlier, glaringly prepared without the benefit of a transcript of witnesses' testimony that led it to recite many inaccuracies. Concerned at what he read, Reed advised Davis that the findings "leave something to be desired as they are written both in form and substance." He also expressed great concern at the lack of due process afforded to the VSP that the board excoriated because it had no way to appeal its findings. In their rush to form this extra-judicial body, its creators overlooked this important right that any litigant appearing before a tribunal deserved and which infected the legitimacy of its work.

While others also appreciated the problems Reed identified, there was another that has not been discussed which also influenced the direction the board took in fashioning its findings. Identifying and resolving potential conflicts of interests early on do not appear of concern to any of the participants. If it did, they never raised them and none of the records of the Irasburg Affair discuss them. Yet, the strong relationships and friendships that Oakes, in the middle of a full-blown campaign for governor, shared with governors Hoff, Gibson and Emerson, board attorney Lt. Gov. Foote, and attorney Kyle T. Brown representing VSP troopers cannot be overlooked. Oakes was a Young Turk and some of those associated with the inquiry, either directly or indirectly through familial ties, also shared that cherished characterization with him. Foote and Brown, together with Judge Gibson's son, the secretary to the Vermont Senate, Robert H. Gibson (1963–1999), all served as his campaign managers in his run for attorney general in 1966. Robert Gibson also acted as Oakes's campaign director for governor in 1968. Further, the examination of Oakes conducted by Foote and Brown during the hearings overseen by Gibson raises substantial questions about how such friendships affected the course of his and others' testimony.

Other examples of the strong ties these individuals shared extended to their wives. On the same day he ordered the formation of a board of inquiry on Sept. 26, Hoff appointed Oakes's wife, Rosalyn, to the Vermont State Housing Authority.[447] She was immediately elected by its members to become its vice-president.[448] A month later, just two days before Gibson opened the Irasburg hearings, Rosalyn joined Barbara Wick, the wife of the second male board member, to co-host a new daily television show broadcast from Burlington covering "the arts, government, education and employment."[449]

Oakes also possessed extraordinary power to influence and direct the work of what was supposed to be a neutral, unbiased process that Reed and attorney Robert Eldredge representing Commissioner Alexander decried as absent. The theater surrounding the hearings and affecting each of these individuals, including the careers of Gibson's law clerk Jerome Diamond and Oakes's assistant Frank Mahady, meant that attacks or slights made by any one of them on the other, or their failure to fall into line condemning the VSP, threatened professional and political suicide. Under the special circumstances of the time, it is reasonable to ask what behind-the-scenes roles did any of them also play in Oakes's campaign and what perks they could expect from him if he became the state's next governor? There is also a sense of intimidation on the part of a few of the participants, particularly attorney Kyle Brown, who chose not to press points with witnesses that could have helped his VSP clients, but who chose to retreat to avoid embarrassing a political peer. Secretary Reed and Gov. Davis certainly recognized these unspoken conflicts. However, as a newly installed governor distancing himself from the problems of Hoff's administration, they too chose a silent path refusing to raise them publicly and thereby avoid the unpleasant taint of the Irasburg Affair.

The friendships clouding the relationships of these men during the hearings presents an additional important conflict that has escaped notice. Recently defeated by Davis in embarrassing fashion during the Republican primary, Oakes now appeared before the board in his role as the attorney general having overseen the prosecution of Larry Conley. However, he also acted as an investigator in that case working closely with Mahady and L'Ecuyer to track down leads the three considered important and as a witness to the actions of the VSP that the board was judging. The combination of a prosecutor, investigator and witness in one individual presents a unique situation, in the judicial arena at least, and is highly unusual. It might have raised eyebrows in another forum, but in the context of a board of inquiry it did not prompt any objections. Nonetheless, even in a governor-created board of inquiry the parties are entitled to a measure of unconflicted due process and the Irasburg board's findings indicates that it took no action to neutralize those that Oakes presented.

What effect Rev. Newell's racist rants about the Irasburg matter, or the letters he received from constituents disgusted at what they understood as fact, had on Hoff's choice of board members is not known. The credibility of his Vermont-New York Youth Project remained, together with calls for him to immediately address the state's widespread poverty and hunger, and to salvage his vision, while also distancing himself from the carnage, meant that a villain must be identified.

His call for a board commanding respect could do that, but also presents questions about what arrangements, or "understandings," were made beforehand in their appointment. With Oakes's blessing, and likely his input on the selection, Hoff found three individuals of "high repute" to serve on his board of inquiry: its chairman, U.S. District Court Judge Ernest W. Gibson Jr. of Brattleboro; Burlington attorney Hilton Wick; and Dorothy M. Collins, a retired Vermont College educator living in Hyde Park.

Hoff's mandate to the board directed that it conduct "a complete and thorough investigation into all of the facts and circumstances resulting from the settlement in Vermont of DAVID L. H. JOHNSON and his family at Irasburg, including, but not limited to, any and all acts of violence or threats thereof against the said DAVID L. H. JOHNSON and his family, *the conduct and performance of any and all state officials and agencies in connection therewith*, the threat of possible vigilante activity and evidence of the relationship between the press and state agencies or the general public." (Emphasis added).

Upon completion of its work, Hoff further ordered that the board submit "a complete and detailed report of this investigation."[450] Professing no interest in the board's efforts lingering into the waning days of his administration, Hoff also directed that it be completed as soon as possible.

Chairman Gibson brought a range of experience to the task. A former U.S. senator, wounded army colonel during World War

II receiving special commendations, state governor and now sitting federal judge, Gibson possessed a unique perspective on the law. At the time of his death in 1969, he was described several ways. They included that he was very personable, a person who tilted at legal windmills and one who worked assiduously on the behalf of plaintiffs harmed by others. From both the bench and in the privacy of his chambers he "scored bureaucrats, law enforcement agencies and lawyers when he felt they were pressing down on 'the little people'"[451] Sen. George Aiken succinctly related that "He was the best man the people who needed friends ever had in this state," characterizing him warmly as "my closest friend."[452] During his own association with both men allowing him opportunities to observe and assess their personal relationship, Oakes told Aiken after Gibson's passing that he "thought more of you than anyone, just as you did of him."[453]

Gibson's esteemed reputation also seems to have affected the outcomes of trials he oversaw where jurors recalled they "based their verdicts on how it seemed to them the judge felt about the evidence being presented."[454] His personal feelings about the merits of the cases meant that his subjective impressions may have allowed for outcomes contrary to law. "Affection for Judge Gibson," one Burlington attorney recalled after his death, "was by no means a feeling shared by all members of the legal fraternity in Vermont. On the contrary, Judge Gibson was an irritant to some lawyers and a savior to others. On the bench, as in the political arena, (he) did and said what he believed was right without regard to whom it may have displeased. I believe that what he said or did while sitting as U.S. District Judge was never calculated to please or satisfy lawyers, but rather to satisfy his own marvelous sense of justice—and every lawyer knew that."[455]

One of those attorneys experiencing Gibson's unrestrained "marvelous sense of justice," Philip Hoff, recalled an earlier occasion when he appeared before him representing an insurance company sued by a woman injured in an accident. Believing he had a solid case refuting her claims, Hoff was taken aback when Gibson was "all over" him attacking his position. The plaintiff ultimately received a favorable, albeit miniscule, monetary award in her favor, but was one that Gibson confided to Hoff the next day only became possible because of the way he treated him. Gibson said he believed she deserved some sort of compensation, but that "If I had not come down hard on you that damned fool (the woman's attorney) would never have gotten a verdict."[456] Personal bias and invoking the power of theatrics seems traits of Gibson's judicial persona.

Before James M. Jeffords succeeded Oakes as attorney general in 1969, he served as Gibson's law clerk between 1962 and 1963. The son of Olin M. Jeffords, a former Vermont Supreme Court chief justice, Jeffords was steeped in the law and held many positions during his career, including as a U.S. senator (1989–2007), placing him squarely in its midst. As Hoff experienced, he also witnessed an instance of Gibson's willingness to intercede in a case that could have gone in another direction without his interference. As Jeffords recounted:

> The law is often impractical and Judge Gibson was a very practical man, so the two were often at loggerheads. He believed that sometimes justice may not quite square with all the facts, so on those occasions, you need to consider common sense, not just a rigid legal point of view to achieve true justice. One time, Judge Gibson was issuing a decision on a strange tort case involving skiing. To my surprise, he blatantly and completely ignored the law. He defended the decision by saying, "Never let the law get in the way of justice; justice is what counts."[457]

Jeffords was struck by Gibson's comment, saying that "here was a man I had an unbelievable amount of respect for ignoring the law." Gibson's intention to provide litigants with his unique "marvelous sense of justice" meant that applying the law in a case assumed secondary importance. It certainly confounded those litigants with legitimate claims losing cases he presided over that they might otherwise have won had he followed the law. Gibson's additional inclination to confront those in positions of authority, including law enforcement, presents another reason warranting a reassessment of the Irasburg hearings he oversaw for the presence of bias.

Because Gibson's personal impressions of right and wrong dictated the course of the Irasburg hearings and writing the board's findings, his attitude about them specifically are of additional importance. While he conducted the public hearings in a generally orderly fashion, sitting silently as witnesses such as Oakes testified and then sniping at VSP investigators, questions concerning his overall objectivity and biases arise. Gibson considered the work odious, saying that he "accepted the unpleasant task of chairmanship" of the board in the first place in order to guide it through the "unpleasant tasks" it faced.[458] Impatient at the conclusion of the hearings, he told the attorneys he wanted them to submit proposed findings for the board to consider and that it be done "the quicker the better. We want to get rid of it."[459] After those findings were issued, he wrote to Hoff to tell him of his relief at having "finished that very difficult and rather unpleasant chore."[460] Comfortable with the board's final conclusions and believing nobody cared any further about the testimony provided by witnesses, he advised Hoff that "except for historical purposes, I am not sure it is necessary for it to be transcribed." Hoff followed his advice at first, but soon backtracked when a firestorm of opposition to the board's work arose because there was nothing transcribed to support its findings.

Gibson also maintained strong relationships with other politicians and the press at the time of the hearings in a practice that began two decades earlier. After his return from the war and receiving glowing acclaim for his service, in 1946 *Rutland Herald* owner and publisher Robert Mitchell suggested he run for governor in the approaching elections. Intrigued at the thought, Gibson conferred with close friend and Windham County neighbor Sen. Aiken about the proposal. He decided to pursue the position and went on to win, assisted by Mitchell's strong backing made possible by his newspaper's resources. A "rare political triumvirate" soon blossomed, composed of the three men who, according to Aiken's wife Lola, "could be said to have run the state of Vermont, or at least pulled most of the strings of power" in the next years.[461] Candidly providing further insights into their close relationship, Mitchell acknowledged that at times their friendship "went beyond the bounds of appropriate activities for a newspaper publisher."[462]

While Mitchell professed to have broken off from such shady practices, at the time of the Irasburg turmoil he continued to maintain extensive contact with Aiken and Gibson in numerous telephone calls witnessed by Vermont Press Bureau chief Stephen Terry. "I know that Gibson and Mitchell talked a lot off-line about the state police and its role in the case," Terry recalled.[463] And what did the three men talk about?

Mitchell was proud of his intolerance for racism that summer, proclaiming in May that Vermont was a "white racist state."[464] To alleviate the problem, he also believed that the *Herald* "in its role as opinion-maker—or at least opinion-influencer—should lay helpful foundation stones in that regard and should establish a model for others to follow."[465] To what extent the many calls between Mitchell and Gibson discussed racism after Hoff appointed Gibson chairman of the board of inquiry able to facilitate the publisher's goal for his paper is not clear. Nor is the effect they might have had in guiding Gibson's ultimate findings the VSP was also racist, but it cannot be discounted. Somebody had to assume the role of scapegoat to alleviate the distraction Irasburg caused to Hoff's youth project that Mitchell so strongly endorsed in his editorials; anything less threatened significant embarrassment to each of them. It must also be of sufficient notoriety able to divert attention away from Hoff's administration's failure to act on the ominous warnings of hunger and malnutrition present in Orleans County. To not find one meant that other embarrassed politicians and pundits could be left holding the proverbial bag. Consequently, adopting the unsavory mantle of racism that Rev. Newell sought to lay on the department provided a convenient avenue to follow. And with the momentum building to condemn the VSP, it was only a matter of time before it all fell into place.

Hilton A. Wick also served on the board with his good friend Gibson, but remained silent throughout the hearings, except to administer oaths, never raising his voice to ask questions. A graduate of the Harvard Law School that Oakes also attended, former head of the Vermont Bar Association and recently named president of the Chittenden Trust Company, Hoff tapped Wick as another of Vermont's elite to investigate the Irasburg matter. Together with Gibson, he provided strong backing to Oakes and figures prominently in the aftermath of the board's report when the two advocated for his appointment to become a federal judge when Gibson stepped down.[466] The political relationship between Oakes and Wick began, at least, in 1966 when Wick circulated petitions on Oakes's behalf in his run for attorney general, earning the latter's appreciation for his efforts.[467] A year later, Wick counseled his friend to set his eyes on the governor's office in 1968 promising that "I would do such as I can in this area to help you."[468] Just two months before the Irasburg violence, Wick promised Oakes's campaign manager to take the candidate with him as his guest to meet members of the Burlington Rotary Club to provide him with further exposure to the state's king-makers.[469]

Dorothy M. Collins occupied the board's third seat and, like Wick, never intruded into the witnesses' testimony to pose her own questions. She was respected and well known in the academic field, with degrees from UVM, and held teaching and administrative positions at Trinity College, Johnson State College and most recently as dean of admissions at Vermont College.[470] Notably, she is the only one of the three board members to pen her personal views in preparing its findings. Neither did she participate in advancing Oakes's post-attorney general career that her male counterparts, the powerful Gibson and Wick, assured.

The accumulating conflicts of interest presented by the board and its principal witness, Attorney General Oakes, began immediately upon its creation on Sept. 26. The mandate from Hoff that it investigate "the conduct and performance of any and all state officials and agencies in connection" with the Irasburg matter meant that his role fell squarely within its scope of inquiry. There was no provision to direct the board when conflicts such as this arose and was of no apparent concern to the participants. Rather than retain the services of an outside, independent prosecutor to guide the board's work, Oakes participated early on as its close confidant and consultant clouding borders that should have otherwise been made clear and honored.

The conflict became more evident the next day when Hoff instructed Oakes to "make available to Judge Gibson and his board of inquiry whatever personnel and material he may deem necessary and appropriate to the conduct of his investigation and to render such other assistance as may be requested of your office by the board."[471]

The same day working from his federal court chambers in Brattleboro, Gibson dashed off letters to Oakes and VSP Commissioner Alexander (addressing him as "Alex") requesting they provide him with "copies of all records and correspondence of your department having to do with this affair." Because of the minimal amount of documentation his office generated during the investigation, Oakes complied within a couple of days. However, Alexander's situation proved more problematic because statutory provisions seemed to limit the VSP from disclosing criminal reports to private citizens that he needed to clarify.

Before complying with Gibson's request, Alexander sought a legal opinion from Oakes approving of the transfer of records and did so immediately after he said it was permissible; delivering the documents "to Judge Gibson 4 Oct. at 6:20 p.m.," a handwritten notation in the records relate.[472] While Oakes expressed no concern over Alexander's caution and routine request for an opinion, it offended Gibson. Upon learning of it, he sent off another letter peevishly telling Alexander that he was acting pursuant to Hoff's executive order. If he wanted a copy of it, Gibson snipped, "I am sure the governor's office will be glad to show it to you." Impatient at the prospect of any delay, he warned Alexander that "I shall expect a prompt reply" and ominously told him that among those expected to testify at the hearing "you will be asked to be a witness."[473]

Alexander had no way of knowing that Gibson would make public the reports he provided to him. He rightfully believed they deserved careful handling in the same confidential manner that police investigations were routinely processed and not, instead, distributed outside of the board's needs. Revealing the many twists and turns that the department's investigation took, the reports identify many individuals, their stories, their alibis, their cooperation and non-cooperation with police. Few of the more than 220 people they interviewed would have wanted that information made known to the public, but Gibson opened it all up causing Alexander great concern. Had he understood Gibson's intention, he said he would have sought a court order beforehand in a position that irked the chairman even further.[474]

Writing in its findings about Alexander's "apparent failure to make available to the Board all matters he had in his file," Gibson's, and apparently his clerk Diamond's, mean assessment only added more unwarranted fuel to the fire consuming the VSP's credibility.[475] In the end, there was never any question that the department ever withheld information from the board; a situation Gibson could not prove otherwise. It provided copies of all the paperwork it generated throughout investigation, evidenced by the stack of reports, accompanied by those from State's Attorney Pearson and the Orleans County Court, that Gibson described as standing "nine inches high."[476] Despite that accountability, questions remain concerning Detective Chilton's report of David Johnson's criminal history that appears tampered with while in the board's possession.

The string of conflicts continued, evidenced by another aspect of the relationship between Hoff and Gibson. While employed as a trooper, 33-year-old Bobby Joe Jackson served as Hoff's driver providing security. They developed a good relationship and Hoff admitted he was "tremendously fond" of him, but they parted ways when Jackson decided to pursue another career as an investigator with the state's Department of Water Resources. He soon recognized his error and sought reinstatement with the VSP, writing to Maj. Davis who told him he would have to take his request up with district commanders for their approval. Jackson never heard back from Davis and a second inquiry with Commissioner Alexander brought an answer that he did not believe it in the department's best interest to rehire him.[477]

Jackson understood that Alexander's refusal stemmed from reports he assisted Caledonia State's Attorney Sten Lium months earlier when Lium lodged the embarrassing allegations that VSP commanders required troopers to comply with ticket quotas to earn favorable evaluations. He denied doing so and asked Hoff to intercede on his behalf in some way.

A week after naming the members of the board of inquiry, Hoff wrote to Jackson. "It occurs to me," he said, "that in the process of doing this investigation, they might well take a look at your situation if for no other reason than to clear you of any involvement. If it turns out this way, I think then I would be in a position to urge the department to re-employ you." Despite being neither employed by the VSP during the Irasburg investigation or playing any role as a witness or in any other capacity in it, Hoff sought Gibson's intervention on Jackson's behalf.

"I am enclosing a copy of my reply to him," Hoff wrote to Gibson, "as well as his letter to me with the hope that in the process of this investigation you might be able to take a look at Bobby's situation. If he comes out well, I find it difficult to believe that the State Police should not reinstate him." Rather than refuse Hoff's extraordinary request to use the board of inquiry in an unrelated matter outside the scope of its mandate, Gibson responded favorably: "We will, of course, take a look at Bobby Jackson's problem."[478] In the end, and unsurprisingly because of its irrelevancy to the Irasburg matter, neither Lium's campaign against the VSP or Jackson's name ever appeared in any of its reports or came up during witness testimony. Nonetheless, Hoff's solicitation and Gibson's willingness to abide his wishes presents another troubling aspect involving those in positions of authority responsible for the conclusions reached in the board's findings.

On Sept. 30, the three board members met for the first time in Montpelier to discuss how to proceed. Oakes also attended, the press reported, and "spoke to the group for a period of time, but did not detail his remarks."[479] Nobody from the other agency the board was investigating, the VSP, appeared to provide its remarks. Regardless, at some point Oakes's former campaign manager, Lt. Gov. Foote, was named as the board's counsel to conduct questioning on its behalf. After their meeting, Gibson traveled to the NEK and met with several people, including Johnson's attorney, Robert Rachlin, and Bernadette Roy's attorney, former governor Lee Emerson. The substance of their conversations is not known.

The board met a second time in Montpelier on Oct. 7 that Foote also attended. By this time, information concerning Angell's and Wade's trip to California seeking to bring Barbara Lawrence back to Vermont for Johnson's trial was known. The fact that they never consulted with Oakes before they left peeved Gibson, making it clear in a letter he wrote to Oakes.†† He authored all of the board's correspondence (perhaps with clerk Diamond's input) to express his displeasure with the trip, telling him that it constituted only one of "several rather unusual things (that) have happened in this matter."[480] Gibson's contentions about the trip concerned him so much that,

---

†† Why Oakes should be consulted about the trip is curious because he emphatically told State's Attorney Pearson he wanted nothing to do with the adultery case.

despite simple explanations of its innocence from the participants and bank officials, and supporting documentation, the late-night meeting between them to obtain the needed money for it seemed so odd he became obsessed with its perceived irregularity. He did not understand or appreciate the challenges that VSP investigators routinely faced at odd hours conducting out-of-state investigations that required them to use their own money and to later seek reimbursement. Nor did he understand that the reimbursement process no longer required the governor's approval that he participated in two decades earlier or the current methods they used pursuant to longstanding approval granted by Hoff and his administration.

In fact, the board's work itself posed a challenge for Hoff's administrative assistant, forced to solicit help from the commissioner of administration to process Gibson's request for reimbursement of his, Wick's and Collins's expenses. "Please advise out of which account," she pleaded, "we can legitimately take these expenses. In fact, I would appreciate it if perhaps your office could prepare the necessary papers."[481]

Each of the board members received the money they sought to support Gibson and his four-member staff (secretary, clerk, crier and reporter) relating to their travel, food, lodging, telephone and copying expenses, totaling some $2,000.[482] Except for the late-night emergency that investigators faced in obtaining funds to travel to California requiring them to personally sign a $1,500 note, there is virtually no difference in the reimbursement process they and the board utilized.

The board also misunderstood the reasons behind troopers creating what it perceived as "a somewhat nebulous organization" that worked on its behalf. Testimony from officials made clear its voluntary nature, funded by members' dues that had no connection with any of the board's mandates. Unwilling to accept such an explanation, it conflated the financial arrangements investigators made for the California trip with the perception that troopers' dues were used to pay for it, insinuating the presence of a bizarre scheme forcing them to contribute.

In its pursuit of what it interpreted as questionable practices, and with an apparent lack of understanding of state law concerning such proceedings, Gibson asked Oakes to conduct an inquest to look into the financing of the California trip and provide it to him. Sharing information gained through secret inquest proceedings without court approval is a violation of law and indicates that the board may not have fully appreciated the ramifications of what it was asking. However, Oakes did and rather than commit to starting an inquest simply advised Gibson that "we are working" on his request.[483] He never did institute one, which, nonetheless, led the board in its final recommendations to have either the attorney general "or a proper legislative committee" investigate the situation further. Additionally, it questioned the legitimacy of the troopers' organization, saying it had "serious doubts as to the legality of any such move on the part of the State Police," and recommended further inquiry into it by a higher authority.[484] Notwithstanding the board's suspicions, neither Oakes or his successor, James Jeffords, or the legislature ever found reason to question the California trip, its funding or the existence of a suspicious troopers' association.[485]

The cooperation between Gibson and Oakes in the weeks leading up to the hearings designed to examine the conduct of both the attorney general's office and the VSP was exceedingly close, facilitated by clerk Diamond. Correspondence between the two men's offices shows that as soon as the VSP provided its files to Gibson, he passed them on to Oakes. By mid-October, Oakes reported back that "Skip Mahady and I are working on our comments relative to the State Police file." Days later, he related that "Greg (L'Eucyer) and Skip are going over (my comments) and when they have done so, I may very well have some corrections, in case my own memory has lapsed because as you know those were fairly busy times!"[486] The three men worked together as a team to scour the VSP files and prepare a polished sixteen-page document for Gibson entitled "RE IRASBURG, COMMENTS OF ATTORNEY GENERAL JAMES OAKES, October 18, 1968."[487]

At the same time, Mahady prepared a second six-page document detailing particular aspects of the case Oakes assigned to him. Together, the two reports show the team closely analyzing the VSP reports to create a roadmap for the board, breaking down the entire episode into three time periods: "Phase I—The Shooting Case;" "Phase II—The Adultery Case;" and, "Phase III—The Harassment Phase." While they concluded that the VSP reports accorded generally with their own recollection, this access to the other party's information beforehand also allowed them an advantage the VSP did not have. It permitted them to raise questions in advance about when and how the department conducted its work and to prepare answers that did not damage their positions.

There are no reports of interviews or other documentation in the extant files demonstrating that Oakes or his assistants contemporaneously memorialized any of their own work during the investigation to back up their later interpretations that the VSP acted in an unacceptable manner. The only corroboration of their allegations comes from what they remembered, a shaky basis that both Oakes and Mahady admitted caused them to recite inaccurate dates of events.

Consequently, several of their observations about VSP's actions on days of particular importance are likewise inaccurate, leading to erroneous interpretations of the department's work. Notably, the VSP was never accorded a reciprocal courtesy to provide its own outline to the board of what happened or was provided with copies of either Oakes's or Mahady's reports. Because of that failure, the hearings turned what was supposed to be a fair inquiry into a lopsided trial by ambush surprising unprepared officers. Closely monitoring events, the press had a field day watching the VSP twist in the wind, its credibility attacked and claims of racism descend on it.

Meanwhile, Oakes remained above it all. Unsurprisingly, he took full credit in his Comments for finally solving the shooting case when Mahady and L'Ecuyer reportedly concentrated their efforts on Larry Conley as the "prime suspect" a week after the shooting, faulting the VSP for not arresting him earlier. To reach that conclusion, Oakes ignored other important aspects of the quickly unfolding case that drove the VSP investigators' efforts in other directions.

These concerned a series of omissions and misstatements he made, including: the work conducted by some 20 officers tracking down and interviewing more than 220 witnesses; that they already identified Conley soon after the event and worked virtually 24-hours-a-day to accumulate additional information to support a warrant for his arrest; and that Mahady agreed with police there was insufficient evidence for the arrest requiring the additional investigation. Neither did he acknowledge that: Mahady and L'Ecuyer interviewed only a single witness (Bernadette Roy) that the police had not already spoken with because she was in California; he agreed with the VSP that Johnson's suspicion someone from Lawrence's family in California may have committed the offense warranted further investigation to omit them from the suspect list; and, despite his allegations to the contrary, the VSP worked with Mahady and L'Ecuyer continuously in the exceedingly complex environment he fostered as a campaigning candidate for governor interceding into a police investigation he admitted he had no authority over.

As the records demonstrate, there is overwhelming evidence to credit the VSP's diligent work to solve the case and little to support Oakes's arguments to the contrary.

As soon as Gibson received Oakes's comments on the VSP files, he forwarded them on to the other two board members.[488] Because the board never invited the VSP to provide its own summary of what happened, it lacked its insights that could have aided its understanding of events and, perhaps, ameliorate the growing impatience Gibson exhibited towards it. After reviewing Oakes's submission, he wrote to Alexander, this time greeting him abruptly as "Mr. Commissioner." The tone of his letter conveys great displeasure with the reports Alexander sent him and said that "it is very apparent to me that these are not complete." Apparently surprised that Alexander had also forwarded him additional information, rather than thank him for his attention, the chairman curtly said "Now you have come up with some more." Uninterested in any delay or working with Alexander to gather the necessary information, Gibson simply told him to "be present the morning of 8th of November at 9:30 a.m. at the District Courtroom in Newport."[489] In advance of the hearings, Gibson's clerk Diamond prepared his lengthy outline that ended on Nov. 7 with the entries that Mahady had submitted his report and "Hearing started but Johnsons didn't show on time."[490]

"LOOPHOLES AND CONTRADICTIONS"

The Irasburg Board of Inquiry conducted five days of hearings between Nov. 7–22; two sessions in the Newport courthouse and the others at Gibson's courtroom in the federal building in Montpelier where he frequently donned sunglasses because of the bright lights. Without the ability to subpoena witnesses, 33 individuals responded to invitations for them to testify, while an unknown number of others simply ignored the opportunity; a void in the evidence contributing further reason to question the completeness of the board's work.

While Foote acted as board counsel assisted by Diamond, St. Johnsbury attorney Kyle T. Brown and his associate, David L. Willis, represented officers Cram, Dean, Duhaime, Green, Heffernan, Hogan, Lessard, MacDonald, Marhsall, Pellon, Potvin, Shanks, Wade and Washburn. Montpelier attorney and former Washington County senator Robert A. Eldredge appeared on the behalf of Commissioner Alexander. Gibson's secretary, Shirley A. Bliss, and his court crier, Ernest T. Johnson, also attended the hearings transcribed by his court reporter, Herman J. Vesper.

Vesper's 753 pages of transcribed testimony available for public examination and evaluation describes only one aspect of what happened in Irasburg. The accompanying 187 exhibits admitted during the proceedings that he carefully itemized tells another side of the story in much greater detail (Appendix E; exhibits 181–187 are not listed).

The release of these documents to the press by Gibson (that he said Hoff ordered), a week after the hearings began presented a huge problem for anyone named in them. Constitutional protections of privacy meant nothing for both those implicated during the investigation and others who were now seeing their names and aspects of their lives published widely. It presents a stark example of the pitfalls presented because of the rushed methods used by the quasi-legal board of inquiry faced with decisions that a court of law could have easily decided by withholding and using them in an orderly legal fashion.

While the press initially relied on the daily testimony it heard to write its bombastic bylines ("Incredible Story of State Cops," the *Times Argus* headlined after the first day of hearings), the withholding of these exhibits for a week only added further mystery when it gained access.[491] All of a sudden, the public heard that many others, including community members, the clergy and those in the media were implicated in some aspect of what happened. This piecemeal release of information, guided by Hoff's political hand, only intensified the suspicions of those outside of law enforcement that the VSP had something to hide.

In this highly contentious series of the hearings so unique and important in Vermont's history, Gibson did not believe it necessary to arrange for the transcription of testimony on a daily basis. Hoff also entered into this aspect of the hearings and ordered that no transcripts be prepared unless he allowed them, apparently agreeing with Gibson that they served no use other than for "historical purposes."

Their decisions presented significant problems for the board when it prepared its findings, forced to rely on its recollection of the testimony it heard. It also affected Hoff himself after he lodged serious allegations against the VSP based on those findings because neither he or the board could recite specific testimony to support their positions. Had Gibson and Hoff allowed this information, and the accompanying documents, be made available on a timely basis, perhaps much of the ensuing rancor, hyperbole and misunderstanding lodged against the VSP could have been avoided. When the documents were released, it was already too late to undo the earlier damaging tone set by the hearings placing the VSP squarely in its crosshairs. Unfortunately, Vesper's work sat unused for the next two months during the uproar after the release of the board's findings in December and the transition of power from Hoff to Davis completed, before he finished transcribing them on Jan. 18, 1969.

Under Gibson's guidance, the hearings appeared to accomplish three things, two for public consumption and the last less obvious: compliance, more or less, with Hoff's mandate; to clarify for a confused public, and Hoff, the chronology of events leading to Conley's arrest and the adultery case against Lawrence and Johnson; and, to post its imprimatur advancing the career prospects of recently defeated Oakes in his campaign for governor. Memorable testimony came from Johnson, Oakes, and Alexander describing their various roles. Johnson's account of the shooting was readily accepted as accurate, while his denial of adultery that the press trumpeted as true, actually suffered significant credibility issues.

Oakes told how he became involved, his appearance in Irasburg after the shooting and, in his interpretation of the facts, directing the effort to charge and convict Conley; making sure to distance himself from the adultery case. Alexander presented additional information about police policies and procedures, his interactions with Oakes and the press while refuting allegations his department was racist. Other officers, attorneys and members of the clergy also testified to tell what they knew to fill in the blanks. Members of the *Newport Daily Express* also explained where the information they printed came from that caused Hoff so much concern, while other media representatives were either never invited or declined to attend.

The *Burlington Free Press*'s James Warren McClure begged off Gibson's invitation to appear between November 7 and 12 because of a pre-scheduled business trip.[492] However, there is no indication that Gibson made arrangements after his return and while the hearings continued for him to attend. The absence of McClure's testimony provided the board with the opportunity to infer there was some kind of untoward relationship between him and Alexander; an allegation that McClure could have refuted. As Alexander made clear to the board and Hoff, that kind of innuendo was untrue and the record corroborates his evidence denying such a relationship.

Lt. Gov. Foote questioned all of the witnesses and repeatedly scored points disparaging the VSP while minimizing any potential harm to his friend Oakes. Court reporter Vesper duly noted 50 pages of questions and answers between he and Oakes presenting a one-sided picture of his relationship with the VSP. When Oakes's other friend and former campaign manager, the representative of VSP troopers Kyle Brown, had the opportunity to ask questions, it provided him with another opportunity to slam the VSP's investigation of Conley.

"Based upon your analysis of the case," Brown inquired in his single question of Oakes, "and the evidence, (do you) have any doubt as to whether or not proceedings were properly conducted against Mr. Conley."

"Absolutely not," Oakes replied. Attorney Eldredge, on Alexander's behalf, received more favorable responses from witnesses mitigating the impact of Oakes's testimony and the insinuations the department was racist or acted improperly.

On other occasions, Gibson challenged officers for not understanding the complexities of the rules of evidence regarding the admissibility of a witness's prior convictions. He swiped at them for inquiring into Johnson's criminal past because they could only find a Florida conviction for his carrying a concealed weapon in 1952.

Vermont law permitted the introduction of past convictions of witnesses if they occurred within the past 15 years, making the Florida conviction inadmissible.‡‡ Notwithstanding, it is curious that someone in Gibson's position, trained and familiar with the intricacies of the law, should bully and try to diminish the work of officers on a legal issue that attorneys and judges often wrangled with. Even if inadmissible, such information assisted investigators in their overall examination of Johnson's checkered past to determine if, as he alleged, other people might have been responsible for the shooting and not Conley. Gibson's theatrics and badgering only succeeded in further painting the VSP as racist and seeking to undermine Johnson because of his skin color.

As the hearings progressed, an intensely interested press continued to attend, including a reporter for *Life* magazine. On Nov. 11, it gained an even larger audience that brought the entire matter full circle. Popular actor Lorne Greene, of the television series *Bonanza*, appeared in a National Educational Television broadcast to express his support for Hoff's Vermont-New York Youth Project.[493] Many eyes around the nation were looking at what was happening in Vermont and the credibility of the board's work was at stake.

Barbara Lawrence did not attend the hearings, safely removed and living on the California coast. But she had a dramatic impact on them when a newspaper account reported her retraction of the confession she made to police months earlier about her affair with Johnson. The VSP immediately contacted the Monterey County district attorney about the allegation. One of his investigators, Edward F. Warner, quickly arranged to meet with Lawrence and listen to her admit that her first statement to the VSP was in fact true and the retraction was not. The VSP's number two, Maj. Davis, immediately flew to California where he met with Warner, Lawrence

---

‡‡ A person shall not be incompetent as a witness in any court, matter, or proceeding by reason of the person's conviction of a crime. The conviction of a crime involving moral turpitude within 15 years shall be the only crime admissible in evidence given to affect the credibility of a witness. 12 V. S. A. § 1608, eff. June 10, 1959.

and her attorney. She repeated her story once again for Davis and signed a third statement, dated Nov. 14, 1968, admitting that police did not threaten or make any promises to her when she first confessed.[494] Warner subsequently appeared in Vermont and testified before the board, but, despite his information and the documentary evidence provided to it, it never acknowledged Lawrence's most recent admission that her first statement was not coerced. Instead, it let the matter that consumed so much time, attention and testimony drop from the record. In its place, it provided only a brief, simplistic statement in its findings referring to her retraction as repudiating her "alleged confession to the State Police."[495]

Hoff understood that in the last days of his administration his papers and all the secrets they held could be opened to public when he left office in January. On Nov. 15, he wrote to UVM Dean Alfred B. Rollins Jr. authorizing their removal directly from his statehouse office to the university where they would remain "closed" and out of the public's eye as legal arrangements proceeded to finalize the transfer.

Security for the papers concerned Rollins and he promised Hoff they would be placed in the university's special collections rather than in its more accessible archives.[496] By disposing of his papers in this manner, Hoff avoided the traditional process that sent governors' records to the secretary of state's office when they left office and where the public could view them without interruption. His secretiveness only adds further questions about the conduct of the inquiry into the Irasburg matter.

Gibson's hearings ended on Nov. 22 after Foote questioned Larry Conley's father, Howard, about his knowledge of the shooting case. Gibson then declared the proceedings closed and requested the attorneys to submit proposed findings "the quicker the better" because "we want to get rid of it."

Alexander's attorney, Robert Eldredge, spoke with court reporter Vesper to order a copy of the transcript only to learn that Gibson prohibited him from doing so. The only way that Eldredge could obtain a copy, he said, would be if Hoff allowed it; and Hoff did not.[497]

Perhaps comfortable with the way the evidence unfolded so strongly in his favor, there is no record of Oakes submitting any of the proposed findings that Gibson requested. However, Commissioner

Alexander did sense something unfavorable in the wind and on the same day submitted a five-page "Statement" outlining the VSP's position on the evidence.[498] His submission is telling because it also indicates the direction that Gibson intended to go with his findings.

A notation in its margin in his distinctive handwriting indicates his concern adjacent to Alexander's account that in his 41 years of police experience no attorney general had ever interfered with the VSP's investigation of a breach of peace case. Below a question mark that Gibson placed next to it, he wrote "AG chief l(law enforcement) off(icer)." Apparently unwilling to acknowledge Oakes's own admission that he had no authority to intrude into a police investigation, Gibson still held tight to a perception that he did.

By the end of the month, a reflective Oakes became uneasy with the strength of his position because of the testimony the board heard. The prospects to open up his own investigation with the power of the judiciary behind him to compel testimony by subpoenas offered a more vigorous forum than what Gibson presided over. His assistant Mahady told the press that Oakes was considering the move in order "to plug certain loopholes and contradictions brought to light in the testimony."[499]

Those specific contradictions and loopholes are unknown, but apparently caused great concern within NEK communities. Local Rep. Arthur Mooney responded to Mahady's statement writing to Oakes asking him not to open a second inquiry. The "people of Orleans County," he said, "as individuals and as citizens groups feel the purposes of the inquiry have been served." Uninterested in seeing Oakes delve more deeply into their lives and secrets, he reported that "they are satisfied to have that inquiry set as a seal upon the matter." It was not just his personal feelings, Mooney said, but also a point of view "held by a considerable majority of people in Orleans County."[500] In a letter marked "<u>PERSONAL</u>," Oakes replied that he shared Mooney's views and promised to wait for the board's report before deciding how to proceed.[501]

Gibson soon relieved the two men of their concerns when the board delivered its scathing report of the VSP removing Oakes from any liability. With the threat of another investigation removed, it is reasonable to ask what Mooney and the people of Orleans County considered so dire that they did not want it exposed? Perhaps they simply tired of the ongoing investigation and hearings, or had other concerns haunting them that might touch on their attitudes towards Blacks. Regardless, Oakes's abandonment of his legal prerogative to delve more deeply into the circumstances behind the Irasburg Affair than Gibson did means that the "loopholes and contradictions" he identified remain to this day undercutting the board's work.

The Gibson-Oakes partnership, influenced by the omnipresence of Sen. Aiken and Mitchell's *Rutland Herald,* intensified in the weeks before the board issued its findings. Gibson floated the idea of his retirement from the federal bench to Aiken who would be instrumental in naming his replacement to the highly coveted position dependent on political patronage that the White House would listen to in making the appointment. Several letters in support of Oakes arrived in Aiken's office, including John Downs, the partner of David Johnson's attorney Robert Rachlin, who wrote a week before the findings were published, followed by Rachlin himself in March.[502]

"Oakes," a newspaper reported about the situation, "has long been identified with the Aiken-Gibson wing of Vermont liberal Republicanism" marking him as a strong candidate to replace his mentor Gibson. A heavy campaign ensued pitting Aiken's backing of Oakes against governor-elect Davis's choice, Burlington attorney John Dinse. Ironically, Gibson's fellow board member, Hilton Wick, was also Dinse's law partner, but he too supported Oakes.[503] The political fighting over the "Oakes-Dinse" matter drew the public's attention in these weeks, including Brattleboro attorney Osmer Fitts writing to U. S. Secretary of State William Rogers seeking his intervention on Dinse's behalf. While he said he respected Oakes, he was irked because of his "swinging his Harvardian knowledge and bearing around" compared to the earned respect that Dinse had from "us older members of the bar."[504] Rogers responded telling Fitts that he referred his letter "to Attorney General-Designate (John) Mitchell for his consideration."[505]

Gibson held on in the next months, refusing to retire unless Oakes replaced him. Working to make it happen, Aiken pressed hard in Washington threatening to obstruct Attorney General Mitchell's agenda unless Oakes received the appointment. However, Gibson did not retire, dying in November 1969 (at age 68) making the position available immediately. By the spring of 1970 Aiken successfully forced officials to consider Oakes to fill the position, paving the way for his appearance before the Senate Judiciary Committee in April. In his statement to that body, Oakes outlined his legal background noting the important cases he handled as Vermont's attorney general. "I represented the state in some important civil litigation," he said, "and, of course, was responsible for the handling of a dozen or so murder cases, 30 to 40 habeas corpus cases and for starting a law enforcement training act."[506] For the person who Gibson said single-handedly solved the state's most notorious race-related case rocking it to its core, Oakes never mentioned Irasburg. Neither did any of many correspondents writing to Aiken on his behalf. Irasburg was kryptonite to Oakes, distancing himself from its effects in the next years after he received appointment as Vermont's second district court judge.

Oakes's accomplishments leading to his ultimate appointment to a judgeship notwithstanding, the pragmatic Aiken viewed other criteria of more importance in deciding who to back, ones involving where he lived in the southern part of the state. As he wrote to President Nixon, Oakes's qualifications for the job included his being "geographically correct" by living where he did.[507] On another occasion, he explained that while "Jim was a liberal and would be a good judge, even more important was his geographic location (as) it would not be good to have both judges from the same location in one corner of the state" where Vermont's second federal judge, Bernard Leddy, lived in the north.[508]

When he finally received the appointment, Oakes effusively expressed his great appreciation to Aiken for his efforts while also recognizing those of his second friend, the departed Gibson. "I will do my utmost," he wrote, "to live up to your, and Ernest's, expectations and hopes."[509] Fortune continued to smile on Oakes thereafter, advancing quickly to a seat on the prestigious Court of Appeals for the Second Circuit in 1971 in yet another milestone facilitated by Aiken.

CONFUSION: BOARD OF INQUIRY'S
FINDINGS AND RECOMMENDATIONS

"Northeast Kingdom Lawmen Clubbed by Irasburg Report," read the headline of Gibson's good friend Robert Mitchell's *Rutland Herald* describing the board's findings made public on Friday, Dec. 13, 1968. Described as a "blockbuster" condemnation of Commissioner Alexander and Orleans County State's Attorney Pearson, their investigation and prosecution of those involved in the shooting and adultery matters was deeply flawed.

"The Board of Inquiry," the article said, also "left hanging heavily in the air the implication that police deflected their (shooting probe) because of some influence and the board's finding was that such an influence sprang from racial prejudice." Gibson's contribution in exposing the presence of racism was, in Mitchell's eyes at least, profound. Upon his death the next year, a glowing *Herald* editorial credited Gibson as "this man who loved Vermont so much (that he) exposed the cancer of racism that had infected parts of Vermont and suggested the necessary surgery."[510]

In sum, the public learned from Gibson's report that the police and prosecutor were racists and there was no way they could prove otherwise. Hoff also agreed and immediately said there was no question that the VSP leadership inflicted "a black eye to the state" committing "inexcusable" conduct in the process, promising to take action in the near future.[511]

Their screaming condemnations notwithstanding, Oakes's and Mahady's "loopholes and contradictions" and Secretary Reed's condemnation of the lackluster findings found an audience in the legislature. There, Elmore Senator Fred Westphal sought the formation of a "blue-ribbon joint House Senate subcommittee" with the necessary subpoena power that Gibson lacked, to conduct another investigation. He argued that Hoff's actions in instituting the hearings "have cast a cloud on the State Police and unless they take legal action to clear themselves, the cause of law and order is bound to be hurt." He further argued that many unanswered questions remained about the board's work because of Gibson's limited authority, insinuating they resulted in findings "intended to harass or whitewash." Future Gov. Thomas Salmon, destined to oversee the approaching Paul Lawrence Affair in a few years, also weighed in discrediting Westphal's proposal. It was, he said, "an exercise in futility calculated to do nothing more than embarrass Gov. Hoff and Judge Gibson."[512]

The concerns of Oakes, Mahady, Reed and Westphal repeated the same impressions reached by the VSP's attorney Eldredge. He said that the board's findings and conclusions simply could not be supported by "any reasonable interpretation of the evidence." He called the report "unwarranted, unfounded, and tragic" and that it harmed the image of the state. "This unnecessary investigation," he said, "and the attending publicity, which was at times inaccurate, has hurt Vermont unjustly and unfairly."[513]

He believed Gibson's "one-sided" hearing unfair causing him to appeal to Hoff to allow court reporter Vesper to finally prepare a transcript so that he could point out its inaccuracies. "It is difficult for me to understand," he wrote to Hoff, "how you could so easily accept the (report) without first reading the transcript of the evidence so that you could determine whether these findings and conclusions were supported by the evidence presented." Eldredge thought that Hoff had not "taken an unbiased view of this matter when it is apparent that you have reviewed only the conclusions and not the evidence."

There was, he said, "serious doubts that a number of these findings and conclusions will find support in the evidence."[514] Faced with such a reasonable request, Hoff finally allowed him to have the transcript, but only if he or Alexander personally paid the $550 that court reporter Vesper required for the work.[515] Backed into a corner and needing it to respond to the charges, Eldredge agreed to meet Hoff's petty demand. Vesper then charged into the task for the next month before delivering it after Hoff left office.

Without the benefit of a transcript and confident in the board's findings, Hoff wasted no time in his administration's last days before blasting Commissioner Alexander for the VSP's pitiful performance. He readily adopted all of the findings and struck out, rashly censuring him and demanding that he take immediate corrective action reforming his department's practices and to institute disciplinary action against Dean, Potvin and Chilton. While he did not accuse

Alexander of racism, he also reminded him of his sworn duty to provide equal justice and protection to "<u>every</u> man." In conclusion, he warned that "Vermont must never again have a case where the fulfillment of that oath may be brought into serious question, as it has been in respect to the handling of Irasburg."[516]

Alexander responded, pointing out he did so without the advantage of a transcript to rely on because of Hoff's refusal to provide him with one. Over the course of 15, single-spaced typed pages, Alexander disputed each of the points made by the board. He effectively dismantled in detail every one of its many allegations against the department based on, he said, its "innuendo and inference" of malfeasance citing ample reasons why he was correct and the board was not. Ending, he told Hoff that "You have accepted the findings and conclusions of the Board and upon the strength of them have felt it necessary to censure me. I regard the censure as unwarranted and I sharply disagree with the findings and conclusions of the Board which cast doubt upon me and members of the Department of Public Safety and which call into question our integrity and the propriety of our acts with relation to the Irasburg affair."[517] Hoff deemed his response an act of defiance that brought him and secretary Benjamin Collins together with Alexander and Eldredge to meet at Hoff's home to quell the discord between them.[518] Hoff seriously considered firing Alexander, but held off when he received a second letter from him promising to look into his concerns after he received a copy of the transcript. "You just don't hit someone with 40-odd years' service to the state between the eyes," Hoff said.[519] Watching closely, the press had another field day at Alexander's expense slamming him for daring to refute the board's findings in his first letter and continuing the call for Hoff to fire him.

Eldredge intervened into the fray with the recently sworn-in governor Davis to explain to him the circumstances behind the two letters that reveals Hoff's duplicity for characterizing Alexander's second letter as a concession.

"I wish to state emphatically," he wrote, "that it was made clear to former Gov. Hoff, not only by Colonel Alexander, but by myself, that the second letter in no way changed the position of Colonel Alexander as stated in his first letter."

At all times, Eldredge wrote, Alexander refuted entirely Hoff's censure as "unwarranted and without justification" and that "the Findings of the Irasburg Board of Inquiry are not supported by the evidence submitted."[520]

Just before leaving office, Hoff appeared in an educational television program broadcast from Burlington with the board of inquiry members to discuss the Irasburg matter. The public expressed intense interest in its findings that led an eclectic number to write directly to Hoff for a copy. They included the extremist right-wing group Green Mountain Rifleman in Bethel, the Jewish Advocate in Boston, Goddard College in Plainfield and Lloyd Hayes at the *Newport Daily Express* who drew such strong ire from the board.[521] Nobody from the VSP appeared alongside the board members during their television interview to provide an additional perspective on the event. Hoff shrugged off any thought that another investigation should take place and said he did not believe any additional testimony was needed because he "had assumed all concerned would be willing to testify at the November hearings." He apparently did not know about those individuals who refused to attend, Gibson's disinterest in pursuing the testimony of James McClure at the *Burlington Free Press* to clarify his relationship with Alexander, or that he refused to allow attorney Angell, readily available in the courtroom, to testify about the supposedly suspicious circumstances surrounding California trip.

Gibson also took the opportunity to discredit three of the state's newspapers for their purported collusion with Alexander, but could not recall which ones they were. According to Gibson, "the state police have been given every opportunity to tell their side of the story." From his point of view as a sitting federal judge and former governor, he said that "It became my conviction state police knew or should have known young Mr. Larry Conley did the shooting but instead they started to investigate the background of Mr. Johnson. They made no background investigation on Conley."

As a result, and in the manner consistent with the experiences of jurors deciding cases in his courtroom taking their lead from his demeanor, he indicated that the board fell into line with his reasoning saying that "It became apparent to us there was racial prejudice involved."[522]

The interview turned to the outcome of the proceedings when Gibson said "As far as I am concerned, we did the best job we could." Wick agreed, saying that "I feel there is substantial evidence to each of the conclusions we reached."

While none of the three believed that Vermont justice had broken down, Dorothy Collins "said it seemed that it stalled."

When the panel discussed Capt. Harold Dean's threat to sue the board for disparaging him, Hoff and Gibson laughed it off. "I might ask Hilton to defend me," Gibson guffawed as Hoff "chimed in that 'in three days I'll be practicing law.'"[523]

In such an open forum with so many television viewers, would they have been so flippant about such an important matter if a member of the VSP had been present to refute their aspersions? The glee the men reveled in exemplifies the problem presented by the board's configuration because of Hoff's neglect to include any provision for due process to anyone harmed by the board's findings. Former attorney general Reed, now paving the way for Davis' new administration, laid out the problem for him as he moved into office and assumed responsibility for the Irasburg matter. He counseled him as follows:

> One very important point which should be made quite soon is the lack of any opportunity for the State Police to test the findings in any way—there is no appeal process or even, apparently, any opportunity to request the Commission to review any of the findings in the light of the transcript evidence. In effect, they are condemned publicly without any processes normally available to either side of a legal controversy. The public censure and the publication of the report by the Governor, prior to any appeal or review, further denies the State Police any reasonable defense as a practical matter.[524]

The pragmatic Reed further recommended a course of action that Davis soon followed: disagree with Hoff's decision to institute a board of inquiry because other avenues could have been pursued "without the widespread publicity and controversy;" recognize that while the board members exercised "fairness and impartiality," their findings are still "subject to being tested against the evidence to determine whether the evidence supports such findings;" say that Hoff's decision to censure Alexander without a transcript constituted "undue haste without regard to accepted legal principles;" and, that Hoff's publication of his censure of Alexander and the board's findings constituted sufficient criticism that he did not need to take any further action against him or his staff. It was not an easy pill to swallow, but Davis abided in the next difficult months to follow Reed's recommendations.

The trauma inflicted by the steady flow of discord also concerned the new attorney general succeeding Oakes who wanted to distance himself from the kinds of problems he and his staff caused for the VSP in Irasburg. When the VSP learned that a member of James Jeffords's staff tried to intrude into an unidentified investigation taking place under Potvin's command that February, it brought Maj. Davis and Jeffords together for a face-to-face meeting. "The attorney general was most apologetic," Davis recounted, and "gave me every assurance that he wanted good working relations and full cooperation between this agency and his and I believe it is truly his desire."[525] It constituted a refreshing change from the way business occurred between the two agencies in the recent past.

The board's findings dropped into Davis's lap presented him with unwanted challenges as he sought to distance himself from them. Its condemnation of the VSP was only because it selectively picked its way through the evidence deciding what to credit and what to discredit; a task accomplished without a transcript to recite for support. Mahady (on the behalf of Oakes), Reed, Eldredge, Alexander and Westphal all recognized its obvious failures. As Alexander noted, the innuendo and insinuations of wrongful behavior infusing its findings made things all the worse because it did not accurately recite witness testimony. Without the transcript, and with rare references to the exhibits in its possession, the board's findings repeatedly recite inaccurate accounts, misinterpret and misrepresent important points, consistently disparaging the VSP to Oakes's advantage.

"We conclude," it wrote, "that failure of the Attorney General of Vermont to vigorously investigate this case would have been a dereliction of duty on his part," ignoring the breach of etiquette he committed intruding into the existing relationships between police and state's attorneys.[526]

"We conclude," further it said, "that Larry Conley might not have been convicted on the shooting episode had it not been for the activity of the attorney general's office in this matter," similarly ignoring all that the VSP had done.[527] In the course of its published 30-page report there is no instance where it does not fault the department's investigation on any important point. The finding's central theme centered consistently on the outline that Oakes and his team provided at the onset of the hearings: the VSP's purported lethargy to investigate the shooting offence and its vigor in pursuing the case of a married Black man involved with a married white woman demonstrating it had racist intentions. How is it possible that Vermont's premier law enforcement agency could have stumbled so badly interviewing over 220 witnesses and tying the many pieces of evidence together resulting in a conviction not done anything right? It flies in the face of reason.

Neither Oakes or the board had to say so explicitly, but just making racist insinuations, ones the press rallied around for months, allowed readers to draw a similar conclusion; a point that Gibson confirmed during his television interview. The findings also cut the department for what it considered its unholy alliance with the press to conduct aspects of the investigation on its behalf that none of the evidence supports. The VSP further failed to coordinate their efforts, the board said, while Oakes admirably brought order to the disarray and a final resolution in an outcome that police could not have accomplished without him. Such a strong endorsement of Oakes could only strengthen Gibson's ongoing effort aimed at retiring and positioning his friend to assume his role as a federal judge.

Gibson's misguided perception of the existence of racial prejudice within VSP ranks strongly influenced him in fashioning the board's findings. Before they issued, he promised to delve into the case because "we want to air this thing out completely. It needs a lot of airing."[528] However, that effort withered because of an absence of evidence directly tying the VSP to any racially-motivated prejudice unless accomplished through the innuendo that Alexander and Eldredge complained about. Undeniably, Lt. Potvin admitted to Rev.

Newell he thought he might have some personal prejudice in dealing with Johnson, but he also thought he conducted the investigation fairly. Both Newell and Father Bouffard said neither of them and ever seen any display of racism by officers. Newell also credited Potvin's candor because he recognized the difference between an individual's own prejudices and those based on racist attitudes aimed at attacking a minority population. But Gibson seems to have conflated the concepts in the process forcing him to qualify its presence to be sure the public understood he thought racism did exist in the ranks. When encapsulating the entire episode of Conley's firing into Johnson's home, he said that "the issue here is not the kind of man the Rev. Mr. Johnson is; the issue here rather involved the safety of a man's home in the state of Vermont."[529]

It is disingenuous to separate out and say that important information concerning a star witness's credibility, in this case a man with questionable credentials and a checkered past, is not relevant in the prosecution of a breach of peace case; it is. The timing of the VSP's investigation into Johnson's background after Trooper Lessard found him in a compromising position with Barbara Lawrence days after the shooting event was simply fortuitous.

There is no evidence it was done to shift the shooting investigation in some untoward way, such as trying to undermine a Black man, that the media and Gibson sought to portray. Johnson was the primary witness and participant in an exchange of gunfire taking place between he and Conley. Prosecutors and defense attorneys alike had every right to information calling into question his, and every other witness's, credibility. The VSP's efforts to comply and ferret it out was only a matter of routine police work, regardless of how anyone unfamiliar with the process wanted to characterize it.

Another document provides additional background information concerning the board's findings revealing that they did not arrive at them unanimously. Neither of Oakes's friends, Gibson or Wick, left behind a paper trail revealing their thoughts about the proceedings. However, educator Dorothy Collins did and they provide a telling window into, as she told her two male counterparts, her impressions from a woman's point of view. (Appendix F).

She recognized that her refusal to adopt media representations adverse to the VSP would surprise some. "I can't help but reflect," she wrote, "how disappointed (the public) would be at some of my omissions." A careful reading of her considered opinions affirms her suspicion and shows that she possessed a much more magnanimous understanding of the challenges the VSP faced than did Gibson or Wick.

Answering the first question of whether some undue influence brought the Johnson family to Vermont to cause problems, Collins said "no"—they just came seeking a better life. She then denied that racism in the form of "a militant majority of the population (seeking) to drive away our colored citizens" existed in the state.

Instead, she believed it present to the extent it encouraged others to engage in lawlessness. She also faulted the lack of educational programs "at home, school and church as unfinished business" contributing to the problem. While the remarks of one officer (Potvin) did "indicate an underlying prejudice," she thought that "the influence of some members of the press was of questionable value to unbiased action of officers."

Collins then tackled the issue of "the quality of police protection" during the investigation. She acknowledged the hard work that many officers provided, but also faulted what she believed was "time wasted due to poor communications, loose organization, some uncertainty about laws, and the reluctance on the part of citizens to become involved."

Understandably, as a lay person, and in lockstep with her male counterparts, she did not appreciate the responsibility of police to investigate felony crimes such as adultery, particularly one committed in the presence of a police officer, and thought that case should have been handled in the civil courts. Why she called the police response in the shooting case (that she characterized as "harassment" without insinuating the presence of any racial undertones) as "slow action" is unknown because the evidence demonstrates the quick work of many officers to identify Conley, chase down all the accompanying leads to exclude other suspects and arrest him.

Notably, at no point did Collins ever refer to Oakes or engage in second-guessing the accounts of police about their involvement with him. While the board's findings repeatedly heaped glowing praise on him, for her personally he seems to have made little impression. For someone outside of the ongoing attempts of Gibson and Wick to advance his career, it is unsurprising that she did not engage in the effort.

While the other board members refused to acknowledge the difficulties that Johnson presented to the investigation, and which Gibson continually shied away from, Collins did not. "The apparent lack of stability in the emerging personality of the Rev. Mr. Johnson," she said, "tended to confuse the issue for officers and public alike." Her assessment that the confusion wrought by David Johnson is perhaps the most candid and unfiltered observation made by anyone in the past half century concerning the Irasburg Affair. She also had no qualms about the background investigation that police conducted to untangle the series of events and seems to have understood its importance. Only Gibson and Wick had problems with it.

Lastly, Collins assumed a motherly persona to calm the upheaval that the Irasburg Affair presented to the state. She wrote that the board's recommendations "should include a warning to the Vermont community to avoid complacency and watch carefully the influences at work within itself especially in its responsibility for the values of its young people." Concerning the police, she called for better coordination of their efforts and that future appointments and recruitments be "carefully screened to insure the high standards evident in most of its present members."

After Alexander received the transcript from Vesper to compare it with the board's findings, reviewed the reports again and conducted another round of interviews of his staff and troopers, he wrote to Gov. Davis to affirm the letter he wrote to Hoff in December disagreeing with his assessments. None of the allegations Hoff lodged could be reconciled with the testimony, he said, repeating that his officers conducted their work in the "most professional and competent manner" under extremely difficult circumstances. They were "strenuous and adverse," he recounted, "imposed not only by government officers, but by irresponsible and inaccurate press reports and irresponsible and unwarranted inference by some members of the clergy as well as irresponsible and erratic behavior on the part of the victims of the shooting incident."

Regarding Oakes, Alexander said the transcript demonstrated that he expressed personal opinions "not based on fact and which were purely conjectures resulting from his inexperience in the field of investigation or were formulated for some purpose unknown to this officer."[530] Earlier he wrote to Hoff more directly to reject Oakes's assertion that the Conley case was only solved because of his intervention, calling it "entirely without foundation" and "wholly unwarranted." The reason for it, he said, was because Oakes "was then involved in a political campaign and for reasons best known to him desired to conduct his own investigation."

In charge of the receipt of the board's testimony and evidence that formed its findings, Gibson likened his role to that of U. S. Supreme Court Chief Justice Earl Warren investigating the Kennedy assassination a few years earlier. However, recent information uncovered by *New York Times* reporter Philip Shenon provides damning insight into its conduct and ultimate findings challenging Warren's conclusion that Lee Harvey Oswald acted alone.[531] According to his staff of attorneys, Warren was a prima donna, standoffish and refusing to engage them in their work. He drove them relentlessly to quickly provide a pre-determined finding that no conspiracy existed because, he said, Oswald worked alone. Despite significant leads showing Cuban involvement and Oswald's contact with its spies in Mexico City in the weeks before the assassination, Warren ignored it; apparently at the urging of an embarrassed CIA not wanting the world to know what it suspected beforehand but failed to act on. Warren stood in the way of his attorneys pursing other leads, continually frustrating them when they uncovered credible allegations worthy of further investigation when they should, instead, concentrate on quickly shutting down their work.

Warren was also highly protective of the Kennedy family and did not want to intrude into their lives, placing Jackie and Bobby beyond the reach of questioning by his experienced investigators. He sought to protect Oswald's wife, Marina, prohibiting his attorneys from pursuing damaging evidence they uncovered against her, leading them to call her "Snow White" and Warren "Dopey" behind his back. Neither did Warren allow any transcripts of meetings between commission members to record for posterity their disagreements and dissents. While he characterized their ultimate conclusions as "unanimous," dissent did exist in the form of Senator Richard B. Russell, chairman of the Senate Armed Services Committee, who seriously questioned the theory Warren embraced. Circumspect in her own opinions that might conflict with Gibson's or Wick's, Dorothy Collins also entered a respectful view distancing herself from the draconian findings of the board. If it was "unanimous" as Gibson insisted, it appears a strained interpretation of the facts.

"Fundamentally dishonest," is the description Shenon assigns to Warren's work. It is also a worthy assessment for the Irasburg Board of Inquiry's mean-spirited *Findings and Recommendations* for the same reasons. Each of the principal points of alleged misconduct the board sought to assign to the VSP crumble when compared to the void of evidence present in the record. Among others, they include: the early identification of Conley as the person responsible for the shooting; the absence of delaying tactics; purported employment of the press to aid the investigation; and, the circumstances surrounding Barbara Lawrence's interview with investigators.

Digging deeply to find flaws where none existed, the board's work unfolded under the supervision of a strong-minded former governor and sitting federal judge communicating frequently during the proceedings with outside, long-time associates, a sitting U.S. senator and *Rutland Herald* publisher about what was happening. He appears personally unconcerned by any notion that the law or uncomfortable facts could interfere to alter what seems a pre-determined outcome, one made possible by the "marvelous sense of justice" one attorney said he pursed. Even in other instances where they did threaten, as his former law clerk Attorney General Jeffords recalled, it did not prohibit him from allowing his subjective feelings to intrude and allow outcomes contrary to law. What effect Gibson's conversations with others had on the final outcome is uncertain. But under the current circumstances involving the future of his good friend Attorney General Oakes, the prospect of a politically motivated hit-job on the VSP remains a viable explanation.

Impatience also marked Gibson's attitude, who found the whole exercise an "unpleasant task" to "be rid" of it as quickly as possible. There is no question of his high standing in the legal community or his integrity, but in the unrestrained environment of the hearings he oversaw the fates of others possessing less standing, hobbled from defending themselves from his influence and forced to suffer in silence.

As a result, the board's work, and similarly Warren's commission, left behind a legacy of unanswered questions. For Gibson, they include: Oakes's and Mahady's admitted, lingering "loopholes and contradictions;" mistakes and omissions caused by his urgency to prepare a report with ready-made conclusions and his impatience with what he perceived as obstruction by Alexander; his protection of a favored witness (Oakes) to avoid embarrassing him and concurrent advocacy to replace him as a judge; his refusal to allow a witness with relevant information to testify (Angell); the steps taken to minimize the unsavory aspects of Johnson's past and present, preventing inquiry into his suspect ordination into the ministry; the incomprehensible assessment that police expended an inordinate amount of effort investigating Johnson for adultery instead of the white perpetrator involved in the shooting when the evidence showed it constituted only .003% of their time; and the absence of a transcript of the proceedings and internal discussions between board members to allow for the public's accurate understanding of their positions.

Further, the board's findings did not alter the innocent circumstances surrounding the formation of the Vermont Troopers Association because Gibson already knew from testimony that some form of representation for officers was already in progress. However, the release of his report propelled the alarmed officers to immediately gather in Montpelier the following week to consider a draft of articles of association and attracting a membership. Their efforts succeeded so well that in the next month 154 out of 185 eligible officers joined.

Low pay ($111.50 a week for long work days), no overtime, ineligibility for Social Security and needing access to legal representation when allegations of misconduct were made against them drove the men to begin the process of separating themselves from the other state employees receiving much better benefits. The initial officers of the organization included some who played important roles in both the Irasburg and future Router Bit affairs, including Harold Dean and Dana Goodnow in the former and James Ryan, Richard Spear, John Heffernan, David Reed and the trooper who killed himself, Howard Gould, in the latter.[532]

Conclusion

The findings of the Irasburg board threatened to have a profound effect on the VSP that Gov. Davis's prescient secretary recognized immediately. In his response to a constituent writing to Davis about the matter that "I am ashamed of the state of Vermont," Reed said he understood her concern. He also called for her to understand that Davis was working under a unique challenge as he sought to bring the matter to a conclusion. "The many fine public servants in the (VSP)," he wrote, "must be given some consideration, because if their morale and willingness to do their duty is hurt too much, the public at large can suffer." "It is important to move carefully," he said, "and not risk loss of confidence of the entire department."[533]

The potential loss of morale within the VSP and its effect on the public's safety weighed heavily on Davis who wrote to Alexander to notify him of his position on the case shortly after Reed's letter. Davis said he studied the board's findings and conclusions closely, the transcript and exhibits and other unidentified "evidence submitted at my request," and met with Attorney General Jeffords, the board's counsel, Lt. Gov. Foote, and his attorney, Eldredge. Alexander and the department suffered significant bad press over the months and Davis thought that, plus Hoff's release of his own scathing letter to him and the more than 1,000 copies of the board's findings distributed widely, constituted sufficient disciplinary action for any perceived missteps. He declined to take any further action against Alexander refusing to require him to discipline any of his officers as Hoff ordered. However, he did direct that in the future he work more closely with the attorney general's office and to monitor his own department to "be constantly on the alert to discover the existence of racial prejudice and if any should be discovered, to treat it as cause for dismissal."

In ending his letter to Alexander, Davis said that "I am satisfied that the Department is composed of able and dedicated men, several of whom, including yourself, have been subjected to lengthy and harsh criticism. The time has come to put an end to the controversy."[534] While the politicians sought to move on, the fallout from the Irasburg Affair and its insinuations of racist cops lurking inside the VSP had already inflicted undue harm to its reputation. The weaponization of racism had begun.

In the next years, the department suffered a form of institutional post-traumatic stress disorder, exemplified by its increasing distrust of its political overseers and the media treating it to the "harsh criticism" Davis described. It did not end the ensuing disagreements between VSP commissioners and the state's governors until a decade later after a trooper committed suicide because of a significant departmental breakdown in the interim.

It proved a very trying time that brought a previously independent VSP to its knees before transitioning into an agency in line with the American policing mainstream.

Vermont Statehouse where VSP Corporal Howard Gould took his life,
July 30, 1979

Governor Philip H. Hoff
(1963–1969)

Governor Richard A. Snelling
(1977–1985; 1991)

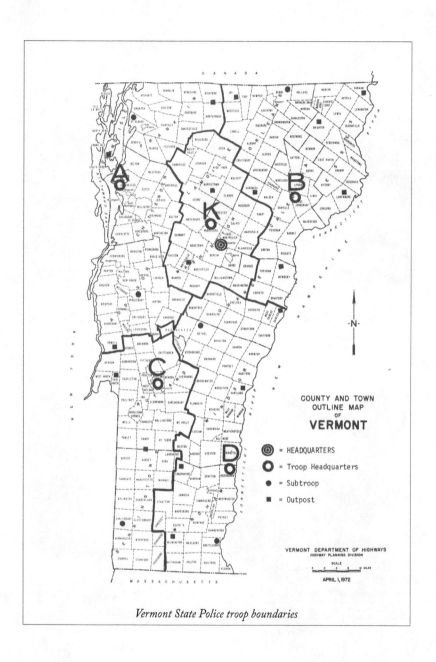

COUNTY AND TOWN
OUTLINE MAP
OF
VERMONT

⊚ = HEADQUARTERS

◯ = Troop Headquarters

● = Subtroop

■ = Outpost

VERMONT DEPARTMENT OF HIGHWAYS
HIGHWAY PLANNING DIVISION

SCALE

APRIL 1, 1972

Vermont State Police troop boundaries

COMMISSIONERS

Merritt A. Edson	William H. Baumann	Erwin A. Alexander
(1947–1951)	*(1951–1965; 1977)*	*(1965–1970)*

Edward W. Corcoran	Francis E. Lynch	Warren M. Cone
(1970–1977)	*(1977–1979)*	*(1979–1980)*

Redstone, Vermont State Police headquarters, Montpelier

Major Glenn E. Davis

Captain Harold Dean

Irasburg home targeted by night-riders, July 19, 1968

Living room windows struck by shotgun pellets

*Second floor window (marked "G") from where David
Johnson returned fire with his 9mm Luger pistol*

*View from inside the living room showing state
police working in Johnson's front yard*

Richard LeClair's white over green 1968 Oldsmobile 442

Lt. Clement F. Potvin

Det. Laurence A. Wade

Det. John B. Shanks

Det. Billy J. Chilton

Det. Dana O. Goodnow

Tpr. Lane F. Marshall

Tpr. Jean G. Lessard

Maj. James H. Ryan

Capt. Richard A. Spear

Capt. John P. Heffernan

Capt. George O. Patch

Lt. Milford W. Ramey

Cpl. Stanley T. Merriam Jr.

Det. David A. Reed

Lt. Edward R. Fish

Howard Gary Gould,
standing center (c. 1960)

Gould promoted to corporal by
Major Davis (1970)

Patrol Commander Gould,
Troop B, St. Johnsbury

Howard and Charlene Gould

Gould (right) on safety education
assignment shortly before his death

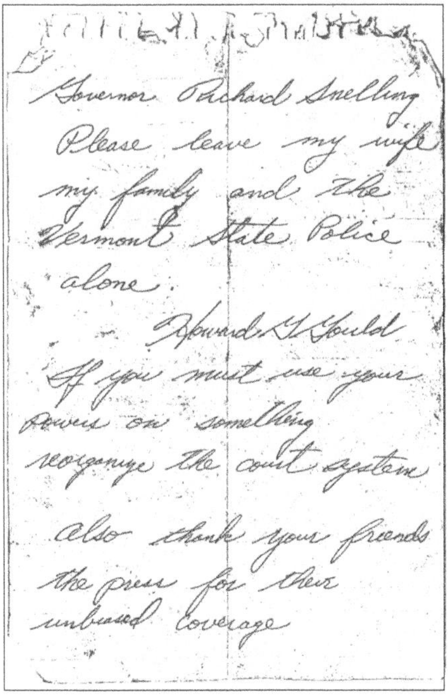

Governor Richard Snelling

Please leave my wife
my family and the
Vermont State Police
alone.

        Howard G. Gould

If you must use your
powers on something
reorganize the court system

Also thank your friends
the press for their
unbiased coverage

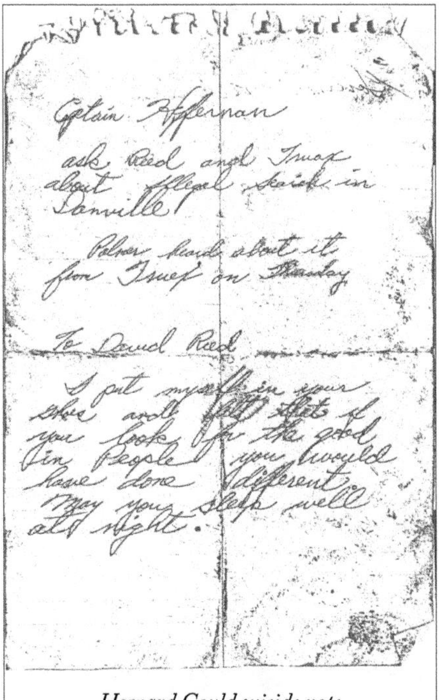

Captain Heffernan

ask Reed and Truax
about illegal search in
Danville

Palmer heard about it
from Truax on Thursday

To David Reed

I put myself in your
shoes and if the state of
you look for the good
in people you would
have done different
May you sleep well
all night.

Howard Gould suicide note

Part II

A Sinister Tragedy

The deceased, Howard Gould, and the members of his family were to be the so-called 'scape goats,' in an attempt to shift the blame for any alleged improprieties upon the plaintiffs herein for the sole and exclusive benefit of the Vermont Department of Public Safety and the individuals and persons therein located and employed.

Charlene Gould, et. al. vs. Vermont Attorney General's Office M. Jerome Diamond, Dale Gray; Vermont Department of Public Safety, James Ryan, Nelson Lay, George Patch, and John Doe as unknown person or persons

Rutland Superior Court, No. S377–81Rc, July 24, 1981

Chapter 8

RETRENCHMENT

FALLOUT

THE RELEASE OF THE IRASBURG BOARD OF INQUIRY'S REPORT in December 1968 appears to have immediately precipitated significant phenomena affecting Vermonters' well-being. Whether it alone caused the problem or not is unknown, but in the following months the VSP experienced great difficulty attracting new officers to its ranks. Already among the last of all the states to provide adequate benefits to troopers, it found recruiting "a touch-and-go proposition" because of the long hours demanded of them.[535]

In June 1969, Alexander wrote to Gov. Davis soliciting his assistance, warning "The department is experiencing a high turnover in State Police personnel and finding it almost impossible to recruit replacements."[536] Whereas only 27 officers resigned since the department's formation in 1947, 17 of them left in the one-year period between May 1968 and May 1969. An estimated 50% chose to remain in law enforcement, but working for other agencies. Their decisions to do so, one VSP press release said, indicated they "basically left for better salaries, benefits, working conditions and opportunities."[537] It also appears that the reputation the Irasburg board imposed on the department further contributed to the sudden exodus.[§§]

The cumulative effects of these stresses on morale and the department's functioning are further reflected in the rising crime rate taking place at the same time. Between January–August 1969, the VSP investigated 1,871 major crimes compared to the 1,303 taking place in the same time period the year before, representing an eye-popping 43.6% increase. Breaking and entering continued as the most problematic offence constituting 55.5% of major crimes, followed by grand and petty larceny (respectively, 15.1% and 22.2%). Crimes against property also increased substantially by 44.4% while those committed against the person rose by only 10%. Revealing the tremendous workload that the VSP suffered under, only 19.4% of all major crimes were solved, a negligible increase of 2% from the preceding year. Losses sustained by victims for all stolen and recovered property during this period amounted to $600,475.46.[538] These figures explain why so many Vermonters and out-of-state second home owners remained frustrated with the state's fiscal inability to remedy the crying needs that law enforcement suffered under.

As the VSP sought to regroup after Irasburg, it grappled with an increasing array of crimes and demands for service. Speeders, accidents, fatalities, burglars, thieves and now the specter of potential racial problems demanded the pressed troopers' attention. At the same time, the completion of the interstate system meant increased presence of drugs threatening the population. "There has been tremendous growth," the VSP's Drug Abuse Control Program reported in August 1968, "in the illegal use of drugs known to law enforcement officers in the State of Vermont within the last 18 months and unless adequate

---

[§§] The vilification of police continues to pose a challenge in assuring the public's safety. In 2021, despite an increase in violent crime, police recruitment efforts in Vermont faltered to such an extent that officials decided to do away with requiring applicants to pass a written examination. https://vtdigger. org/2021/08/08/citing-crime-rise-federal-prosecutor-calls-for-stepped-up-police-recruiting-and-retention/ and https://vtdigger.org/2021/08/10/written-exam-nixed-for-new-recruits-at-vermont-police-academy/. In the state's largest city, Burlington, politicians ordered police to reduce the number of officers resulting in the rationing, and unavailability, of assistance able to respond to calls for help. https://vtdigger.org/2021/05/24/burlington-police-roll-out-response-plan-based-on-degree-of-urgency/

enforcement and educational programs are immediately established the people of Vermont will suffer greatly."[539]

Drug investigations in 1967–1968 numbered 56 with only 9 arrests and rose substantially between 1969 and 1970 when 374 took place, resulting in 192 arrests.[540]

Traffickers' easy access to the interstate system allowed them to facilitate the flow of drugs from Montreal to coastal Boston and New York. According to state's attorney Sten Lium, the New York State Police cracked down so hard on traffickers in 1966 that the next year they shifted their operations into Vermont. "By 1967," he wrote, "Highgate Springs, Vermont was the principal Stateside entry point for these drugs. From there, the route ran through Franklin County to Burlington, thence to Montpelier and White River Junction, and into New Hampshire."[541]

During the next decade, Vermont law enforcement continued to see its highways used as a corridor to facilitate the transportation of drugs going in both directions, described further by VSP Commissioner Francis Lynch testifying before a senate committee in 1978.

"We do have a hell of a lot of people evidently traveling through (Vermont)," he said, "there is a whole lot of traffic, extraordinary serious drug traffic now emanating from Maine. The Coast Guard has raised so much hell in the Florida area that people transporting their hard drugs from Colombia by boat, beginning to bypass Texas, bypass Florida, come all the way up to Maine."

"There is a whole lot of passage through Vermont.," he said, and "the days of Vermont being a beautiful little place tucked away in New England, and no problems developing is changing. We have a lot of people coming here, we are so close to Boston, we are close to New York, people aren't fools down there and they bring their problems with them."[542] The availability of drugs in the 1970s became so prevalent that it overwhelmed the ability of unprepared and unsophisticated rural police agencies on the local, county, and state levels to muster sufficient forces to attack the problem effectively. Similarly, it also impacted their ability to internally monitor their own conduct to assure the legality of their actions during drug investigations.

The state's police community faced further challenges to their very existence. In the spring of 1968, as he grappled with the poverty and hunger problems around the state, Gov. Hoff formed a special committee to provide a list of the most important challenges facing state agencies. Number 15 on its list concerned "Public Safety" as the group of high-ranking officials looked beyond the interests of the VSP to creating an entirely new form of policing, one that could threaten the mandate the department worked under since 1947. Regional, or some kind of district, policing seemed more appropriate to the committee and it recommended that Hoff pursue it to increase "local law enforcement and protection to individuals."[543]

Moving away from the traditional local, county and state methods of organizing public safety resources to create this new form of regional police remained an attractive alternative to the frustrations that an undermanned VSP offered. Gov. Davis later embraced aspects of the recommendations and in 1971 moved to create a "super agency" encompassing a variety of state-level, traditional law enforcement functions. Called the "Agency of Enforcement and Protection," he planned for a single cabinet-level member to take charge of the departments of Agriculture, Banking and Insurance, Labor and Industry, Motor Vehicles, Public Safety, and Liquor Control.[544] In 1974, local police faced a similar challenge to their independent authority when additional proposals similar to those made by Hoff's committee sought to advance the creation of regional police forces that threatened their very existence.[545] Neither Hoff's or Davis's proposals considering the formation of an all-inclusive agency or the consolidation of local agencies succeeded. However, they did remain a viable option for future governor Richard A. Snelling to follow in the late 1970s when he seriously considered abolishing the nagging existence of an independent VSP.

THE KING AND DUKES OF THE MIGHTY KINGDOM OF REDSTONE

The resolve of VSP commanders to respond to the changes Vermont society faced following the taint that the Irasburg Affair inflicted on them meant the implementation of a strong hand. Alexander remained in office for the time being, aided by the department's executive officer, Maj. Davis, and Capt. Dean overseeing enforcement operations, constituting the principal troika.

Upon Gov. Davis's announcing Alexander's retirement in August 1969 (contending it had "nothing to do with the so-called Irasburg incident"), he received a letter from Dr. William L. Meyer, an assistant professor of biochemistry at UVM and president of the executive committee of the Burlington branch of the NAACP. The organization, he warned Davis in no uncertain terms, had great concerns regarding his selection of a new DPS commissioner and issued a set of demands.

"As black and white citizens of this state," he wrote, "we demand that the next Public Safety commissioner be fully dedicated to protecting the rights of black citizens."

Next, "we demand that he be determined and active in assuring that all the men under his command behave likewise," followed by "we demand that the new Commissioner be instructed in no uncertain terms that the Governor of the State will be most unyielding in determining that the principles of police impartiality are strictly adhered to."

Lastly, the organization demanded that the next commissioner "have no record of public or private complicity in or condoning of the unquestionably racist attitudes and behavior of a number of State Police officials in the so-called Irasburg Affair."

"We present these considerations," he ended, "not as requests, not as expectations, but as demands. When a record of police neglect and racism exists, a man cannot be polite about threats to his personal safety. He has the right to demand these things from the governor of all the people and to fully expect that the governor will make no compromises, public or private, in meeting these demands."[546]

Davis did not receive Meyer's letter kindly, writing back requesting he be clearer with regard to the purported racist officers participating in the Irasburg matter. Meyer should, he said, "state directly the names of such individuals, rather than to refer to them indirectly" and offered to meet with him personally if he wanted to discuss the matter further. There is nothing in the record indicating any further interaction between the two men.

Retiring Commissioner Alexander's attorney, Robert Eldredge, also wrote to Davis with his recommendation for the next commissioner, suggesting Waterbury native and former commandant of the U. S. Marine Corps, Gen. Wallace M. Greene Jr. "He is an accomplished administrator," Eldredge said, "disciplinarian and I am sure would be a distinct credit to your administration."[547]

Returning control of the VSP back to a person with a military background after Alexander's tenure with the DMV and then as a trooper presented an attractive opportunity to regain the public's trust in it. It started out well enough upon the DPS's creation in 1947 when Gov. Gibson appointed former U. S. Marine Corps Major Gen. Merritt "Red Mike" Edson as its first commissioner. A respected, decorated hero of two world wars and native Vermonter born in Rutland fifty years before, Edson abandoned his rising military career to return home and assume this new civilian role. Thereafter, he set a sad example that others in the department followed when, four years after his departure as commissioner in 1951, he committed suicide at his Washington, D.C. home, sitting in his garaged, idling car succumbing to the effects of carbon monoxide poisoning.[548]

Two men without military experience assumed the commissioner's position after Edson, William Baumann and Alexander, but Davis now agreed that a stronger hand should become involved. While Gen. Greene turned down Davis's invitation, he soon settled on another military man, former Bennington resident, Col. Edward Corcoran, to take the position. Corcoran's 30-year tour of duty with the U.S. Army serving in various capacities as a provost marshal of Dwight Eisenhower's headquarters during World War II, at West Point, in South Korea and in Europe seemed to make him the ideal person for the job.

After retiring from the Army in January 1970 from his most recent duty station at Fort Ord in Monterey where David Johnson and Barbara Lawrence lived before coming to Vermont, Deane announced Corcoran's appointment in April 1970; it is unknown if Davis considered any of the demands made by the NAACP's William Meyer in the process.

"Col. Corcoran," Davis said, "is considered to be one of the ablest and most experienced police officers in the armed services. He will bring to his new position a wealth of experience and a record of success."[549] As Corcoran later learned to his great detriment, using military tactics to control civilian police forces could cause significant problems.

Even with a new commissioner, Maj. Davis and Capt. Dean continued as the VSP's most influential members overseeing the arrivals, departures, promotions and disciplinary action of officers for the next several years. Remaining unrepentant in his criticism of the VSP high command insisting that Davis and Dean be "neutralized," state's attorney Lium lambasted it for its recent performance in the NEK. "When it comes to administering a large-scale investigation into a serious act of vandalism (Irasburg)," he wrote, "their lack of judgment and expertise is only too evident."[550]

In his wide-ranging criticism of the department (he unsuccessfully approached Hoff to name him as its commissioner), Lium provides additional insight into the quality of officers working under Davis and Dean in 1968. "The general calibre of State Police recruits," he said, "in the past three years is not what it was."

Whereas the Kentucky State Police hired one man for every 15 applicants, Liam said, Vermont picked one for every two to three applying; a significant downgrade from years earlier when it was "extremely selective" and chose one for every 25 to 30 applicants. Because of their love for "shoulder leaves and bars, and their organization charts" and "with an abundance of Captains and Lieutenants," Lium accused Davis, Dean and their cronies of empire-building and self-aggrandizement emanating from their VSP Redstone headquarters. "The King and Dukes of the mighty Kingdom of Redstone," he said, "are parade-ground soldiers, garrison guerillas" watching over their voiceless lowly troopers suffering at the hands of a top-heavy organization, forced to abide their fascination with high numbers of arrests for motor vehicle violations. The power that rested with Davis and Dean, Lium predicted, would remain for the next several years.

Their close association dated back to the department's birth in 1947. After Gibson swore in his new commissioner on the Capitol building steps (only feet from where a trooper would commit suicide three decades later), Edson administered oaths of office to Alexander and Dean. Fifty-five new troopers, 27 of them transferring into the new department from the DMV, also took their respective oaths at the same time.[551] Initial training meant a heavy emphasis on motor vehicle law with the expectation they would develop their crime investigative abilities "through on-the-job" experience.[552]

Beyond taking their oaths of office and allegiance, and promising to comply with generally stated "departmental Rules and Regulations," there is no evidence until the tragedies unfolding in the late 1970s that the VSP ever instituted meaningful ethical considerations into its training curriculum. Neither did it adequately alert personnel of their obligation to report to superiors instances of questionable conduct coming to their attention. Even if they had received such instruction, in this "go along to get along" atmosphere it is doubtful that misconduct ever received the attention it deserved out of fear of publicly embarrassing the department.

The backgrounds of the men assuming control of the VSP in the 1970s and the roles they played in the future Router Bit Affair varied. It is largely distinguishable by when they gained employment during three waves, or cadres, coinciding with their personal coming of age in their twenties. Davis, Dean and Robert E. Field (1947) and Nelson R. Lay Jr. (1949) constituted the first round, followed by a second when the state faced an immediate need to bolster its ranks because of an increase in crime. This introduced others, including John P. Heffernan and Richard A. Spear (1954) and James H. Ryan (1955) into the fold.

A third group began its service in the early 1960s that included Milford W. Ramey (1960) and George O. Patch (1962). While some had military experience during World War II and the Korean War (Lay, Patch, Ramey, Ryan, and Spear), none appear to have obtained any formal education beyond graduating high school; Lay did obtain an associate's degree from Champlain College in 1975.[553]

The tight affinity that developed and bound these men together as early employees of the VSP when it coalesced into a functioning department conferred on them a special distinction in the eyes of others. Those who came afterwards could never claim their presence during the department's formative years as they could and the unspoken authority and attending respect descending on this group provided each with an aura of respect allowing them to assume a uniqueness few dared to challenge. They maintained a rigid chain of command structure among them requiring many problems identified in the field be reported upwards to Redstone for resolution. The process they utilized surprised a 1975 legislative committee examining their methods leading it to conclude that the "utilization of intermediate decision-makers does not appear to be what it should be."[554] Unconcerned with such guidance from outsiders and proud of their roles and the tight grip they maintained, these early men created and fostered the perception of what it meant to be, as they each considered themselves, a loyal "company man."

An attribute of the company man mindset included vigorous opposition to allowing the employment of anyone with a college education, made clear by Capt. Dean in 1975. While reported as a personal view, but one no doubt shared among his peers, he unhesitatingly made it publicly known "that he does not approve of college graduates on the force because they are too independent." Obliquely referring to the desired company man they could tolerate, Dean explained that someone with a college education was unwanted because he could "not fit in with the 'establishment.'"[555] Similarly, when Maj. James Ryan assumed temporary leadership of the department in 1979, the press identified him as a member of the "old school," described by his friends "as a man known for his experience, a natural who relied little on police textbooks."[556]

The atmosphere within the VSP fostering opposition to enlightened thinking in the ranks instilled in the minds of others the perception that anyone who tried to advance their education and sought monetary assistance from federally funded programs designed to make that possible participated in, according to Capt. Heffernan, "a big farce."[557]

In an insightful display of one's expected knowledge of basic criminal law, even some holding high rank could not define one of its most basic concepts. When the head of the department's Bureau of Criminal Investigation (BCI), Capt. Richard Spear, was asked to define "exculpatory evidence" (information able to minimize or refute an allegation), he swore under oath that "I don't know what that means. Don't ask me; I don't know what it means."[558]

The closely held dislike these men reserved for anyone receiving an education beyond the immediate needs of law enforcement proved so successful that in 1971, in a department of 228 sworn officers, only 4 had college degrees.[559] At the same time, in an apparent attempt to show itself as forward-thinking while silently practicing a separate agenda, the VSP reported to the governor that "some 40 officers" had taken advantage of federal programs to further their education as part-time students.[560]

Public perceptions were one thing, but Sten Lium was not fooled by the VSP high command's machinations. In 1972 he issued another of his scathing assessments concerning the extent it had fallen, describing the department as "like Alice in Wonderland on a bad trip," run by a "tinhorn dictatorship" made up of Davis, Dean and Commissioner Corcoran. They constituted a "Mickey Mouse administration," he said, "using "a 19th century Mexican Army mentality (of) an army at war with the people."[561]

Unstoppable in their practices, the culture developing among these early arrivistes occupying Redstone meant sharing a winking, unspoken privilege where some viewed lower placed officers with the initiative to better themselves as a threat to the status quo. While those first men began to rise within the organization, new faces began to appear in the next decade offering the prospect of enlightenment able to penetrate into an increasingly wooden command structure. Both Edward R. Fish (1962) and Howard G. Gould (1964), who later killed himself at the statehouse, served in the Navy and went on to obtain college degrees following their employment. While Gould gained an associate's degree in law enforcement from Champlain College in 1976,[562] the much admired and respected Fish received a B.A. from Goddard College, a master's degree in education administration from Johnson State College, and attended a lengthy, nine-month long course in police administration at Northwestern University. Following his retirement in 1989, he became the chief of police in Barre.[563]

Fish was distinctly ahead of his time and arguably the best-educated, enlightened command officer in the VSP. He played a critical role in the 1979 disruptions after Gould's suicide when he headed a panel of officers bravely bucking the efforts of Redstone superiors seeking to save face for their own involvement in the debacle when they tried to railroad detective David A. Reed with bogus charges of neglect associated with his death. A high school graduate, Reed served three years in the U.S. Army before joining the VSP in 1965 and later made detective, promoted to the rank of corporal in 1971, serving in the NEK in the following years.

Fish's admirable efforts on Reed's behalf removing the unwarranted cloud of suspicion from above him did not go unnoticed by his superiors. Soon after, Fish experienced silent ostracism from the high command when he walked Redstone's hallways watching doors close quickly to bar his entry because of his brazen willingness to have, as Fish characterized it, the "audacity to contradict the hierarchy" in exonerating Reed.

"Fortress Mentality"

Retrospectively viewing the conduct of the VSP command in the 1970s after the trauma Irasburg inflicted reveals a new way of operation. It demonstrates an undeniable path showing that its members defensively withdrew behind Redstone's walls protective of their status and reputation. They repeatedly revealed in quiet, and not so quiet, ways their distrust of governors and legislatures, dismissive of the tight grip they tried to impose on their operations. They also expressed a clear resentment of an intrusive press unwilling to move on from the Irasburg board of inquiry's findings insinuating their racist inclinations, repeatedly reminding them they constituted damaged goods.

Davis and Dean remained in place and many viewed their presence with disfavor believing that, despite whatever commissioner a governor might install, they alone controlled the department's operations. None of this kind of internal suspicion existed before Irasburg when the command staff was, comparatively speaking, more open and trusting. Now, post-Irasburg, a new world presented itself to the department's bosses, circling their wagons in self-protection as demonstrated during the approaching Paul Lawrence and Router Bit affairs.

Two other VSP officers with no direct involvement in the circumstances surrounding Howard Gould's suicide in 1979, but whose legacy contributed significantly to its surrounding disruptions, also joined the department in the 1960s. The names of Stanley

Tucker Merriam Jr. (1964) and Paul D. Lawrence (1967) intertwined throughout the 1970s because of their association in investigating the increasing use of drugs that the new interstate system introduced. The intrusive "shiftless ski bums, part-time college students and drop-out students" that a VSP supervisor identified in 1967 as the cause of the problem drew the attention of law enforcement at all levels across the state. The incredible, lingering impact that Lawrence had in investigating those complaints came to sully the reputations many, putting them on the defensive, including the VSP. His history of drug arrests based on the untruthful affidavits he filed for arrest and search warrants, planted evidence, and perjured testimony was so blatant, so wrong, and so egregious that 71 individuals eventually received pardons from Gov. Salmon in 1977.[564]

After Gould's suicide in 1979, it is instructive that Lawrence had no intention of shedding any additional light on what happened in these earlier years. When a Connecticut State Police (CSP) officer investigating the death tried to contact him at his place of employment in South Burlington, he received a chilly response. As his report describes, Lawrence "refused to come to the telephone, and told the receptionist to tell this officer that he does not give interviews and did not want to talk to me."[565] Regardless of Lawrence's lack of cooperation, the legacy he left behind touched all of the state's law enforcement practitioners, succinctly recounted in 1979 under the newspaper headline "The Ghost of Paul Lawrence Poisons Faith in Vt. Justice."[566]

The VSP employed Lawrence for four years before he left the department under a cloud of suspicion in 1971. Prior to his departure, he publicly blasted aspects of its administration that, in retrospect after Gould's suicide, ring true despite his abhorrent conduct. Lawrence had a contentious relationship with his superiors, singling out Davis and Dean, calling them "martinets" because they interfered with drug investigations. His ire stemmed from their refusal to allow investigators to pursue investigations at ski areas and southern Vermont colleges, and prohibiting their use of updated techniques to go after major dealers.

Tellingly, Lawrence explained that the problem with the state's drug enforcement operations lay within the VSP itself where "no one wants to assume responsibility for the program." As a result, he admitted that "the undercover men run the drug program at random" out of necessity, but that "If it were better supervised it would be much more effective." He blamed Davis and Dean in the same manner that Sten Lium did for causing morale problems within the department and said that they enforced petty "outmoded rules and regulations" on troopers "with a vengeance."[567]

After his departure, Lawrence gained employment as the chief of police in Vergennes and went on to launch his own form of drug investigations on an unsuspecting public. Author Hamilton Davis conducted an extensive inquiry into Lawrence's career during this time, recorded in his explosive book published in 1978, *Mocking Justice: America's Biggest Drug Scandal,* subtitled *The shocking true story of Paul Lawrence, a corrupt narcotics cop, and the hysteria which led a frightened town into wrecking the lives of its children.*

His account appeared precisely as the events leading up to Gould's death unfolded and conveys the author's crushing assessment of the VSP management style during Lawrence's tenure, blaming its neglect for the havoc he caused.

Despite Lawrence's dishonorable discharge from the Army for character and misbehavior problems in 1966, the VSP conducted only a cursory background investigation failing to uncover it before hiring him. By 1970, Lawrence worked in Brattleboro alongside Gould's brother-in-law, Albert J. Ravenna, who recalls the two of them working together on drug matters. Ravenna also worked beforehand during the Irasburg matter when he and other troopers received assignments to guard Johnson's home in an exercise he called "a joke."

At some point, he became suspicious that Lawrence was planting evidence when they executed search warrants. He alerted the Windham County state's attorney, and former law clerk to Irasburg chairman Judge Gibson, M. Jerome Diamond of his concerns. Diamond also had reservations about Lawrence and chose to decline prosecuting cases he was involved with that led his VSP supervisors to reassign him to the Rutland office.

When additional questions about Lawrence's credibility appeared in 1971, he left the VSP without facing any consequences. Author Davis inquired closely of Maj. Davis about Lawrence's actions and the circumstances of his departure, but received only evasive responses. Trying to understand why the VSP continued to protect Lawrence, Davis concluded that the major possessed a "fortress mentality," an "us against the world" feeling, on the department's behalf placing him in a defensive position seeking to protect its reputation in the face of uncomfortable questioning.

Assessing the consequences of such a position, Davis wrote "It may be true that when a member or former member of a supposedly elite organization gets into trouble, the organization is unfairly placed in a bad light." "But," he accurately concluded, "covering up such incidents can have devastating consequences." His prescient warnings came true in the year following the publication of *Mocking Justice* when an avalanche of additional embarrassing revelations charged into public view. They were ones attributable, in large part, to the VSP's allowing Lawrence to leave its employment without accountability for his actions and his reputation intact because it viewed him as "no longer (its) problem."[568]

In August of 1973, Lawrence obtained employment in law enforcement with the St. Albans Police Department. Over the course of the next months, he lodged a staggering 106 drug charges against purported dealers in the community, including one involving the assistance of a member of the VSP's Drug Abuse Unit, Cpl. Stanley Merriam. The specific details of his personal relationship with Lawrence outside of their working together during the latter's employment with the VSP are clouded. However, records indicate that concerned superiors, including Maj. Davis, reportedly warned him to distance himself from the rogue officer which he refused to do.

When questions arose about Lawrence's drug investigations setting up innocent people, in February 1974 Attorney General Kimberly Cheney became personally involved. He contacted Corcoran and, together with Davis, the officers agreed to arrange for an undercover officer from the Maine State Police to come to Vermont to see if Lawrence could be compromised in a drug purchase surveilled by other officers. Despite repeated reassurances from Corcoran and Davis they had the operation well in hand and scheduled to begin in July, Cheney later found out that they had done nothing. In his telling recount of the incident, he concluded that the two men lied to him and were, in his assessment, "bad cops."[569]

Despite Corcoran's and Davis's inaction, Lawrence's fall from grace happened on July 10, 1974 with his arrest by Burlington police for falsifying an affidavit to support the arrest of a person— an undercover out-of-state officer—that he accused of drug dealing. Months before, Merriam allegedly concealed his knowledge that Lawrence reportedly planted evidence during a search conducted in February 1974. He remained an avid supporter of his friend after his arrest when the department assigned him to serve as a bodyguard for Lawrence's attorney because of threats he received.[570] Five years later, in 1979 during the firestorm of investigations into the VSP's conduct following Gould's death, Merriam, with a personal file opened to CSP investigators revealing two reprimands (one for firing a warning shot and the other erased) and who gained promotion in the interim, entered a no contest plea to a reduced administrative charge in connection with his failing to notify his superiors of Lawrence's actions.

While Merriam steadfastly denied wrongdoing, other concerns arose about his suspected perjury during inquest proceedings investigating Lawrence and the results of an important lie detector test administered to him in August 1974. Attorney General Cheney insisted that Corcoran arrange for the examination, one so extraordinary it was the first time in VSP history that one of its officers underwent a process requiring the use of an outside examiner from the Maine State Police to conduct. It provided a predictable ending after two hours and four tests (with Merriam walking out during questioning) when the examiner concluded he was untruthful.

The tortured history of his report of the examination in the following years, stored away in an unmarked envelop in a VSP file cabinet and finally "discovered" in 1978, constitutes a critically important event to understand the department's culture and insular practices leading up to the Router Bit Affair in 1979 and Gould's suicide.

Other highly placed officials in addition to Cheney (who calls Merriam the third VSP "bad cop" involved in the Lawrence matter) also recognized the department's internal problems.[571] In 1980 Vermont's U.S. Attorney William B. Gray confided to Gov. Snelling's aide, R. Paul Wickes, that "The State Police has an institutional interest in maintaining an inference of credibility whenever an officer testifies in court, and that Merriam's credibility problems may damage that inference even with respect to other officers."

Merriam's troubles presented such concern to federal authorities that Gray said he "suspects that Merriam may have himself have planted methamphetamines during a search in a drug case in St. Albans" and would not have used him as a witness had the defendants not pled guilty.[572]

The favorable treatment that Merriam received following his no contest plea to administrative charges of concealing information in 1979 allowing him to remain on the force enraged Gov. Snelling trying to deal with the aftermath of Gould's death. Disgusted with the department's antiquated internal controls over its members, he succinctly called the treatment that Merriam received a "miscarriage of justice."[573] The result also indicates the continued presence of a "fortress mentality" within the VSP stretching back to the wreckage wrought by the Irasburg Affair.

Chapter 9

STORM WARNINGS

POLICE TRAINING (AGAIN)

THE WARNING LIGHTS FLASHING DANGER concerning the VSP's management style lit up well before it imploded in 1979. A legislative committee examining it in the aftermath of the Lawrence matter in 1975 characterized its supervisory staff at the time as believing that troopers were "subject to their unchecked command and having few personal rights," deserving of immediate corrective action.

Among its many recommendations, it strongly urged that the department obtain expert outside help in the area of "internal management."

A second investigating committee ordered by Gov. Salmon a year later to inquire into Lawrence's havoc similarly agreed that problems existed internally. Ironically, it also provided observations consistent with Lawrence's warnings in 1971 about the need for the VSP to take responsibility and provide direction to drug investigators. The committee noted that, with the exception of the Burlington Police Department, no Vermont law enforcement agency had sufficient policies in place (calling them "extremely poor") to assure the integrity of those types of investigations. Concerned that Lawrence "was not a single case of the 'bad apple,'" and that there may be larger, systemic problems, the committee reiterated the need for change.[574]

Among its recommendations, one particularly difficult obstacle concerned the failure (euphemistically called "unjustifiable hesitancy") of some "working within Vermont's criminal justice system to investigate Lawrence." To overcome that problem, it recommended that "special emphasis" be placed on additional training for officers so that "there will be no hesitancy in taking appropriate action whenever there is reason to believe the integrity of the criminal justice system may be suspect."

Practically, at the same time the VSP faced an onslaught of drug investigations consuming the full attention of its thinly-manned Drug Abuse Unit conducting 629 inquiries in 1975 involving 900 people. The extent of any education these officers and others in the department received concerning their obligation to report instances of misconduct uncovered during their work is unclear. Allegations of ethics violations must be founded on clear rules identifying what one constituted and describe a process of how to report it, but the department's records do not identify any such concerns. At most, after initial recruit training officers attended periodic in-service sessions focused on the practical day-to-day aspects of law enforcement. Recognizing that a problem existed in providing timely notice of the department's expectations of its officers, Corcoran suggested that "a general Departmental policy bulletin" be distributed to address any issue of concern.[575]

In the face of the Lawrence Affair and urging of Gov. Salmon's committee, the inaction of the VSP command staff to seriously accept its guidance more aggressively than simply issuing policy reminders demonstrates an insular attitude dismissive of outside intrusions into its operations.

As the VSP dithered, in 1978 Secretary of Administration Richard Mallary, one of Hoff's fellow Young Turks, shared with Gov. Snelling his frustrations with the DPS.

He was upset over its budgeting processes and pointed to the agency's "turmoil, indecision and lack of management" where, he said, "the organizational structure and lines of communication are exceedingly unclear."[576] His comments incorporated the findings of a recent analysis conducted by the state's Cost Control Council examining the overall training of the state's law enforcement personnel where palpable tension existed at various levels. Those investigators identified a distinct phenomenon within the police community at large reaching back at least a decade, repeating the warnings of Attorney General Oakes in 1967 about the disruptive relations between police agencies. This more recent study identified the resentment that municipal and county officers felt towards the VSP at their perceived "elite" status, a "green shirts" versus "blue shirts," or "we/they feeling," mentality fostering division between them.[577]

The state's disjointed law enforcement training methods presented such conflict and discord that the report's authors took the extraordinary position the VSP's independent status be abolished. In its place, they recommended that it, a training council, police communications, civil defense, a criminal information center, and, "if legal, the Military Department," be incorporated into a single overarching Agency of Public Safety. Their refreshing analysis (one replicating Gov. Davis's earlier in the decade) promoted Snelling, struggling to find a way to resolve the infighting, to write approvingly in its margin "Good idea."

The administration's consideration of a doomsday scenario ending three decades of VSP independence had severe consequences in the next months when its defensive command staff learned its authority was under attack. This, in turn, led it to engage in more of the petty "fortress mentality" conduct that author Hamilton Davis identified the same year.

Training continued to pose problems in the years following Irasburg after the DPS acquired the former tuberculosis sanatorium in Pittsford in 1971, where it moved its operations. The Law Enforcement Training Council that Oakes sponsored, coming into existence the same month as the Irasburg shooting, also moved into the same facility.

In 1974, the legislature intervened once again into the training fray to reshuffle and thereby increase the strained relationship between the two agencies. This time, it removed some of the LETC's independence and "reversed itself and required that all LETC training recommendations be subject to the approval of the Attorney General."

At the same time, it left the DPS in control of its administrative functions prompting Snelling to scribble in exclamation, "Problem is here!" next to the Cost Commission's summary. While its funds remained under the control of the DPS, the LETC, now renamed the Vermont Criminal Justice Training Council (VCJTC), saw its authority increased to recommend training regulations "for all criminal justice personnel rather than law enforcement personnel only." Recognizing this as an additional threat to its independence, the VSP objected to any further consolidation efforts or oversight of its own training that predictably caused "an irritant to both groups."[578]

Compounding the differences between the VSP and 60 other criminal justice agencies in the state, the creation of the Vermont Crime Information Center in 1970 provided another forum for their disagreement.[579] Recordkeeping placed under the control of the VSP allowed it to expand its responsibilities and incorporate an increasing number of employees, which garnered further resentment from local agencies resistant to abandon that similar function they used in their own decades-long practices. Training and recordkeeping continued to drive police agencies apart and pose challenges to Snelling and a legislature continually trying to bridge their differences.

Within the VSP, the average trooper continued to experience the same onerous working conditions they did in the 1960s. Salaries paying $134 a week hardly kept pace with the long hours demanded of them, reaching as many as 100 a week, and which did not allow them to receive overtime pay.[580] Working to correct such disparities, in 1970 one of the four college-educated officers on the force, Trooper Michael G. Sullivan, tried to make their displeasure known to their superiors. They included the department's third in command, Capt, Dean, continually unrepentant in his open displeasure with having educated officers working alongside those who were not. After serving in the U. S. Marine Corps and graduating from the University of Connecticut with a degree in English in 1969, Sullivan began his employment with the VSP the following year to begin a two-year period of unblemished service earning him a "fully satisfactory" rating at the end of his first year.

However, he also drew the attention of an irritated Dean when he and another trooper sought to revive the moribund Vermont Troopers

Association, started in the Irasburg days to serve as a voice calling for change. Sullivan received a great shock when he read his next evaluation significantly downgrading him in each of nine categories "sprinkled with charges that he spent more time on association work than on actual police work." When Sullivan met with his superior, Sgt. Richard Spear, who approved the rigged assessment, and later played a significant role in the travails of 1979, and provided him with evidence contrary to the allegations threatening to file an unfair practice complaint, he backed down. Spear's blatant conduct exposed, he admitted that he approved it at Dean's direction.

Despite receiving an amended, glowing assessment recommending him for future promotion, the damage was done and Sullivan resigned saying that he "could no longer stay around and observe what was happening to honest young men, like himself, with their whole lives and careers ahead of them."

Sullivan's immediate supervisor, Sgt. Russell Patnode, one of the first officers to join the department in 1947 and not a part of the high command clique, agreed with him. In 1975 on the eve of his retirement, Patnode acknowledged his own frustration that he would never receive a promotion. "After I accepted that fact," he said, "I reached a certain level and that is where I stayed. If you have to fight the people at the top every minute, it destroys an officer."[581]

Patnode's observation reiterated the opinions of others concerning the unacceptable situation within the VSP. Gov. Salmon's effort to remove both Davis and Dean because of low trooper morale ran into a stonewalling department that met without success. Accompanied by the accumulated displeasure the department generated in the aftermath of the Lawrence Affair, the legislature entered into the fray. In the spring of 1975 House Appropriations Committee Chairman Emory Hebard (who served as Hoff's gadfly during the Irasburg Affair) headed an 11-person inquiry of the department that included two future governors, James Douglas and Madeleine Kunin. While the solons diplomatically concluded in their final report that VSP command personnel did not act out of any "sinister motives," they made 17 recommendations for change from practices they deemed outmoded and harmful to the good of the department. Among them, replacing deteriorating cruisers, correcting an unacceptable distribution system that allowed 300 shirts and trousers "in various stages of deterioration" to sit unused at Redstone, and hiring female troopers.

The committee also found that a rigid chain of command structure run by superiors viewing troopers as "enlistees subject to their unchecked command and having few personal rights" resulted in much secrecy instilling great distrust in the lower ranks. Transfers occurred at-will without the reasons behind them being stated or subject to review. From 1972–1975, 83 troopers were transferred, 8 for disciplinary reasons that the leadership deemed necessary "to save him from himself."

Extra-marital affairs and circumstances where superiors believed a trooper's reputation was in danger meant a transfer that often included uprooting his family without explanation because their superiors believed "the less that is said about the reasons for the transfer the better." Sten Lium, still leading the charge against the VSP leadership, opined to Hebard's committee that these transfers constituted "'muscle flexing,' designed to show a recalcitrant trooper who's boss, or worse, to run him out of the department."

Hebard's committee also faulted the promotion system that included an assessment of a trooper's merit conducted by a panel of higher-ranking officers unfamiliar with him personally. As Maj. Davis later admitted to CSP investigators, favorable actions by officers were rarely considered by superiors making promotions. Instead, it was a matter of "cussing and discussing" a potential candidate's reputation and general word of mouth they received via the department's grapevine controlling their decisions.[582]

However, what Davis did not disclose until it became public knowledge in 1980 concerned the department's practice of keeping two sets of personnel files on officers. One was available for them to review, while a second "secret" file remained in a separate cabinet under the control of the commissioner and available only to a select few. While none of this information was known to the solons in 1975, they comfortably concluded nonetheless that the promotional assessments made by these senior officers were "meaningless." The "central question," the committee posed in its ignorance of the true extent of secrecy within the VSP was "whether the present leadership can alter its management philosophy and exhibit the good will required to regain the confidence in the field." "At stake," it wrote "is the morale and retention of a large number of good state troopers, and the continued effectiveness of the department in serving the state." In the end, after recommending that the department mend its ways, the committee repeated what other studies concluded, in diplomatic fashion, that Vermont was well-served by an ethical organization and applauded its "devotion to duty, courage, dedication and courtesy."[583]

Anxious to show he understood the enormity of the problem, Corcoran transferred Dean out of Montpelier and into a small trailer in Burlington in charge of the VSP's snowmobile enforcement program. While he maintained his captain rank, Dean did not take lightly what he deemed a demotion and soon retaliated. He filed a lawsuit in federal court naming Corcoran and Hebard as defendants alleging they violated his right to due process because of the unilateral transfer without his input. The suit later settled in 1977 after Dean's retirement.

Absent any enforcement ability, the Hebard committee's recommendations for change, that included the way the VSP conducted internal investigations, languished. In February 1976, the department did revise its confidential internal rules and regulations to some extent, including prohibiting officers from receiving gifts or engaging in "conduct that causes a scandal," but never defined what constituted a scandal. By inference, the changes also placed authority to conduct internal investigations solely into the commissioner's hands following receipt of a complaint made "in triplicate." The process directed further that "The original and first copy shall be forwarded to the commissioner labeled 'Personal,' and the second copy shall be retained by the complainant."[584] Each of these seemingly mundane, innocuous provisions affecting both an internal understanding of who was responsible to initiate an internal investigation and the flow of paperwork had a substantial impact precipitating Gould's suicide in 1979.

Before his death, the effectiveness of the 1976 rules on officers' conduct was soon tested in a widely known incident when a trooper reportedly threatened a public defender who then lodged a complaint with Corcoran expressing his displeasure.[585] In addition to Corcoran's own internal review, the allegation drew the attention of the attorney general's office and the ACLU also demanding a full investigation.

Other witnesses came forward to express their own involvement with the officer, but Corcoran soon dismissed their complaints, viewing them as "a personal feud."[586] The incident appears to have impacted other actions of the department as only months later he was transferred out of the field and into the crime laboratory assigned to the photography section.[587] He continued to draw additional attention when he and another trooper became involved in a late-night fight outside a St. Johnsbury bar in June 1978 that led to his hospitalization for facial injuries and the other officer reportedly "disciplined for filing a false report about the incident."[588] In 1981, after the seismic changes within the VSP and the way it conducted internal investigations, he was again the first officer charged pursuant to new rules imposed by the legislature for strip-searching a hitchhiker.[589]

"WE GOT AWAY WITH A TON OF SHIT"

After the great upheavals the department experienced because of Gould's suicide, yet another legislative study in 1980 examining its organization, structure, and administrative and management policies returned to the work conducted by their predecessors in 1975. Regarding the changes the VSP made for internal investigations in response to that earlier guidance, this second committee cast aside diplomacy and unhesitatingly expressed its displeasure at what it accomplished. It faulted the command staff once again for its bumbling efforts concluding that its attempt to provide needed instructions to officers to guide their conduct "were often incomprehensible and frequently disregarded."

Echoing Capt. Dean's complaints and the words of Paul Lawrence, it found due process protections for officers (the same complaint lodged by others concerning the Irasburg board's proceedings) inadequate to allow them to defend themselves against allegations, themselves questionable because the procedures lacked sufficient definition to guide anyone's conduct.

"Indifference paid to legislative recommendations" this second committee wrote, in essence, allowed insulated VSP command officers to continue with their defiant conduct obstructing unwanted inquiries from an outside organization.[590]

Robert Gensburg, a St. Johnsbury attorney and special prosecutor investigating the Lawrence affair, had significant interaction with the VSP during these years and expressed a similar opinion immediately after Gould's suicide. A destructive mind-set existed among the high-ranking members, he reflected, that refused to publicly acknowledge internal wrong-doing because it could "cast a bad light on the state police." A "don't make waves" attitude prevailed and he related that "wrongdoing has for a long time been tolerated and condoned by top level officers as long as it can be handled quietly" conveying to "idealistic, young troopers entering the organization" they must play by the rules so they "don't give state police a bad name."[591]

Recently, a highly placed officer familiar with the state police hierarchy during this time confided to the author, "You have no idea how much HQ brushed under the carpet. We weren't all that clean and Paul Lawrence was just one of many."

"You've got to remember," he related, "those were the 'old days' and we got away with a ton of shit. Everyone covered for each other and any waves were met with disgust as not being a team member. Founders of DPS were still on board and if they black-balled you, you were never going anywhere except the Island Pond airport outpost!," he said.

Clearly, the high command learned nothing from either the embarrassing Irasburg or Lawrence affairs that blossomed into a full-blown crisis with Gould's suicide. In the end, prosecutor Gensburg provided a chilling assessment of a VSP command staff responsible for a "common and unsettling theme" minimizing misconduct constituting "a massive failure of the state police to do what they are supposed to do."

As the VSP underwent scrutiny by legislators, county sheriffs sought to solidify their own role in the overall scheme of law enforcement. Despite two centuries of history and a sympathetic legislature watching out for their interests, coordinating efforts between themselves remained lackluster in the mid-1970s.

Additionally, vague laws governing their conduct brought questionable interpretations leading to bizarre challenges. In January 1975, defeated Washington County Sheriff Mark Brown refused to accept the prospect of his removal from office and, relying on an obscure law allowing town selectmen to appoint police chiefs, enlisted the support of area towns to name him as their own.[592] The effort would allow Brown to conduct business that might otherwise go to the competing sheriff seeking contracts for the work. Newly installed sheriff Malcom "Mike" Mayo objected to Brown's efforts and soon raised a number of concerns as his own conduct fell under suspicion. Mayo's purported questionable actions in 1975 (falsifying records and fighting) resulted in the legislature, for the first time in its history since 1785, conducting impeachment proceedings seeking his removal alleging three counts of maladministration of office, but was ultimately acquitted after days of fiery hearings.[593] Allegations that Mayo was not able to work with the county prosecutor also arose, exemplifying the tensions and persistent, petty bickering existing among the various components of Vermont law enforcement in the 1970s.

Within the VSP, obsessive secrecy, persistent allegations of "green shirt" versus "blue shirt" elitism, unintelligible rules and regulations, inconsistent treatment of instances of misconduct exposing favoritism, and forced transfers only compounded these challenges calling for change.

Virtually none of this existed before the new world wrought by Irasburg.

Chapter 10

THE LYNCH DEBACLE

THE MERRIAM FACTOR

AFTER HIS ELECTION IN 1976, Gov. Richard Snelling began to address the crying need for change in Vermont's criminal justice system. The problem presented such challenges that he mentioned its lack of direction in his inaugural address.

"We must substantially increase our capacity to protect people," he said, "by strengthening and harmonizing all elements of law enforcement, the state police, and sheriffs and local police. Improved morale and delineation of roles and functions of police officers is a first step that must be accomplished by a new attitude towards the process of prosecution, corrections and parole, ensuring that police, judges, state's attorneys and parole boards proceed with shared objectives."[594]

Citing the repeated complaints of "low morale" inside the DPS (calling it a major priority), Snelling had no intention to reappoint Corcoran as commissioner. He deemed him responsible for the mess Hebard's committee uncovered and made it known he wanted someone much younger to replace him. He had no interest in repeating the missteps of his predecessors by appointing someone with a military background. Instead, he sought a person with charisma and a background able to allay legislators' concerns over the department's inept management style and raise its reputation in the public's eye.

Snelling's assistant described the new administration's ideal candidate, "We're thinking of looking for someone in their 30s or 40s who could rethink and restructure the entire department, someone who could walk into a room full of people and be immediately recognized as Vermont's top cop."[595]

While the search for Corcoran's replacement proceeded, in January 1977 Snelling appointed the department's second commissioner, William H. Baumann (1951–1965), to return and assume the role on an interim basis.

Baumann enthusiastically seized the opportunity and immediately moved to address some of the Hebard committee's concerns of an organization he found "in deplorable shape."[596] Resolving waning morale remained a top priority and he ordered that delayed promotional exams be scheduled, while seeking ways to invigorate a VSP presence where needed. Believing that "the state police were losing their identity" in Lamoille County and listening to executive officer Maj. Davis tell him that the department had to get "back what (it) had lost" because of a lack of supervision and advancements made by an invigorated sheriff's department, Baumann adopted his recommendation that Cpl. Stanley Merriam be assigned to oversee the effort.

Significant disputes later arose in the weeks prior to Gould's suicide concerning the circumstances surrounding Baumann's decision to appoint Merriam that provide additional evidence of the disarray within the department at the time. The results of his polygraph exam conducted in 1974 during the Lawrence Affair indicating his untruthfulness were withheld and never passed on by Davis to Baumann proceeding under the assumption that the officer was "a good supervisor who inspired men and got the job done." In fact, the adverse exam indicating troubling facts that could have affected his decision remained hidden from view. It was never recorded in logs kept by the Polygraph Unit, within the commissioner's office, or in Merriam's personnel file. For some unknown reason in his particular case, and perhaps others, the VSP maintained this additional layer of secrecy beyond the concealed second files it kept on its officers. Until the polygraph report's subsequent discovery five years later in 1979, just Corcoran, and Davis who witnessed it, were apparently the only ones who knew of its existence.

Regarding his role in making the appointment and the effect that Merriam's unfavorable polygraph report could have influencing Baumann, Davis told investigators that, while aware of the unfavorable assessment he was untruthful, he disingenuously asserted the results were "inconclusive." No investigator examining the favorable consideration that Merriam received ever accepted Davis's explanation that undercut the department's credibility in the next months.

In making the appointment, neither was Baumann apparently aware of the significant concerns that former Attorney General Cheney had of Merriam's truthfulness that led to Gov. Salmon's extraordinary petitioning the Supreme Court to appoint a special prosecutor to investigate it in conjunction with the Lawrence Affair.

That effort did not result in any action taken against Merriam, but after his election as attorney general, the former Irasburg law clerk M. Jerome Diamond (1975–1981) conducted his own investigation in 1979. His blistering report that June condemned the VSP command personnel for not pursuing the allegations against Merriam that allowed it to fester for years. Diamond's office unequivocally determined that both Corcoran and Davis knew of the exam's results and that Corcoran's failure to take action as commissioner "represents a serious breach of the public trust."

The record of the department's conduct revealed, "at best" the attorney general's redacted report described,

> Command defensiveness and indifference to charges of police misconduct. A malaise has replaced what should be a departmental response characterized by a professional desire to quickly identify and discharge persons unfit to enforce the criminal laws of this State. Our investigation found little evidence that certain command officers with the Department have displayed or now display any level of earnestness in determining whether a high-ranking officer of the Department had concealed evidence of criminal

wrongdoing and (deleted). The lackadaisical response by the Department when confronted with substantial evidence (deleted) can be seen as an institutional offense of significant gravity.[597]

Summing up, the report left an indelible impression that "the actions of a few police officers and commanders have betrayed even modest public expectations; their failure is reprehensible."

Blissfully unaware of the cloud over Merriam's head and not otherwise privy to the scheming of his immediate subordinates at Redstone, Baumann followed Davis's recommendation to aggressively move to enhance the VSP's prestige, jumping on the suggestion of Troop K commander Lt. Richard Curtis in Middlesex.

Curtis advised him to move quickly to establish a robust state police presence in Lamoille County in order to disadvantage the admirable work conducted by the county sheriff. The persistent competition and bureaucratic infighting among police agencies remained on full display when Curtis learned that selectmen in Johnson planned to abolish their police force at the March town meeting.

"This would be a good time," Curtis suggested, "for us to get our feet in the door before the County Sheriff gets a contract with them."[598]

Baumann agreed and days later he and Davis, apparently without considering other candidates, approached Merriam with a plan to relocate him from where he worked in Franklin County to Lamoille County to supervise four troopers.

If he agreed, they promised that upon his obtaining satisfactory results and passing a promotional examination for sergeant that he would be promoted and allowed to remain in Lamoille County without fearing a transfer.[599]

Merriam agreed and an excited Baumann directed Davis to assign him "ASAP with instructions to go-go-go-go." Merriam did as directed and soon clashed with the county sheriff when he instructed his troopers "that the State Police were going to reign supreme and they were going to reign in Lamoille County one way or the other."[600]

His aggressive behavior, endorsed by Baumann and Davis, also caused further problems with the county state's attorney that soon gained attention in the highest levels of state government.

FRANCIS LYNCH

While Baumann, Davis, and Merriam worked, Snelling pushed ahead to find his next DPS commissioner able to mitigate the discord these others fostered behind his back. A search committee reviewed more than 200 applications for the position, recommending five individuals for Snelling's favorable consideration that 53-year-old Francis "Frank" E. Lynch ultimately received on June 20, 1977.

A Massachusetts native and graduate of Holy Cross College, the trim, silver-haired Lynch, straight out of central casting, presented a striking appearance commanding attention. He also bore a resume Snelling described as "one of the most impressive careers in law enforcement of anyone in the field today."

From 1950–1977, Lynch served in several capacities as an FBI special agent, an inspector for the American Express Company, on the Indiana Crime Commission, as commissioner of public safety in Omaha, Nebraska, and director of security at Texaco, Inc. and Owens-Illinois, Inc. FBI Director Clarence Kelley, a role that Lynch was also recommended for by the National District Attorneys Association, reported to Snelling that Lynch was "one of the finest men ever to serve the Bureau." He also provided Lynch with an autographed picture of himself that later hung in his Redstone office, inscribed "Law enforcement is much better because of you and I hope you remain with us for many years to come."[601]

Based on those recommendations, Snelling expressed full support for Lynch in rebuilding the state police facing a high number of anticipated retirements during "this critical period."

Regarding the need to mend fences within the law enforcement community, Snelling trusted Lynch's ability where, he said, "In a state of our size, there is the greatest possibility to meld the capabilities of the State Police, sheriffs and local law enforcement agencies into one of the finest police networks in the nation."[602]

Notwithstanding its glowing recommendations on Lynch's behalf, the search committee examining his past failed to conduct a full inquiry that could have uncovered a significant episode soon repeating itself in Vermont with momentous consequences.

Lynch never worked as a police officer handling the public's everyday complaints directly. Regardless, his stint as an FBI agent seems to have awed others when he received appointment in Omaha as its director of public safety overseeing police, fire and other public safety departments. It lasted for only a brief period from 1965–1966 when the city mayor fired him for "insubordination" and a "lack of cooperation," attributed to his "uncontrollable temper."

While Lynch had his supporters from among the police ranks who liked his take-charge attitude, he failed miserably as an administrator. "His basic problem," the mayor recalled, "is he can't tolerate any supervision. He's got to be the boss of everything, and you've got to do it his way or nothing."

Trying to quell rioting within the city's Black community in the summer of 1966, Lynch overstepped his authority as director intruding into that of the city's police chief when he went "charging up and down the streets wearing a white hat, shouting orders, inflaming the situation" trying to quell, as Lynch put it, the "hoodlums."

The chief had little tolerance for Lynch and described him as "just one of those guys who wants things done his way and if things aren't done his way he won't go along. He's probably his own worst enemy."

Lynch's impact extended elsewhere and an official handling fire safety matters complained that he "continually meddled even though he admitted he knew little about firefighting" and that "it seemed to me like he was a frustrated would-be policeman." After he was fired for interfering with the police chief once again, the mayor said that "There is no place in this administration for either dictators or a Bull Connor (referring to a racist Alabama law enforcement official). Mr. Lynch has insisted on being both director and chief (and) has bypassed the chief several times."[603]

Such information could have significantly aided Snelling in his effort to find a suitable commissioner for Vermont's DPS able to back up his optimistic hopes for change. However, that failure quickly crashed just two years later when he fired him for the same kinds of conduct forcing Omaha city officials to send him on his way.

Soon after Lynch's swearing-in on July 20, 1977 (scheduled for later Senate confirmation), he received a visit from Court Administrator Michael Krell and former Paul Lawrence Special Prosecutor Robert

Gensburg. Both men participated in Gov. Salmon's study in 1976 calling for the pardons of dozens of people because of the rogue cop's actions based on the thorough investigation Gensburg oversaw. He minced no words in his own findings of the affair concerning who was at fault in the disaster, writing that "there was a very substantial question at the onset that the Vermont State Police were seriously in cahoots with Lawrence or their lab, which enabled Lawrence to operate in the fashion that he did."[604]

Krell and Gensburg had every reason for continuing concern whether the situation had been remedied and, as the attorney general's account of their meeting describes, they came "to discuss some of the serious negative consequences to law enforcement caused by the Paul Lawrence affair."

They also wanted "to direct (Lynch's) attention to instances of missing state police reports which came to light during the investigation." The savvy Gensburg already knew beforehand the department maintained second, secret files on officers that it did not want him to see and which it never provided to him pursuant to a subpoena seeking information during the Lawrence investigation. When he raised the problem with Lynch, he recounted that "It went in one ear and out the other."[605]

Little of this consequential, important information conveyed by highly respected officials with first-hand knowledge of the department's internal problems meant much to the newly arrived Lynch. He appeared uninterested in their report, lacking any sense of urgency or inquisitiveness, later telling an investigator that "he did not comprehend the purpose of their visit."[606]

But perhaps he did know the sordid details well because he was already privy to the secret files under his control and chose, instead, to adopt a Cheshire Cat persona to protect them in response to Gensburg's probing questioning.

Additional concerns arose over Lynch's attention to detail and intention to address the department's problems surrounding Merriam's unfavorable polygraph examination. The results of that report were so explosive that when Merriam's direct supervisor, the respected Lt. Fish, learned of them he admitted "you could have knocked me over with a feather," incredulously asking "why in the hell was this allowed to just sit on the backburner."[607]

While Lynch said he first became aware of the situation in March 1978, Maj. Davis provided conflicting accounts about the timing to attorney general and CSP investigators. He told one that he warned Lynch right after his appointment a year earlier, but that "he did not feel the importance of the polygraph was understood" by Lynch. Gesturing "with his hand over his head," Davis conveyed to the interviewer that "the information probably went over Lynch's head," and to a second investigator he never mentioned it.[608]

Davis, also an experienced polygrapher, understood the critical role that polygraph examinations played in investigations. The attorney general noted their importance, specifically addressing the "high degree of reliance" the VSP command placed on them allowing them to make "grave and substantial decisions" and where a separate unit dedicated to administering them existed.

However, unlike Corcoran, Lynch had no intention of requiring any sworn officer to submit to one. When CSP investigators pointedly inquired of him if "he would ever use a polygraph in an administrative inquiry regarding his personnel," Lynch emphatically responded "that he would never, ever use a polygraph" because its "only possible use was as an investigative tool."[609]

When Lynch did become aware of the Merriam report, whether after his appointment in 1977 when he gained access to the secret files or in 1978 as he professed, the investigating Keyser Commission expressed its own dismay in assessing his inaction and whether it rose to a level warranting criminal charges. Ultimately escaping sanctions because Snelling had dismissed him by that time, the Commission made its own dissatisfaction known and wrote that when advised of the results Lynch "was incredibly nonchalant about a possibly serious breach within his department, to which he took no action."[610]

Soon after Lynch assumed office, the "turmoil, indecision and lack of management" within his department that Secretary of Administration Mallary decried became readily apparent. Only days afterwards, Lynch moved quickly and on Aug. 1, 1977 promoted Merriam to the rank of sergeant on a probationary basis.

After testing conducted that April shortly after his transfer to Lamoille County, Merriam placed fourth out of 39 applicants making him eligible for consideration. Despite his high ranking, it appears to have been an extraordinary move by Lynch because, according to Maj. Davis, he warned him that "there was no room in the (department's table of organization) for any promotions." Unwilling to listen to his caution, Davis said that "Lynch went ahead and made them anyway."[611]

A second, bizarre example of the latitude other VSP senior officers believed they possessed, and which Lynch's attitude emboldened, involved another officer seeking promotion to sergeant. The course of this individual's travails also had significant ramifications for his brother, David Reed, the VSP detective in St. Johnsbury who played a central role in the approaching Router Bit Affair.

Fifteen-year veteran Corporal Cornelius Reed participated in the same process as Merriam in which a 9-member promotional potential review board evaluated his suitability for the position, but that he was not allowed to attend; the same kind of process that the legislative panel condemned in 1975.

Unknown to him, Lt. James Ryan, whom he had never met, appeared before the board to provide it with an allegation of an "an undocumented rumor" concerning Reed's purported misconduct. It was "neither investigated nor ever reflected" in his personnel file and which must have come from the secret file kept on him. When Reed's supervisor learned of Ryan's unsupported allegation, he said he was dumfounded. Calling himself "flabbergasted," Reed soon learned that the untrue information led the panel to place him far down on the promotion list.

Reed appealed the adverse decision to then-commissioner Baumann, but was denied relief and after Lynch's appointment was again rebuffed. A further appeal to Gov. Snelling resulted in his appointing Labor and Industry Commissioner Joel Cherington in December 1977 to conduct an inquiry.

Cherington's subsequent report, reciting Ryan's admission he provided an unsubstantiated rumor to the panel, lambasted him for his conduct. He deemed it "a gross and prejudicial deviation" from established procedure that was "so gross and undisputable that defense was unreasonable." Despite Cherington's order that Reed receive promotion, Snelling overruled him and instead ordered the promotional process be revised. Reed's attorney took great offense ("I'm quite bitter," he said) to Snelling's decision, believing that his client was being victimized for political purposes in an effort to "screw the lid down" on the department's growing problems leaking into public view.

"It was done," he said, "as a calculated effort to shore up the office of the commissioner of public safety" and "to quash it and ride it out."[612]

In 1978, Reed participated once again in the promotion process only to have Ryan and other officers implicated in the Router Bit Affair, captains Heffernan and Spear, sit in judgment of him. It was a foregone conclusion that he receive a low rating and Reed attributed it as "silent retribution" for his audacity to appeal his case both administratively and to the Vermont Supreme Court. As the parties awaited the court's decision (rendered in February 1979 dismissing it on jurisdictional grounds) and the sordid facts surrounding Merriam's polygraph and the St. Johnsbury matter involving his brother festered, department heads launched a secret investigation of Reed. He learned of it in early 1979 after friends told him Spear appeared at the Rockingham office inquiring about him, advising that if anyone had any questions to contact the commissioner's office.

After he requested his attorney to contact Lynch for more information, Reed received a blistering letter from Lynch demanding that he explain to him "why a lawyer was inquiring about internal state police matters."[613] While nothing more was ever said to Reed about the investigation and it never appeared in his personnel file, the entire affair remained in the minds of all the participants contributing to the significant changes finally imposed on the department in 1980.

Disillusioned troopers in the field also watched Lynch's actions closely after his arrival, witnessing other unwelcomed acts they viewed as favoritism allowing for the promotion of less qualified officers placing much further down the list to leapfrog ahead of others. They called it "the 40-to-1 man" rule, meaning that someone who scored in the 40th position jumped over those above him and received higher rank before those with better scores; a process that Labor Commissioner Cherington found "not proper."

This occurred particularly with those working at Redstone, as recounted by Trooper Dennis Bouffard, described as one of the most important witnesses in the coming troubles and a person the Keyser Commission found highly credible.

"Most of your higher-ranking promotions," he explained, "come out of the Montpelier office, and it has an awful tendency to appear that if you're in with the right crowd in Montpelier and you're in Montpelier, you tend to go places and if not, you're not going to get promoted."

The attitude of those highly placed officers opposed to innovation under Lynch's command continued to fester and interfere in making the department more effective.

"There's no place, no room in the department," Bouffard protested, "for troopers to have an open mind. We have absolutely no rights. In fact, when they hire us at the academy, they tell us to give our souls to the lord because our ass belongs to them. Our private lives are closely ridiculed. Our working life is governed quite rigidly and we're not allowed to open up any ideas. If we say something that we think might better the department, might aid the department in either saving money or being efficient or something like that, they pay absolutely no attention. We are the working force of the department and that's the way we're supposed to remain."[614]

Lynch's conduct in making other promotions also drew the attention, and ire, of the legislature because it had not made the necessary appropriations beforehand to pay for them. When called to account for his rushed actions during his confirmation hearing in the Senate, Lynch disingenuously told the committee of his concerns about the department's finances from the very beginning. He also omitted any mention of his overruling Davis's caution to not make promotions because there was neither a place for them in the table of organization or money to pay for them. "I wasn't here three weeks," he testified, "when I wrote a letter to the budget and management and told them 'Hey, what the hell's going on, the budget is going to be short; if we spend not a nickel more than what we are doing, we are going to be way over the budget.' I repeatedly brought that question up, repeatedly, because I could see what was happening. The budget was short."

Incredulous at what he heard, Vice-Chairman Donald L. Smith inquired of Lynch why his experienced staff had not made him aware of the shortfall immediately after his appointment. "We have trouble understanding," Smith said, "why somebody wouldn't explain it. Some of those men up there (in Redstone) have been there quite a few years and they have participated in several budgets."

Receiving an insufficient answer, Smith expressed his frustration again: "It's hard to understand why someone up there wouldn't explain it to you. Some of those men, some of the higher-ranking officers have been there a long time."

"We have had a hard time with management up there for several, for the past several commissioners," he continued, "and it is hard for me to understand what the problem is. We all know that at the top level, there have been problems."

Smith also sought an explanation from the department's second-in-command, Maj. Davis, about its lack of communication with the legislature in conveying the needs of the state police.

"I said," he recounted, "'Glenn, you never even told us. We are the committee that was appointed to handle police matters and traffic matters and all of us are on this committee because we asked to be here, and we're supposed to be your friends, and you never told us. How can you get there if you didn't tell us?'"

"I've never been able to understand" the conduct of VSP administrators Smith said, wondering why "other department heads seem to have a much closer relationship with the committees than does the state police, and it has always been that way, for several years."[615]

A review of the VSP's relationship with the legislature in the 1960s reveals none of these kinds of problems between them that became a reality only after the Irasburg Affair.

Pushing on after making his inexplicable promotions, the first few months of Lynch's administration saw significant restructuring of the department's chain of command creating future confusion in the field concerning officers' responsibility.

Whereas in the past the BCI detectives fell under the authority of each of the individual troop commanders, Lynch separated them out and put them under his personal supervision. Capt. Spear (who oversaw and then retracted his deceptive evaluation of Trooper Sullivan in 1970), in charge of detectives and his second-in-command, Sgt. Milford Ramey, reported directly to Lynch as they oversaw the work of their 40 plainclothes detectives.

Because Maj. Davis prepared to retire in 1978, Lynch brought in Lt. Ryan, promoting him to captain as Operations Officer and placing him in charge of the Field Force (uniformed personnel), laboratory, staff services, and administrative and civil defense personnel. Reportedly religious, Ryan's friends teasingly called him "the bishop" when he was the station commander in Rutland, but with his new assignment they deemed him "the pope."[616] "You take care of those uniform guys," Lynch told Ryan, "You know them. I'll take care of the BCI."

When Davis retired in the spring, Lynch placed Ryan into the number two role as major answerable only to him, but who continued to display little regard for the niceties of rank.[617]

As Lynch admitted to the CSP, he did not conform to the established chain of command, explaining that when he moved the BCI to Redstone he intentionally situated its office "in such a position that he could see the entrance" from where he sat in his own office. This allowed him to monitor those coming and going and when he wanted to talk to someone "he would holler to them to come into his office." "He apparently violated the chain more often than not," the investigator wrote.[618]

The muddled process of shuffling so many officers from one chain of command to another failed to specifically address their vague responsibility to report misconduct to superiors when it became known.

Conducting internal investigations always presented a ticklish problem for an agency fiercely protective of its reputation never wanting to publicly acknowledge misbehavior in its ranks. Until the problems arose under Lynch's command, internal investigations were things that the VSP did for other police agencies requesting its help, not within the department itself.

An internal investigations unit did exist at one time, but was disbanded when it "became bogged down" responding to requests for assistance from outside police agencies and "apparently was not effective."

As Ryan explained to the CSP, the practice within the VSP meant that "basically Troop Commanders handled their own (local) internal problems" in traditional fashion and did not bother headquarters. At the same time, consistent with his philosophy of not using polygraphs in internal investigations, Lynch refused to reinstitute an internal affairs unit believing that headquarters personnel could handle other allegations of misconduct.

While the current rules and regulations provided that only the commissioner could initiate an internal investigation, Lynch implemented his undefined practice on a case-by-case basis without any sense of continuity from what was expected in the field offices.

Lynch's policies did not address the concerns raised by Hebard's legislative committee in 1975 calling for change in the way internal investigations were conducted. Notwithstanding that two different procedures governed at the local and headquarters levels, the Keyser Commission attributed Lynch's actions directly to his dissatisfaction in the way that the Merriam investigation was conducted. The consequences of his unguided practice conducting internal investigations were immense, the commission concluded, and constituted "an administrative failure of major proportion" that "was a disaster." Ryan also contributed to that assessment, but sought to vindicate his own conduct telling the CSP investigators that "When Colonel Lynch came on board any semblance of internal affairs capability disappeared."[619]

In its place, the more than 200 VSP officers answerable to the two different chains of command ordered by Lynch earnestly sought to abide by the existing rules that did not make such distinctions, leaving them relying on, as one senior official expressed, "tradition." This grey area where allegations of misconduct could be reported and handled either locally or at the headquarters levels between two chains of command, dependent on subjective interpretations of their severity guided by the ad hoc determinations of superiors, caused significant confusion for officers. It ultimately contributed directly to the death of a one mired by the confusion they wrought, all because of Lynch's disastrous nonchalance, inconsistency and lack of regard for the chain of command.

Lynch's attitude failing to appreciate the need to maintain good relations with other police and state's attorneys prosecuting their cases also caused considerable problems for the department's image throughout the state. In Lamoille County, where Merriam worked to elevate the state police above the sheriff, the rift became so great that a delegation of county officials made up of businessmen, a judge and a senator traveled to Redstone in the fall of 1977 to make their concerns known.[620] In a telling explanation of his feelings about the relationships they complained about, Lynch made several observations to CSP investigators after his dismissal about why state's attorneys were "taking a shot at him." As their report relates:

> He said the community of lawyers in the State of Vermont is quite plentiful. He said that since there are numerous lawyers and very little crime that lawyers often become involved in politics. He said that they really only have a couple of things to do: either get involved in politics or go to work for the government. He said that the State's Attorneys as far as he is concerned, don't want a really professional State Police Department. He said they want to keep it small so that the Sheriff's offices and the local police departments are not outshined by the State Police. He said it's a known fact that the public defenders prevail in criminal prosecution about six to one over prosecutors. And it is for this reason that he feels that a truly professional police department would increase these odds.[621]

Such an assessment did not surprise the unimpressed, experienced officer from Connecticut conducting the interview characterizing Lynch as being "as candid as Lynch can be," inferring he could also be dissembling in his answers.[622]

The blanket allegation by the head of the VSP that county prosecutors favored sheriffs and local police to the disadvantage of their state counterparts constitutes, perhaps, one of the most bizarre positions ever expressed by one holding such high office. It also shines a light on the environment those working within the VSP faced abiding by the conditions that Lynch fostered. It exemplified the "fortress mentality" infesting Redstone's management style that author Hamilton Davis identified in the years after the Irasburg and Lawrence affairs that soon contributed to Gould's suicide.

ATTACKING THE PROSECUTORS

Any hope by Snelling his new commissioner could steer the VSP out of troubled waters soon evaporated as the strained relations between the suspicious Lynch and two elected states attorneys became evident shortly after his appointment and Merriam's promotion. They involved Merriam's deteriorating relationship with Lamoille County state's attorney P. Scott McGee and a concerned Dale O. Gray in Caledonia County that a trooper committed perjury during testimony about a case and his suspicions that other officers in the St. Johnsbury barracks were involved in criminal conduct.

The situation was so extraordinary that the two seasoned prosecutors each experienced retribution from the state police when it turned its resources to investigate their personal lives instead of the substantive complaints they made. When they reported their concerns to Snelling in the spring of 1978, they requested Merriam's immediate suspension and that "necessary steps (be taken) to commence a full scale investigation" of the VSP to determine if "supervisory officials are guilty of actionable nonfeasance or malfeasance in the handling of allegations of misconduct by Vermont State Police officers."[623]

As McGee explained, they constituted "serious law enforcement matters with statewide implications."[624] The two attorney's prescient warnings of accumulating problems within the VSP only accelerated, convulsing the department to its core soon after.

Unaware of suspicions over Merriam's past involvement with Lawrence who so tainted the public's perception of law enforcement, McGee initially endorsed his assignment to Lamoille County advocating on his behalf. He provided Merriam with space in his office allowing him to move out of the sheriff's department where troopers also worked, but which came to interfere with his own operations.

When McGee asked Merriam to not use his office as a meeting place, it promoted a stinging response that he could "bite my ass."

As their relationship deteriorated, in November 1977 the circumstances surrounding a seemingly innocuous late-night, single-car accident snowballed to shed light on Merriam's past conduct hidden from general knowledge to that time. The situation between McGee and Merriam became so strained following the accident that Merriam's supervisor, Edward Fish, notified the department's most senior official, James Ryan, that unless Lynch resolved the problem, "I respectfully request we contact the Attorney General's Office."[625]

Personally unaware of Merriam's past at the time, Fish's warning came to fruition in the next months when McGee and Gray forced the matter out of state police hands and into the governor's.

On the evening of Nov. 20, 1977, off-duty Hardwick Police Chief Michael Lauzon drove his vehicle off the road where it overturned, coming to rest on its wheels. He received non-life-threatening injuries and was found sitting on the ground by one of Merriam's officers dispatched to the scene, Trooper Kenneth Strong. The accounts provided to investigators of what happened afterwards made by Strong, deputy sheriff Donald Stubbs who arrived shortly before Strong, ambulance personnel summoned to the scene, state's attorney McGee, and Merriam tell an inconsistent story based upon their particular perspectives, and interests. Stubbs recognized that Lauzon had been drinking and told Strong that he "would not touch it with a ten-foot pole because the Chief of Hardwick Police Department was involved."[626]

While Strong also noticed that Lauzon smelled of alcohol, he decided he was not sufficiently impaired to warrant processing for driving while intoxicated, attributing the accident to excessive speed. Shortly afterwards, Strong advised McGee of the incident and who expressed concern that evidence of a motor vehicle violation avoided prosecution because the trooper did not process Lauzon for DUI.

After explaining his reasoning for not doing so, Strong reportedly admitted to McGee that, since Lauzon was a fellow police officer, "one hand washes the other" because "you'll never know when you may be in someone else's territory."[627]

McGee expressed his displeasure and immediately spoke with Merriam who reacted with surprise that Strong would have made such admissions to the prosecutor, but adding that he thought them appropriate. After speaking with Strong, Merriam was satisfied he acted appropriately and dismissed McGee's contention of any favoritism extended to Lauzon.

After conducting his own investigation and speaking with ambulance personnel, McGee became convinced that Lauzon showed sufficient signs warranting processing for DUI.

On Dec. 30, 1977, he wrote to Strong describing his disappointment that Lauzon was not processed and that the fact he was a police officer "should have had no bearing on your decision to request a breath sample."[628]

McGee sent copies of his letter to both Merriam and one of his superiors, Lt. Curtis, and days later received a response from Merriam. Exhibiting the ongoing VSP policy of dealing with problems at the local level and not involving superiors, Merriam took strong offense to both McGee's admonishment of Strong arguing that the trooper never said the things McGee reported and that he did not merit the letter "nor do I feel that a copy should have gone to Lt. Curtis."[629]

Days later, an incensed McGee took the extraordinary step of writing a blistering, three-page letter to Merriam setting the record straight concerning his conversation with Strong. The prosecutor also condemned Merriam for speaking with Lauzon about the matter while it remained under review by his office, calling it "improper and highly irregular."

Concerned that Merriam was twisting the facts, McGee wrote that "In light of what I perceive as a deliberate misstatement by you of the facts and in light of other unfounded comments in your letter, I am sending a copy of this letter to your troop commander."

He also explained why: "As a matter of policy, I send copies of written communications to field officers concerning performance of their duties to supervising officers. This ensures that the command officers are aware of the problems or developing problems among the troopers."

Upset at being in this position, McGee ended, "We've all got more than a full-time job on our hands to help keep the public peace and well-being. It is unfortunate to have to devote time to problems such as this one." This time, he sent copies of his letter to Curtis, Fish, and Lynch.[630] McGee's efforts earned him a rapid response from Fish taking strong exception that in going over his head to the commissioner he "did not follow accepted management procedure" and violated the chain of command.

"I hope I have made my point," Fish wrote, "You run your office and do not ask me or my men for advice," calling for the end of this "childish bickering." He also warned that "I will continue to do what I feel is right and will not be intimidated by you complaining about me or my men to my commissioner or anyone else."[631]

Refusing to be intimidated himself by what he viewed as VSP intransigence and defensive posturing, McGee wrote directly to Lynch. The sarcasm contained in Fish's letter, he wrote, and the "more serious matter" of Merriam's willful misstatements of facts, together with his "outrageous" language when asked to cease using his office, led him to request Lynch to take "appropriate disciplinary action."[632]

The timing of McGee's demand could not have been more fortuitous because on Jan. 20, 1978, Lynch appeared before a Senate committee to confirm his earlier appointment as commissioner. During the hearing questions arose about the department's past failures in not communicating with the legislature about fiscal and disciplinary matters. Caledonia County Sen. Gerald Morse explained that when VSP headquarters lingered in responding to an inquiry he took direct action that reveals the lax protocol existing between members of the legislative and executive branches in such matters.

"We called St. Johnsbury (the VSP barracks) and we called the trooper," Morse said, before continuing, "He stopped in and told me that we would get a full report, and we haven't had any report on that." In explaining why there might have been a delay, Lynch responded that "My policy is, whenever there is a complaint, from any source, justified or whatever, involving a state police officer, immediately, a command officer investigates the case."[633]

What Lynch did not understand at that defining moment was the unfolding consequences of his recent reorganization of the department with its two chains of command lacking definitive guidance to officers on how to implement his policies. However, he did have a general understanding about the circumstances of the case Morse referred to when he said he met with a trooper because the senator told him about it when they conferred outside of the committee hearing room. It concerned Morse's meeting with St. Johnsbury detective David Reed whom he knew since he was a child calling him "a good cop and the type that would arrest his own mother if she did anything wrong."[634]

As Morse recounted his meeting with Reed to CSP investigators, the officer told him "about troopers being involved with stolen router bits at the St. Johnsbury Troop" and nothing more. In his version of meeting with Morse, Lynch explained that the senator only told him "that the FBI was involved in a 'big thing' in St. Johnsbury."[635]

When Lynch inquired of his former employer about the allegation, he said they reported "they had nothing going in St. Johnsbury at the time." However, Lynch soon learned more about the situation and contacted Morse to tell him he "would take the necessary steps."

Lynch also had much on his mind about the allegations of misconduct taking place in Caledonia and Lamoille counties when he met personally with McGee just days after his confirmation hearing. He listened to the prosecutor repeat his complaints about Merriam, seeking his transfer out of Lamoille County because he could no longer trust him due to his "intentional distortion of facts" in the Lauzon matter and "recent activities in attempting to alter the known facts" (reportedly trying to discourage Deputy Stubbs from accurately describing his discussions with Strong at the accident scene) about it.

McGee also wrote to Merriam to tell him what he was doing, lamenting that the officer's actions had "shattered" his trust in him.[636] Lynch responded to McGee's concerns immediately and had a meeting with Strong, Merriam, and Fish, attended by "the appropriate supervisory officers."

Afterwards, he wrote to McGee refusing his request to transfer Merriam. He also reportedly emphasized his policy to those in the meeting that: all citizens receive equal treatment; professional courtesy be extended to others; and, importantly, "Problems as to procedure or policy are to be referred through assigned channels to me for resolution."

Lynch's positioning in this instance may not have satisfied McGee, but they put on record, in a manner consistent with his recent promise to the Senate committee, that through the actions of his unnamed supervisory officers he would address problems associated with VSP procedure and policy. Those representations faced a dire test in the next months as the approaching Router Bit Affair percolated.

In the meantime, on Feb. 6, McGee banned Merriam from his office unless he had an appointment, instructed him not to call after hours unless for an emergency. He also refused to accept any of his, or other troopers', paperwork for cases they submitted unless approved by a supervisor.[637]

Refusing to accept inaction by the head of the state police, the determined McGee branched out and sought additional information on Merriam that resulted in his discovery of explosive evidence surrounding the missing 1974 polygraph exam. After receiving guidance from individuals that Merriam lied during both the exam and inquest proceedings and that proof of it could be found in the sealed Paul Lawrence files in a St. Albans courthouse, McGee met with Fish at his office on March 3, 1978.[638]

He told him he had strong evidence from "highly credible sources that Merriam had failed the polygraph," but Fish denied it. He said he already knew that Merriam had taken a polygraph exam because he told him, but that he had passed it. Fish promised to look further into the matter and contact him, but, as the attorney recorded, he "never heard back."

The reason for Fish's failure to respond is because he apparently alerted his Redstone superiors that McGee found something threatening to harm the department.

As a part of its later investigation into the actions of the VSP concerning Sen. Morse's report of the router bit matter in St. Johnsbury, when the attorney general's office examined the companion matter of Merriam's polygraph exam, it admitted that this "peculiar saga has not been resolved." Meeting with obstruction in its efforts, the attorney general attributed the problem to "persons within the Department (who) have not been straightforward."

Questions arose over the timing when Lynch became aware of the missing report and who explained that upon learning of it in

March 1978 "he ordered a full search." When asked about its scope, Lynch told investigators "Everybody was looking. See, for anything involving the Merriam polygraph, any damn thing."

But he did not do the most obvious thing, the attorney general reasonably noted, writing that "for a police agency, the search was either not professional or earnest. It apparently occurred to no one to get a copy from the most logical, certain source: the (Maine State Police) examiner."[639]

Adding to the drama, the attorney general's report also revealed the curious fact that, despite the supposedly confidential inquiry, "Merriam was kept informed" of its progress.

Three days after McGee met with Fish and only three days before his probationary promotion to sergeant expired and became final, on March 6 Merriam met with McGee. The officer admitted to him that, while "there had been a conflict between his testimony and another officer's," he took and passed a polygraph.

However, none of the information that McGee had uncovered and conveyed to Lynch and Fish, his reports of Merriam's misconduct and his dissatisfaction, the complaints of Lamoille County officials, the frantic search for a polygraph examination showing Merriam's dishonesty existed and was known by Maj. Davis and in the possession of the Maine State Police meant anything.

On March 9, Lynch ignored it all and made Merriam's promotion permanent, noting that his performance evaluation rated him "excellent, exceeds job requirements."[640]

McGee charged ahead to gain access to the polygraph report in the court's files and contacted Lawrence investigation special prosecutor Gensburg, Attorney General Diamond, a deputy sheriff and a court clerk. He also spoke with a local defense attorney who told him of incidents in which it appeared Merriam may have lied and his apparent attempts to discourage other officers from dealing candidly and openly with him.

After alerting Gov. Snelling's aide William Gilbert about the situation in early April, Lynch immediately called McGee to inquire if he "had information relating to possible illegal conduct by a trooper." The attorney declined to answer.

Soon after, unsuccessful in his efforts to obtain his transfer, McGee had had enough with Merriam and told him unequivocally that "I do not want you to participate in criminal investigations in this county," because, no doubt influenced by the cascading avalanche of information he accumulated, "I am unable to rely on facts related by you in presenting a case for prosecution."

Delivering him a direct slap, McGee told Merriam that one case he had recently forwarded to his office would not be prosecuted and that he would advise the defendant not to appear in court.[641] The following day, in a caution already well in progress, Fish wrote to Ryan that unless Lynch resolved the boiling problem, the attorney general should be advised.

After receiving permission from a judge on April 20, 1978 to look at the sealed Lawrence files, McGee traveled to St. Albans, located the Merriam polygraph report and made a copy of it. Demonstrating how well Merriam remained abreast of what McGee was up to, he boldly appeared in the prosecutor's office to confront him. According to McGee's secretary, Merriam inquired of her if he "had gone to Maine," and that neighboring county state's attorney Gray "must have some friends in Maine DA offices" because "they were checking into his polygraph and were talking to the person who ran it."[642]

Merriam had no involvement with Gray in neighboring Caledonia County at that time, but the circumstances surrounding a sworn affidavit filed by Trooper Thomas Truex in St. Johnsbury concerning an unrelated matter led the prosecutor to suspect its truthfulness. The affidavit involved a 1977 burglary case where Truex recounted a set of facts from an interview that the witness later recanted, leading Gray to become suspicious and institute a complaint with the VSP in October 1977. Seeking to exonerate himself, Truex sought permission from Lynch to allow him to take a polygraph examination to show his truthfulness.

However, Lynch refused because "he did not and would not use the polygraph" in internal investigations.[643] It took many months before the cloud of suspicion was removed from above the innocent officer's head after Truex successfully completed a polygraph conducted by an outside examiner. Concerning the VSP's internal investigation of the matter, the CSP wrote that it was conducted with "no supervision and direction" and could have been resolved in Truex's favor early on had Lynch approved the polygraph in the first place.[644]

Gray experienced further frustration with another VSP internal investigation that summer when Lynch refused him access to one concerning the conduct of a trooper injured in a late-night fight outside of a St. Johnsbury barroom in June. Attempting to ascertain as much information as possible to guide his prosecutorial duties, Gray expressed his displeasure at Lynch's interference that allowed the problem to "fester and boil" instead of finding a resolution.[645]

As uncomfortable information about the VSP threatened to surface, a vindictive Lynch, aided by members of his command staff, decided to launch investigations into the two problematic state's attorneys. The popular and repeatedly elected (since 1970), and president of the Vermont State's Attorney's Association, Caledonia State's Attorney Gray, became the subject of one of them. After Trooper Carol Kostelnik (one of the first two females hired by the department in 1976) was assigned to his office as an investigator in 1978, Lynch summoned her supervisor, David Reed at the St. Johnsbury barracks, and ordered him to conduct an investigation into their "social relationship."

The married Gray had taken a trip to Pennsylvania with Kostelnik to interview a witness in a rape case and Lynch told Reed, in Ryan's and Spear's presence, that he wanted to do an investigation on the two, but which Reed viewed instead as an effort to "get something on Gray."

Reed later spoke with Spear and declined to conduct the inquiry "because it would get them into trouble." Abuse of authority entered into Reed's mind because, as the attorney general's report described, he "had cause to believe that the Department had a policy of using its facilities to retaliate against a person suspected of trying to impeach the Department."[646]

Regarding McKee's complaint concerning Merriam, this second investigation focused instead on the prosecutor. As the attorney general's report noted, this investigation "pursued any avenue which held out the possibility of discrediting the State's Attorney rather than pursuing that information and those leads with direct bearing on the announced purpose of the investigation."

The report further concluded that "Responsibility for the improper direction of the internal investigation must be apportioned not only among the investigating officers but their superiors as well."[647]

The oversight that Redstone exercised concerning McGee's complaints was facilitated by the extraordinary process it employed. Merriam was now a sergeant and past practice meant that any investigation of him should be conducted by officers of a higher rank. Instead, Lynch tapped two corporals, Gordon Adams and Edward Farmer, to, as Adams recounted of his conversation with him, "Get your ass going in Lamoille County to see what's going on" concerning McGee's questioning Merriam's integrity.[648]

The assignment of corporals to investigate a superior officer was so unusual that former Commissioner Baumann told investigators "I would never do that" and Lt. Fish advised "That's not typical at all." When asked if he could explain why this process was used in the Merriam matter, Fish responded "No, I can't. I certainly can't, department procedure is to assign senior officers."[649]

Justifying their decision and the ticklish questions it posed, Lynch and Ramey later sidestepped the issue and told investigators that this was not an internal investigation, but a "fact-finding investigation."[650] Regardless of how they wanted to characterize the situation by focusing on McGee's concerns over Merriam's "integrity," the central issue remained the officer's credibility which by its very nature involved his personal conduct and whether or not he should remain a member of the VSP.

The attorney general's report into Adams's and Farmer's investigation provides a scathing assessment of unimaginative, biased police work performed over the course of ten days resulting in a final report submitted on April 25, 1978 exonerating Merriam. Had they conducted a truly professional inquiry, the attorney general describes, they could have very easily uncovered, and made known to their purportedly uninformed superiors, the ticking timebomb that Merriam's polygraph report presented.

Advised by McGee during an interview that special prosecutor Gensburg might have relevant information about Merriam, Farmer contacted him. When asked if he had any recent contact or information about Merriam, Gensburg replied that he did not. However, he offered to Farmer that he had information about Merriam's involvement in the Lawrence matter, but was immediately cut off when Farmer told him he was "not interested in that."

Refusing to be treated in that manner, Gensburg pressed on and said, according to McGee's account of a call Ginsburg made to him immediately afterward, "he was going to tell him anyway." Gensburg then "proceeded to tell Farmer about Merriam's inquest testimony and the conflict (with other witness testimony) as well as the fact that Merriam had flunked the polygraph examination."[651] When Farmer was later interviewed about his comment to Gensburg, he simply said that he "didn't know" if he had said something like that.[652]

Farmer and Adams conducted other interviews, but the attorney general's overall assessment of their efforts concluded that they concentrated on inconsequential matters as they "cavalierly discarded" information about Merriam's polygraph and did not focus on McGee's concerns, but, rather, in finding information to discredit him. Condemning the process and results of the investigation, the attorney general wrote, "These matters relate to the integrity of those in command of the (DPS). If any in a command position have violated their public trust by withholding crucial information or by actively seeking to conceal or distort evidence demonstrating serious misconduct by a member of the Department, the basis for their continued association with the Department has been compromised and their positions should be surrendered or terminated."[653]

Assessing the totality of the case against Merriam, the attorney general unequivocally concluded that he "be dismissed from the Vermont State Police for gross misconduct."[654] Unconcerned, the VSP command found nothing to fault with the Adams-Farmer investigation. As Lt. Fish recalled, one of the BCI supervisors told him that "Stanley came out looking like a hero."[655]

The brazenness of Lynch, Ryan and Spear to utilize department resources in an effort to undermine political opponents represents one of the most unsavory aspects of how members of the VSP high command conducted themselves in this post-Irasburg and Lawrence time period.

Pivotal Meeting

Confident that substantial evidence of misconduct existed, McGee and Gray sought a meeting with Snelling's attorney, William Gilbert. On May 1, 1978, the two prosecutors, Gilbert, governor's assistant John Gray, Attorney General Diamond, his chief of the criminal division, Assistant Attorney General Paul Hudson, and Lynch gathered. McGee objected to Lynch's presence because his conduct provided the reason for their gathering, but was overruled by the governor's representatives. They discussed Merriam's performance in the Lauzon matter and when McGee brought up the subject of his 1974 polygraph examination it drew a curious response from Lynch. Apparently taken aback, according to McGee's three-page account of the meeting, Lynch said this was "the first time he had heard anything" about it.[656]

His statement made little sense when compared to his later statement to investigators that just weeks before their meeting he ordered a search of Redstone and that "Everybody was looking for anything involving the Merriam polygraph, any damn thing."

As the meeting continued, and Lynch had time to reflect on his comment, he changed his story. Now, he said that "all he remembered about the polygraph was that someone had told him about it and that the results were 'at best,' inconclusive and, at worst, inconclusive."

McGee pressed him as to why he first denied any knowledge of the test only to reverse himself and acknowledge it, but "Lynch gave no explanation."

For Attorney General Diamond, Lynch's amateur performance left him with the clear impression "that he acted shocked."[657] McGee then produced the report and allowed Lynch to read it, observing that he did not convey "any notable facial or other expressions," had "virtually no reaction" or "express verbally any surprise or concern about the report's contents."

Neither did Lynch ever relate, McGee wrote, "that he had previously ordered a search for the polygraph report or had attempted to locate a copy to review personally."

Clear that the VSP had significant problems, the attendees decided that Diamond's office should conduct an investigation into

Merriam that Lynch agreed to because, he wrote, they were "of serious import to the State Police, the State's Attorneys and the public."[658]

Unable to avoid doing otherwise, Lynch also agreed to remove Merriam "from all functions in Lamoille County" and "from any involvement whatsoever with matters involving criminal investigation, the handling or preparation of evidence, or any other matter involving criminal cases such as chain of custody."[659]

When an alarmed Gov. Snelling learned of the situation, he specifically warned Lynch against any interference telling him "To let the Attorney General handle the investigation and not to get involved."[660]

The press actively monitored the situation in Lamoille County and when Lynch was questioned about the high-level meeting a couple of days later, he adopted a decidedly defensive posture mischaracterizing what happened. "Nobody investigates my department," he said, "If it needs investigating, I do it" and that if anybody questioned VSP procedures, they had "better come and see me."[661]

A contentious war of words immediately followed when McGee told the press that Lynch "was being misleading," drawing a dismissive response, "I am not going to comment on Mr. McGee's statements."[662]

The date when Merriam's polygraph exam was finally found remains unknown. Two secretaries working for Maj. Davis and Lynch provided conflicting information that could have clarified when he became aware of it. One said she found it in April in Davis's files and another said she was mistaken in her recollection.

Regardless, days after his meeting with attorneys and governor's representatives, on May 11 Lynch wrote to Hudson that, following a search of state police headquarters "some days ago," it was located on May 9.[663]

The report, according to Lynch, "had been filed in a plain, unmarked vanilla envelope with no cross reference or other identifiable data in a section marked 'Polygraph.'" As the attorney general's report of the matter found, despite the confusion in 1978, Lynch never answered the overriding question of why he finalized Merriam's promotion on March 9 when so much evidence of the report's existence and its disqualifying contents, particularly in the files of the Maine State Police, was known.

Lynch's policies reinforced pre-existing practices prohibiting any interference from outside the department questioning its conduct. Nor did they allow for legislatively recommended changes in the way that internal investigations were conducted because of his adamant refusal to allow either a separate unit charged with that responsibility or permit polygraph examinations of officers.

Rather than a new face with fresh perspectives able to turn the VSP around and foster better relations with police and prosecutors that Snelling hoped for, the brash, easily-slighted former FBI agent served as a lightning rod drawing off critical attention from the overall needs of the state's law enforcement community. His defensive, turf-protecting attitude squandered many opportunities calling for him to rise above the discord and extend an olive branch to those who disagreed with him and watched as he descended into the siege mentality that author Hamilton Davis reported in the department in 1978.

While the cops on the beat from all agencies sought to work together, Lynch, in particular, drew the ire of the Vermont Police Chiefs' Association (VPCA) that year. Attempting to establish uniform training for all departments, the organization ran into continued opposition from Lynch who believed that state police should stand apart from them in an attitude characterized as "parochialism" standing in the way of everyone's increased professionalism. Lynch's "current views and philosophies are counterproductive," they wrote, "to professionalism of law enforcement personnel and management system in the state of Vermont." "Our disagreements," the president of the association offered in a qualified manner, "are only with the commissioner and his top advisors, perhaps."[664]

Lynch's inability to bend to the demands calling for change in the years immediately after the pivotal Paul Lawrence debacle offered yet another opportunity for discord marking 1979 as the Vermont State Police's *annus mirabilis*.

Chapter 11

BLOSSOMING WEEDS

CONTINUING DISCORD

LYNCH'S CONTENTIOUS RELATIONSHIP with many in the law enforcement community significantly tainted what should have been one of mutual respect and cooperation. However, as a front-page *Rutland Herald* headline blared in October 1978, "Lynch Blasts Back At His Detractors," accompanied by an image of the civilian commissioner wearing a crisp uniform, all was not well among them.[665]

Three months earlier, on its 10th anniversary, the press reminded the public once again of the department's purported discriminatory actions during the Irasburg Affair.[666] Could it ever escape the findings of the that board of inquiry and the pundits' persistent lambasting of its reputation? Now, calling critics of his policy that the state police deserved treatment apart from other police "divisive" and "suspect," Lynch garnered little sympathy in return.

Rather than quietly declining to assist in a misdirected effort that could avoid embarrassment, Lynch publicly lashed out at Montpelier Police Chief Douglas Franks for approaching him with a "damn fool witch-burning enterprise."

Franks had met with Lynch and offered up a harebrained proposal seeking VSP assistance to investigate, as Lynch reported to Snelling, "homosexuality in the Montpelier High School as well as sex misconduct at the Vermont Legislature."[667]

In his defense, Franks turned on Lynch and said he "was way off base" and only refused to participate "because he could not be in control of it."

At the same time, Lynch also questioned Attorney General Diamond's proposal to create an organized crime strike force in Chittenden County and said that he "was not the "chief cop'" in the state, or possessed the competency to run such an operation. Lynch drew so much suspicion from police leadership in general that when the head of the VPCA, Winooski Chief Roger Willard, met with him, he carried a hidden tape recorder. Willard admitted he did so because "I distrust him."[668]

Growing increasingly cautious and paranoid when speaking with reporters, Lynch confided to Snelling one particular insight.

"On a small bulletin board next to my desk," he wrote, "where I post a variety of notes to myself, for some months I have had a piece of paper with three (reporters') names on it. The reminder is for me to be very careful with these three individuals who have scorched me in the past."[669] Lynch's caution reflects the continuing attitude of the VSP command staff to remain leery of the press in this post-Irasburg environment, unwilling to experience a repeat of that harsh time when they received a barrage of derogatory ridicule surrounding that investigation.

Lynch's other conduct within the VSP constituted a growing crisis in the governor's mind after reading this latest communication when his advisors made their own feelings known. In an alarming memorandum, counsel Gilbert wrote to Snelling on Oct. 2, 1978, that in light of "the obviously growing problems of (DPS) internal administration" that "Lynch is badly managing, in part, because he is badly managed."

Whereas "we thought we had a hero," he said, "instead we have a normal human with some advantages and many disadvantages." Gilbert expressed his frustration at the executive department's inability to penetrate into the internal workings of the "completely insular" state police to allow it to understand what was going on so that they could provide direction. Instead, he wrote that "we deal only with the tip of the Pyramid" in the form of Lynch who "always says 'everything's ok' or somebody else is wrong and/or is attacking his department and men." The time had come, Gilbert and fellow advisor John Gray thought, to reorganize the DPS and move quickly to engage the legislature.[670]

Snelling received further encouragement from one of Vermont's most iconic figures: Vermont Country Store founder, Vrest Orton. In a letter marked "Private and Confidential" written two days after Gilbert's memo, Orton reminded Snelling of his service as a past member of the Law Enforcement Training Council when it suggested changes within the DPS to then-Gov. Salmon.

Orton repeated his concerns and said that while Lynch "is an excellent officer of the State Police," he was "not necessarily a Commissioner of Public Safety." Orton called for significant change in the form of a "re-organization of the whole police system" and that as a result "everybody would be happier."[671]

At the same time, Gray sent Snelling a memo describing another communication from Lynch that was "a defense of State Police activities in particular against the characters involved in this continuing scenario." After asking Snelling to "review quite carefully" its contents, the exasperated governor returned the memo to him, pleading with emphasis in large script, "John—Please don't <u>do</u> this to me. Please review it yourself if it is worth it and tell me what is important!"[672]

The DPS faced continuing budgetary problems in 1978–1979 because of significant bureaucratic obstacles within state government impeding the flow of federal dollars down to those actually delivering police services. Maj. Ryan explained to the VTA that any differences the press reported between the department and sheriffs and local departments were actually few and "personal" in nature.[673] Instead, the problems that law enforcement faced, he said, stemmed from an ongoing "budget crunch" pitting various interests against one another.

The U. S. Department of Justice, through its Law Enforcement Assistance Administration (LEAA), provided the states with significant funding for police services, but only if they abided by strict criteria yielding measurable results to assure their compliance. In 1977 and 1978, plans submitted by Vermont officials were so deficient the LEAA's top administrator wrote to Snelling that "at a time when the vast majority of the states were receiving multi-year approvals, (in 1978) we awarded Vermont only single-year approval in the hope that the plan would improve." That did not happen for the 1979 plan causing him to lament that it had actually "deteriorated in quality" from the prior year's plan forcing him to refuse its funding request because of "substantial non-compliance" with the law. Offering help to correct the problem, he ended on a positive note hoping that "Vermont's criminal justice system would benefit from an improvement in comprehensive planning and (I) hope that you see this as an opportunity to take advantage of that benefit."[674]

The principal bureaucratic impediment to Vermont's ability to disperse federal funds rested with the Governor's Commission on the Administration of Justice (GCAJ), headed by former DPS commissioner Baumann. He was not himself the obstacle, but, instead, the cumbersome, 21-member board, made up of individuals that Snelling characterized as "bleeding hearts favoring idealistic rehabilitative and juvenile programs" stood in the way.[675]

Lynch derided them as "professional educators, social workers, experts in grantsmanship" with no experience in law enforcement. Further, the heavily staffed operation, manned by thirty individuals, drew off so much money in salaries that it left little for actual police services. Lynch said that when he attended their meetings "small cliques banded together to obtain funding for their own projects," that the staff "had a long standing posture of opposition if not actual feuding with the State Police," and that their records revealed "of the million dollars (of federal money) to be allotted only some $35,000 to $40,000 can be traced to going to State Police operations."[676]

Ryan agreed with his assessment and explained that "the vying for funds between state and local police could well be the source of aggravation that has resulted in the deterioration of relationships between the two levels of law enforcement."[677]

Based on recommendations by Gilbert and Gray echoing the recent calls by the Cost Control Council, and no doubt guided by Gov. Deane Davis's call in 1971 for the creation of a "super agency,"

Snelling moved forward with a similar plan. Police instruction remained the crux of the problem as Snelling sought uniformity of training throughout all levels of law enforcement while Lynch argued that the VSP deserved separate consideration that did not place it under the control of another entity.

"Unfortunately," Snelling told the press, "Our current system leads to confrontation, public charges of bad faith and elitism and provides no convenient mechanism for the resolution of the dispute, without legislative intervention in the form of budget action." Singling out the sole problem to his mind, he emphasized that "A new management structure is badly needed if the public safety of Vermonters in future years is to be assured. The organization of the (VSP), at the State level, no matter how well executed, inherently fails to require that the interest of local law enforcement be taken into account."

In short, he said that the department "has been unable to meet a dual responsibility to both the Vermont State Police and the interest of local law enforcement." The solution required the creation of a single "Public Safety Agency" headed by a cabinet-level civilian secretary to whom the Commissioner of State Police, the Adjutant General, a Director of Communications and Records, a Director of Training and Certification and a Director of Administrative Services reported.[678]

Snelling's proposal immediately earned praise from the Vermont Police Chiefs Association believing it could "alleviate the parochialism present in some law enforcement circles within the state."[679] However, on Feb. 23, 1979, he faced tough questioning from the press about its effect on the VSP. By then Lynch had time to digest and consider what it meant to his independence and made his great displeasure known widely. He surprised and publicly embarrassed Snelling's aides Gilbert and Mallary who believed he had already agreed to the proposal but then backtracked and railed against it before a legislative committee.[680]

While Snelling acknowledged to the press that "there is some justification in the charge of elitism" within the agency, he emphasized where the problem lay. When he discussed aspects of the proposal with Lynch, he said that he "made it quite clear that he feels that the State Police must not only guide their own training, but should not be called upon to follow the same rules and regulations as other levels of law enforcement and should, in fact, be in charge, really, of all training of all law enforcement officers."

Concerning the new agency itself, Snelling said that "I am afraid I lost his confidence."

> Reporter: So, he is not too thrilled with that particular proposal.
>
> Snelling: He hasn't told me directly how badly he feels about it, but he has told others how badly he feels about it and Vermont is a very small state.
>
> Reporter: You have a policy disagreement with the Commissioner of Public Safety.
>
> Snelling: That would appear to be the case.

While Snelling did not challenge Lynch's advocating a position contrary to his, he related frustrations with his public stance: "Commissioner Lynch is very unhappy with the present training circumstance. He is making that displeasure clear to almost anyone who will listen. And I, frankly, believe his attitude is exacerbating the conflict between the local police and the State Police. I am as much a supporter of the state police as he is, but I think his conduct in this affair is not helping the image and the support of the general public for the state police."

Regardless of how the proposal proceeded, Snelling said that he expected Lynch "to obey the law" and to "arrange his budget and his forces in order to live within those ground rules."[681]

Meanwhile, the attorney general's investigation concerning Merriam proceeded fostering yet additional discord between his office and Lynch. Four days after Snelling's press conference, Diamond wrote to warn Lynch. In a letter marked confidential, he said that, "it is my opinion that Sgt. Stanley T. Merriam has violated his oath of office as a Vermont State Police Officer" and referred the matter back to Lynch to handle administratively.[682]

Lynch dallied and, contrary to his promise on May 1, 1978 to not allow Merriam to handle law enforcement matters, placed him in charge of the state's drunk driving and truck weighing projects. After months of not responding to Diamond's recommendation, Lynch disingenuously explained that he had not done so because he did not receive a memorandum of law to support his conclusion.[683] Lynch's explanation left the attorney general "baffled," but willing to meet and let him review a draft of the report.[684] However, Lynch "repeatedly postponed meetings" and never saw it until it came out in June.[685]

The next months brought increased pressure, headed by Gilbert, to bring members of the legislature on board with Snelling's single agency proposal. Calling it "an important legislative priority of the governor," he gained the support of two senators to sponsor Senate Bill 156 to make the new agency a reality and went on to solicit further approval from other state leaders.[686] Troubles for Snelling persisted as he directly intervened to obtain backing from another senator, reiterating in May that "the underlying problems facing law enforcement in Vermont continues."[687]

Snelling also faced concerns about his personal safety leading Lynch to assign a trooper to his office for the duration of the legislative session.[688] When an instructor at the Pittsford training academy controlled by the VCJTC ran afoul of his superiors for badmouthing his former employer, the Bennington Police Department, alleging low morale, he was fired. Questioned by the public asking why the VSP did this, Lynch predictably distanced himself and pointed out that the VCJTC was a separate agency.

"Hell," Lynch said, "I didn't fire anybody. This whole thing is none of my business." Unwilling to leave the subject in a gracious manner, he went on to interject his own interpretation about facts he had no information on and disparaged the VCJTC administrator for firing the trainer: "That's a hell of a note, isn't it? What in the world is that poor guy going to do now?"[689]

Meanwhile, other aspects of Vermont law enforcement imploded with the election of former Orleans County deputy sheriff Leroy Null to the position of state's attorney.

Null exploited a loophole in the law that did not require state's attorneys to have a law license and campaigned on a platform appealing to voters to elect someone from outside the legal establishment. People were tired of attorneys dictating to them, Null said, and he promised to treat them differently leading to his defeat of an attorney backed by the county legal profession. Only days before his appointment on Feb. 1, 1979, he was involved in a bizarre incident working as a security guard in which he fired two shots at a car leaving a dance. Nobody was harmed, but his actions brought the VSP in to conduct an investigation to forward to Diamond's office.[690]

In the week following Null's swearing-in, the legislature considered his peculiar situation. In a move the press described as "a strong show of dislike for the legal profession," the House overwhelmingly rejected any requirement that a state's attorney be a lawyer by a vote of 122–21.

One of its members said the reason for the action was because "electing a lawyer to be county prosecutor is no guarantee of getting a qualified person."

"A turkey is a turkey," she said, "no matter what his profession."[691] Null's tenure over the course of the next year faced many challenges when a judge refused to allow him to handle cases in his courtroom and irate citizens and members of law enforcement expressed their displeasure at his dismissal of dozens of serious matters they believed involved his friends and supporters. It also caused hardship in neighboring Caledonia County where State's Attorney Gray provided him with support drawing off needed resources from his office ("too damn many hours," he said) preparing cases for him.

"There is no enforcement up there," Gray said, "It's gotten out of hand: he can't do anything up there."[692]

The incredible situation lasted throughout 1979 that saw a grand jury launch an investigation into allegations of misconduct by the Orleans County sheriff and Null, resulting in Null's indictment that December on five counts of perjury and the destruction of evidence. The situation became so untenable that the legislature became involved to consider, for the second time in three years after the Mayo fiasco in Washington County, his impeachment.

It all ended in April 1980 when Null died of natural causes leaving a legacy, described by one newspaper as "one of the most bizarre and controversial chapters in recent Vermont history—one that saw the wheels of justice in this remote NEK county grind to a virtual halt."[693]

ROUTER BITS

While Snelling and his assistants considered their path forward with the new Agency of Public Safety and squabbled with Lynch's "badly managing" the VSP, on Jan. 12, 1979, 28-year-old Nelson Lee Charron appeared in Caledonia County district court. He came to resolve a minor criminal charge investigated by BCI detective David Reed and brought against him by State's Attorney Gray. It concerned his involvement in the theft of some 30 router bits, valued at about $40, from his place of employment at the Northeast Tool Division of the Vermont American Corporation in Lyndon.

While the otherwise seemingly trivial charge was resolved with Charron's plea of no contest to a single count of petty theft and a minimal fine of $50 imposed, the story behind it irrevocably changed the lives of many people, convulsing the VSP to its core.

Before his plea, Charron's case percolated with varying intensity within the VSP since the beginning of the prior year when county Sen. Morse learned of it from Reed that led to his questioning of Lynch about it during his confirmation hearing in January 1978.

As Morse and Lynch confirmed, they had discussed Morse's misinterpretation of Reed's information that the FBI was investigating "a big thing" in St. Johnsbury concerning "troopers being involved with stolen router bits."

Lynch professed no knowledge of the matter and subsequently confirmed with that agency it had no such investigation underway. James Ryan, who accompanied Lynch during the hearing, quickly dismissed the allegation as simply "politics" because he thought "the committee, including Morse, didn't particularly care for Lynch." Ryan also displayed disinterest in a similar report at the time made by St. Johnsbury station commander Sgt. Robert Fields, whom he considered a "tale-carrier."

When questions later arose concerning when Ryan became aware of the problems surrounding Charron, his questionable response to CSP investigators reported it was not until over a year-and-a-half later in July 1979. It constituted a clear misrepresentation of what happened when the evidence revealed he knew something was amiss much earlier during Lynch's confirmation hearing constituting much more than the "tempest in a tea pot" scenario he tried to portray it as.[694]

However, by that later date the damage caused by his, Lynch's, and other commanding officers' failure to take seriously allegations of misconduct within their ranks had been done. During the eighteen-month interim, Reed sought to abide by the department's ambiguous internal regulations to report to his superiors what he knew of the situation early on while abiding by the jumbled chain of command caused by Lynch's recent changes. Those confusions, exacerbated by the attitude of VSP senior officers scurrying for cover when their actions surrounding the Charron and Merriam situations came to light at the same time, resulted in other investigations frustrated at their inability to obtain clarity on what happened in each instance. As the attorney general's investigation about their responses relates, "There are more versions of the sequence of events than there are persons involved in them."[695]

It made reconciling their varying accounts so difficult that it interfered in pursuing charges against deserving individuals. It also demonstrated the fortress mentality that infused a command staff seeking to deflect the incoming tide of bad press in this post-Irasburg environment.

Despite the neglect of VSP officials and the destruction of their records in the next decades documenting their involvement, the substance of what occurred in Caledonia County from 1978–1979 can be reconstructed with reasonable accuracy because of the ensuing official investigations.

Nelson "Ticker" Charron began work at the Vermont American plant in 1976 as a grinder on an assembly line producing between eight and nine million router bits a year for the company's principal customer, Sears & Roebuck.

Conflicting accounts report that employees could remove defective bits freely for their own use from a discard bin, while others say it could be done only with permission, which Charron did not have. Rumors within the community related that so many bits became available because of the company's lax policy that nobody purchased any at the local Sears store.

Even Maj. Ryan knew years earlier of the practice when he worked in the St. Johnsbury area. "My wife came home with a bag full of oh probably eight drills," he recounted in sworn testimony, "that a friend of hers had given her."

When she told him who they came from, Ryan related, "I knew" the person because "he worked up there and said they were seconds and that they gave them away." Not wanting his wife to face the prospect of any embarrassment for receiving the bits, Ryan admitted that "I didn't want them and didn't want anything to do with them, so I threw them away."[696]

The same year Charron started grinding drill bits he became an auxiliary trooper during the winter months working in the VSP's snowmobile enforcement program. He obtained the position after Cpl. Howard Gould, from the St. Johnsbury barracks, recruited him allowing Charron opportunities to interact with other troopers under Gould's command. When the conduct of all the troopers later fell under suspicion because of their association with Charron, Gould became immensely embarrassed, blaming himself for the resulting mess. A quiet and proud man, Gould was profoundly and deeply affected by what happened because of this trivial event that spun out of control and took on a life of its own, ending in the loss of his.

Howard Gary Gould was born in Fitchburg, Mass. in 1942 to parents Howard George Gould, originally from Danby, Vermont, and Thelma Gould, from Mansonville, Quebec. He graduated from Rutland High School in 1959 where, showing an early interest in maintaining order, the faculty selected him to serve on the Monitor Squad. The group identified itself by prominent armbands showing their authority in order to assure "that student traffic moved in smooth and orderly fashion" through the building's corridors.

Nicknamed "Ace," Gould's efforts earned him additional monikers of "Stern monitor," "delightfully different," and, because he served as both Shop Council chairman and elected treasurer of industrial arts, "Shop Shark"[697] Following the example of older brother George who joined the U.S. Air Force two years earlier, Gould enlisted in the Navy after graduation and headed to the Great Lakes Naval Training Station for basic training.[698] After completing additional instruction at the Naval Air Technical Training Center in Memphis, Tenn. in 1961, he went to the Naval Air Station in Sanford, Florida as an aviation fire control technician third class assigned to Heavy Attack Squadron Seven aboard the *USS Enterprise*.[699]

After his discharge in 1963, Gould returned to Vermont, working temporarily at a Springfield machine manufacturing company before joining the VSP on Feb. 24, 1964. After training, the freshly minted Second Class trooper's first assignment took him to Troop K working in the Montpelier-Barre area.[700]

A year later, he earned promotion to Trooper First Class and on June 7, 1965 transferred to Troop A in Burlington. In October 1966, Gould began a new assignment in the opposite end of the state as a detective trooper assigned to the BCI in Brattleboro.[701]

In May 1967, he married Charlene Ann Ravenna, a 1964 graduate of Rutland High School whose parents lived near his in a working-class section of town.[702] Charlene's two brothers, Albert (AJ) and Donald, followed Gould's example and both joined the VSP in, respectively, June 1964 and December 1973. They all maintained a close relationship in the following years, regardless of where the work took them. After AJ received promotion, assigned to BCI in Brattleboro, in 1970 (where he participated in drug investigations with Paul Lawrence), he worked for a period alongside his brother-in-law. Gould was already known as a "perfectionist" by that time and so attentive to detail that he sometimes delayed submitting reports because they needed, in his mind, more attention.

"Slow and steady, always taking his time," AJ recounted to the author, led him to nickname Gould "Flash" that they both laughed about right up to the day of his death.[703]

On June 8, 1970, Gould received promotion to corporal as a patrol commander in St. Johnsbury's Troop B supervising line troopers. Lt. Nelson R. Lay, who superseded Lt. Potvin, assumed responsibility for the entire NEK region and joined him upon his own promotion.[704] Lay described Gould as "a good steady individual," "very stable," "dedicated and very reliable," who "would work 20 hours a day if you asked him to."[705]

His fellow patrol commander, Cpl. Claude Hebert, recalled that the two of them became "very friendly" and believed him "a tremendous and very dedicated police officer" as they "fought the department on a lot of procedural problems and won most of them."[706] Upon entering into his new duties, Gould also attended a three-week course of instruction at the Command Training Institute at Babson College in Wellesley, Massachusetts.

The presence of these officers in St. Johnsbury marked a period of needed change after the Irasburg Affair when that office had become the department's "punishment station." It suffered in the next years, gaining a sordid reputation within the department "that if you screw up they would send you to St. Johnsbury."

That peaceful interim changed however, according to Trooper Truex, in 1977 with the arrival of one of the department's most senior officers, Sgt. Robert Field (1947), assigned as station commander that May and the promotion of David Reed to sergeant in BCI in August.

After that, Truex recalled, a feeling of paranoia infested the office where "it seemed like a conspiracy all the time. Field and Reed were always in each other's offices with the doors closed and this is something new because when the door was closed you knew something was going down."

Newly arrived officers noticed the change immediately from their prior assignments, shocked that "they had never seen an office like this where everybody is talking about everybody else and you have got to have your back against the wall and they just didn't feel comfortable." "Everybody had the opinion," Truex explained, "that they had to watch their back (because) Field and Reed were just cultivating other troopers trying to get information about what the other troopers were doing. I think their whole dam philosophy was divide and conquer."[707]

Festering paranoia within the ranks fostered by the seeming mistrust held by their superiors only increased in the St. Johnsbury office throughout 1978 before exploding in 1979.

For the last three years of his life, Howard Gould worked as a member of the department's Safety Education division that largely removed him from the day-to-day operations at St. Johnsbury. It allowed him many opportunities to put a much-needed compassionate face on a police agency that saw its credibility eroded because of the Irasburg and Lawrence affairs, the latter so prominently portrayed in Hamilton Davis's *Mocking Justice* released in 1978.

Fellow corporal Dean George worked closely with Gould for a year until early 1979, just months before his suicide, as the only two officers traveling throughout the state to conduct community relations and described their relationship in glowing terms. The two attended numerous state fairs (seven in one year that often involved working 12-hour days), school picnics, and other events where large numbers of people gathered that allowed George to witness Gould interact with "hundreds of small children."

"It seemed that most everywhere we went," George recounted, "Howard had already made an impression, and people were excited to have him return." Gould took his responsibilities toward the children very seriously, particularly those working on school safety patrols, "because he felt very strongly that most of those kids would look at the Vermont State Police in a positive manner, and with a great deal of admiration and respect. It seemed that whatever Howard did in Safety Education he did with the utmost pride and love for the Vermont State Police." In ending, George expressed his highest regard and respect for him: "As a friend, Howard will be missed by many of us; as a Vermont State Police trooper, he will be missed by all of us."

Many others agreed and at the time of his death Gould's personnel file held "numerous letters of commendation from both within and outside" the DPS.[708] His direct supervisor, Lt. Edward Prescott expressed a similar sentiment and told CSP investigators he "was an excellent police officer, a hard worker, always devoting more time than he should have to the job."[709]

In 1979, Howard and Charlene lived in Waterford, a town located on the New Hampshire border at the Connecticut River and a short distance from the state police barracks in neighboring St. Johnsbury. They also owned a 287-acre tract of land the industrious Gould arranged to have logged allowing him to consider purchasing an additional 1,000-acre lot for further clearing, but never took place.

Before moving to Waterford, the savvy speculator purchased and logged other tracts of timbered land that he sold off for a modest profit, including one parcel to another trooper.[710] The two lived within their means and as Charlene, who recently began work at an area business in December 1978, described their situation to investigators, they "had no bills and no real problems."

Howard's "Number One thing," she said, "was pride in the Vermont State Police," and that he was "super dedicated."[711]

The size of their family increased between 1969–1972 to include three children as they moved around the state to accommodate VSP demands. Their youngest son, Jason, recalls his father's life revolving around the needs of the state police, as well as other community interests. He remembers watching him prepare exhibits and washing "Monty," one of the department's first vehicles, in their driveway that he took to the fairs. He also recalls that in the wintertime Howard participated with the Vermont Association of Snow Travelers, a snowmobile organization maintaining trails for its membership.[712]

Gould knew Ticker Charron as a local deputy sheriff who interacted with troopers on occasion and, impressed with him, convinced him to consider joining the VSP snowmobile patrol. He agreed and Gould conducted an investigation into his background that revealed no reason to suspect his honesty that soon led to his employment.

Beginning only months after he started in 1976 and until early 1978 when David Reed learned of the situation, Charron engaged in a misplaced sense of friendship, ingratiating himself with his newfound friends and eventually pulling six unwitting troopers, including Gould, into his criminal conduct.

Concealing the fact that he was stealing router bits from his employer, the situation began innocently enough when Charron asked Trooper Victor Theriault if he wanted any. Charron explained he could get them from where he worked because of their inferior quality, so-called "seconds," and lied that he had permission to remove them. Theriault agreed and over a period of three months Charron provided him with around forty bits that the trooper had no reason to believe were anything other than what Charron represented them to be. Confident that nothing was amiss, Theriault made no secret of his receipt of the bits and displayed them openly on his desk drawing questions from other troopers asking where he got them.[713]

Patrol commander Cpl. Hebert became aware of the bits showing up at the office when Theriault gave him a dozen of them. He also had no reason to suspect any problem, but later questioned Charron when he offered to provide more to him directly. As with Theriault, Hebert was satisfied with the seeming innocence Charron portrayed and accepted a few that he offered. However, they burned out quickly and he refused to give Charron a rifle he wanted in trade.[714]

In the next months, other unsuspecting officers became involved that included Sidney Adams (bits valued at $9), Dennis Bouffard (unidentified value), and Truex ($72) receiving bits either from Theriault or Charron.

When any asked if they could get into trouble for receiving them, Charron reassured them that it was alright. Poorly paid troopers could already receive discounts in other transactions that did not raise any official concern within the VSP. Gould's brother-in-law, AJ Ravenna, recalls it was commonly known throughout the VSP that any of its members could travel north to Beecher Falls on the Canadian border to purchase deeply discounted furniture from the Ethan Allen Furniture Company.[715] Other concessions by various businesses also accommodated the hard-working troopers in quiet ways that officials certainly knew about but never punished.

While Charron, perhaps defensive and wanting to distance himself from the troubles he caused in distributing his stolen goods, later recalled that he and Gould did not have a close relationship, Bouffard disagreed. He recalls that they had a "very, very close" friendship that included their visiting and cutting wood together.[716]

They also interacted at Gould's home where Charron expressed an interest in a pistol Gould owned and agreed to exchange for some bits, valued at $78, for them. On none of these occasions did the extensive investigations conducted by the CSP, an interim DPS commissioner or the Keyser Commission ever find that any of these officers had reason to suspect Charron was doing anything illegal. But they all paid a high professional and personal price for having their names connected to his.

The tortured path leading to Gould's death in July 1979 began in early January 1978 when Bouffard had an innocent conversation with David Reed at the St. Johnsbury barracks. Reed was a no-nonsense, 12-year veteran of the state police who consistently earned performance evaluations marking him as fully satisfactory to outstanding. Descriptions of him by fellow officers ranged from admiration for his investigative abilities and honesty ("a super-honest cop" according to Bouffard) to grudging respect ("a good cop, just a lousy individual," Truex said).[717]

In Montpelier, Commissioner Lynch had no qualms about Reed, promoting him to sergeant just months earlier in August 1977 saying "we should have 250 Sgt. Reeds."[718] Even after he learned that Reed improperly communicated information about the problem in St. Johnsbury to his friend Sen. Morse that led to their exchange at his confirmation hearing, Lynch continued to rely on Reed asking him several times to stay in contact with him in order "to cement department relationships with members of the Legislature."[719]

Bouffard's general conversation with Reed followed his observation of a box in his office bearing a picture of a router on it. They had a discussion about what the tool could do and Bouffard suggested that if Reed was ever interested in obtaining bits, he should speak with Charron because he could get seconds from where he worked. Unaware that they were stolen, Bouffard innocently told Reed that Charron also provided bits to other troopers in the office piquing Reed's interest because he had not heard that before. Curious about Bouffard's statement and suspecting Charron did not have authority to remove bits from his employer, Reed recalled that he telephoned his superior, Lt. Milford Ramey at Redstone, about it. "I just told him," Reed testified, "that one of the auxiliary troopers appears to be stealing router bits and it appears as though the troopers are receiving it," but did not identify any of them.[720]

While Ramey expressed concern, he provided Reed with no direction on what course of action to take.

Reed proceeded to the Vermont American plant on Jan. 9 to speak with its president, Dale Gibson. Gibson told him that company officials already suspected, despite a policy allowing employees to obtain bits with permission, that large numbers of them were being stolen. So many were unaccounted for that the local Sears store constituted an anomaly in the national Sears chain because the numbers of bits it sold did not correspond to the numbers of routers purchased that otherwise usually matched because one could not be used without the other. Gibson suspected that people buying routers without the necessary bits somehow had access to those missing from his inventory. Interested in halting the thefts and surprised to hear that Charron might be involved, he agreed to assist Reed.[721]

RESPONSIBILITY ADRIFT

Reed faced a growing conundrum unanswerable by the VSP rules and regulations. He did not have enough information to implicate any troopers, but reasonable grounds to suspect that an auxiliary trooper participated in criminal conduct. He had no authority to institute an internal investigation into the troopers' conduct because only the commissioner could approve that.

"The department policy," he later explained, "is that we don't investigate our own people like within our office. We notify our supervisors whom supposedly initiate investigation and have an investigator from another area come in" to conduct it.[722]

However, nothing prohibited Reed from looking into Charron's actions to see if any troopers might have known the bits he supplied them were stolen. This, in turn, could then trigger a separate internal investigation into their conduct.

Significant discrepancies in the accounts of senior officers concerning when Reed advised them of the situation made it impossible for any of the resulting investigations to accurately recreate what happened after he met with Gibson at the Vermont American plant. Reed testified that after their meeting he conferred with the two detectives he supervised in the St. Johnsbury office only to learn that one of them was Charron's brother-in-law, leading him to believe he had to shoulder the investigation personally for the time being.

However, he did share with station commander Sgt. Field and troop commander Lt. Lay what he had learned and thought he would see if Charron might try to provide bits to him. Reed understood the delicate task before him and need to avoid the appearance of entrapping Charron to engage in a crime he was not otherwise willing, or pre-disposed, to commit.

He reportedly shared his plan with Field and Lay and neither of them entered any objection. However, when their conduct was later questioned, they and other senior officers, recalled the situation differently.

As the attorney general's report examining this particular issue determined, "Reed's action was clearly not entrapment" and that "it is very disturbing that a contingent of high-ranking State Police officers (specifically naming Ryan, Spear, Ramey, Field, and Lay) continued to refer to the act as possible entrapment. This suggests that the higher-ups had formed an 'attitude' about Sgt. Reed that was not based upon careful regard for applicable law or facts. Although many of these men knew of Reed's plan none raised the entrapment issue with Reed beforehand."[723]

Their questionable defenses waited for the future and, believing his course of action appropriate, Reed proceeded.

Soon after meeting with Gibson, Reed went to the local Sears store and spoke with its manager who confirmed "they sold almost no router bits but he'd sold a large quantity of routers, which is unusual because one is not good without the other."[724]

The manager agreed to loan Reed a router for his investigation, now aimed at providing Charron with an opportunity, if he initiated it, to offer to provide Reed with bits. He displayed the router openly on his desk and on Saturday, Jan. 14, when routine, weekend snowmobile patrols took place, Charron arrived to take the bait. Walking past Reed's office, he saw the router and engaged him in conversation, telling him it was a Christmas gift he was returning to get another model.

When Reed explained that he was also waiting for the expensive bits to come on sale, Charron told him "not to worry, he would get me some," because "I can get you a good deal on them, you don't have to buy any." Reed responded that he would rather just wait until they came on sale, but Charron reached out, patted him on the stomach, and repeated "don't worry about it, I'll take care of it, and walked down the hallway."[725]

Several weeks passed until March 4 when Reed found a bag containing 30 bits on his desk that he took to Gibson at the plant to confirm they came from his factory. Gibson told him they were indeed from his facility and of first quality and not seconds, repeating again that Charron did not have permission to take them.

Within hours, Reed went to Sen. Morse's house where he shared the latest twist with him.[726]

Reed met with Charron two days later at his home and offered to pay him for the bits that Charron admitted he left on his desk, but declined saying "What do you want to do? Get me for stealing?"

He continued to refuse accepting any money and when Reed left told him "Don't tell anyone where you got the bits."[727]

On March 7, Reed met again with Charron, this time to tell him that he was part of an investigation into the theft of router bits from his place of employment. Charron admitted his conduct and said he had done so on other occasions in the past two years and given some to troopers identifying "Truex, Palmer, Hebert" and Gould as recipients. After that, Reed recounted, realizing "that I was out to find out which troopers were getting them he seemed to clam up on that" and refused to provide any further information.[728]

Knowing that Reed planned to send the case to State's Attorney Gray for prosecution, Charron panicked and immediately contacted Bouffard telling him he "wanted the bits back." He told him that "he was going to destroy the bits and was going around to each of the other troopers about them."[729]

Charron also called Gould's home and spoke with Charlene since Howard was away at the academy in Pittsford. He told her that Gray already had the investigative papers and he "was worried about losing his job and how he was going to feed his children."

Aware that her husband also received bits from him, Charlene called the academy to advise him of Charron's news.

Listening to her crying, Gould said he knew nothing about what was happening and, expressing no concern, told her she was being "overdramatic."

She asked him to call Charron directly, but he refused and told her "he could not."[730] Distraught at what was happening, Charlene asked him if she should call the state's attorney directly, but knowing that "regardless what he said, she would probably call Gray anyway" Gould told her that if she did to tell him "she was calling on her own and not for him."

Charlene immediately contacted Gray at his home ("more or less screaming at him," she admitted) and caught him unawares of what she was talking about or even who Ticker Charron was.

He soon recalled after Charlene told him what Charron advised her and then disclosed that Gould had received some of the bits from him. She was extremely upset with Charron's account of what Reed had done and accused the detective of setting him up. It made no sense, she said, to prosecute Charron when there was so much theft taking place by others at the manufacturing plant.

Gould went to the St. Johnsbury office the next day and, after returning home and kicking a door, recounted to Charlene what happened. He had spoken with Reed, calling him "the snake," after he walked into his office "with a big grin on his face and said, 'Guess what? I busted your buddy.'" When Reed told him it was for stealing router bits, Gould responded that "You did a big stroke of business picking up Charron" and told him that even he had a box of bits at home and asked if Reed wanted him to bring them in. After Reed reportedly gave him "a dirty smile" and walked away, Gould went to Lt. Lay asking what he should do with the bits and Lay told to just hold onto them.[731]

Gould's anger notwithstanding, Reed recounted that when the two met he agreed to withhold filing his report with their superiors to allow Gould time to "take care of the problem before I would tell headquarters, so if headquarters asked why he was permitting it, he would have a chance to take care of the problem."[732] In the meantime, Charron recognized his difficult situation and on March 15, 1978 submitted his resignation to Gould citing the time his auxiliary work took away from his family and "one or two more reasons but I do not wish to bring them up at this time." He also acknowledged with appreciation the "past and present law enforcement officers" he worked with and from whom "I have learned a very, very lot about the laws." He ended thanking Gould and wrote, "I hope you give future (greenhorns) (sic) your time and knowledge as you have given me."[733]

Beyond Reed's verbally advising Lay and Field, and possibly Ramey, at the investigation's onset, a lack of documentation about those notifications of what he found posed significant obstacles to future investigations providing Redstone commanding officers sufficient cover to explain their own actions. In addition to Reed's March 8 standard report of the Charron investigation, the only other two documents he wrote concerned memos addressed to Ramey and Lynch on March 13. Writing to Ramey, he advised that he completed his investigation into thefts at the Vermont American facility and that court action was pending against an auxiliary trooper who had provided stolen property to several unnamed troopers. He did not specifically indicate that the troopers committed crimes, but alerted Ramey that "the circumstances surrounding the Troopers receiving this stolen property indicate a strong possibility that the items they were receiving were known to them to be stolen" and that he had "taken no action" with regard to them.[734]

In his memo to Lynch, Reed simply identified Charron as an auxiliary trooper-defendant with a pending case accused of theft and the investigation's case number, indicating that copies of it went to Lay, Field, and Gould.[735] Recreating the tortured paths of these two documents proved impossible because the recipients either blamed inefficiencies of the department's internal mail system and refused to acknowledge their receipt or, in this environment of jumbled responsibilities across the chain-of-command, simply assumed that they were not the ones responsible to follow up on Reed's explosive disclosures. Meanwhile, concerned troopers named by Charron approached Reed and told him they had received bits from him. When they offered to turn them over and asked what was going to happen, he refused to accept them because he said he had referred the matter to Redstone.

The denials of Reed's superiors that they did not know notwithstanding, all evidence points to the fact that notifications were made in March because on April 20, 1978 he had a meeting at Redstone with his superior officer, Capt. Spear. Spear confronted Reed and, referring to Charron, told him that he "was picking on the poor kid or had set the poor kid up" and should have handled the matter locally and not create a "problem in the department involving the troopers and the auxiliary." Uncomfortable with what Spear said, Reed told him "I didn't believe this was the end of it. I said that you know this is going to come back and haunt us." He then inquired of Spear, "Well, do you want me to cover-up for it?" and received a response that "No, I ain't saying that, but you could have took (sic) care of it." Unconvinced at his true intention, Reed told him "you're saying you wanted me to cover up for the whole thing."[736]

Spear also advised Reed that the "old man," referring to Lynch, was mad because he spoke with politicians. This took Reed by surprise because Lynch specifically instructed him to meet with them to improve the department's image with the legislature. In the next months Reed received further confirmation his superiors knew about the allegations because State's Attorney Gray, who Reed also advised about their inaction, told him his reports were being flagged at Redstone to keep abreast of the situation. Others also confided to Reed that Redstone was upset he did not handle the matter on his own at the local level instead of referring it up the chain of command.

On Aug. 31, 1978, Reed provided sworn testimony in Charron's theft case. When questioned by his attorney about the notifications he made to his superiors and whether he thought it "a little unusual that no one has taken any action on any of your reports?," he responded "yes." Still curious if his superiors knew of the situation, when Reed accompanied Lynch to a meeting on Sept, 6, he quizzed him if he was aware of it. Lynch quickly brushed him aside and said that he was, that "the troopers were foolish," and left him with the impression that "he didn't want to discuss it."[737] That fall, Lynch was also confronted by a reporter who told him "something to the effect that the word was out that an investigation (referring to Charron) may have been mishandled and some of the troopers investigating the thefts were part of the process." In response, Lynch told him he was "aware of the incident and was going to re-check to make sure proper action was taken."[738]

Reed's concerns about the department's lines of communication and inaction by his superiors coincided precisely with observations made by others from outside the agency. While Secretary of Administration Richard Mallary noted in July 1978 its "turmoil, indecision and lack of management" style where the "organizational structure and lines of communication . . . are exceedingly unclear," three months later Snelling's attorney William Gilbert wrote that Lynch was "badly managing." Each of those factors continued into the next year, accelerating at a pace that the Redstone commanders could not match before exploding into public view to inflict unnecessary widespread damage attributed to their collective malfeasance in the preceding months.

Chapter 12

"Only One Option"

Firing Lynch

"Have you heard the news?" Gould asked Charlene when he returned home from work on July 24, 1979. She had not. He then told her that Snelling just "axed Lynch" and "passed the word to all the State's Attorneys in the State to dig up any wrongdoings about State Police since Lynch came in to justify his firing" him. A year and a half had passed since his and other troopers' involvement with Ticker Charron intruded into their lives and, hearing nothing from Redstone in the meantime, Charlene believed "the whole business (had) blown over."[739] However, Gould appeared uneasy in the days before and on July 20, while in a "very depressed state," he confided to Dennis Bouffard that he thought "everything was going to roll downhill right into his lap." He felt very responsible for the problem because he hired Charron and feared he "was going to take the brunt of the whole thing," becoming the "fall guy" and lose his job over it. According to Bouffard, the despondent Gould kept telling him "how he had done the background investigation and how (it) showed how honest Charron was at that time."[740]

But the festering problem had not blown over as Charlene hoped and now its connection stretching from Gould's hiring him all the way to Lynch became clear in news reports consuming the state's interest for months. It became the press's number one story for the entire year, a period "long remembered by the Vermont State Police." "In 12 turbulent months," the *Rutland Herald* wrote at the end of 1979, "Public Safety Commissioner Francis Lynch was fired, two officers were suspended, and several others were disciplined, sweeping accusations of political interference and of a press vendetta, and a state police corporal committed suicide."[741] After the news broke of Lynch's dismissal, Gould had only days to live as the sleeping details surrounding Charron's and the troopers' conduct that nobody wanted revealed splashed across the news. The events in late July eerily resemble the frenzied activity taking place the same month eleven years earlier when police investigated the Irasburg nightriders.

The pressure on the VSP was immense for the first half of 1979. Ranging from the ongoing disputes between Lynch and Attorney General Diamond over the missing Merriam polygraph report and the favorable treatment Lynch accorded him to Snelling's push to create his Agency of Public Safety to stop the never-ending squabbling inside the law enforcement community that Lynch continued to inflame, the problems seemed to never go away. On May 10, Snelling met with sixty troopers in White River Junction at their request to hear them express their displeasure with the new agency proposal, warning that they "are prepared to step into the political arena in order to ensure our well-being as State Police Officers."[742]

In June, Diamond's office released its long anticipated 102-page investigation into the VSP's involvement with Merriam based on the serious complaints made by state's attorneys McGee and Gray a year earlier. Diamond's number two man, thirty-one-year-old Deputy Attorney General Gregory McKenzie, authored the report providing a withering assessment of the department. His review described the ineptness of commissioners Corcoran and Lynch in charge of an institution crying for change, unwilling to detect and remedy internal wrongdoing as they and their immediate subordinates sought to obstruct a full inquiry into their actions. There was, McKenzie determined, in its treatment of concerns about Merriam, a "legacy of command indifference to the knowledge of criminal wrongdoing on the part of a line officer."[743]

Just days before Lynch saw the report, on July 3 he received the American Legion's Policeman of the Year trophy, awarded in a tie with a municipal officer.[744] Perhaps emboldened with such a display of public support, and consistent with his conduct in Omaha when he openly fought efforts to supervise his actions, Lynch lashed out against Diamond's report on July 19 attacking any insinuation he acted inappropriately. He vehemently denied its substance alleging that "it contains countless instances of a complete disregard for uncontradicted facts and of the author having jumped to conclusions which, in turn, are based on illogical inferences, drawn from nonexistent facts."[745] He followed up his attack confronting Snelling in the same way he did to Diamond just weeks earlier when he demanded a memorandum of law to substantiate his belief that Merriam should be dismissed. Now, he told Snelling he wanted the governor to provide him with "copies of interviews, omitted exhibits, (and) inquest transcripts referred to in the report" supporting its claims.[746]

Snelling faced other concerns the same day with his new agency proposal as officials from within government, the judiciary, and law enforcement weighed in on its far-reaching impact. Lynch's strong opposition and the legislature's refusal to approve it earlier in the year did not sway Snelling from continuing to pursue it. He contended that while he still believed "strongly that this is a good idea," he quizzed Gilbert "whether we really want to do it."[747]

For the tiresome Lynch and his unacceptable dismissal of Diamond's report ("the straw that broke the camel's back," Snelling said) and after receiving confirmation from trusted confidant, and former member of the Irasburg Board of Inquiry, Hilton Wick, on Saturday, July 21 Snelling decided it was time to fire him.[748]

Moving quickly, he arranged for the appointment of a special five-member commission headed by former Supreme Court Justice F. Ray Keyser Sr. to further investigate Diamond's findings and assure the public "that there will never be a coverup of police wrongdoing in Vermont." He then summoned Lynch and Ryan to be in his office at 8:30 a.m. on July 24.[749]

That day started out with fireworks when the *Barre-Montpelier Times Argus* newspaper published the first of many stories about the Router Bit Affair. Apparently frustrated at VSP commanders' inaction to investigate troopers' conduct in prior months, State's Attorney Gray took the highly unusual step of providing the press with a copy of David Reed's Aug, 31, 1978 deposition describing in detail his investigation into Charron, the receipt of router bits by troopers and inaction of his superiors to institute an inquiry. Reed later denied any part in its disclosure and an independent investigation by a Burlington law firm in 1980 confirmed his account before assigning Gray responsibility for the debacle.[750]

The newspaper's salacious article describing Reed's testimony laid it all out and specifically identified the troopers involved (Bouffard, Gould, Hebert, Palmer, Theriault, and Truex), the people Reed said he notified of the allegation (Field, Lay, Ramey, and Spear), and his surprise that nobody from Redstone took it seriously enough to initiate an investigation. "The Reed deposition," another newspaper described, "is a vivid document which describes in stark detail the bewilderment and dismay of a veteran state police officer who discovers what he believes to be a coverup by his superiors."[751]

The article also surprised Reed's fellow troopers at the St. Johnsbury barracks with no reason to believe their actions had fallen under suspicion months earlier. Now, they found their names splashed across the state under a headline shouting "Evidence of New State Police Cover-Up Linking Officers to Stolen Goods."[752]

In his office that morning, a sober governor who, only two years before, profusely acclaimed Lynch's appointment with expressions of hope for a better future for the state's law enforcement community, asked for his resignation.

Accompanied by Ryan, who waited outside, Lynch unsurprisingly refused the request prompting Snelling to hand him a prepared "terse one-sentence letter stating that the commissioner was being removed from office 'immediately.'"[753] After dismissing Lynch and inviting Ryan back in to consider whether to place him in temporary command, and no doubt prompted by that morning's article, he asked him if he was involved in a "coverup."

Mincing no words, Snelling inquired point blank, as Ryan recounted, if "he might be involved in some sort of problem too." The governor also wanted him to explain "if there was any problems in my background that would cause further discredit to the state police" mentioning "the possibility of St. Johnsbury and something involving a number of troopers."

Snelling already had further reason to suspect Ryan's credibility at the time because of his conduct during the Cornelius Reed promotion proceedings in 1977 when he provided false information, apparently from a secret second file the department maintained on him, that Labor and Industry Commissioner Cherington condemned as "a gross and prejudicial deviation" from accepted practices. As the attorney general's subsequent report into their meeting related, Ryan "said that he told the governor that he'd had some information that there was an investigation by Sgt. Reed, but that Ryan had not done anything about it and that Ryan's conscience did not bother him, nor was he embarrassed or concerned."[754]

"This evidently was the information that the governor was looking for," Ryan recounted. Regardless, Snelling asked him to "submit a memorandum, or what have you, outlining what my memory was of that time in regards to my involvement in it and I did."[755]

Later that day, Ryan provided Snelling with a three-page explanation of his conduct in the St. Johnsbury matter. It only created more confusion because of factual inaccuracies and inconsistencies that arose in later statements he made to Connecticut State Police investigators. Ryan's memo also marked the first time that Gould's name appeared as the person supervising Charron. He further inserted a reference to Charlene's conduct, identifying her as Mrs. Howard Gould, when she called Gray to tell him "that the prosecution (of Charron) should not go forward."[756]

Now, not only had the press identified Gould as the recipient of stolen property, but the governor himself had reason to suspect he and Charlene had a role in an attempt to impede the prosecution of a crime. Ryan ended telling Snelling that he assigned Capt. John Heffernan, the only person without a direct connection to the St. Johnsbury allegations (for now), to conduct an internal investigation "as prescribed by Department Rules and Regulations."

His "tempest in a teapot" was about to turn deadly.

Of the several concerns that Ryan's various accounts presented, his contradictory explanations of when he first learned of the St. Johnsbury problem constituted the most difficult to reconcile with the evidence. He told Snelling that he learned of it at the time of Lynch's confirmation hearing in early 1978 when Sen. Morse brought it up and that he instructed Ramey to stay on top of it (which Ramey denied).

However, he later contradicted that account when interviewed by the CSP and explained he first became aware of it "as a result of a memorandum he had received from Attorney General Diamond on 7/24/79."[757]

While the Keyser Commission discounted that later time and ultimately found that Ryan knew of the situation in March 1978, it did not find that he had participated in a cover-up because of these conflicts.[758]

Regardless, Ryan's inconsistencies in other testimony provided at inquests and hearings made it impossible to answer that question with certainty. For the conspiratorially minded Ryan, the timing of the damaging disclosures in newspapers of the St. Johnsbury problems and Lynch's dismissal painting the department as a kind of Keystone Cops slapstick farce was nothing more than a political ploy to undermine and embarrass the VSP.[759]

The rush by concerned command officers to find out what Snelling knew began later that morning after Ryan left his office and drove the short distance to Redstone. There, he presided over a previously scheduled meeting attended by troop and station commanders, BCI sergeants that included David Reed, and other staff officers. They discussed Lynch's dismissal, but not the router bits matter.

After the meeting, at 11:30 a.m. a waiting representative of the attorney general met with Ryan and handed him a letter demanding that documents concerning the Charron investigation be turned over to his office. It also reported, to Ryan's apparent surprise, that they were contained in a sealed file located at the St. Johnsbury barracks. Ryan then convened a second meeting at 12:30 that included Heffernan, Spear, Patch, Lay, Reed, and another detective, Harold Kinney. When Ryan asked Reed why there was a sealed envelope in St. Johnsbury, he explained that because the matter involved troopers, he did not want anyone in the office to have access to it so he secured it in that fashion. The attendees' accounts conflict concerning whether Reed actually identified the officers involved in the alleged misconduct at that time, but Ryan reported he did and "I was shocked at that point."

When Ryan confronted Reed asking why he had not reported this before, the officer responded that he already had. What Reed did not tell him was that he possessed a second copy of the file he kept at his home that included not only the Charron investigation and his notes, but also copies of the two memos he sent to Lynch and Ramey on March 13, 1978 advising them of the situation. At some point during the meeting, Ryan turned to the St. Johnsbury troop commander Nelson Lay and said words to the effect "I told you to take care of this," demonstrating his knowledge about the problem before July 24.

With Reed and Kinney excused from the room, the remaining officers spent the next twenty minutes discussing what to do. In an early expression revealing how they planned to handle the avalanche of bad publicity and try to cast blame elsewhere, "the question of Sgt. Reed's integrity came up."[760]

This entirely unwarranted insinuation questioning Reed's character by seeking to cast doubt on an experienced criminal investigator with an unblemished record reveals a dark underside of the VSP command staff ready to turn on its own to protect itself in a classic example of shooting the messenger. Shelving that defense for the moment, but which soon served as a rallying point for the stressed senior officers, Ryan ordered that Reed and Kinney go to St. Johnsbury, retrieve the sealed file, open and copy it to send to him, and turn the original over State's Attorney Gray.

Perhaps confused in the rush of events in the order of executing Ryan's directions, Lay, Reed, and Kinney drove to St. Johnsbury, retrieved the sealed file and took it to Gray. However, the prosecutor refused to meet with all of the officers together and insisted on seeing Reed alone. Probably already suspecting Gray had released his deposition to the press that caused all the havoc that day, Reed refused.

After Gray threatened to issue a subpoena for him to hand the file over, the three officers immediately left and returned to the barracks where Lay called Ryan for further instructions. Making contact, Ryan told him to have a disinterested person open it, make two copies of its contents and return them to the envelop, sending one copy to him and leaving the other in the St. Johnsbury files.

Subsequently, a dispatcher performed the duty in front of Lay and Reed and wrote on the file "I made two copies of each item in this envelope (consisting of twenty-six pages) and resealed same on 7/24/79 at 1542 hours at St. Johnsbury."

Meanwhile, Gray prepared his subpoena and had it served on Reed to bring the file immediately to court, which he did. There, he also provided testimony at a secret inquest; a process that eventually involved the testimony of thirty-three other individuals telling their particular stories.

After Ryan received the file later that day, he called a meeting for 8 a.m. the next morning and summoned Ramey, Spear, Patch and Heffernan to attend. While the evidence strongly indicates that Ryan and Lynch had indications of the router bit problem as far back as January 1978 at the time of Lynch's confirmation hearing and their subordinates knew of it in the following months after Reed's March 13 memos to him and Ramey, expressing their collective "surprise" at Reed's recent revelations of the sealed file the men now concentrated their efforts trying to identify the specific dates when they became aware. As the attorney general's report of their meeting describes, "Ramey and Spear were thinking out loud trying to recall," and "said they had never seen" Reed's memos, which Patch voiced a similar belief.

Disingenuously, knowing that allegations of trooper misconduct could only be instituted by the commissioner, Spear and Ramey also "wondered why Reed hadn't handled the matter himself since Reed was a sergeant in the State Police, and would have had both the authority and obligation to do so."

Meanwhile, Ryan "said that he talked to someone about the incident" and that it might have been a passing conversation with Reed but who had "indicated there was no evidence of State Police involvement."[761]

Similarly, Lynch distanced himself from the problem during a press conference after Snelling fired him and said that he "may" have learned of a potential problem at some point by a reporter, but failed to reveal that Sen. Morse alerted him to it over a year beforehand.

All Lynch could say was that he knew virtually nothing about it "until I read it in the newspaper the other day that there were troopers involved." When asked about any investigation by the department, he continued to place the responsibility elsewhere. "To the best of my recollection or knowledge," he said, "if there had been at a lower level, it was never brought to my attention."[762]

Despite their collective "inability," or refusal, to acknowledge receipt of Reed's memos, the overall atmosphere of the Redstone staff on July 25 conveys an appreciation of their shared guilt in failing to follow up on the St. Johnsbury allegations that nobody cared to acknowledge.

Now in temporary charge of the DPS, an emboldened Ryan revived a prior plan abandoned by Lynch to discredit the department's troublesome nuisance, State's Attorney Dale Gray, using a ruse.

"After Lynch was fired," the attorney general's report describes of this moment, "Ryan sent down a memo, ordering the investigation of (Trooper Kostelnik) be conducted. The order directed Reed to sign the investigation."

Ryan and Heffernan already disliked Gray's female investigator whom Heffernan previously conferred with Redstone about dismissing for unspecified conduct in Shaftsbury, but, instead transferred her to St. Johnsbury. There, she garnered further dislike after an off-duty trooper "buzzed" her on a motorcycle at what she claimed was over 100 miles per hour while she dealt with a motorist she had stopped. She reported the incident that resulted in station commander Sgt. Field, whom Ryan disliked, sending a memorandum to Redstone describing it. Field also convened a meeting of all the office troopers because he sensed "a lot of friction" in the air with her fellow officers who believed she was trying to get someone in trouble for an incident that could have been handled at the office level.[763]

Reed had already avoided Lynch's earlier command that he look into Kostelnik's relationship with Gray, but now, despite having already questioned his "integrity," Ryan believed him credible enough to conduct an extraordinarily sensitive inquiry and to sign his name to the effort. While it all smacked of a set-up, Reed did as directed and prepared the report. However, Ryan refused to accept it because it did not focus sufficiently on Gray and ordered him to rewrite it to show that he "was the subject" of the investigation.

But after Heffernan reviewed the revised report, he too declined to accept it and, according to the attorney general, "directed Reed to rewrite the report to indicate that (Kostelnik), not State's Attorney Gray, was the subject of the investigation" and which Reed did.[764]

Ryan's and Heffernan's hounding of Kostelnik soon convinced her to resign, effective Aug. 31, 1979, complaining that while she believed herself "one of the better troopers on the department, her work is not appreciated."[765]

Ryan's willingness to try and corral Reed into conducting an inquiry into a personal relationship he had no authority over reveals further the depths to which the new overseer of the VSP had sunk. It also failed to derail Kostelnik's relationship with Gray when the two married in 2003.

While the VSP command staff charted their future course, Howard and Charlene Gould experienced immense stress. The press called their home repeatedly, appearing on their doorstep where a reporter questioned their young son if he had any router bits. Angry at the press's brazenness, Gould told Charlene that if it was just himself, he could handle it, but involving his wife and children was too much. He was incredulous to see his and the other troopers' names published and told her that "depositions do not belong in the newspaper and that he would like to know who leaked all this 'garbage.'"

"Look at that," he exclaimed, "There are our names right there and we haven't even been invited to an inquest. We haven't been served with papers and here we are tried and convicted right on the front page. This is incredible!"

Someone was leaking information and Gould thought it came from either Gray's office or someone in the courthouse.

The Goulds soon received subpoenas to appear at the secret inquest on July 26 and which only increased their anxiety. While Gould tried to downplay the seriousness of the proceedings, Charlene reported to investigators that neither of them could sleep.

She would wake up crying, she said, and let out her emotions, but that "Howard just kept it all inside" because he was an "introvert."

He kept repeating to her that "There's a black cloud hanging over our office and it's all my fault" and that "people should know that being a State Policeman is all he knows, and that for 16-and-a-half years he did the best job for the State Police that he knew how. And that now, all that had been ruined." "Not only was his career ruined," he told her, "but also the careers of all those other troopers involved because of what the press had done to them."

When she told him it would all "blow over," he said that was impossible.

She recalled him saying, "People who read about a person being tried for murder one day, ten years from now won't recall whether or not he was found guilty or innocent. All they will remember is that he was tried for murder. He told her for that reason there is no way that he and his fellow troopers could now carry on in their job. He especially could not carry on in his since his job was safety education which required close contact with people."

They also "discussed his leaving the department, selling their home and what they would live on without his salary coming in."[766]

While Howard and Charlene waited anxiously and Ryan, Spear, and Ramey huddled at Redstone to compare their accounts, a bizarre situation arose. A previously scheduled ceremony for the promotion of thirty officers was set to take place on July 25 and, unconvinced of the legality of Gov. Snelling's dismissal of him the preceding day, Lynch "showed up for work, outfitted in full state police regalia, and went about his business as the state's top law enforcement officer."[767]

His blatant actions contrary to Snelling's order dismissing him touched off a firestorm with Attorney General Diamond who quickly filed papers with the local court seeking a temporary restraining order banning Lynch from state property. A clear need for the order existed, he said, because of confusion "not only among the higher-ranking officers of the department, but among the more subordinate members particularly in the areas of the proper lines of authority, accountability, and uncertainty as to whose orders, directives, and policies are to be followed."

Lynch did not respect Diamond or his office and dismissed their allegations as "unnecessary paranoia" showing "no class," but also resulted in the cancellation of the ceremony upon the court granting the order. The legal wrangling over Snelling's authority to dismiss a DPS commissioner continued until November when the Vermont Supreme Court ruled his actions lawful and Lynch disappeared from sight.[768]

Placed into an uncomfortable position defending himself, Snelling attended a press conference the day after the restraining order issued to describe in further detail the many problems Lynch posed to the effective administration of criminal justice in the state. He said he suggested to Lynch several times in the preceding months he should resign, but the recalcitrant commissioner refused. Only after Lynch summarily dismissed the findings of the attorney general's office concerning Merriam and cast himself as the victim, stonewalled and refused to address the percolating issue, repeatedly disparaged other law enforcement agencies with defamatory language, and lodged several serious, false allegations against other public officials did Snelling decide that he could no longer maintain any confidence in him.[769]

The VSP was in crisis and Snelling demanded change in its leadership.

As that bewildering scenario unfolded in Montpelier, Howard and Charlene appeared at the court in St. Johnsbury on July 26 to provide their testimony and where they met other officers also waiting their turn. They included some of the local troopers as well as their superiors from Redstone, including Spear, who waited the entire day before the court dismissed them late in the afternoon and ordered their return on Saturday, July 28.

The next day Gould did not go to work because, he told Charlene, "If he saw David Reed he knew that he would punch him out," and remained at home where the news media continued to hound him throughout the day.

When Charlene got out of work that afternoon, she discovered her car had a flat tire and called Howard. He came to fix it and told her that "he thought someone had let the air out of it because of the recent publicity."[770] She also experienced troubles at work where, she recounted to investigators, "a man came up to her and told her what a thief her husband was and a no-good SOB" and that "she slapped" him.

Tensions remained high and on July 28 Spear and Ramey returned to the court and sat alone in a waiting room. Soon Dennis Bouffard, who first alerted Reed about troopers receiving router bits, entered and found himself in the presence of two of the department's highest-ranking officers. In an account of their interaction that the Keyser Commission determined accurate, Bouffard explained what happened.

"I walked in," he said, "and I took my Stetson off and I said to, just generally, the only two that were in here, Capt. Spear was on my right and Lt. Ramey was on my left. And I was looking out the window and I said 'this is going to be a great day, isn't it?' Capt. Spear pointed his finger at me and made kind of a smirk on his face or something and said 'this is all your fault.' He said 'you're the complainant.' He kept that kind of a smirk on his face."

Then Ramey spoke up and "looked at me and he looked at Capt. Spear and he said 'you know, years ago it would be damned awful hard to fuck another trooper.' He looked out the window and he said something to the effect that 'we would have a talk with him and if that didn't work we would give him a blanket party (a form of punishment where a victim is covered by a blanket and beaten by anonymous assailants).'"[771]

While both Spear and Ramey later denied these comments, Lt. Fish reported being present a day or two afterwards at the BCI office at Redstone when Ramey regaled others about the account after it appeared in the press. Ramey, Fish reported, said "that he had a telephone call at his home the evening before, after Bouffard's testimony had been printed in the *Rutland Herald*, I believe, that his mother said something to the effect that 'You didn't threaten that young man with such a thing, did you?'" and that his father said, "'Well, Milford, it sounds just like you,'" whereupon Ramey "just laughed."

From Fish's perspective, there was no question of the accuracy of Bouffard's account that the exchange took place and Ramey's conduct confirmed it.

Howard and Charlene both testified on July 28, preceded by his having breakfast with Trooper Truex beforehand to discuss giving an award to the local Jaycees.

As Truex recalled, Gould acted "very relaxed and having a cup of coffee, shooting the shit, relaxed, that's all."[772] He testified first and then went to the St. Johnsbury office where Charlene showed up after she was done.

As the CSP report of their conversation reveals, it was a particularly difficult moment for the two of them: "She said she started to tell him about her experience at the inquest when he admonished her not to talk about it since she was under oath not to talk about her testimony. She said that she told Howard that was not fair; that they were husband and wife. He said the court rules were not set up with that consideration in mind. He insisted that they must not discuss their individual testimony. She said that he did remark that 'It was cruel and inhumane treatment for a husband and wife who were going through hell not to be able to talk to each other because of the fear of going to prison.'"[773]

Cpl. John Palmer, one of the officers who received bits from Charron, also testified on July 28 and provided a sworn statement of what happened after he left the courtroom. State's Attorney Gray met with him and advised that both his and Gould's credibility "were untarnished and that there was nothing to worry about." He also told him that "the problem lays further up in that something should have been done back when the initial investigation was conducted."

Truex was also present and recounted that Gray told them "You guys aren't in any trouble and went on to imply that the inquest was successful in developing information that would be harmful only to high-ranking State Police officers."[774] In a second meeting with Gray, also attended by Assistant Attorney General Paul Hudson, the two men told Palmer that "the problem laid much higher up than the troopers involved personally. Both agreed that the main reason there was no problems with the troops who possessed (router bits) was that they felt we were the only ones telling the truth."[775]

On Sunday, July 29, the day before his death, Gould became more reclusive and told Charlene to cancel a prearranged outing with friends. That day the newspaper reported more information, including quotes of witnesses testifying at the inquest, that agitated Gould even more. These were supposed to be secret proceedings and whoever was leaking it committed a criminal offence.

He told her he would answer the phone so she did not have to experience any further problems in dealing with the intrusive calls that continued to invade their privacy throughout the day. His paranoia increased as he tried to divert his attention and attend to small household chores and sought to envision their future after Snelling appointed a new commissioner.

According to Charlene, he thought that the new appointee "would be under his thumb and the only way to make Snelling look good and make it look like he cleared this matter up would be to get rid of all the troopers involved in the router bit matter."

He believed that Snelling would use the affair and "anything else that he could get" in order to justify his firing Lynch. They also talked about what they should do and, after examining their savings, concluded that subtracting their debts from their assets left them with only $1,000.

"She said he told her," an investigator wrote, "that they wouldn't be able to afford the house payment; that they would have to move. She said he also said that he wouldn't be able to get a job because the State Police would say that he was let go because he had received stolen property."

Gould also made a telephone call sometime that evening when he contacted his brother-in-law, and fellow trooper, Donald Ravenna, that has never been reported. "He was really depressed about the whole deal," Ravenna recounted to the author, "and was blaming himself for the whole affair" because he hired Charron that "ended up bringing this cloud over the state police."

Ravenna asked him if Charron "went through the normal hiring process (polygraph, interview, etc.)" and Gould told him that of course he had.

However, "There was no getting him off the 'it's my fault for dragging this huge cloud over the state police' no matter what I said," Ravenna related. "I told him to get some sleep and call me the next day so we could set up a meeting someplace where I could treat him to lunch. He said he would. Never heard from him again. Next call was from my brother saying he was dead."[776]

Saying Goodbye

Using call sign "310," Howard Gould radioed into the St. Johnsbury dispatcher from his driveway at 6:41 a.m., on Monday, July 30, 1979, to begin his last shift. Without her own vehicle that morning, Trooper Kostelnik also telephoned into the office requesting that someone pick her up at her home so she could get to court by 8 a.m., which Gould volunteered to do. This was, Kostelnik recalled, "very unusual" because it was out of the way for him and the two shared a strained relationship. She believed Gould felt threatened that she was trying to intrude and take over his safety education job. She also had a much different impression of Gould than others did characterizing him as "a worrier," "insecure," a "wheeler-dealer always involved in buying and selling things," and alleged that his nickname was "Chicken," a derogatory term that nobody else ever reported during any of the ensuring investigations.

According to Kostelnik, "when he picked her up, he was very cheerful and greeted her warmly," which she sensed as "unusual." After Gould dropped her off, he volunteered to handle a second transfer and picked up Sgt. Arthur Yeaw, who also recalled he appeared "cheerful" that morning.[777]

While Ticker Charron attended State's Attorney Gray's inquest that same day to provide a noteworthy 70 pages of testimony (second in length to David Reed's 98 pages days earlier), Gould experienced a difficult time when he finally reached the office.

Between 8:30 and 9, he shared coffee with a BCI detective and another trooper who reported that he "didn't appear to be himself that day."[778]

Between 9–9:30, Gould called his supervisor, Lt. Prescott, in Montpelier to talk about a public safety exhibit he "was going to set up at the Champlain Valley Fair in Essex Junction." The huge, week-long extravaganza was a month away and many nationally known entertainers planned to attend, including Mel Tillis, the Oak Ridge Boys, Minnie Pearl, and the Up With People Show, together with the Jack Kochman Hell Drivers, AMA Motorcycle Races, and a demolition derby that Gould's exhibit would be a part of.[779]

The two also talked about the current difficulties in St. Johnsbury and Prescott told Gould he would stand behind him and he felt he never did anything wrong.[780]

Soon after they talked, as Howard recounted to Charlene later that day, Reed repeatedly appeared at his office door, looked in, and "gave him a dirty sneer." He said he had done nothing to cause this and feared that Reed was going to "dump the whole thing on him because he was the one who hired Ticker."

Upset and unable to concentrate, Gould left the office to return home. According to Charlene, he called her and said that he had done so on four separate occasions that morning in between encounters with Reed in order to "get his head together so he wouldn't punch (him) out."

He also asked her to come home as they had a problem because someone from the press approached their seven-year-old son and asked him if his father "had router bits." Charlene was unable to return so, at 12:40 p.m., he "called in via telephone to the St. Johnsbury Troop to say that he would be home the rest of the day."[781]

When Charlene arrived home at 4 p.m., Gould told her to call the friends they excused themselves from meeting days earlier and to "tell them to come over." She did so and then shared their last moments together with a CSP investigator who wrote out her account of his anguish.

> He then asked her to go for a walk with him. She said as they walked, (he) told her that he was worried that (St. Johnsbury troop commander) Nelson Lay was also going to dump the router bits matter in his lap. She said he remembered how 18 months ago when he had told Nelson about his having bits from Charron, Nelson told him to sit on them and how none of that (information) surfaced. She said he had the feeling Nelson would deny having said that. She said that Howard also told her that he watched the kids swim in the pond for a while and that he took them for a two-hour ride in his truck. She said that he then told her that he had to get gas for the

truck, whereupon she reminded him that they had company coming.

Gould then told her that "he really would like to talk to David Reed to find out how he could sleep when 29 lives were going down the drain."

When she questioned him what he meant, he said "add up their families: the 'boys' families; and Charron's family and you'll come up with 29."

Charlene warned him that if he tried to contact Reed "he would only get into more trouble" prompting him to respond that "she was lucky in that she could vent her frustrations by throwing chairs and banging on walls, but he could not."

Pausing, he spoke his most ominous words about the whole situation and told her "There is only one option open to me. Do you know what I'm telling you?" Still believing he wanted to physically strike out, she said "Yeah, you're going to beat the hell out of Dave Reed. Right?"

"No," he said, "think about it."[782]

Gould then got into his truck, stopping his daughter who tried to get in and told her he was going for gas and would be right back.

His last words to Charlene were to make sure that their friends came over and then he drove off. When he did not return, and after their friends' arrival, Charlene made several frantic phone calls to try and find him, including to the St. Johnsbury barracks, but without any luck.

Finally, Lt. Lay drove into the driveway later that evening to tell her the news.

Unsubstantiated rumors reported that Gould had gone to Montpelier earlier in the day and then went looking for Reed "to kill" him.[783]

However, it soon became clear that, instead, Gould drove the 45 miles from Waterford to Montpelier arriving in the capital around 6:30 that evening. He dressed simply, clad in, according to a bystander when his body was later found, "a black tee-shirt, brown trousers and bedroom slippers."[784]

He appears to have found a telephone booth and called his other brother-in-law, good friend, former trooper, and now Attorney General Diamond's chief investigator, AJ Ravenna, at his apartment in nearby Barre.

Ravenna related to the author the call lasted about 15 minutes and that its full contents have never been disclosed in the past. While there are sparse indications in the extant files that it occurred, for some inexplicable reason none recite its particulars. Strangely, despite all of the ensuing high-level investigations, Ravenna also reports that nobody ever talked to him about any of it in detail or, surprisingly, summoned him to appear at an inquest in order to get the full story of the moments before Gould's death.[785]

A newspaper article immediately after the suicide reports that Ravenna said Gould "was upset with the press, totally upset with the press, because of the press' cutting and drying and convicting everybody right in the newspaper."[786]

But there was more to the conversation that Ravenna did not disclose at the time beyond saying "We had a normal brother-in-law conversation, interspersed with a number of things."

Ravenna can remember their discussion now because of what happened soon afterwards that left such an impression on him. While the press reports the two planned to meet at ten o'clock the next morning, Ravenna says that Gould told him matter-of-factly, without any sign of despondency, that he had to go away for a few days and asked him to check in with Charlene and the kids to make sure they were alright. They also discussed the problems in St. Johnsbury and that Gould told him Reed had been smirking at him earlier in the day.

Most notably, he did not express any concerns about his personal liability in receiving any of the stolen bits. Instead, he feared what Reed's actions did in the eyes of the troopers he worked with ("undermining him in the office," Ravenna recounted) who would then view him in a lesser light and thereby diminish his authority.

Gould was "a perfectionist" and proud to be a trooper, Ravenna said, and that during their conversation he continually looked inward, asking himself what he missed in hiring Charron and allowing the problem to fester and get to the level it did.

"I should have done a better job," Gould told him, blaming himself for bringing "a blemish on the badge." He also thought that state's attorney Gray believed everything that Reed was telling him. Ravenna did the best he could to console him and said not to worry, that "I didn't think things were as bad as he thought," and they would meet the next morning to talk further.

The two hung up and Ravenna reiterated that throughout their conversation Gould sounded normal and provided no indication he intended to harm himself.

An hour later, Diamond called him with the news.

After the two talked, Gould drove his truck to the rear of the statehouse, parked and walked a short distance to an archway, the so-called "Tunnel" separating the building from a cafeteria at its rear. AJ Ravenna thinks that the meticulous Gould did not want to leave a mess in his recently refurbished truck and that is why he walked away from it. Nobody witnessed what happened next, but someone heard a shot ring out shortly before 7:00 and an unidentified teenager passing by found Gould on the ground lying face up with "a gun in his hand, and his chest saturated in blood."

The Montpelier Police Department was summoned, but neither its responding officers and a local ambulance squad were able to revive him.[787]

The police quickly cordoned off the area and the local medical examiner and Washington County State's Attorney Gregory McNaughton arrived at the scene reporting that Gould's death appeared to be a suicide. Maj. Ryan was also notified and he, together with Patch and Prescott, came to coordinate with Montpelier police which agency should handle the investigation. Between them, they decided that the police department should take care of the actual suicide inquiry while the VSP crime lab handled the forensics.

At some point Lynch showed up, but, "was not permitted to enter the area."[788] The mobile laboratory arrived shortly thereafter and removed Gould's weapon from his right hand and a 1977 letter of commendation signed by Lynch from his pocket, placing them into evidence. Two pages from a stenographic notebook were also found over the sun visor of his truck. Around 10:30 p.m., his body was removed and taken to Burlington for an autopsy.

A ballistics test later confirmed that Gould used his .357 caliber service revolver to inflict, according to Chief Medical Examiner Eleanor McQuillen, a chest wound that entered mid-thorax and exited left back resulting in laceration of his heart with shock & hemorrhage—and death within seconds.[789]

Further tests confirmed Gould's fingerprints on the papers from his truck that quickly drew the attention of investigators because of their explosive contents. The first page was addressed to Gov. Snelling and the second to Capt. Heffernan and David Reed as Gould expressed his different thoughts to each.

To Snelling, he pleaded "Please leave my wife, my family, and the Vermont State Police alone" before signing his name.

He added additional language below signaling the impact that the inquest process and devastating revelations in the newspapers he could not respond to posed and which damaged his cherished reputation.

"If you must use your powers on something," he told Snelling, "reorganize the court system," followed by "Also thank your friends the press for their unbiased coverage."

His displeasure with Snelling constituted a valuable tool that the VSP command staff soon recognized it could use in its titanic struggle to assure its independence, threatened by the proposed new public safety agency.

The second page of Gould's note presented a different challenge to command personnel because it implicated the actions of other troopers about an event that nobody in authority knew anything about and which could further damage their already tarnished image. To Capt. Heffernan, the head of the field force, Gould wrote, "Ask Reed and Truex about illegal search in Danville" and that "Palmer heard about it from Truex on Thursday."

He also addressed his nemesis David Reed, who smirked at him on multiple occasions earlier in the day: "I put myself in your shoes and feel that if you look for the good in people you would have done different. May you sleep well at night."

His comments to Reed aside, Gould's revelation that there was more to the story than had been told seems to have sent the VSP commanders into their well-established secretive "fortress mentality."

It allowed them time to fashion a story able to remove questions about their integrity or further blemish the department's reputation.

Chapter 13

REAPING THE WHIRLWIND

SHIFTING BLAME

AFTER PATCH, RYAN AND PRESCOTT left the statehouse, they went to the St. Johnsbury office and directed an officer to go to his house to pick up his cruiser and bring it to the barracks. When Patch searched it immediately afterwards, he found a steno notebook with pages resembling the ones Gould's suicide note was written on.

While Patch's find did not reveal any conclusive connection to his death, in exhibiting the loose ways that some of the evidence was handled, he kept the notebook in the trunk of his car for the next month. Only after being questioned by investigators on Aug. 30 did Patch turn it over to the VSP laboratory for analysis.[790]

Patch also went to the Gould's residence the next day together with several others including Attorney General Diamond and his wife. Diamond was a friend of the Goulds from their time together in Windham County when he was state's attorney and Gould worked in the Brattleboro barracks. "We go back a long way," Diamond recalled, and had come to console Charlene when, at one point, he overheard Patch ask her if they could talk in private.[791]

The two went outside and when the Diamonds left, they took a path passing near where Patch and Charlene talked, but who did not realize their presence. Diamond recalled that he "overheard a conversation" as they passed and that "the part of the conversation I overheard was Capt. Patch trying to convince Charlene to give the Department permission to release the suicide note that her husband had written."

Patch wanted to do so, Diamond recounted, "because if it were released it would be embarrassing to the Governor and could be used to defend the Department at a time when the Department was coming under increasing negative publicity."

But, "at that point," he continued, "I guess Capt. Patch noticed me within hearing distance and immediately stopped the conversation."

Referring to this incident in his office's later report of the department, Diamond's deputy Gregory McKenzie described Patch's comments as consistent with the VSP's "policy of using its facilities to retaliate against a person suspected of trying to impeach the Department," repeating "a theme which some have seen in the Merriam case."[792]

It also presented a continuing example of the kind of petty retaliatory action the VSP command staff engaged in against people it felt threatened by, including state's attorneys McGee and Gray, and troopers Kostelnik and Cornelius Reed that repeated in the near future against another of their targets, David Reed.

In the following weeks, Diamond spoke with Charlene who called him and his wife to share her feelings and describe the pressure she felt deciding whether or not to release the note. Diamond recognized that "there, indeed, was a power play, so to speak, between the State Police and the Governor going on," and counseled her not "be dragged into it."[793]

In fact, Charlene's permission was never in issue because portions of the note soon reached the press that immediately made them public.

From her perspective, while she acknowledged speaking with Patch, Charlene could not recall the specifics of her conversation with him. When Patch was questioned about their conversation, he denied ever seeking to disparage the governor.

The "power play" that Diamond identified was very real as Snelling pushed forward with his proposal for a new Agency of Public Safety. The battles taking place within his Commission on the Administration of Justice also played out immediately after Gould's death when discussions over funding for the state's criminal justice information system unfolded. Fearful that their divisions could halt a $125,000 grant necessary to push the new agency forward, Sec. of Administration Mallary warned governor's counsel Gilbert to be careful about the "highly sensitive subject" and suggested he contact commission members to reiterate the importance Snelling placed on the grant.

It was "very important" they meet beforehand, Mallary wrote, so that they could discuss how to deal with those not "completely happy" with the proposal.[794]

The power struggle played out elsewhere involving the VSP and its interactions with the attorney general's office for reasons beyond the ongoing problems it had with Lynch. Diamond's chief investigator, AJ Ravenna, recalls that as soon as information about his conversation with Gould before his death became known, his routine interactions with the department's BCI conducting investigations were immediately cut off.

"BCI hated Diamond," Ravenna said, and that whenever he appeared at Redstone "its office doors were quickly closed" to bar his entry.

Ravenna already bore a disadvantage because of a grudge the department's high command held against him that began in 1977 when he left its ranks to work for Diamond. They viewed his new employment an act of "betrayal" because people did not leave the VSP to work for some other agency they believed seeking to undermine its authority.[795]

The 13-year BCI veteran detective corporal placed in the top three for promotion that year, but when he learned that Maj. Davis wanted to transfer him back into the uniform division as a patrol commander and move his family north to Middlesex, he saw it as a vindictive demotion.

No reason existed to transfer an experienced, qualified officer who worked his way up the chain of command to a position of prominence in this manner unless for some reason unrelated to his job performance. Ravenna could not be certain, but believes he fell into Redstone's disfavor after an encounter with Ryan.

When Ryan had occasion to walk into his Brattleboro office one day and found him writing a report with a radio playing quietly in the background, he confronted Ravenna asking how he could possibly do that. In what he believed a lighthearted response, Ravenna responded, "Well captain, I can also walk and chew gum at the same time," whereupon Ryan pivoted and walked out.

From that time on, Ravenna seemed to encounter disfavor from headquarters and Davis's order for him to move back into the uniform division made such little sense he spoke with Diamond who welcomed such an experienced officer to join him.

On Aug. 1, two days after Gould's death, almost the entire VSP high command descended on the St. Johnsbury office to attend meetings reverberating soon afterwards affecting the careers of several of them. After their arrival, Ryan, Heffernan, Spear, Prescott, Lay, and Lt. Gordon Mooney separated to conduct two meetings. In a one-hour gathering of all the officers that Ryan attended, the focus was, as he recounted, "to learn the frame of mind of the troopers and counsel them to seek medical help with the Department's funding in order to prevent a reoccurrence of the Gould suicide."[796] After the meeting, Ryan walked into the second meeting in Lay's office where David Reed underwent questioning by Heffernan and Prescott about Gould's report of his involvement in an "illegal search in Danville." Before Ryan entered, Reed asked Heffernan if he could have an attorney present and was told he could not; a situation that repeated itself when he underwent additional questioning by Heffernan on Aug. 8 and 9.

After Ryan arrived, the intensity in the room increased substantially when he confronted Reed and engaged him in what he called "close questioning" that Reed characterized instead as "aggressive" and "almost an attack."

When the attorney general's office examined their encounter, it characterized it as more of an intense, angry, slanted, accusing interrogation than, placing quotation marks around the word for emphasis, an "interview."[797]

Just as Ryan had participated in his rushed meeting with Heffernan, Spear, Patch, and Lay a week earlier after Lynch's firing and the subject of Reed's integrity came up, on this occasion after Gould's death the stakes were even higher. In the interim, the VSP command staff had time to assess how to address its increasingly apparent inaction on the router bit investigation and settled on Reed as their convenient scapegoat in an effort eerily mimicking the faultfinding efforts of the Irasburg board of inquiry a decade earlier.

Now, the issue of his integrity became of secondary importance as they focused their attention instead on a more personal level and attacked, without any discernable or justifiable reason, Reed's mental capacity. It was only the beginning of what proved a concerted campaign to undermine and destroy the credibility of an otherwise honorable officer to drive him from the ranks. And it backfired in spectacular fashion.

The lack of any department rules or regulations that legislators and other officials clamored for in past years now had a significant impact on a rudderless command staff unobstructed by the interference of a functioning internal affairs unit able to navigate the thorny issues such work entailed. As the Keyser Commission concluded in examining this time period, "There are no regulations of the Department which deal with the level of command that should conduct internal investigations" allowing them to happen "on an ad-hoc basis."[798]

Of the abuses uncovered and among the several departmental charges later instituted against Ryan by Commissioner Paul Philbrook in 1981 was one involving his conduct with Reed as a result of their interaction at St. Johnsbury.

"Acting singly and/or in concert with others," Philbrook alleged, Ryan had "ordered David Reed to undergo psychiatric examination when he knew or should have known that there was no substantial basis for such examination."[799]

In recounting their exchange leading up to his decision to require Reed to undergo the examination Philbrook recited, Ryan prepared a three-page memorandum (some of it redacted from public view) explaining what led him to question his mental state. In it, he related that after entering the room he engaged Reed "in conversation in an attempt to determine his state of mind."[800]

Reed was clearly distressed and told the three command officers that he "felt isolated," he "might just as well resign," that he "would not recover from the damages to his reputation incurred as a result of the release of the deposition," and "he wished he could be suspended so he could get it over with."

Continuing in his effort to inquire into, Ryan reiterated, Reed's "frame of mind," he quizzed him on other matters indicating his probing intention to undermine Reed's accounts rather than to ascertain candidly what happened. Perhaps Ryan never intended such an interpretation of his account, but it forcibly demonstrates that he did not believe anything Reed had to say and that his ultimate decision concerning his fate was already pre-determined.

When Ryan asked him about his notification to Redstone about the router bits and Charron incident, Reed told him he was "paranoid about headquarters" because of the unfavorable reception he received from Spear when he confronted him about it. Reed told Ryan of his conversation with Lynch about the matter during their time together when he drove him between meetings.

Ryan also confronted him with having confided in Sen. Morse about the St. Johnsbury matter and Reed admitted that he did. When Ryan "questioned closely" why he had not pursued "the investigation of the suspected troopers," Reed told him that they never investigate troopers in their own offices.

This led Ryan, already aware of the problem a full year beforehand and who certainly knew that internal investigations only started when the commissioner ordered them, to disingenuously record that "This is either a calculated lie or a gross misconception of the real-life situation."

He reached this conclusion, he wrote, because Reed had previously investigated Truex who worked in his own office which would, to a struggling Ryan seeking justification, "seem that it could be a lie."

When Ryan summarized his interaction with Reed, he made serious allegations that do not appear supported by the evidence.

"The impact of this conversation" Ryan wrote the day after, left him "with the opinion that Sergeant Reed was either a devious, scheming manipulator or suffering from a personality disorder."

Rather than a candid assessment about the problems that Reed revealed and proposing a way to resolve them, Ryan's report constituted little more than yet another effort by VSP command staff to attack an unfortunate messenger.

The same day that Ryan wrote these words, former Navy admiral, and Woodstock native, 56-year-old Warren M. Cone "vaulted from peaceful retirement obscurity into the middle of what has become one of Vermont's most emotional controversies."

With a background in communications and none in law enforcement, Snelling was unhesitant to appoint the recently retired sailor as Vermont's next commissioner of public safety for a brief period in order, he hoped, to bring much needed stability to a department in turmoil.

Additionally, Cone must have also agreed not to interfere with his plan for a new Agency of Public Safety before receiving the assignment.

Faced with the attorney general's recent assessment of the department's deficiencies, Cone promised to conduct his own investigation. "I want to find out exactly what the facts are," he said, "and put them into perspective."

Utilizing the same words that Gov. Hoff used in establishing the Irasburg board of inquiry, Cone said "I will not conduct or permit a witch hunt to be conducted."[801] He immediately sought outside assistance and asked Snelling to contact Connecticut Gov. Ella Grasso and solicit her help providing officers from her state police force to conduct an investigation.[802]

As the VSP command staff considered their next moves, the accolades on Howard Gould's behalf rolled in. Former Gov. Hoff had past involvement with him and described him as "first class, polite, nice, orderly, prompt—all the good things a trooper is."[803]

The recently dismissed Lynch also added his thoughts, "I'm heartsick. I'm heartbroken. I weep for his family. In my opinion this tragedy should never have happened."[804]

Facing his own internal problems, Ryan described Gould graciously as "hard-working and capable and extremely proud of the department." "I have known him for years," he said, "and consider him a steady and dedicated police officer in love with his job." Connecting Gould's suicide directly with the problems in St. Johnsbury, he said further that "When you're exhausted emotionally, God knows what happens. It was not a small thing to him obviously."

He also acknowledged the difficulties that all six troopers named by the press faced and said that "These guys are just at a loss as to what to do. Their pride, honor and careers are a very big thing."[805]

Gould's supervisor, Lt. Prescott who spoke with him earlier in the day about the department's exhibit at the Champlain Valley Fair, expressed similar feelings, describing him as "a devoted family man, who built his own home and loved to hunt."

"No question in my mind," he said, "he was as fine a young man as you would want to meet."

From the public, one former neighbor also expressed her feelings and said that Gould was a "very easy-going guy, a very nice guy, but quiet. He wasn't the type to make enemies."[806] And another said that "You had to know how intense this guy was. His work had taken him to the edge of his grave."[807]

Reluctant to make any kind of a public statement, Charlene offered simply that "All that my husband has lived for and felt so deeply is embodied in these few words: He died as he lived—a good, honest man. There is nothing more to say."[808]

Even before Gould's funeral a chorus of indignation rose up from various levels of government and throughout the state's law enforcement community.

"Vermont State Police," the *Rutland Herald* reported, "shocked and bitter over the suicide of a fellow trooper, moved to have the Supreme Court investigate prosecutors' handling of a secret inquest which is believed to have played a role in the suicide."

There was no doubt in anyone's mind that the leaking of deposition and/or inquest testimony to the press led directly to Gould's death because, Ryan said, he believed it "detracted from his image and the image of the department."[809]

Future governor and former member of the 1975 legislative committee investigating the VSP Lt. Gov. Madeleine Kunin also condemned the leaks and said they "were to blame for Gould's death."[810]

Washington County State's Attorney McNaughton agreed and said that "To him, his integrity was important, and to him, the way the public was reacting, he didn't have any integrity left, whether he was guilty or not."[811]

He went further, accusing that "Those responsible for the media coverage bear a heavy responsibility for his death."[812]

He did not mention either Gray or Diamond for their possible involvement with the disclosures, but strongly insinuated the fault lay with one of them. The conspiratorial-minded Ryan also blamed the disclosures on others and angrily said that "This is another step on the ladder of somebody's long-range plans."

Had Redstone's delay in investigating the circumstances in St. Johnsbury or Ryan's order to Reed to investigate Gray's relationship with trooper Kostelnik caused the prosecutor to, in turn, disclose secret inquest information to the press in the same way he had already done with the detective's deposition in order to take the pressure off of himself? Unfortunately, none of the ensuring investigations ever resolved that question. Regardless, the leaks reported in the press were, McNaughton said, the "catalyst" for Gould's suicide and the fact that he committed it at the state house bore "symbolic overtones."[813]

Lynch weighed in with his characteristically earthy commentary to condemn, using Ryan's words, the "tempest in a teapot" situation in St. Johnsbury that prosecutors pursued ("busily engaged in turning over every rock") and the publicity the department received ("character assassination") in a press conference that one newspaper reported as "impassioned" and "rambling." A "common dog of a criminal," Lynch said, would get more due process and legal protections than troopers, "Every day after day they pick up the paper and there they're flagellated, there they're indicted, there they're tried, and there they're hanged."[814]

More than 900 mourners from throughout Vermont and New England, including at least seventeen police departments, appeared at St. Peter's Church in Rutland on Aug. 2, 1979 to attend Gould's funeral. It was described as "the largest crowd in anyone's memory" packing into the church. The brief service lasted only a few minutes as the crowd listened to a pastor "read from the Book of Lamentations, saying of the man who took his own life Monday: 'My life is sadness, I tell myself my future is lost.'"[815]

Afterward, "one of the longest processions in recent times" accompanied the casket bearing his body, clad in his full-dress uniform, to Evergreen Cemetery to receive military honors before being laid in the ground.[816]

While the fired Lynch appeared at the church and characteristically assumed his customary showman position occupying center stage alongside the Gould family ("still a member of the Vermont State Police," he said), Gov. Snelling was conspicuously absent "in accordance, his aides said, 'with the wishes of the family.'"[817]

However, he did release a statement reiterating that Gould's suicide was "a tragic element in what was already a very sad and complex situation," and that it "highlights the urgency of dealing properly and promptly with the current events and controversy about the state police."

Barred from attending, Snelling prepared an extraordinary document addressed simply to "Vermont State Troopers." Across six single-spaced pages, the state's governor spoke directly from his heart to each of the men and women of the VSP in a way never done before. He outlined what had taken place to this time, how his office conducted itself, and sought the troopers' understanding and support ("I need your help," he wrote) as a complicated investigation process was about to unfold that could not be characterized as either a "witch hunt" or a "cover-up."

He told them about his meeting in May 1978 with two unnamed state's attorneys (McGee and Gray) who first conveyed to him their concerns about "wrong-doing by a member of the Vermont State Police" (without naming Merriam as the subject) that, if true, would "indicate a problem which no reasonable and responsible person could or should ignore."

He described Lynch's dismissive attitude towards those allegations, the attorney general's report into the situation that he received on June 29, 1979, and then learned, for the first time just weeks later the serious reports of wrongdoing in St. Johnsbury. He acknowledged Lynch's "very favorable impression with the troops," but also reminded them that he was a civilian member of the governor's cabinet acting as their commissioner and, by definition, was "not a 'trooper.'" Writing that "the courts and history will decide" the propriety of his actions, Snelling explained his dismissal of Lynch because "of my lack of conviction that he would dispose of the complaints and allegations" swirling around the VSP. He planned to pursue further inquiry, he said, "in such a way that reasonable men and women would conclude that an objective investigation had been made, and that the actions taken were right and fair in accordance with an impartial reading of the evidence."

Once completed, he said that "the trivial will appear clearly to reasonable people (to) be trivial, and the important and substantial problems, if any, will have been clearly dealt with in such a way as to warrant public confidence."

Snelling also expressed his great appreciation for the hard work of the "99.9 percent of the members of the department" and told them he stood firmly behind them.[818] However, his solicitations for peace between his office and the VSP seem to have meant little to some of the conspiratorially-minded members of the VTA responding in anger against him for firing Lynch.

"This leaves .1 percent of our organization in a questionable grey light," its president complained, "and also leaves a question mark in the minds of the Vermont taxpayer."

As recounted on the frontpage of the *Rutland Herald* under the headline "Snelling Condemned by State Troopers," the association further charged him with an agenda aimed at exploiting the St. Johnsbury problem to his advantage and allow him "firm political control" over the state police. "This .1 percent," the president continued, "is the basis that the governor is using to create an urgency for completion of this investigation (into alleged police wrongdoing). This .1 percent is the embryo from which is to be born a new 'Vermont Police Organization,' a new 'Super Agency' under the direction of many appointed departmental heads, all answerable to none other than the governor."[819]

Meanwhile, lawyers in the attorney general's office debated whether the release of its report on the Merriam matter to substantiate Snelling's statements would expose the governor to a lawsuit by Lynch for damages.[820]

On Aug. 3, Assistant Attorney General Hudson contacted the newly installed Cone to schedule a meeting with himself and State's Attorney Gray to, as Cone wrote, "talk with me relative to an investigation they were conducting."

They met late in the day at Hudson's office to discuss the growing number of investigations, believing it necessary to come to an agreement between them how to resolve any conflicts that might arise. Cone told them that if they ever thought any problem existed to contact him directly and he would do the same and call Hudson. "Let's not fight each other," Cone told them.

The two attorneys also advised they planned to use the services of a Massachusetts polygrapher to examine Reed "to find out if what he told them was the truth or not," and requested that Cone provide them with a vehicle, which Cone could not promise. He also told them that, as of that day, Reed had been re-assigned from St. Johnsbury to Redstone to work in the training division preparing curriculum for an upcoming state police class. After Cone told them that he would be working for Patch, the attorneys advised him that "you know that they don't get along." Cone said he "didn't know they didn't get along," but told Gray "I understand what you are saying."[821]

A second assistant attorney general in Diamond's office, David Putter, also met separately with Cone to discuss the fallout from the turmoil Gould's suicide posed to the department. In a meeting that has never been reported before, Putter recalls the two of them talked privately in Cone's Redstone office; a building State's Attorney Lium soon dubbed "Redgate" in this post-Watergate period for its role in the persecution of David Reed.[822]

Watergate is a particularly apropos analogy providing further insight into the mindset of Redstone's occupants similar to a Nixon White House where paranoia boiled inside its walls. Cone was particularly careful in these highly unusual times when dealing with people he had no experience with and confided with Putter a secret that nobody knew anything about. In what Putter recalled was a "dead serious" tone, he told him he installed tapping devices in the building that nobody knew about, including his office and other locations he did not care to identify.[823]

There has never been any evidence that Cone did as he said, but his sharing of such highly sensitive information with Putter deserves significant credibility in light of the stakes at that moment.

Cone also spoke with Ryan who conveyed to him his recent interview with Reed in St. Johnsbury and the purported "inconsistencies and unique attitudes" he presented. Ryan sought Cone's consent to allow him to provide a profile of the officer's background to "a proper person" to determine if a "psychiatric examination would be in order."[824] The timing of Ryan's request is not clear because Cone met with Reed on Aug. 7 and came to his own conclusion that he "was going to be a critical witness." Contrary to Ryan's account, Cone took credit for the decision, writing that "I decided that it would be best to eliminate any possibilities of legal problems with respect to the validity of a witness and have David Reed visit a psychiatrist" and told Ryan to arrange it.[825]

Regardless of who had the idea, the Keyser Commission expressed its "serious reservations" about Ryan's conduct after his interview with Reed because of the way he disparaged him as a "devious, scheming manipulator" and one "suffering from a personality disorder." "Major Ryan's presentation of a psychological profile," the commission concluded, "could hardly be unbiased."[826] At the same time, it did not fault Cone's decision to allow Ryan to pursue the examination because he reasonably believed that Reed suffered from "tremendous pressure" by what was happening and the timing of Gould's suicide.[827]

Ryan's presentation occurred only hours after Cone met with Reed when he and Patch proceeded to the Waterbury State Hospital and met with Dr. Nancy Collett, Psychiatric Clinical Director of the Willard Geriatric Unit.

Their hour-long meeting included Ryan's presentation of his version of a "profile" of Reed that he wanted Collett to consider and then render an opinion "as to whether or not the background as depicted could be a symptom of a mental disorder" and, if so, how to proceed. Ryan's account of the meeting reports that before providing her with information about the St. Johnsbury matter, he told her about another incident that never appeared in any of the investigations and which may have been maintained in a secret, second file that nobody beyond the VSP high command knew about; his actions replicated the same efforts he took to undermine the promotion of Cornelius Reed in 1977 when he provided unsubstantiated rumor to a board.

Ryan recounted to Collett his personal involvement with Reed "about an incident that occurred a number of years ago in Rutland where (Reed) made it a point to inform (him) that the officers in the

Rutland area were committing minor infractions." Nothing more on this matter was disclosed, but Ryan apparently thought that because "this information was unsolicited" it was of value in making an assessment about Reed's sanity. Or, could Reed have simply provided Ryan with his suspicions about the activities of Paul Lawrence that Ryan did not want revealed at this later time because of Redstone's delay in acting on them?

Ryan then expanded on his "profile" to Collett describing a series of seemingly innocuous events twisted to infer that Reed had devious motives indicative of decreased mental capacity. They included Reed's belief that his superiors "intentionally covered up" the St. Johnsbury matter; a "confrontation" he had with Trooper Truex about his "playing penny ante poker at his residence on his time off;" an internal investigation that Reed conducted into Truex in another matter that he did not complete; the apparent reversal of Reed's position regarding the investigation Lynch wanted him to conduct into state's attorney Gray's purported "immoral conduct" when he refused to disparage the attorney in his relationship with trooper Kostelnik; and, in reporting matters "such as the Kostelnik and router bits incidents that he would not sign" his written statements. Absent from his account, Ryan never told Collett what actually happened with Reed's report into the Gray-Kostelnik relationship when he ordered Reed to rewrite it to disparage Gray and then Heffernan directed him to rewrite it again to take the onus off of Gray and place it onto Kostelnik. His selective recitation of facts of Reed's conduct provides further indication of his intention to place the blame for the VSP's high command negligence onto someone who did nothing wrong.

Ryan answered several of Collett's questions and told her that Reed was about 35-years-old, married for two years and about "the recent tragedy in his life due to the still born death of his first child."

At the end of their meeting, Collett recommended that Reed be examined by a psychiatrist and suggested he meet with Dr. William Woodruff.[828] In light of the rushed series of events taking place over the past days and Gould's death, Collett's assessment based upon the slanted representations made by the VSP's second-in-command cannot be necessarily be faulted. As a result, they provided Ryan with additional cover in his effort to disparage Reed and escalate his devastating attacks in the next months.

However, it did not meet all of the high command's approval and Capt. Spear later acknowledged that "Yes, emphatically yes I feel (Reed) was unfairly treated" as a result."[829]

Events moved quickly elsewhere in the governor's office and Redstone in Montpelier and with inquest proceedings pursued by Hudson and Gray in St. Johnsbury. On Aug. 6, 50 troopers of the VTA met with Lynch and his attorney at the Berlin Armory where he "reassured them I'd fight this thing through to get my job back."

Unconvinced of the purity of Snelling's intentions for the department, the group issued a two-page statement questioning his reorganization efforts, accusing him of engaging in a "witch hunt" resulting in Lynch's firing. "Our department has become a political billiard ball being thrust into various pockets for the sake of public notoriety recognition," they said.

While the organization expressed little fear at what their members might have done in the current environment, they also lamented the revisiting of instances of police misconduct occurring years earlier. "Let the cold light of day and the Vermont taxpayer again be our judge," they wrote, "We have no political ambition. Can all involved in this investigation make the same claim?"[830]

Fears of politicization of the department was indeed a significant challenge for Snelling, who received specific warning from former commissioner Baumann in June about the problem in conjunction with the creation of his Agency of Public Safety.

Concerning the internal operations of such a department, Baumann wrote to counsel Gilbert, "I do not want to have politics interfere in the appointment, promotion and apprehension process in the state police. It does in the local and county process but never, I hope, in the Vermont State Police."[831]

Faced with growing opposition to the new agency proposal, Gilbert wrote to Snelling on Aug. 6 that it was "extremely important" that he postpone his efforts "so that troopers and others will not feel that the current instability is being used as a time for the Agency to be rammed through."

"Right!," Snelling agreed with emphasis after circling Gilbert's words and that it was a "<u>Very</u> important consideration."[832]

The turmoil also had an immediate effect on the legislature itself where a committee recommended to Snelling on Aug. 3 to convene "an early meeting of the Emergency Board" to consider a $17,000 allocation to the DPS to help alleviate space problems in its laboratory.[833]

Every branch of government faced some kind of challenge because of Howard Gould's suicide and the next months presented the opportunity for each to share some part of the agony.

INVESTIGATIONS

Excluding the secret inquest proceedings conducted by state and county prosecutors examining potential criminal conduct and the recently released attorney general report on Merriam, two more investigations of the VSP took place in the last half of 1979. An additional one conducted by the legislature followed in early 1980.

Aside from the messy shotgun approach, unsurprisingly yielding inconsistent results, the most reliable contribution from any of those efforts came from Connecticut State Police officers assigned to its Statewide Organized Crime Investigative Task Force. The seriousness and complexity of the challenges surrounding Gould's suicide became so interwoven that on Aug. 9, 1979, on orders from Gov. Grasso following Cone's request to Snelling, Connecticut's Commissioner of Public Safety Donald J. Long assigned the task force's commanding officer, Director Lt. John F. Bardelli (hired in 1966), also a third-year law student, to head the investigation. Following his assignment in Vermont, Bardelli returned home to complete law school, retire from the state police in 2001 after a stellar career taking him to its highest rank as commander of the entire force, finally serving as United States Marshal for the District of Connecticut from 2003–2008.

Two other task force members, Sgt. Martin A. Ohradan (1958) and Trooper Laurent C. Guillot (1964), assisted Bardelli in the investigation. The highly trained and experienced team, each with a military background, soon provided much needed expertise examining

Vermont's quagmire of problems. They provided an unbiased probing perspective to a challenge requiring their concerted attention for the next two months before concluding their work in October.

It marked the first time that any CSP officers ever participated in an internal police matter outside of their state.

The same day Commissioner Long assigned them to the task, Lynch and Ryan appeared in court to undergo questioning at an inquest conducted by Hudson and Gray.

On Aug. 13, Bardelli and Ohradan arrived in Montpelier and met with Cone and Ryan to begin their assignment. Their work space consisted of a "small office beneath the Barre office of Attorney Joseph Palmisano, the special attorney appointed to assist the (DPS) in the investigation."[834] "Specific instructions were provided to them in writing," Bardelli wrote in the first of many reports, "which directed the investigators to look into several areas of questionable practices" of the DPS.

"Additional oral instructions" directed them to also "pursue any other avenues of investigation which would assist in a comprehensive evaluation of the (DPS) performance record and its procedures for internal controls" and "to report on any incidents of wrongdoing including apparent coverups."

After speaking with Cone and Ryan and reviewing some of the reports they provided, the investigators identified eight areas to focus on. As listed by Bardelli, they included references to the well-known router bit problem, matters referred to in Gould's suicide note, and additional allegations of misconduct unconnected to his death:

A. Charron Investigation

B. Garfield House Search

C. State vs. Brown Matter

D. Kostelnik Matter

E. Priest Investigation

F. Merriam-McGee Controversy

G. Merriam Polygraph Incident

H. Gould Suicide[835]

To assure the confidentiality of their reports, Bardelli explained to Cone that a single, multi-page carbon "snap-out" form utilized by his agency would be used, identified by SOCITF case number 37–10.

The initial reports would be stored in a locked safe at the task force office in Meriden, Conn. where only Bardelli and Long could have access. When their work was completed, he told Cone, "We will deliver to you the entire form intact" and that "No photocopies will be made."[836]

The fruits of their labors eventually found their way into the records of the Keyser Commission. They reveal that they interviewed over 100 witnesses, half of them VSP officers, supplemented by fifteen polygraph tests conducted by a Washington, D. C. examiner that Cone called in. Departing from their lodging at the Sir Anthony Motel in Barre at 8 a.m. each day and working late into the evening, the officers' reports reveal the many different avenues their investigation took.

They logged thousands of miles around the state ("on a task no one had ever undertaken before") as they assiduously identified and doggedly tracked down new witnesses directing their inquiries into other areas of potential concern that nobody knew about before they asked their probing questions.[837]

Bogus allegations that potential witnesses committed other crimes and indiscretions (arson and infidelity) were thoroughly investigated in textbook fashion to determine their credibility before moving on to the next potentially explosive revelation. Their careful efforts duplicated the kinds of actions taken by VSP investigators during the Irasburg Affair that also ran down many leads in order to gain as much information as possible. The Connecticut officers also encountered resentment from within the VSP ranks when its members conveyed the attitude that they preferred to "handle their own problems" internally and an impression of "why the hell don't they leave us alone and let us do our job."

Bardelli understood their displeasure at the intrusive nature of their work but also recognized the legitimacy of the allegations being made. While identifying several "gray areas" of concern and concluding that a probe was "definitely needed," his team ultimately determined, in a qualified manner, that "the greatest majority of state police (are) dedicated law enforcement officers who intend to do a good job."[838]

The quality of the work conducted by these experienced, no-nonsense organized crime investigators makes their efforts the most reliable source of information for this time period as nothing seemed to escape their eyes. In comparison, the VSP's work paled and when the Keyser Commission examined the work of corporals Adams and Farmer during their inquiry into the Merriam-McGee fray, it identified noticeable differences from their out-of-state counterparts examining the same set of facts. "The Connecticut State Police investigation," it wrote, "is actually much more thorough. Many more people were interviewed, including all of the ambulance personnel, the State's Attorneys' investigators, other troopers, other persons with complaints about Merriam, Michael Lauzon and, in addition, the personnel files of Merriam were reviewed." Despite Cone's questionable conclusion in his own parallel inquiry taking place at the same time that the two VSP corporals "did a thorough job of investigation," the commission found otherwise. "The contrast between (the Connecticut) investigation and the Adams and Farmer investigation," it wrote, "certainly suggests that the Adams and Farmer investigation could have been much more vigorous."[839]

The high standard set by the Connecticut men seems to have satisfied the commission because it relied overwhelmingly on many of its reports in reaching its conclusions. Even Snelling looked to Connecticut investigators for help, prevailing on them to assess the quality of security at his Shelburne home and measures needed for the "protective security at the Governor's office."[840]

Cast in a seemingly subservient role in providing adequate protection to the state's highest elected official, the VSP had additional work to do to maintain his confidence it could protect him.

While Cone pursued his own internal investigation relying on and meting out discipline based on the work conducted by his VSP investigators, the Keyser Commission assembled to consider how to accomplish its mandate. Snelling cast a wide net in setting it up and while its reputable members possessed an admirable amount of experience, consistent with the members of the Irasburg Board of Inquiry, none had any in the demands of routine police work. Its five members included 81-one-year-old, former supreme court justice, F. Ray Keyser, former attorney general Charles E. Gibson Jr., attorney and chair of the University of Vermont Board of Trustees Peter P. Plante, vice president of one of the state's largest insurance companies and former mayor of Burlington Francis J. Cain, and the former editor of the *Burlington Free Press* Gordon T. Mills.

On Aug. 10, Snelling formally welcomed the commission members to their work, writing that "Vermont is very much in your debt for agreeing to serve her in helping to arrive at sensible conclusions concerning a matter of very great public policy importance."

"The broadest charge I could give you," he said, "would be to assist the state of Vermont with an overriding goal of justifying public confidence in government and in particular in the operations of the Vermont State Police."[841]

Snelling set out several ambitious goals for the commission to accomplish, described in five single-spaced pages. They reveal his great hope it could unravel and solve the complex and contentious environment the VSP had fallen into and evaded his own efforts to remedy.

He still had hopes of success for his Agency of Public Safety proposal at some point, but the times demanded immediate, drastic changes. His far-reaching assignment to his commission included: reconciling the findings of the attorney general's latest report with whatever conclusions Cone reached in his internal investigation; the adequacy of VSP rules, procedures and regulations, whether they met constitutional standards and to make recommendations for change; a thorough examination of the St. Johnsbury situation and whether a coverup took place; look into other reports of wrong-doing to see if they were handled appropriately; examine existing statutes and make recommendations regarding the appointment and removal of commissioners; how to resolve problems of statutorily imposed confidentiality concerning (inquest) documents hindering the ability of state's attorneys, the attorney general and executive branch to share information; examine the leaking of confidential information to journalists that has "become the subject of great speculation injurious to the orderly process of factfinding and to the determination to protect the civil rights and reputation of individuals whose conduct became the subject of speculation;" and, finally, provide guidance regarding the public's right to know about government operations.

In addition to this herculean list, Snelling sought the commission's guidance in whether an "independent review commission" was needed outside of the VSP to examine its internal problems.

"The extreme damage to the morale of the Vermont State Police," he wrote, "and to the families of troopers, as well as to public confidence" called for change and he asked if such a review body "or some other structure" could remove such concerns out from under VSP control and into another arena. Snelling further advised the commission that in its work it should "take the testimony of any witnesses" and to avail itself of any documents it could find to accomplish its goals.

Chapter 14

"ABSOLUTELY A FARCE"

ABUSING AUTHORITY

BEFORE THE KEYSER COMMISSION COMPLETED ITS WORK, David Reed experienced further discomfort as the VSP relentlessly scrutinized his purportedly defective mental state. Based on Ryan's interview with Dr. Collett, Cone directed Reed to submit to a psychological examination and polygraph test. He complied and met with Dr. Woodruff who found him sane and attended a polygraph examination providing inconclusive results.[842] Next, prosecutors Gray and Hudson sought their own examination and arranged for Reed to go to Massachusetts to meet with another psychiatrist and undergo a second polygraph examination.

While that psychiatrist determined he was "extremely anxious over both the serious consequences of events in which he was embroiled and over his wife's health," he found that Reed was "certainly rational and aware of the consequences of his behavior."[843]

The next polygraph took place in two sessions between Aug. 14 and 15. Its inconclusive results reported that Reed was both untruthful in some regards and evasive in others. It further determined that "based on the continuous vacillations" he provided to questions, "this case consists of facts and features that were perhaps <u>overstated</u> at one time and are <u>understated</u> or vaguely stated."[844]

On Aug. 24, Reed underwent another evaluation in Burlington that included both a stress test and a third polygraph.

This time, the polygraph examiner found Reed "truthful in every regard" and that the exam conducted in Massachusetts could not be accepted because the operator "gave a non-standard test which was not properly conducted" and that any inconclusive findings should be resolved in his favor. Apparently dissatisfied at those favorable results, his supervisor, Capt. Patch, immediately ordered Reed to undergo another psychiatric exam with Woodruff to purportedly assure his sanity before taking yet another polygraph.

While he complied, and Woodruff determined him sane once again, Reed reasonably believed that the repeated examinations constituted "a harassment tactic rather than true concern for his mental state."[845]

However, it did not stop and on Sept. 1 he underwent another stress test ordered by his superiors. Cone and Woodruff discussed Reed on several occasions between September and October. Woodruff told him that the officer was indeed sane, but, according to Cone's notes, "saw things only in black and white and was troubled because he could not remember things that happened with respect to (the router bits matter)" that led him to believe Reed "needed further consultations." When Cone called Woodruff on Oct. 17 to advise he planned to charge him in the near future, the doctor told him "you know, David Reed believes that he is being blamed for the whole thing." After Cone told him "I would expect so," Woodruff ended the conversation saying "O.K., Admiral, you have the quarterdeck."[846]

The VSP continued to hound Reed and on Oct. 24 he underwent another stress test.[847]

Finally, on Nov. 1 Reed was examined by a psychologist who found him truthful, but who also determined he "had serious limitations of memory with the passage of time."

The examiner also faulted the conclusions drawn from the first two polygraph tests because of all the questioning Reed underwent about events that took place such a long time ago and that the two psychological exams he underwent caused him to be "uncertain as to what he could remember with certainty and what he could not."

In the end, the Keyser Commission simply discounted virtually all of it because none of the tests were acceptable evidence in court and that "no test standing alone is conclusive."[848]

The ham-handed attempts by Reed's superiors to discredit his sanity by making him participate in so many examinations and tests failed miserably. They also incurred the wrath of one of Howard Gould's close friends and frequent critic of the VSP dating back to 1967 during the Alexander regime, now NEK's Essex County state's attorney, Sten Lium, formerly of Caledonia County. Incredulous at what Reed went through, Lium blasted the process attacking Ryan as the instigator of an orchestrated campaign to belittle and force him to leave the department.

The letter Ryan sent to Collett setting off the series of examinations was, he said, a "complete and utter fabrication" precipitating concerns within the ranks that Reed should be institutionalized. Even after the department's own psychiatrist found him sane on two occasions, Lium alleged that his superiors continued to try and make him the sacrificial lamb for their problems and to bear the burden for Gould's suicide.

"The exploitation of a man's suicide to destroy a man's reputation is the most vicious thing I've ever heard of," Lium exclaimed. Ryan, Patch, Heffernan, Spear and Ramey were "not qualified" to lead the VSP Lium said and that "There's no way to exaggerate the pathology in that agency. No department in this state has ever misused its power like this department." Lium wanted the men removed or else "the granite-like integrity and superb reputation of the (VSP) will continue to be eroded and no new officers will ever dare to report corruption or wrongdoing."[849] The scapegoating the department faced during the Irasburg Affair had now come full circle to implicate the involvement of VSP commanders themselves as the instigators seeking to assign wrongdoing on an innocent victim when none existed.

From the existing records, it is not possible to ascertain specifically what Cone relied on in determining whether or not to administratively charge members of the VSP. Concerns later arose about his conduct during his short time as commissioner when Lium charged him with engaging in another coverup to protect members of the high command. Rather than exercise sufficient independent control of the department, Lium condemned the powerful cadre of entrenched officers who "took (Cone) in and made him a clone," calling their conduct "sick."[850] Their influence over Cone was so overwhelming that in a very short time, without waiting for the full results of the extensive CSP investigation then underway, and contrary to his earlier promise to not engage in a witch hunt, Cone made up his mind to punish the St. Johnsbury troopers. On Aug. 31, 1979, he met with Cpl. John Palmer at an exit on Interstate 89 to apprise him that, even though he passed a polygraph showing he did not know he accepted stolen property, "he would be punished at the appropriate time for having router bits that did not belong to him in his possession."

The next day, Trooper Truex went to Cone's home where he similarly learned that although he too passed a test showing he did not know they were stolen, he planned to punish him "for having router bits in his possession not belonging to him" and for conducting an unrelated, questionably illegal search that Gould referred to in his suicide note.[851]

Had Howard Gould lived, he no doubt would have received a similar warning, despite the absence of evidence of his own wrongdoing.

Cone's willingness to punish the officers so quickly for engaging in conduct devoid of any evidence to intentionally commit either a criminal act or violate departmental rules without the benefit of the CSP report is noteworthy. It strongly suggests an absence of independent judgment and, instead, displays the power and pre-determination of Redstone's occupants to offer up the troopers as sacrificial lambs to show that something was being done and remove the onus of their own neglect from over their heads.

While Heffernan did some of the work leading to Cone's decision to punish the troopers, the commissioner also shared what information he had with the department's attorney, Joseph Palmisano, who also had access to reports prepared by the out-of-state investigators and video tapes of Reed's examinations. After reviewing the materials, on Oct. 2, 1979, Palmisano wrote a confidential letter to Cone recommending that Reed "be charged administratively (for violations of regulations and) should also be subject to dismissal for conduct unbecoming a state police officer based upon the totality of the circumstances."[852]

Interestingly, neither "conduct unbecoming a state police officer" or "totality of the circumstances" appeared in any of the department's rules and regulations that Palmisano cited as authority. Regardless, moving quickly and believing in his guidance, Cone met with Gray and Hudson on two occasions in the next week before a general strategy meeting took place on Oct. 10 attended by the two prosecutors, Cone, Attorney General Diamond and his deputy, Gregory McKenzie. "At this meeting," Cone recorded, "it was agreed that no criminal charges would be filed against any of the current State Police; however, that I would conduct the administrative functions commensurate with the degree of culpability of those concerned."[853]

On Oct. 11, Cone summoned the four St. Johnsbury troopers still working for the department to his office in Redstone to mete out their punishment. In this environment devoid of comprehensive, workable, and understandable rules and regulations to guide officers' conduct and unable to cite a specific reason to punish them, Cone made his own subjective assessment of their guilt. It represented a serious departure from any notion they received appropriate due process for their alleged missteps.

It is even more concerning when each of the officers already passed polygraph examinations and Cone specifically concluded "that none of these people knew that the router bits were stolen."[854] The only provision of the deficient rules instituted in 1976 possibly applicable to their guilt concerned Section 5.16, "Minor Offenses." It made disciplinary action available for an unspecified "offense considered minor in nature," but without defining what constituted such an infraction.[855]

Handing troopers Bouffard, Palmer, and Truex a piece of paper, Cone advised each that "Pursuant to our conversation in my office this date, you may consider this memorandum a reprimand for conduct contrary to the good order and discipline of the Vermont State Police."

For some unidentified reason, Cpl. Sidney Adams received only a verbal reprimand.

Other officers received punishment from Cone that day for offenses also considered "minor" pursuant to Section 5.16. Captain

Patch received an "admonition" for his reported deficient oversight of an internal investigation concerning Truex, while Ryan received his own piece of paper. "Pursuant to our conversation in my office this date," Cone advised the department's second-in-command, "I consider that you used poor judgement in March of 1978 in not causing an investigation and/or follow-up to be conducted relative to the St. Johnsbury router bit allegations. This memorandum is to be considered a reprimand."[856]

Months later, Cone explained why he chose to sanction Ryan in this manner. He cited, much to the surprise of the attorney general who listed nine additional reasons warranting more severe punishment, his failure to "confirm or put to rest" reports from Field and Lay at St. Johnsbury that Charron was distributing router bits to troopers.[857]

Notwithstanding these actions, Cone concluded that "I do not feel that the problems (in the department) are with personnel, but rather with the system. The sworn officers and civilians employed by Vermont's Department of Public safety are, in general, very competent, professional and of high integrity."[858]

Cone also faulted the inaction of former commissioners Corcoran, Baumann, and Lynch, and second-in-command Maj. Davis concerning the problems with Merriam, but had no authority to impose punishment on any of them. Aside from giving a nod to Lynch's additional delay in dealing with the St. Johnsbury matter and Ryan's reprimand for a "minor" offense, he exonerated the rest of the Redstone high command from any liability and found that no cover-up occurred. However, his decision to punish the four troopers, papering their personnel files with damning allegations of misconduct able to derail future hopes for promotion, even if characterized as "minor," appears little more than a cruel face-saving measure to show something was being done.

Cone's actions also appear to have had political connotations because at the same time Snelling pushed forward with his Agency of Public Safety providing a beacon of opportunity to anyone in Cone's position seeking advancement. His temporary assignment as commissioner would expire in the spring and, just a week after the troopers were punished, on Oct. 18 Snelling and counsel William

Gilbert conferred if he might be the right person to assume control over the new agency should it gain legislative approval.

Cone's actions against the troopers constituted the clearest evidence that he could handle a difficult challenge and appears they influenced Snelling to consider him for higher position. However, the astute governor cautioned Gilbert, writing with emphasis in this politically charged environment, to discuss it with him before he talked with legislators "so I can make sure you understand the dangers to this approach!"[859]

Two months later, while vigorously pursuing discipline proceedings against David Reed, Cone continued to garner Snelling's favorable attention when his Planning Office solicited his input on the complexities surrounding the formation of the new agency (described by one planner as "a curious business') consolidating the Vermont Commission on the Administration of Justice, civil defense, motor vehicles, DPS, and their bureaucracy into a single entity.[860]

At the same time Cone wrote to VSP officers to assure them he had an "open door" policy welcoming them to share their concerns and to always remember an old sea saying that "illegitimus non carborundum (don't let the bastards wear you down)."[861]

When the Keyser Commission reviewed Cone's findings and actions and compared them to the conclusions of the attorney general in the Merriam matter in compliance with Snelling's instructions, it accorded Cone's work great deference. Its report did little beyond giving a respectful, appreciative pat on the back to the former admiral now under consideration to head the new agency, but much to the consternation of the attorney general expecting a more vibrant and comprehensive assessment of the department's problems.

Other than his decision to punish Merriam that became public in November, the details of Cone's report remained a secret throughout the winter until it was fully reported on March 27, 1980, a full month after he submitted it to Snelling, but who already knew what it contained beforehand. The delay provided an additional benefit to the VSP high command, now exonerated by their new boss, but unaware he worked behind their backs to assist Snelling in planning the new agency they despised.

In their blindness, they now turned their attention to David Reed to deliver the most forceful action possible to destroy his reputation and remove him from the department. The trick for Cone apparently required him to carefully push that effort forward and exploit its advantages to position himself for further advancement, while not offending them or the attorney general because he would have to work alongside them should he succeed.

PERSECUTING DAVID REED

The sloppy effort launched by Cone and the VSP high command against Reed was doomed from the beginning. The palpable tensions between the department, the attorney general, and governor's office and the political overtones surrounding the controversial new agency mandated that any charges against the detective be unassailably ironclad. The department's reputation and credibility were at stake and the consequences of any missteps devastating if they failed. The case against Reed must be based on provable facts able to establish he committed offenses of clearly expressed rules and regulations uniformly applied to all members of the DPS. The herculean challenge fell to department attorney Palmisano to weave together a comprehensive, understandable list of violations Reed committed that would be determined internally and overseen by a three-member panel of ranking state police officers drafted for the assignment.

The pressure was immense and Cone made it even more difficult because, according to Palmisano, he pushed Reed's prosecution to get it done as quickly as possible.[862]

Former commissioner Baumann's observation in June 1979 fearing the politicization of the department became a reality as the rush demonstrates the importance of timing related to Cone's possible consideration to head the new agency. The tensions between the VSP and attorney general also made Palmisano's efforts to obtain additional legal advice from the latter (similar to the unsuccessful attempts made by attorney Pearson during the Irasburg Affair) more troublesome. When he confronted the attorney general's office after his efforts fell apart alleging that attorneys from that office assisted him in drafting the charges, a canvas of its lawyers failed to substantiate his claim. "I have to conclude," one of Diamond's deputies wrote in a devastating report placing blame for the debacle elsewhere, that "unless Palmisano can present real evidence to the contrary, that no one from this office assisted Palmisano in the drafting of the charges against David Reed and that no one was aware of the charges which would be brought against Reed until after they were filed."

Beyond providing some assistance on a procedural question, he observed that "there was no participation of this office in the Reed disciplinary hearings."[863]

Palmisano's efforts incorporated a bloated laundry-list of seventeen questionable allegations of misconduct against Reed. He described them in a four-page Bill of Particulars based on twisted, unsupported interpretations of the facts found in the many reports of investigators. A legislative committee examining his work concluded that VSP commanders counseled Palmisano in preparing the charges against Reed and had "scraped the bottom of the barrel to discredit" him in the process. The similarities to what happened with the unsubstantiated findings of the Irasburg board of inquiry a decade earlier are striking.

Nonetheless, and satisfied for the time being, Cone adopted and formally lodged Palmisano's allegations against Reed on Nov. 9, 1979, listing them in an abbreviated two-page memorandum to him. They included his purported false testimony during the August 1978 Charron deposition alleging that he notified his supervisors of the router bit problem, his failure to complete two reports pertaining to it and "the Priest case" thereby "causing unnecessary scandal," and that he "conducted an illegal search of the Garfield residence."

Cone's references to Priest and Garfield pertained to the report contained in Gould's suicide note to "ask Reed and Truex about illegal search in Danville." It involved a convoluted set of facts surrounding a purported sexual assault, a theft of property, and whether a victim gave Reed consent to search her home for evidence and which Truex unwittingly became entangled in.

Lastly, Cone returned to the Charron deposition and alleged that because Reed provided false testimony he thereby "jeopardized the efficiency and discipline of the (VSP) command" that "caused a scandal and reduced your effectiveness as a member of the (VSP)." The catch-all offense applicable to "conduct that causes a scandal" was listed in the department's rules (Section 5.3.B.2), but provided no guidance of what "scandal" meant. The term referring to actions that could generally "offend propriety or established moral conceptions or disgraced those associated with it" appeared in no controlling legal context for the department to follow.[864] Just what constituted a "scandal" and did Reed deserve to have his fate rest on subjective interpretations, or "eyes of the beholder" kinds of impressions, to make those kinds of decisions?

Moving ahead, Cone immediately suspended Reed with pay, who made it known he thought the department was making him a scapegoat because he had done nothing warranting the charges.[865] The public also heard of more state police misconduct at the same time that caused further concern with the VSP. In St. Johnsbury, Lt. Lay again fell under scrutiny when reports that more than 100 expense accounts filed by troopers for meal reimbursements could not be found in office files that led one of them being charged with insubordination for his alleging that a supervisor told him to falsify his records.

Upon learning of the problem, Ryan admitted in marked understatement during embarrassing public testimony that "accountability has become a major problem for state police."[866]

On a second occasion, Ryan acknowledged that another officer's egregious conduct during a bizarre court hearing amounted to "a first for the state police," the same observation he made of Gould's suicide.

This time, a state police corporal testifying at a civil hearing concerning his failure to pay child support took aim at the legal profession. Angry at the treatment he received, the officer attacked and called attorneys "pocket-picking parasites" as part of a judicial system that "protects only bums and lawyers."

Repeatedly admonished by a surprised judge telling him to control himself and threatening him with jail after being ordered to make the payments ("I am astounded at this from a state trooper," he said), the officer stormed out of the courtroom, slamming a door behind him. Rising to his feet, the judge ordered the bailiff to "go get that man" and, after he returned, charged him with contempt.[867]

The officer later avoided punishment after writing the judge a letter apologizing for his actions. Expressing the same kinds of emotions that Howard Gould did regretting his own involvement in conduct that brought a dark cloud over the VSP, the officer similarly referred to his actions reflecting back on the department and its commanding officers, saying that "I feel bad about causing them this problem."[868]

As the VSP high command pursued immolation and an embarrassing public reckoning, a bright moment took place that fall. The Vermont State Grange served as an exemplary beacon of service in the agricultural community and decided to recognize the important contributions that Gould made by establishing a Safety Award in his name that it planned to hand out yearly. A dinner and award ceremony took place in Bennington attended by Charlene Gould, Commissioner Cone, Gould's supervisor Lt. Prescott and many others.

Charlene spoke on her husband's behalf offering sincere thanks before confiding heartfelt feelings about what had happened to her and her three children since he died.

> This honor you bestow on Howard Gould tonight, is for his family, the 1st step out of the midnight darkness of the past three months. I cannot thank you enough. This occasion when the focus of events is defined by a single word—honor.
>
> In establishing this award in Howard's name, you will annually honor someone who best serves the State and its citizens each year in the vital area of safety.
>
> You also honor the concept of devoted public service. A concept to which my husband dedicated his life. In conferring this award each year, for long years into the future, you will keep Howard's name alive, by honoring the man or woman who meets the high standards of excellence. But, to Howard's family, and to all who loved him, you have, in naming this award for him, honored the life he lived and the unflinching high personal goals by which he lived— service, dedication and honor.

Howard's name was linked to his honor, he died rather than have it unrightfully wrenched from his life.

You have helped reforge the link. You have, in large measure, also restored to me and our children what was always his and should never have been in doubt—the honor his life and the name of a 'good and honest man.'

The events of the past week have further dispersed the darkness, but yours, the Vermont State Grange, was the 1st ray of light and we will always be grateful.

Thank you ever so much.[869]

The 32-year-old mother, left with three children to feed, clothe and educate, but unable to continue making mortgage payments was forced to move out of their home and return to Rutland to live with relatives.

When she contacted the VSP for assistance to pay for transporting their possessions, she recalled that a high-ranking officer refused her request. He told her that the department did not want to set such a precedent in the event another trooper ever committed suicide and then his family sought similar treatment. He had troopers to train, he said, but no funds to assist her.

Unmoved by her plight, the family however remained closely connected with the St. Johnsbury troopers and when its first Christmas without Howard approached, she recalled their friendship.

On past Christmas Eves, Gould routinely took their eager children out to his cruiser in the driveway and radioed in to the dispatcher to ask where tracking showed Santa's location. Now, with their father gone, one of her sons feared that Santa could not find them because they moved and he wrote to the St. Johnsbury officers asking them to be sure and tell him where they went. Sorry for their loss, and distinctly different from the cold treatment she received from their Redstone superiors, the troopers sent her money to purchase gifts for the children.

The feeling of ill-treatment Charlene received from her husband's superiors lingers to this day, dismayed that someone so dedicated to the VSP could have their legacy dismissed so easily. "My husband lived and breathed Vermont State Police," she told the author, "his life was black and white—no grey—such dedication (and) for what?"[870]

"Snelling: Merriam Case A Miscarriage of Justice" the headlines blasted on Dec. 1, 1979 announcing the governor's response to the discipline Cone meted out to the suspended, demoted VSP officer.[871] Two days earlier, Merriam entered a no contest plea to an administrative charge that in March 1974 he failed to notify his superiors of the allegation that Paul Lawrence planted evidence during a search in Swanton. His offense fell under another of the department's vague rules prohibiting conduct that "jeopardizes the good order of the command."[872]

In reaching this conclusion, Cone agreed to drop more serious charges that Merriam lied during two inquest proceedings and demoted him to corporal, suspending him for three months. This allowed him to return to work the following March assigned to the special services unit in Colchester performing maintenance on the department's fleet of cars. What reliance Cone placed on the secret files pertaining to Merriam or any of the other officers he reprimanded is unknown, but he was aware they existed.[873]

Apoplectic at the outcome with Merriam, and unaware of the extraordinary secrecy the VSP exercised, Snelling slammed the lenient treatment of someone he, and other prosecutors, believed deserved outright dismissal from the ranks and barred from ever again testifying in a court of law because of his lack of credibility.

He told members of the press, "I personally am not prepared to trust Merriam in the uniform of a Vermont State Police officer." An "absolutely flabbergasted" State's Attorney McGee echoed a similar sentiment and said it was unthinkable that Merriam could remain on the force because "his misconduct in the nature of false swearing or encouraging another officer's misconduct goes to the core of the criminal justice system and cannot be tolerated."[874]

Defensive at the unfavorable reporting of the VSP, department attorney Palmisano struck back.

"We're not in Iran," he said, referring to the unrest that resulted in the U.S. embassy takeover in Tehran a month earlier. "We're still the United States of America and people are entitled to due process." Snelling understood the limitations imposed by the department's deficient rules and regulations that Palmisano referred to and absolved Cone, possibly still under consideration to take over the new Agency of Public Safety, of any negligence. Cone's hands were tied, Snelling said, because of the "very serious shortcomings" of the existing disciplinary regulations. Despite his punishment, Merriam garnered statewide support when some 2,000 people signed a petition calling for his return to the rank of sergeant. He also received a vote of confidence from his Elmore friends in March elections for selectman where he defeated an incumbent by a vote of 71–25.[875]

Reed's fate rested with three officers selected from a standing list that included: Chairman of the Disciplinary Board Lt. Edward Fish (Assistant Field Force Commander), Lt. Eugene Edwards (Troop A commander), and Sgt. George Nickerson (Bethel station commander). Their findings at the conclusion of the evidence would be used by Cone to determine what, if any, punishment Reed received.

Fish and Edwards each served directly under Field Force commander Capt. Heffernan, now assigned to assist Palmisano as prosecutor on the department's behalf. When the appearance of similar conflicts of interest arose because of possible tensions within the chain of command making such determinations arose during the Merriam matter, Ryan came out in strong defense of the process. He "staunchly supported" it, he said, rejecting any notion that the department needed an internal affairs unit in its place.

When you go outside of the chain of command, he said, "You've relieved the command staff of their responsibility and, quite frankly, they're getting paid for it."

In the trade off, he offered that "We're quite willing to be reviewed any time, in terms of the command staff."[876] Reed's case tested his wish when that group came under blistering review that included Ryan's refusal to provide Reed's attorney with his second file that only piqued the public's interest at the department's secretive internal practices.[877]

Conflicts of interest did not appear of concern to those sitting in judgment of the VSP during the Irasburg hearings where Attorney General Oakes occupied conflicting roles nobody dared challenge. But now, a decade later, where officers judging Reed's guilt or innocence remained answerable to Heffernan appeared so compelling, his counsel, the highly capable Barre attorney Oreste V. Valsangiacomo Jr., raised his strong objection directly with Cone and Snelling seeking their intervention.[878]

Neither of them chose to do so, but Valsangiacomo did succeed in getting a postponement until January because of the complexity of the charges and his need to prepare. On Dec. 20, the parties met to resolve pre-hearing issues where Valsangiacomo faced an uphill battle on several fronts to convince the panel to order the department to produce evidence. It involved his access to information about Reed's superiors, including the personnel files of Lynch and Ryan (each of them "implicated in a coverup," he said), Heffernan and other high-ranking officers, Cone's internal investigation and all polygraph tests administered during the investigation.[879]

He also experienced substantial interference interviewing witnesses, explaining to the panel that "I'm absolutely getting nowhere at this point in time."[880] It did not help that he had to also deal with an avalanche of additional witnesses when Palmisano disclosed the names of 37 individuals he expected to testify.

Reed's long-anticipated hearing opened at 8:30 a.m., on Jan. 21, 1980, in the U.S. District Court in Montpelier, the same location where Judge Gibson conducted the Irasburg hearings a dozen years before. Some 30 spectators attended, including three NEK legislators and members of Reed's family and friends wearing "We support David Reed" cards.[881]

Assisted by Heffernan, Palmisano led off the proceedings providing the panel with an outline of the evidence he planned to introduce against Reed.

Valsangiacomo responded that the 17 allegations his client lied during the Charron deposition were "incomprehensible" and only brought against him because "in my opinion, Redstone wanted him to resign." The problem with Palmisano's "incredible" allegations, Valsangiacomo said after the proceedings, was that he had "misadvised" the department telling it to dismiss Reed when he never actually "read the evidence before he prosecuted (him) and that's why his case came off poorly."[882]

Reed, an experienced and trusted officer assigned to conduct confidential internal investigations in the past, had all of a sudden become a suspect leading Valsangiacomo to pointedly question the panel why he was now deemed so unreliable that he faced losing his job.

"David Reed," he said, "has been an honest and good cop for fifteen years. He was rated outstanding in departmental evaluations time and time again."

Now, "You are being asked to conclude he is a liar, a schemer and a manipulator."[883]

The two attorneys engaged in a fierce dog-fight over the next several days arguing over procedure and evidence requiring the legally-untrained panel to confer with Berlin attorney Robert J. Kurrle, appointed by Cone to assist it, for guidance. Despite Palmisano's efforts to limit Valsangiacomo's cross-examination of witnesses, he severely undercut the allegations he authored. Procedural missteps, missing evidence, statements by Palmisano's own witnesses contrary to the allegations, Capt. Patch's admission that a "looseness" existed at Redstone in handling internal investigations, and the observation by investigating CSP officer Sgt. Martin Ohradan that even he did not understand the charges against Reed did little to advance the department's efforts.[884]

"Complete whitewash," "farce," "snow job," "absolutely shocked," "rotten," and "indescribable," legislators said of the proceedings, listening in disbelief at the inadequacy of the evidence and making their great displeasure known. The "Public Safety Department got themselves into a box," one said and they couldn't get themselves out as indications of a cover up by the high command became evident and proof of their sacrificial scapegoating of Reed made clear. Incensed at what they heard, one threatened that if the VSP did not do something about its command problems, "we will."[885] Another expressed his outrage at the expense of the hearing where "the taxpayers are being bled to death for something that's absolutely a farce." Even Cone admitted that he did not have the money to pay for it and said he planned to go to the legislature "and ask for it."[886]

Matters only got worse when Ryan took the stand and testified for four hours before an audience that included ten legislators. When cross-examined by Valsangiacomo, his testimony concerning many issues, including his admission that he misled Gov. Snelling in his July 24, 1979 memo when Lynch was fired and that he provided incorrect information to investigators, differed so substantially from other witness's statements they severely undermined his credibility.

It was absolutely clear from what he heard, one legislator said, that Ryan could not be trusted and that Palmisano had provided "absolutely zero" evidence to substantiate his charges against Reed delivering, according to one newspaper, a "severe blow" to his case.

After the panel listened to 18 witnesses for the prosecution over six days and Valsangiacomo moved for dismissal of the charges, it recessed on Jan. 29, agreeing to meet the following day. Fish, Edwards and Nickerson gathered at Kurrle's office the next morning and went over each of the individual charges carefully to see if Palmisano met the easiest of hurdles demonstrating sufficient evidence to support them. He had only to establish proof by a preponderance, meaning that the weight of the evidence tipped ever so slightly in his favor, in order to succeed.

However, after four hours of deliberation, with the exception of one allegation concerning the Garfield search where Fish parted from the panel's other two members, they exonerated Reed on all remaining counts. Fish's decision meant that the hearing would continue the next day to allow Valsangiacomo to put on evidence, but which went quickly awry because of an extraordinary move by Cone.

Soon after Kurrle conveyed the panel's decision to the parties, he received a call from Cone asking to meet with its members so that he could tell them "what was going on."[887]

Kurrle refused and told him the panel already rendered its decision and that "it would be inappropriate" to allow them to meet together. Minutes later, Cone abruptly summoned panel chairman Fish to his office and "communicated certain claimed evidence on the St. Johnsbury router bit case (to him) which was offered as damaging as against Reed."

None of Cone's information was introduced during the formal hearing and his attempt to do so afterwards outside of the process constituted wholly inappropriate conduct. After Kurrle learned what happened, he directed Fish not to convey any of Cone's allegations to the other two panel members. When his actions became known afterwards, Cone unabashedly avoided any insinuation he tried to sway Fish and said that he only spoke with him because the panel's findings "did not reflect that they had considered certain evidence of which I was aware."[888] Disgusted at what was happening, the same day a legislator called on Snelling to remove all of the VSP high command, naming Ryan, Spear, Patch, Heffernan and Ramey because of their suspicious, inconsistent testimony and to replace them with "another staff at Redstone" to better serve the department and the citizens of Vermont.[889]

His neutrality now tainted because of Cone's inappropriate contact, Fish abstained from any further discussions on the Garfield search that allowed the panel to proceed and verbally enter its decision absolving Reed of all charges. While the public learned only generally of the outcome, the panel's final written decision did not appear until days later. The delay provided the department's misguided prosecutor, Capt. Heffernan, an opportunity to engage in yet another display of embarrassing conduct by a senior VSP officer adding additional proof of the disciplinary hearings' circus atmosphere. On Feb. 7, in his role as the department's field force commander, Heffernan went to the St. Johnsbury office to meet troopers and convey his impressions of how the hearings were going. "Heffernan told the troopers," the attorney general's report of the incident described, "'You will never have to worry about Reed, he'll never be a problem to you anymore. The panel is going to do the right thing and find him guilty and the Commissioner is going to do the right thing and fire Reed.'"

Confident in the seemingly pre-determined outcome, he turned to Dennis Bouffard who first spoke with Reed about Charron's providing router bits to troopers. In dripping disgust with the testimony Bouffard provided to the panel, he told him "I thought you learned your lesson—Reed fucked you twice or three times and you still don't learn. Reed lied and all the Redstone people told the truth." He then proclaimed to his audience, "You would have been proud of your Major (Ryan)—he was magnificent."[890]

Unwilling to abide by protocol to keep unsubstantiated information about Reed from becoming known and apparently referring to what Cone conveyed to Fish he also suggested to the troopers that "damaging evidence on Reed was never released." He also reportedly expressed support for and praised the recently demoted and suspended Stanley Merriam.[891]

The attorney general's report into Heffernan's statements coming from someone so high in the chain of command provides additional information about his role in prosecuting Reed. In a succinct description of his involvement, he said:

> He agrees that he knew of no rule, law, regulation or order from a superior which Reed violated in failing to complete the Truex or Router bits internal investigations. When asked why, as a prosecutor, he allowed a prosecution on disciplinary charges which constituted no legal violation and which had no factual support he replied that he was merely a 'figurehead prosecutor.' The actual prosecutors, Heffernan replied, were Commissioner Cone and Attorney Palmisano. When asked why he allowed his name to be used for charges that were supported by neither law nor fact, Heffernan replied that he did not examine the charges for these elements at the time but followed the Commissioner's orders and trusted in the Department's attorney. Heffernan agrees that he is a "company man."[892]

The longstanding "company man" mindset infesting the department's command staff also existed with at least one member of Reed's disciplinary panel. When questioned about his impressions of the evidence he heard from high-ranking officers, Sgt. Nickerson, hired in 1954 and a classmate of Heffernan and Spear, carefully parsed his response about their truthfulness.

"I feel that everybody wasn't truthful," he said, "I am sure they weren't. I don't believe some things that were said were quite right or truthful." "I sat there and listened to it all," he continued, "and I don't think it all came out the way it should have. I think straightforward honesty would have settled it right then and there." However, he also believed that such things should be forgotten "for the good of the Department."[893] For another perspective on the same testimony, State's Attorney Gray described it simply as a "quagmire" of conflicting statements.[894]

The panel hearing Reed's case issued its final ruling on Feb. 8, 1980 completely exonerating him of all charges and wholly refuting Palmisano's assertion he was a "schemer" responsible for bringing down a scandal on the department. Its sixteen-page decision addresses each of the allegations he and Heffernan tried, but failed, to prove. They repeatedly found no evidence of Reed's misbehavior and that, to the contrary, many witnesses testified about his truthfulness and credibility. In concluding, it recommended that he "be reinstated to his previous assignment with full rights and privileges" and that Cone recuse himself from any further participation in the case because he "is personally involved and has entertained information beyond the scope of the evidence."

Learning of its decision, a relieved Reed expressed his own disbelief at Cone's attempt to intrude into the process and said of the suspension he imposed on him that "If the thing that happens is David Reed goes back to work, then I don't think any good will come out of it. But if the department learns from it, and there's an overall improvement in administration, then maybe there's been some value in the whole fiasco."[895]

While Palmisano said he was "flabbergasted" at the panel's decision and took responsibility for the debacle, Cone moved ahead, still refusing to remove himself from the fray. Instead, he took an entirely different tact accepting its decision inviting Reed to Redstone to discuss his future. After offering him positions at headquarters and the attorney general's office, Reed turned them down, accepting a return to St. Johnsbury as its new station commander. Happy with the change of events, the vindicated officer recognized the discomfort some of the troopers he worked with might feel at his continued presence. However, he refused to run and thought that "It's just a matter of them understanding the circumstances of what happened and why I did what I did."[896]

In the end, the disastrous hearing personally cost Reed over $8,000 to defend himself. For the department, it "ran up a bill of over $25,000," all wasted on a ridiculous display of Redstone's impaired power and none of it directed to assist Howard Gould's struggling wife and family.[897]

Chapter 15

FALLOUT

IMPLEMENTING CHANGE

THE FALLOUT FROM REED'S DISCIPLINARY HEARING was immediate. Concerned at the many inconsistencies in the testimony of the officers, Attorney General Diamond assigned Assistant Attorney General Putter the task of assembling the thousands of pages of witness statements to determine if any of them committed perjury. It took Putter an entire year to untangle before issuing his 207-page report in January 1981, on the eve of Diamond's departure after the fall elections. State's Attorney Gray sought the appointment of a special prosecutor to sort through the conflicting statements, unwilling to expend any more of his own time on the matter because his office "went to hell" the preceding summer conducting the extensive inquest proceedings.[898] The Legislature quickly entertained four different resolutions calling for additional investigations into the VSP high command drawing a wry response from a recalcitrant Ryan welcoming the prospect ("tickled pink," he said).[899]

Angry at the treatment Reed received, the solons also debated whether to delete $35,000 from the DPS budget to avoid paying

Palmisano's bill and associated costs, repeatedly calling it a "witch hunt," but was defeated.[900]

While everyone awaited the report of the Keyser Commission they hoped could shed additional light on the culpability of command personnel, refusing to be sidelined the legislature stepped further into the fray to identify any structural deficiencies within the VSP and render its own recommendations. Snelling did not embrace the creation of yet another inquiry fearing a duplication of efforts, but recognized the legitimacy of the legislature's concerns.

"Gee," he said, "the whole subject is fraught with danger, but (it) clearly has a right to ask questions," warning that his own cooperation in the effort had its limits.[901]

Notwithstanding Snelling's concerns, on Feb. 26 a committee composed of four Republicans and three Democrats headed by Representative Thomas Costello of Rutland was created. Its mandate required it to determine "whether the organization, structure and management policies of the (DPS) are adequate" and that it quickly accomplish its work by April 1 before the legislature adjourned.[902]

Its frenzied work began immediately when, just hours after their naming, the committee members plunged into their assignment receiving a crash course in state police procedures. During the next three weeks they conducted 23 public meetings, received over 40 hours of testimony from 31 witnesses documented in more than a thousand pages of transcripts, and obtained 82 responses from troopers to a 9-page questionnaire sent out to 249 members of the department.

The committee heard from a variety of sources, with officers from the rank of sergeant and below providing some of the rawest, most heartfelt, responses.

"Here we go again," one said in characterizing yet another legislative inquiry, while another thought the effort wouldn't "amount to a yellow hole in the snow."

Bitter and angry responses addressed the favoritism displayed by some of their superiors to undeserving individuals calling for a complete overhaul of the management system. Officers believed the rules and regulations dictating their personal lives were biased and demeaning. "Some that would insult the intelligence of a moron," one wrote, while another said the rules "are interpreted, jockeyed, and dismissed almost at will, at times. Yet at other times they are enforced to the word, depending on who is enforcing." Another officer believed the rules were only used "to convict rather than to support the men in the field." A feeling of helplessness permeated their responses reflecting their shared belief that superiors abused their positions and power and where, one wrote, "things flow down from the top but rarely in the opposite direction."[903]

During its hearings, the committee received testimony from Reed's attorney, Oreste Valsangiacomo. He expressed his view that the problems in the department rested with only "a couple of people," ones that State's Attorney Lium said operated with "arrogance" towards outsiders and "viciousness" against troopers, calling Redstone a "shark's nest" answerable to no one.

In the same manner that author Hamilton Davis wrote about the department in 1978, counsel to the panel, Robert Kurrle, cited the continued presence of a "siege mentality" and "paranoia" present among the top brass. Interestingly, former St. Johnsbury station commander Robert Field, also implicated in the Router Bit Affair, expressed the same opinion and said that there was a lack of leadership in the department where the mentality of his superiors was "to get those who bucked the system." Perhaps, he said jokingly, it was time to "bury" Redstone, but then seriously stated that "I think it's regrettable that they can set out to destroy a man like they did with David Reed."[904]

Despite the enormity of the challenge, the Costello committee's relatively brief preliminary 11-page report issued on March 12 provided an important pathway to guide the department out of its problems. They were ones largely defined as "an impaired capacity to deal expeditiously and justly with allegations of wrongdoing."[905]

Three recommendations for "structural changes" followed, the first faulting the department's failure to competently respond to the Hebard committee's call in 1975 to revise its rules and regulations. While some were drafted thereafter, the committee members found them unresponsive to the recommendations and those that it created "often incomprehensible" and "frequently disregarded" resulting in "abuses and injustice."

After calling once again for an overhaul of those regulations, the committee advanced perhaps the most contentious aspect of its work.

The overriding problem with investigating allegations of wrongdoing was that they remained internal functions of the department with inherent conflicts of interest avoiding any oversight that diminished their credibility. An external review, or the imposition of an "open window" policy, it argued, shedding light into the process could alleviate the problem by allowing review by some other authority such as a state's attorney and/or attorney general to examine whatever internal review took place and report its findings to the governor.

The committee cited two examples to support its recommendation: the report of perjury by Stanley Merriam that remained hidden in department files for years and, unwilling to officially recognize Howard Gould's suicide as work-related calling it instead "an unfortunate complication," the failure of Redstone officials to intervene in a timely manner after learning about the St. Johnsbury allegations. Only after this "unfortunate complication" occurred, a chain of events, the committee wrote, suggested that "an orchestrated effort to clear (the) high command of failure to carry out their responsibility" (also characterized as "an inexcusable abuse of common justice") took place. This involved the prosecution of David Reed facing trumped-up charges assembled by a command staff who "scraped the bottom of the barrel" to find reasons to punish him and remove the taint from themselves. Each of these misfortunes could have been avoided, the committee wrote, had action been taken at the time an allegation of misconduct became known and not, instead, delayed.

In the same manner of the Irasburg matter denying the VSP due process protections in responding to the board of inquiry's slanted findings, the committee's third recommendation addressed the procedural failures of the Reed disciplinary hearing. It proposed various changes to allow an accused officer more latitude to demonstrate his innocence and to obtain the same kinds of protections available to municipal officers.

One provision provided for the introduction of evidence relating to the discriminatory practices of the department where inconsistent application of the rules in the past varied "depending on the favor or lack of favor the particular officer enjoyed."

Pressed for time with limited staff available to it, the committee could not follow up on testimony it received revealing the presence of the department's secret filing system that maintained two sets of records on officers, one they knew about and the other they did not.[906]

As the Costello committee conducted its hearings, on March 6, 1980, the Senate delivered a fatal blow to Snelling's dream to create an Agency of Public Safety when the solons expressed little appetite to pursue a statewide consolidation of police services and, by a vote of 16–13, killed it.[907]

The president of the VTA said it was "one of the greatest things that could have happened" for police morale.[908] The past months brought great stress to the ranks of officers unhappy with Snelling, its president said, a man who "tries to dictate to us." It resulted in the association, for the first time in its history, becoming directly involved in politics giving its backing to a new governor who "will not go off half-cocked" because "the track record of the others shows they have gone off half-cocked." Concerning the publicity surrounding the two candidates for governor, Snelling's and Diamond's statements about Merriam angered many officers and the VTA spokesman said "What right did they have to say his character was no good?" Upset at the treatment the department received from the legislature, he expressed further frustration and said that "The whole thing has been so sickening—investigation after investigation all trying to find something of a major sort and they can't do it."

Citing "enormous damage" inflicted on the VSP in the preceding months, Snelling moved to find a new commissioner to take over from Cone.[909]

Unwilling to repeat past experiences that allowed those with police or military experience to occupy the position and to make it clear that the department fell under civilian control, he found the perfect candidate heading the state Employment Security Department. Quiet, unassuming and no-nonsense, 49-year-old Paul Philbrook drew Snelling's attention because of his long, distinguished service to the state.

He was further described in one newspaper editorial as "a man with considerable talents as an administrator and virtually no record as a quasi-military commander" compared to his predecessor Francis Lynch who upended his own reign because of his "insubordination and arrogance."[910]

Whereas Lynch "automatically thought in terms of leadership and command," it continued, "to the point that he got into a power struggle with (Snelling) and erroneously conceived of himself and the State Police as a semi-independent agency answerable only to their own internal standards and rules," Philbrook offered a much different persona. Now stood a wholly different man, the consummate "career bureaucrat schooled in the value of the chain of command" able to return the agency to unquestionable civilian control.[911]

The timing of Philbrook's appointment as the Costello committee wrapped up its work played directly into Snelling's hands. Unwilling to abide its recommendations, efforts that he said were of "limited merit" conducted under the "extreme pressure of time," and which he believed rested more appropriately with the executive department, on April 1 he signed an order establishing the Vermont State Police Advisory Commission (SPAC).

The new commission's seven members served, Snelling said, "as citizens of the state of Vermont" and not representing any special interests.[912] While ostensibly created to guide the newly-appointed Philbrook in his work, for the first time in VSP history an outside entity appeared on its doorstep with the authority to penetrate directly into its secret inner workings. The commission's mandate tracked that of Costello's committee, charged with reviewing internal investigations, assuring that promotions were conducted "objectively," and to review citizens' complaints. Snelling's actions angered some members of Costello's faction deeming it "a slap in the face," "sideshows and window dressing" and an effort that did not deal directly with "problems that should have been addressed long ago had the governor, or somebody, listened to the Hebard Committee report" in 1975.[913]

For Costello, Snelling's intrusion into what the legislature thought its own prerogative constituted an issue of constitutional dimension pitting the authority of the two branches of government against one another.[914]

Others took a more light-hearted view of the times that led Snelling's aide and later governor, James Douglas, to ask the person in charge of state buildings to erect a new reserved parking sign for him, located so near the statehouse, but without the word "Governor" at its head. It seems that people were stealing the signs and Douglas believed a less conspicuous identification of its owner could alleviate the problem.[915] Despite the opposition to Snelling's appointments, the legislature authorized the SPAC, codifying its authority, effective July 1, 1980, that continues to the present day.[916]

When a legislative committee conducted additional hearings in the first half of 1980 receiving testimony from troopers about the conduct of their superiors, Ryan set off another firestorm. Without telling Philbrook, he issued an order prohibiting officers from testifying in the future unless they received his or the commissioner's permission.

Calling it a gag order, legislators expressed dismay at his attempt to interfere with their work that Costello characterized as "a continuation of the wagon train mentality of trying to avoid disclosure of problems that exist" in the VSP. Sen. Thomas Crowley, one of the members of the newly created SPAC, also received information that troopers were told not to talk—especially to his commission.[917]

Its chair, Alfred Beauchamp, remained determined to correct the department's past inclination to turn inward "without having public responsibility" and "attempt to open up the operations of the state police so they can't become isolated, nor can they become insulated."[918]

The momentum of change within the department continued and new rules and regulations went into effect later in 1980, but only after several difficult months as it conceded some of its past authority allowing officers to receive more protections during internal investigations than in the past. Since then, the head of the Office of Internal Investigations within the DPS receives allegations of misconduct to scrutinize whether they violate any rules or regulations and/or rise to the level of criminal conduct. If the former, they are handled administratively, while in the latter case, the matter is referred to the local state's attorney, the attorney general, and, finally, the governor for appropriate action; in any event, the matter is also reviewed by the SPAC. Before the law took effect, and already recognizing the need for such change, in 1980 the VSP received a total of 122 complaints against officers, but only five determined to be of a criminal nature and referred elsewhere as the law later required.[919]

Simultaneous to the battle between the legislature and Snelling, the Keyser Commission finally concluded its work. Despite the wide-ranging assignment and authority he tasked its members with the preceding August, the public learned nothing of its efforts in the next nine months.

Contrary to the rushed methods utilized by Judge Gibson in the Irasburg hearings, it met in private throughout this time, ultimately costing taxpayers $25,000 in addition to the money already spent on the disastrous Reed hearings. Its report could have been released earlier, but the five commission members refused over fears of retaliatory lawsuits for libel from anyone it named and sought immunity for their actions. Only after the legislature agreed to their demand and allowed them to obtain insurance coverage as "state employees" did they finally release the fruits of their work.

The 105-page report that former supreme court justice and chairman F. Ray Keyser Sr. handed to Snelling on April 1, 1980 generated a decidedly lukewarm reception. Legislators and newspaper editorials repeatedly expressed their disappointment at its findings, deeming them wholly inadequate and unable to fulfill the high expectations placed on the commission by Snelling's mandate. While it had virtually free reign to make whatever inquiries it deemed necessary, the conservative, cautious commission members chose, instead, to narrow their focus and avoid making the hard decisions its challenge posed.

It received no public testimony from any witnesses both because they did not believe they had the authority, or "mechanism," to do so, and, as Keyser related, they "didn't see the need." Nor did they seek authority to gain access to any of the voluminous testimony provided during inquest proceedings conducted by the attorney general and State's Attorney Gray.[920]

Instead, members relied on an estimated 10,000 pages of documents and other testimony, conducted principally by the CSP investigators. Rather than try to resolve the many conflicting witness statements that Snelling hoped they could untangle, and the attorney general identified in its report of the Merriam matter and Cone's report, it did so only minimally. While the commission did make an effort to reconcile some of them, in those instances when it could not Keyser admitted simply that it was "anybody's guess." Instead, it took a middle of the road stance avoiding embarrassing Cone and essentially adopted his findings that no high-level officers committed any criminal offenses and finding that the punishment he meted out to troopers appropriate.

Ultimately, the commission concluded that most of the problems it identified could be attributed to Lynch's tenure, that there was no coverup and, in marked understatement, believed they could be chalked up to "largely institutional failures."[921]

It also declined to entertain any thought of interfering with the public's right to know because the members believed it "represents one of the prices we pay for the First Amendment rights we enjoy." The hands-off, measured assessment of the press' reporting of the Router Bit Affair differed substantially from the condemnation that the Irasburg board of inquiry chose to lodge against the media during those proceedings; a prospect Keyser's commission no doubt wanted to avoid. The commission also refused to provide Snelling with any guidance regarding the appointment and removal of DPS commissioners, leaving it up to the legislature and courts to resolve. While the commission also avoided making any recommendations concerning the department's problematic rules and regulations, admitting it did not conduct an "in-depth study" of them, it did agree that an internal affairs unit should be created and oversight authority instituted.

"Like the mythical Hydra," one newspaper wrote of the collective findings released by the attorney general, Cone, and Keyser, "a serpent that grew two new heads for every one lopped off, each report has sprouted new questions to extend the life of the controversy."[922]

While one newspaper deemed it a deficient effort, the *Rutland Herald* blasted it in an editorial under a headline "No Blue Ribbon, Just Another Whitewash."[923]

Keyser and his fellow commission members, it wrote, failed "to muster the intestinal fortitude and moral outrage" needed to remove Ryan and Merriam from the VSP ranks that by their continued presence served as continual "flesh-and-blood reminders of state police wrongdoing." Keyser's work "was worse than the Cone report," one legislator said, while another lamented that "They really haven't resolved the issues. We know there was a coverup, but they've just skirted the issue."[924]

One member of Costello's committee took the commission's findings to task in comparison to the work he participated in and said it "flies in the face of the other two reports, and I don't think we were that far out to lunch."[925] However, Snelling and Philbrook both took solace in Keyser's work vowing to abide its recommendations. For State's Attorney Lium, Snelling's blind acceptance of the report and refusal to take action against the state police high command in his haste to put the St. Johnsbury debacle behind him entitled him to receive the "Glowing Horseshoe Prize" for 1980 from the "New England Society of Blacksmiths," given "to a person who has shown an unsurpassed speed in dropping hot objects."[926]

While Snelling derided Lium's various observations on state government as "fantasy pieces," he could not escape the evidence that Redstone demanded a severe housecleaning or explain why he refused to do so.[927]

SECRET FILES AND LAWSUITS

In October 1980, the SPAC pursued its mandate to examine VSP internal procedures setting off another round of controversy when it uncovered one of its most outrageous practices. Known to only a select few, Redstone officials maintained a confidential filing system that appeared to date back to its founding in 1947 separating out derogatory information concerning an officer from his personnel file. Nobody in the lower ranks had any idea it existed and its impact proved devastating for anyone entangled in its web. The practice meant that even innocuous, unsubstantiated complaints later dismissed by internal investigations that troopers thought resolved actually never disappeared.

Two officers testifying before the SPAC learned that month that their decades-long careers were derailed after Philbrook accidently disclosed their secret files to the commission.

"All of a sudden I saw tears coming down (his) cheeks," one member said as he watched veteran Cpl. John Krupp look at his file. It included some information that Krupp suspected existed, including two prior internal investigations, but which the department refused to admit or disclose to him in the past. "My god, 21 years and I've never seen this," he said with emotion and that "the file was full of allegations of wrongdoing (on his part) that he had never even been asked about."

Passed over repeatedly for promotion, Krupp said he "had never understood why he was on everybody's hit list."

Cpl. Cornelius Reed was the second officer and provided information about his treatment from Ryan when he appeared before a promotion panel in 1977 bearing "unsubstantiated rumor" of his purported misconduct that did not appear in his personnel file. Subsequent findings by the labor commissioner hearing Reed's appeal concluded that Ryan's indefensible actions constituted a "gross and undisputable" violation of the rules. Both Krupp and Reed had been "shafted," one SPAC member said, characterizing the department's dual filing system as "Gestapo tactics."[928]

While Commissioner Philbrook denied its existence at first, and later backtracked protesting he did not know the files he turned over to the SPAC came from a secret system, his predecessors clearly knew about it. Neither did they ever disclose its presence in any of the other investigations conducted during the Irasburg, Lawrence and Router Bit affairs. Lynch's successor, interim commissioner Warren Cone never referred to it in his report to Snelling and when confronted after Philbrook's disclosure said he had no problem with it because such a practice "is normal when you have a military or semi-military operation."[929]

Even a SPAC member, retired captain Lloyd Potter, knew of the practice when he "accidently" learned of it following his promotion and transfer to Redstone rendering suspect protestations by the high command to the contrary.[930]

Beyond the unfairness the dual filing system posed to officers themselves, the willingness by the VSP command staff to engage in such secrecy displays a woeful ignorance of the law and understanding of their overall role and responsibility in the criminal justice system. Even before its well-known Miranda ruling in 1966 mandating certain rights for criminal suspects, in 1963 the U.S. Supreme Court made it abundantly clear that prosecutors had an affirmative, constitutional-level, duty to provide defendants with any information in the government's possession possibly favorable to their defense.[931]

This includes information about the misconduct of any witnesses that could impact their credibility, even if it might adversely affect the government's case. Such information is considered exculpatory, or able to clear someone accused of a crime, but was a term that, surprisingly, even BCI head Capt. Spear admitted he did not know what it meant.[932] This basic requirement of fairness in prosecuting individuals appears little appreciated by the VSP high command and could have impacted, and undercut, literally thousands of criminal cases the department investigated from 1947–1980 when information concealed in their secret files was never disclosed to defendants.

Special Prosecutor Robert Gensburg in the Paul Lawrence affair, also a member of the SPAC, knew of the problem in 1975 and confronted Lynch about it in 1977, but was dismissed out of hand. "What they produced in court," he recalled of his investigation, "was not the complete files. I knew that what I was looking for was in the files, but it was not in the files they produced in court."[933] The exposure of this unsavory aspect of the VSP underbelly alarmed Philbrook and he immediately discontinued the practice, assuring the SPAC of its termination.

While Philbrook instituted no substantive administrative charges against any of the other Redstone hierarchy, the allegations of Ryan's misconduct drew his particular concern. He retained the services of Burlington law firm Downs Rachlin & Martin to examine the evidence and make "recommendations regarding discipline (or further discipline) of DPS personnel, if such were warranted."[934]

Its 10-month investigation, overseen by David Johnson's attorney during the Irasburg Affair, Robert Rachlin, cost taxpayers an additional $77,000 above that already spent on the proceedings. It resulted in a number of findings centered principally on Ryan's actions recommending that administrative action be taken against him. For Snelling, already deeply immersed in conversations with the attorney general over the standard of proof needed to charge Ryan, the law firm's conclusion only reinforced his hope that, finally, the state police controversies neared an end.

The principal difference between the other reports he received and the law firm's efforts, which Snelling said carried more weight, was that the latter was conducted by lawyers looking at specific violations of departmental rules that the others did not.[935]

Just days after he received Rachlin's report, on April 23, 1981, Philbrook instituted three charges against Ryan. They alleged that: he made inaccurate statements to Snelling in his July 24, 1979, memo at the time of Lynch's dismissal describing the extent of his knowledge of the router bit matter; he caused David Reed to undergo unwarranted psychiatric examination when "there was no substantial basis" to require it; and, he testified untruthfully during Reed's disciplinary hearing.[936]

Ryan contested the charges and after a fourteen-day disciplinary hearing in November he chose be conducted in secret out of public view, a three-member panel of state police officers exonerated him of all charges. While his relationship with Philbrook thereafter appears amicable, on Friday, July 13, 1984, the commissioner walked coolly into his office at the end of the day and handed him a piece of paper. Resistant to accept mandatory retirement when he turned 55-years-old the prior December, Philbrook had enough and simply dismissed him, curtly asking, "Any questions?"[937]

Other members of the high command involved in the controversies of 1979–1980, captains Heffernan and Spear, also saw their careers end in 1984 because they too reached the same age barrier.

None of them were missed by the rank and file obstructed in their own promotions because they occupied the positions they sought. According to Reed disciplinary chairman Lt. Fish, "99 %" of the force backed Philbrook's decision and that Ryan's refusal to depart until then imposed a "very demoralizing" atmosphere on younger troopers.[938] Ryan did not leave without further controversy, and later filed a lawsuit alleging he was the victim of age discrimination.

The departure of these company men did not mean that past discriminatory practices suddenly ended. Even after all of the troubles that Lynch imposed and the legislature sought to correct with the promotion process, their old habits died hard.

One experienced officer recently recounted to the author an important moment in his life in the mid-1980s when he sought promotion to a high rank. "The first lieutenant's test that I took I scored pretty well on the written part (I think I was 4th or 5th highest in the state)," he recalled. "The oral board made up I think maybe 30 or 40% of the score. I took the oral board and I can't remember the captain that was the lead on the oral board, but I do remember VERY WELL that he commented on the fact that I had a master's degree and he said something like, 'What did you do that for and what are you going to do with it?' I was a taken a little off-guard and said something like 'I plan on working hard during my career and perhaps achieving the rank of captain, as you did.' Well, he about exploded at me and in a VERY loud voice said, 'I got the be a captain with a high school diploma — what do you think off that?' I knew that things were not going to go well after that and I think that I ended up with about a 30 on the oral board—enough to drop me way down on the list."

Unwilling to be bullied and face the kind of career-ending stagnation Trooper Sullivan experienced in the early 1970s, the officer resigned.

Lawsuits marked, marred, and convulsed the VSP as a result of the Router Bit Affair. Lynch left his commissioner position only after the supreme court ruled Snelling acted appropriately in dismissing him, leaving him stuttering he planned to sue for breach of contract.

While Reed filed a $300,000 lawsuit against Cone, Ryan and Heffernan on various grounds, Charlene Gould chose a higher target to attack on the behalf of herself and her three children. On July 24, 1981, exactly two years after her husband came home from work to ask her if she heard the news about Lynch's firing, her attorney filed a 16-page complaint alleging six separate counts against Attorney General Diamond and State's Attorney Gray as the lead defendants, followed by VSP officers Ryan, Lay and Patch.[939]

Demanding $250,000 for each of the plaintiffs, the complaint painted a devastating picture of misconduct committed by both of the attorneys for their failure to protect confidential information from being released (Reed's deposition and inquest proceedings) and the collective, untimely response of the others in investigating the St. Johnsbury allegations that unjustly reflected on Howard Gould.

As a result, their actions, and inactions, it alleged, affected his reputation and caused him "great mental injury and damage, along with his wife and children." The complaint further alleged that the three "so-called officers and supervisors" engaged in a cover up and attributed Gould's death directly to them as "a direct and proximate result" of their actions.

Although the extant records do not establish who said it, Charlene's attorney alleged further that the DPS obstructed his access to Gould's files hindering his ability to specifically identify the person or persons within the department who met with Gould before his death and accused him of a crime he had not committed.

This person, or persons, he alleged, also reportedly told Gould that "the responsibility for all of the public allegations concerning the alleged improprieties (in St. Johnsbury) was entirely (his fault) and that he would be dealt with severely by the DPS and would suffer the blame."

Their intention, he said, was to make Gould and his family "so-called 'scape-goats' in an attempt to shift the blame for any alleged improprieties upon the Plaintiffs."

The explosive allegations generated significant opposition from attorneys representing Diamond, Gray and the DPS defendants who further hindered Charlene's access to her husband's files, some that a DPS attorney admitted were "destroyed inadvertently late in 1979." The litigation lasted until late 1983 when Charlene, tired of the fighting and now living in another state, capitulated, agreeing to accept $15,000 for herself and $1,400 for each of her three children to end it all, leaving her attorney's allegations lingering and unanswered. The small amount of money she received only came with a noticeable provision that she released each of the defendants from any further liability for her husband's death.[940]

In the end, it was the "scapegoats," the innocents of the Irasburg and Router Bit affairs ranging from the VSP itself in 1968 to David Reed and Howard Gould and his family in 1979 who fell victim to the more powerful and well-placed able to successfully avoid accountability in each of these tragedies. The arc of misfortune descending on each of them began in Irasburg with the unfounded allegations of racist police imposing consequences on those who followed in ways that none could have imagined thereafter.

Part III

RENEWAL

Omne initium novum alio initio est ab aliquo fine est scriptor

Every new beginning comes from some other beginning's end

Lucius Annaeus Seneca (54 BC–39 AD)

EPILOGUE

CPL. HOWARD GOULD's SUICIDE IN 1979 constitutes a cymbal-crashing Wagnerian Götterdämmerung-type ending to a cyclic play beginning in 1968 with the Irasburg Affair. Over the course of 11 years, the VSP he devotedly worked for experienced dramatic change, transitioning from a relative state of innocence into one facing a cataclysmic reckoning with the Router Bit Affair that cost him his life.

The "Northeast Kingdom" that Sen. George Aiken deadpanned in 1948 where it all unfolded fostered the creation of a second realm that began in 1968. State's Attorney Lium's imaginative "Kingdom of Redstone" sprouted then upon the release of Judge Gibson's Irasburg report that December. Occupied by a "King and Dukes" (and the "parade ground soldiers and garrison guerillas" that the discredited Paul Lawrence called "martinets"), this quasi-military organization assumed unquestionable control over a loyal body of men. It included both Gould and his peers, all devoid of any ability to raise questions with their policies if they disagreed.

Unwilling to stand by and see them victimized, Lium acted in their stead as their strong advocate during the next challenging decade raising a telling number of concerns not easily dismissed. Gov. Snelling attempted to do so, calling them fantasy pieces, but from his political vantage failed to acknowledge the practical truths behind them. Despite passionately embracing aspects of the absurd in making his points, Lium was not the crackpot Snelling insinuated. Like Attorney General Oakes, he too was a Harvard-educated, elected official and privy to confidential information, but not the kind Oakes or other high-level politicians received. Lium's insights came from the perspective of the common trooper and other state's attorneys handling their cases corroborating the accuracy of the uncomfortable truths he exposed.

The VSP's separation from its past, Lium identifies, began to simmer in the mid-1960s under the watch of Maj. Glenn Davis and Capt. Harold Dean grappling with the new types of crime arriving in the state. The definitive break finally came with the Irasburg Affair that set the stage for the Lawrence Affair, mending only after Gould's death forcing internal change on Redstone's insular command staff.

Pundits have expressed a range of thoughts about the importance of the Irasburg Affair setting off this sad chain of events, but isolating it from its consequences as though it stood alone in the stream of time. They range from citing the presence of outside conspiracies causing a racial problem in the state to law enforcement's failure to prioritize the types of crimes it investigated and pursued.

On its tenth anniversary in 1978, some still believed that David Johnson came from California as "the advance man for a party of Blacks whose mission would be to cause social uproar in the region." Described as "fiercely conservative," the *Newport Daily Express's* unrepentant Lloyd Hayes, author of the most inflammatory articles about Johnson in 1968, made that claim, but without adding anything further. Notwithstanding, stirring the pot further he ominously warned that "There's more to that affair than meets the eye."[941]

For Attorney General Diamond, then in the throes of dealing with VSP Commissioner Lynch's shenanigans, the fallout from the Lawrence Affair and the percolating Router Bit Affair, Irasburg presented the opposite end of the spectrum. The board of inquiry's former young law clerk continued to blame the VSP for the problem repeating positions he embraced years before. "The significance of (Irasburg)," he said, "lies in the breakdown of the justice system. Selective enforcement of the laws, as illegal as it is, can occur anywhere, unless you're on guard."[942]

Undefined conspiracies that have never been proven and obtuse police working with an equally obtuse state's attorney picking and choosing what laws to enforce on particular people because of race seems to occupy the perceptions of many others beyond Hayes and Diamond viewing the events in Irasburg. Such easily expressed opinions, without citing credible evidence to support them, does not require their acceptance. Allegations surrounding the explosive topic of race demands deeper introspection because of their potential to mislead and effect the perceptions of later generations about what actually happened.

Taking a larger perspective of the times offers another, more ameliorating explanation that does not place the blame for Irasburg on anyone, other than on those "beered up" young people lighting the fire by sending shotgun blasts into a home occupied by a Black family.

That event did not turn Irasburg or Vermont into a racist hotbed policed by a racist state police. Instead, it was the flames that clergyman Gordon Newell and a frenzied, sensation-seeking media fed with their combined incendiary language making them grow that inflicted undeserved harm on the reputations of many.

Others behind the scenes appear to have also contributed to the circus atmosphere leading to the condemnation of the VSP enabling the ensuing elevation of Attorney General James Oakes to a federal judgeship. They included Irasburg board chairman Ernest Gibson Jr. (invoking his personal "marvelous sense of justice" detached from accepted legal norms), *Rutland Herald* owner and publisher Robert Mitchell and Sen. George Aiken; the "rare political triumvirate" that Lola Aiken identified and which Mitchell admitted had a history of engaging in questionable conduct. Their shared, pre-existing feelings about race and pressing concern for Oakes's political future after his election loss and frequent conversations about Irasburg and the VSP's investigation (witnessed by reporter Stephen Terry) in the midst of Gibson's hearings strongly suggests these outside influences had some effect on the board's findings; ones unsupported by the extant testimony and exhibits.

While the VSP did not start out with the intention of creating a separate "kingdom" of its own after Gibson released his findings, the seeds for division were present. In the mid-1960s, the department struggled to address the growing crime rate with a stagnant manpower level it could neither adequately pay or train because of the bureaucrats it answered to. Telling Commissioner Alexander to find the funds in his existing budget to conduct needed training and denying him authority to establish a facility to make it possible, a parsimonious

Hoff administration set the tone for future failure. They worked their troopers hard demanding significant personal sacrifices of them and their families for the good of the department. They also exploited their goodwill providing compensation with some of the worst salaries and benefits for police in the country while rejecting anyone bearing proof of a college education threatening to upset the status quo.

Still, despite the stressful working conditions threatening mass resignations in 1965, the idealistic blue-collar, high school educated young men flocked to join this rank-driven organization; one that those with military experience understood and fiercely protected. They included a slice of American society ranging from the dedicated Howard Gould living and breathing (and bleeding) all things VSP to the likes of Paul Lawrence who did the worst of any of them victimizing a bevy of innocent people.

Politically, Attorney General Oakes recognized the same need to effectively train the young men that Alexander was denied. As an elected official, he did not require Hoff's permission and successfully pushed the legislature to create the Law Enforcement Training Council that began operations just weeks before the Irasburg shooting. Police training became a common battleground fought over by his office and the VSP in the next years until formation of the Vermont Criminal Justice Training Council in the early 1970s brought some semblance of order.

However, that relatively peaceful interim came to an abrupt end with the appointment of Francis Lynch in 1977, arguing that no outside agency should dictate to the VSP how to conduct its training. Neither did he, or his predecessor Edward Corcoran, appreciate the call from other government officials over the years for the department to remedy its secret practices, so clearly demonstrated by the separate files they kept of their troopers, and implement understandable internal rules to guide them. Their neglect contributing to the Lawrence Affair after Irasburg continued to grow until the Router Bit Affair exploded, representing a form of uncompromising extremism that Alexander would not have recognized before 1968.

In 1968 the NEK presented a "perfect storm" of events combining to affect the psyche of the Vermont's population. In April, Irasburg's Orleans County gained embarrassing national notoriety that it was a "hunger county" where too many of its residents suffered from poverty and malnutrition. Blindsided and shocked at the report, Hoff sent officials into the region in early June on a "poverty tour" to listen to residents and try to understand how Vermonters could possibly replicate conditions seen in Appalachia.

They came away equally shaken at what they witnessed and called on Hoff to immediately institute huge changes in how the state provided for its citizens. At the same moment, Hoff was heavily committed in advancing Vermont's role nationally in the racial unrest problem plaguing large cities calling on its citizens to look into their hearts to find solutions. Working with New York City Mayor John Lindsay, they created the Vermont-New York Cooperative Youth Project destined to bring hundreds of inner-city youths, predominately Black, into the Green Mountains for a taste of an alternative life style.

Hoff was a visionary and his good intentions unassailable as he threw himself into the effort heading a non-profit organization to make it happen. But he also seems to have had trouble prioritizing the other calls within his administration to first address the crying needs of Vermonters seeking food and shelter, bouncing from one crisis to the other. As his wife complained, "We hardly get used to one idea, when you throw another at us. It's more than we can take."[943] Poverty in the NEK and bringing poverty-stricken Black people to Vermont in a program that essentially duplicated the state's century-long experience with the Fresh Air Fund already doing much the same thing made little sense to many.

As the youths arrived and spread out across Vermont, events in Grafton in July jolted the state's officials further when rioting involving outlaw motorcycle gangs from outside the state arrived to wreak mayhem. Working closely with the Army National Guard as it had in recent years, the VSP coordinated a response that Hoff, unhesitant in his micromanagement of the department, viewed as inadequate, blaming Alexander for the problem.

The same weekend, Black teenagers attending his youth program in Barton were confronted by white locals, including Larry Conley home on leave from the military, calling them names and harassing them to leave.

David Johnson, moving his Black family into Irasburg just two weeks earlier that included a white woman and her two children accompanying them, posed another aspect of the rising storm threatening the community. The new arrivals were all initially welcomed by the locals, attending a church event where Black teenagers danced with white women drawing the raised eyebrows of some.

Just days following the Grafton incident, shortly after midnight on July 19, the front windows of Johnson's home were shattered by shotgun blasts coming from unknown assailants driving by and then speeding off into the dark. A rapid response by the VSP brought troopers and detectives from throughout the NEK where they immediately began an investigation lasting for the next several days to identify and finally charge Conley with the offense.

In the midst of campaigning for governor, Attorney General Oakes took a personal role in the Grafton troubles and assigned one of his assistants to conduct an investigation into its causes. When he learned of this next significant event in Irasburg a few days later, he appeared alongside VSP commanders who conveyed the status of their investigation to him. The ensuing work of a board of inquiry appointed by Hoff to look into how the two agencies coordinated their efforts ultimately concluded that the VSP withheld information from Oakes and obstructed his involvement. However, a close examination of the primary documents reveals a much different situation contrary to the report's one-sided condemnation of the VSP faulting virtually its every move that allowed only Oakes to shine alone in solving the case.

The discovery by a trooper guarding Johnson's home that he and his white female friend engaged in a compromising situation presented an additional twist to an already complicated series of events. Significant fallout came from the ensuing adultery prosecution that saw race, sex and community mores mix with late-night shotgun blasts in an environment where politicians seeking advancement fought it out with a police agency cowed by the power they held over it.

Johnson's claiming discrimination and unsubstantiated vocal charges lodged by the clergy that racism infused the VSP's work only inflamed the many problems that eventually led the board of inquiry to agree with them, but expressing that delicate finding in a more circumspect manner. While it sought to portray its conclusions as unanimous, its sole female member understood the situation in a manner considerably less severe than the language its chairman used to craft its scathing document. The presence of glaring conflicts of interest, political maneuvering and a void of evidence of racism in the VSP's ranks poses serious questions about the motivations behind the document's allegations.

As others noted at the time, a means to test those findings by affording the department even minimal due process protections allowing for appeal could have alleviated those problems, but were ones that Hoff and board chairman Gibson denied it. The albatross of racism that the board of inquiry hung around the VSP's neck with its hit job, and which Hoff permitted to remain, began to rot soon after and further affect the public's perceptions of it.

Lium's Kingdom of Redstone took on a different persona from the one Commissioner Alexander knew. Now, its current occupants began to construct the "fortress mentality" that author Hamilton Davis recognized in 1978 in the runup to the Router Bit Affair. Its leaders began to retreat inwards, viewing suspiciously the politicians and media excoriating them so severely with repeated references to purported racism and misconduct during the Irasburg Affair.

The explosive Lawrence Affair in 1973–1974 only intensified their discomfort because of its potential to reveal further secrets implicating them in a coverup of his conduct. A puzzled legislature recognized the reserved manner that Redstone treated it in these years making its budgeting decisions so difficult after Irasburg, confronting Lynch in 1978 with its concerns because of the ever-present problem. Why did Redstone maintain such distance from the very people trying to help it, they asked?

Occupants of the Kingdom of Redstone remained silent, presenting no explanation for their malfeasance in the time after Irasburg. For years, repeated calls for change fell on deaf ears refusing to engage in meaningful reforms threatening to undermine the independence its occupants believed they deserved. Their attitudes can be traced to the history of the VSP in a rural state, set apart from its very beginning from other forms of law enforcement that distinguished it from the state's centuries-long experiences with constables and sheriffs. Towns and cities lacking funds made it difficult to train and equip local officers while, at the state level, money flowed to provide those advantages that others in law enforcement envied, and resented. VSP commissioners and their immediate subordinates with military backgrounds enforcing a top-down chain of command meant further distinction existed that seemed to separate troopers from the rest of the state's law enforcement community.

In their insulated, rarified Redstone environment, commissioners believed it their prerogative to handle internal complaints in quiet and confidential ways to protect the department's reputation. No doubt embarrassed by the revelations of the Irasburg and Lawrence affairs exposing the VSP nationally in an unfavorable light, Commissioner Corcoran concealed the Merriam polygraph report concerning his involvement with Lawrence and took no action, while he and his confidants adhered to their secret filing system. Francis Lynch continued to maintain and protect its dirty secrets and then precipitate further discord during his stormy two-year tenure, marked by a clear disregard for protocol and disdain for outside interference. His refusal to embrace changes crying for implementation and inability to overcome strained relations with other law enforcement agencies as he pushed to make the VSP the dominate police agency and exacerbate the "green shirt" versus "blue shirt" contest only made the problems worse. The finding by the Keyser Commission that Lynch's policies constituted "a disaster" was not far off the mark.

Charlene Gould's release of key players from liability in her civil suit for her husband's death during the Router Bit Affair represents a determination made in a legal setting, a forum wholly separate from a moralistic assessment of blameworthiness.

CSP lead investigator, and law student, Lt. John Bardelli made this specific distinction when he apportioned responsibility for those involved with Gould's suicide. Pointing to the length of time it took for the VSP to look into the St. Johnsbury matter, he wrote that, "The fact that this investigation was dragged out for a long period of time and the fact that much of it was made public undoubtedly contributed to Corporal Gould's feelings that death was the easiest way out."

He also qualified his opinion concerning who was at fault, finding that while "it cannot be said that suicide was a logical step, nor can it be said that other members of the (DPS) are culpable, *legally*, for (his) death." (Emphasis added).[944]

While interim Commissioner Cone (perhaps utilizing his hidden Redstone tape recorders secretly recording the conversations of others) certainly appreciated the differences between the legal liability and moral responsibility, he refused to engage in any fault-finding by the DPS. "All areas (of Gould's suicide)," he wrote briefly, skipping entirely over the subject, "were covered and no deficiencies were noted by any of the personnel involved. It is felt that there should be no further action taken in this matter and the investigation was terminated."[945]

The Keyser Commission adopted a similar hands-off approach determining that "There was no wrongdoing on the part of anybody in the (DPS) that led to Howard Gould's death."

However, it also noted the effects that the department's delay in investigating the St. Johnsbury matter played beforehand. "If the internal investigation into the router-bits matter had taken its course back in early 1978 as it properly ought to have, the results might have been very different, but this is pure speculation."[946]

Attorney General Diamond's report further inferred the department's delay in contributing to Gould's suicide. "We express no opinion," it said, "as to what effect a prompt report and evaluation of the allegation that state troopers received stolen router bits would have had on preventing the suicide of Howard Gould. The matter could have been easily resolved and quickly put to rest by the State Police themselves."[947]

When the legislature's Costello committee prepared its report, the most courage it could muster in making any connection between investigative delay and his death was to say that "an unfortunate complication" arose.

For Gould's fellow troopers, the connection between the allegations of misconduct within their ranks prompting his decision to kill himself could not be clearer. "Please leave my wife, my family, and the Vermont State Police alone," Gould pleaded to Snelling before turning his service revolver on himself. What more proof of his anguish did they need?

In calling this event "this most sinister of tragedies," his peers obliquely inferred that his desperation arose only because of the actions of higher ups that included a domineering governor, a Redstone command staff they still answered to and did not want to disparage directly, and a legal system unable to protect its secrets. Lt. Gov. Kunin and State's Attorney McNaughton blasted the leaks of secret testimony and slanted press coverage disparaging troopers ("the boys," Gould called them) in a controversy Gould felt responsible for and that destroyed each of their careers.

McNaughton also noted the "symbolic overtones" of his actions taking place only feet away from where the legislature convened and Snelling worked, and a short distance from where his superiors operated at Redstone.

Gould's forlorn expressions and his use of violence against himself in a symbolic location forced the call for outside investigations that tore back the mantle of a purportedly competent DPS management system. It exposed a "company man" mindset among commanders that had no place in a responsible police organization. The rank and file were not the problem, their superiors were.

Their domineering influence infused the troopers' working environment with such toxicity it threatened their reputations if any ran afoul of their dictates. The aura of authority that infused the high command because of both their intimidating rank and longevity stretching back decades to the department's founding made questioning their conduct an impossible task as the events of 1979 proved. Any trooper thinking of challenging the status quo did so with their hands tied behind their backs, unaware that their careers could be upended because of information they knew nothing about resting in secret files their superiors kept on them.

After the otherwise innocuous router bit problem became known, the honorable and devoted Gould had every reason to believe he was in Redstone's crosshairs for causing the disruptions; despite the absence of evidence that he or any of the St. Johnsbury troopers engaged in improper conduct. While his suicide succeeded in removing him from the ensuing fray, it did not delay Redstone from looking for others to bear the burden in his stead in a "shoot the messenger" form of retaliation.

It was the same thing they had done in the unwarranted investigations launched against state's attorneys McGee and Gray, trooper Kostelnik, and the Reed brothers. Personnel in Redstone may have ultimately avoided legal responsibility for their actions, but on a moral plane they cannot be excused for their collective neglect to provide a working environment with meaningful rules allowing honest, hardworking troopers the ability to fulfill their law enforcement duties without becoming victims themselves. Tragically, an excess of "fortress mentality" and "looseness" infused the Kingdom of Redstone after Irasburg and throughout the 1970s that only responded to change thrust on it after the violent death of one of their own.

Too many police have died needlessly by their own hand, shown by a sad statistic in 2019 disclosing that 228 individuals did so around the country; falling to 171 in 2020, attributed to the COVID-19 pandemic.[948] In 1938 when they debated whether or not to have a state police force, Vermonters read about the peculiar phenomenon that in the past four years took the lives of 69 New York City police officers.[949] In 1955, they learned that their first DPS commissioner, Merritt Edson, died by his own hand, inhaling carbon monoxide in a closed garage, followed by Gould in July 1979. Then, trooper Alvin H. Hoyt fell in 1982, followed by David B. Wilson in 1990, each taking their lives using their service revolvers in the month of July; the same month that Irasburg occurred.[950]

One of the officers that Gould transported the morning of his own death, the well-liked Derby station commander Sgt. Arthur "Bud" Yeaw who graduated with him at the same time from Champlain College in 1976 and received their degrees in law enforcement together, also died by gunfire in 1983. A Korean War veteran celebrating 30 years of employment with the department, Yeaw was alone, on duty and in uniform, reportedly cleaning his gun in his office when it discharged while reloading, inflicting a fatal neck wound.[951] Several have questioned that "official" account to the author asking how such an experienced officer could die in that manner?

Instead, they have expressed their belief that Yeaw's sympathetic Redstone superiors sought to avoid the uncomfortable appearance of yet another suicide so soon after Gould's and Hoyt's passing. Could the story have been sanitized to characterize it as an accident and thereby protect his reputation and allow his family to receive benefits that might not otherwise have been available? It is unknown if their suspicions are true or not, but in the VSP's refusal to assist Charlene Gould after her husband's death and a decades-long resistance to recognize it as a job-related event (as it did with Hoyt and Wilson) its reasons become suspect.

While Yeaw has rightfully received recognition for his contributions to the department, the only difference between his passing and the others is whether or not they were actually on-duty and in uniform when it happened. In Gould's case, it also depended on whether the decedent was perceived as the instigator of an embarrassing scenario that the department did not care to highlight. While the current DPS commissioner, Michael E. Schirling, has assured the author that the department has "a robust employee and wellness program now," the VSP should go further.[952] It needs to return to its past and examine the deaths of each of these officers, and any others that might have occurred because of violence to themselves, to ascertain if they took place during their term of employment.

If they did, they may deserve the same recognition that Yeaw has received and not have their memories discarded in the way that the department has treated its records of Howard Gould by destroying them immediately after his death; along with all the evidence of the department's involvement in the Irasburg, Lawrence and Router Bit affairs.[953]

Inspired by his father's example, Jason Gould has pursued his own career in law enforcement and become a Washington County deputy sheriff stationed at the Vermont Supreme Court, just feet from where he died. Seven-years-old when he last saw his father, Jason can recall the circumstances of that day: "I still remember the day my father left and never came back as he told us that he was leaving to go fill up gas cans and run some chores. I still remember the look on his face when I asked him if I could go with him, as I normally did when he was running chores." He also recalls the impact that the router bit affair had on his father's mind, "I distantly remember conversations my dad had with my mother at the kitchen table. About how all officers have is their good name, and how his was tarnished. I never really truly understood that until I became an officer myself."[954]

Honoring his father's legacy, Jason also works to raise the issue of police suicide in the consciousness of the state's law enforcement community and provides training on it. He is affiliated with a national organization, Call for Backup, to advance that work seeking to remove the stigma of suicide that so many first responders resort to in times of distress.[955] While Jason was unable to convince Gov. Phil Scott to recognize these efforts with a formal proclamation from his office, he did acknowledge the importance of dealing with police suicide. "I've always admired those," Scott wrote to its national representative, "like our brave first responders, who run towards a problem when they see one, when most would instinctively run away. As a result, many struggle with post-traumatic stress and other mental health challenges. The work you and Call for Backup do has saved lives, and we are grateful for the services you provide."[956]

Each of these individuals that Gov. Scott identifies also deserve wider recognition for their sacrifices to the state. It requires a new generation of officials to engage in serious introspection with a willingness to reject past superficial assessments of whether or not someone was actually on duty at the moment they decided that living life was simply too much. Times change and despite the advances made by the VSP since 1979, it remains to be seen if it will now officially recognize the passing of officers such as Howard Gary Gould, a victim of "this most sinister of tragedies," in a manner commiserate with their proven dedication to public service.

Gould's suicide marked the end of a long trajectory of change within the VSP stretching out over eleven years beginning in Irasburg. George Aiken's Northeast Kingdom still exists, while Sten Lium's Kingdom of Redstone has evaporated in a new era of police management the Vermont legislature forced on it in 1980. Those changes remain today serving the VSP and the people of Vermont well.

However, the taint of racism pinned on it so many years ago is one not easily erased and will no doubt continue on in the minds of some. Revisiting those times may cause discomfort to those wanting to avoid opening old wounds. However, it provides sufficient reason to question why the lead police agency in the state, with no history of racism—recognized in 2009 as the first such agency in the country to establish an Office of Fair & Impartial Policing and Community Affairs—to have suddenly abandoned its mission providing public safety and engage in a course of conduct alien to its culture. Fifty-year-old proclamations of racism and misconduct contained in the politically-motivated, suspect 1968 Irasburg Board of Inquiry's report, infused with its many unanswered loopholes and contradictions, are too serious to ignore in this age when police and distrustful minority populations find themselves at odds and violence ensues.

Social movements, like Black Lives Matter and calls to defund police operations, work to make their voices heard, demanding a seat at the table asking if the past should dictate to the future. The stakes are too high and call on us to engage and test ourselves whether our modern-day perceptions of what happened in Irasburg rests on accurate accounts. Many will continue to believe that they do. But for those who consider the primary sources closely and find that they do not, perhaps it presents an opportunity for all parties to adopt a more enlightened mindset to bring about corrective change in the current toxic environment.

Appendices

Appendix A

Irasburg Witnesses

DATE   AGENCY   NAME   REASON

(Dates are approximate because many witnesses were contacted multiple times)

#	DATE	AGENCY	NAME	REASON
1	7/21/68	VSP	Alexander, Doris S.	Shooting
2	7/21/68	VSP	Arkin, Cy	Shooting
3	7/27/68	VSP	Babcock, Roy E.	Shooting
4	7/23/68	VSP	Bailey's Esso	Shooting
5	7/22/68	VSP	Barlow, Vera	Shooting
6	9/4/68	VSP	Baus, Robert	Shooting/adultery
7	8/12/68	VSP	Beaton, Vickie R.	Shooting
8	7/21/68	VSP	Belanger, Dianne	Shooting
9	7/26/68	VSP	Berdwick, Edward	Shooting
10	7/26/68	VSP	Besaw, Frederick A.	Shooting
11	7/24/68	VSP	Besaw, Roland J.	Shooting
12	7/21/68	VSP	Bezio, Charles D.	Shooting
13	7/20/68	VSP	Blake, Wayne H.	Shooting
14	7/20/68	VSP	Bottum, Edward J.	Shooting
15	7/19/68	VSP	Boucher, Alan	Shooting
16	7/19/68	VSP	Boucher, George and Cora	Shooting

17	7/24/68	VSP	Broom, Bruce A.	Shooting
18	7/24/68	VSP	Brow, Lonnie P.	Shooting
19	7/19/68	VSP	Brown, Bruce A.	Shooting
20	7/23/68	VSP	Brown, Linda Lou	Shooting
21	7/19/68	VSP	Brown, Ross Lee and wife	Shooting
22	7/29/68	VSP	Brown, Steven E.	Shooting
23	7/23/68	VSP	Brusseau, Mrs.	Shooting
24	7/26/68	VSP	Burkewitz, Paul R.	Shooting
25	7/22/68	VSP	Butler, Stanley	Shooting
26	7/23/68	VSP	Carl's Equipment	Shooting
27	7/23/68	VSP	Carl's Shell	Shooting
28	7/23/68	VSP	Chadburn, Iris	Shooting
29	7/23/68	VSP	Chadburn, Wayne G.	Shooting
30	7/26/68	VSP	Chadwick, Janet J.	Shooting
31	7/26/68	VSP	Chaffee, Sherman C.	Shooting
32	7/30/68	VSP	Champagne, Gilles J.	Shooting
33	7/21/68	VSP	Chase, Rolinda R.	Shooting
34	7/24/68	VSP	Chauvin Garage	Shooting
35	7/24/68	VSP	Clayton Sherlaw Citgo	Shooting
36	7/28/68	VSP	Cline, Kenneth	Adultery
37	7/19/68	VSP	Coderre, Marcel M.	Shooting
38	7/24/68	VSP	Coe, Henry G.	Shooting
39	7/20/68	VSP	Collins, Donald	Shooting
40	7/20/68	VSP	Conley, Bruce	Shooting
41	7/29/68	VSP	Conley, Howard	Shooting
42	7/20/68	VSP	Conley, Larry Gene	Shooting
43	7/25/68	VSP	Conley, Rodney D.	Shooting
44	7/25/68	VSP	Conley, Royce J.	Shooting
45	7/22/68	VSP	Conway, Marion	Shooting
46	7/26/68	VSP	Cooms, Gene	Shooting
47	7/22/68	VSP	Cooper, Ben	Shooting/adultery
48	7/20/68	VSP	Croteau, Frederick J.	Shooting
49	7/20/68	VSP	Croteau, Leo J.	Shooting
50	7/23/68	VSP	Croteau's Auto Parts	Shooting
51	9/11/68	VSP	Crowe, Brian G.	Shooting
52	7/24/68	VSP	D'Arcangelo, Lois	Shooting/adultery

53	7/20/68	VSP	Davis, Malcolm R.	Shooting
54	8/2/68	VSP	Davis, Natalie E.	Shooting
55	7/24/68	VSP	Davis, Oscar	Shooting
56	7/20/68	VSP	Davis, Robert A.	Shooting
57	7/20/68	VSP	Decker, Kenneth L.	Shooting
58	7/23/68	VSP	Degrenia, Treffle J.	Shooting
59	7/24/68	VSP	Descheneau, Roger	Shooting
60	7/24/68	VSP	Desmaris, Rene	Shooting
61	7/24/68	VSP	Desmaris, Reo	Shooting
62	7/24/68	VSP	Desmaris, Roger	Shooting
63	7/26/68	VSP	Dion, Wayne T.	Shooting
64	7/22/68	VSP	Drake, Harry	Shooting
65	7/22/68	VSP	Drake, Leda	Shooting
66	7/23/68	VSP	Emery, Jesse A.	Shooting
67	7/29/68	VSP	Faust, Romeo J.	Shooting
68	7/22/68	VSP	Fisher, Merle and wife	Shooting
69	7/23/68	VSP	Ford Motor Company	Shooting
70	7/21/68	VSP	Fortin, Roger R.	Shooting
71	7/24/68	VSP	Fox, Preston E.	Shooting
72	7/27/68	VSP	Ft. Belvoir, Virginia	Shooting
73	7/24/68	VSP	Galipeau, Bob	Shooting
74	7/20/68	VSP	Gates, William	Shooting
75	7/19/68	VSP	Girouard, Moise	Shooting
76	7/21/68	VSP	Girouard, Simonne G.	Shooting
77	7/22/68	VSP	Gleason, Ole M.	Shooting
78	7/24/68	VSP	Green Valley Restaurant	Shooting
79	7/24/68	VSP	Griggs, Sally	Shooting
80	7/20/68	VSP	Grodins, Bernard J.	Shooting
81	7/24/68	VSP	Hanson, Dale	Shooting
82	7/20/68	VSP	Hayes, Lloyd T.	Shooting
83	7/20/68	VSP	Hill, Terrill E.	Shooting
84	7/22/68	VSP	Hodgdon, Lois L.	Shooting
85	7/22/68	VSP	Hodgdon, Wilfred	Shooting
86	Undated	AG	Hovey, Don	Shooting
87	7/23/68	VSP	Howard's Auto Sales	Shooting
88	7/26/68	VSP	Howley, Edward	Shooting

89	7/30/68	VSP	Hunt, David J.	Shooting
90	7/22/68	VSP	Ingalls, Maurice T.	Shooting
91	7/22/68	VSP	Irasburg Post Office	Shooting/adultery
92	7/19/68	VSP	Johnson, David L.	Shooting
93	7/19/68	VSP	Johnson, David L. Jr.	Shooting
94	7/19/68	VSP	Johnson, Ophelia	Shooting
95	7/24/68	VSP	Kelley, Norman D.	Shooting
96	7/27/68	VSP	Kennison, David	Shooting
97	7/19/68	VSP	Kennison, Elwood and wife	Shooting
98	7/26/68	VSP	Kerr Buick	Shooting
99	7/20/68	VSP	LaCross, Michael A.	Shooting
100	7/21/68	VSP	LaFleur, John H.	Shooting
101	7/24/68	VSP	Laliberty, Roland	Shooting
102	7/19/68	VSP	LaMadelaine, Leo G.	Shooting
103	7/20/68	VSP	LaMonda, Roy H.	Shooting
104	7/24/68	VSP	Lanphere, George	Shooting
105	7/30/68	VSP	Larmee, Roland B.	Shooting
106	7/24/68	VSP	LaRock, Francis	Shooting
107	7/20/68	VSP	Larose, Carl T.	Shooting
108	7/22/68	VSP	Larry's Sport Shop	Shooting
109	7/26/68	VSP	Lawrence, Barbara	Adultery
110	7/26/68	VSP	Lawson, Robert C.	Shooting
111	7/23/68	VSP	Lawson, Robert G.	Shooting
112	7/26/68	VSP	Lawson, Winston E.	Shooting
113	7/24/68	VSP	Leblanc, Bernard	Shooting
114	7/29/68	VSP	LeClair, Earl D.	Shooting
115	7/21/68	VSP	LeClair, Richard	Shooting
116	7/26/68	VSP	LeClair, Terry	Shooting
117	7/24/68	VSP	Leclerc, Earl	Shooting
118	7/24/68	VSP	Leo Gaigle's Gulf	Shooting
119	7/20/68	VSP	LePage, Robert	Shooting
120	7/22/68	VSP	Lessard, Jean	Adultery
121	7/20/68	VSP	Little, Douglas S.	Shooting
122	7/26/68	VSP	Little, Douglas T.	Shooting
123	9/7/68	VSP	Lively, Mrs.	Shooting/adultery
124	7/22/68	VSP	MacDonald, Bruce	Adultery

125	7/29/68	VSP	Macleay, Douglas F.	Shooting
126	7/24/68	VSP	Marcotte, Donald J.	Shooting
127	7/20/68	VSP	Marcotte, Gary	Shooting
128	8/3/68	VSP	Marcotte, Gary D.	Shooting
129	7/20/68	VSP	Marcotte, Russell V.	Shooting
130	8/3/68	VSP	Marcotte, Wendell E.	Shooting
131	7/31/68	VSP	Marinello, Frank	Shooting/adultery
132	7/22/68	VSP	Mate, Glena	Shooting
133	7/21/68	VSP	McCann, Leonard	Shooting
134	9/1/68	VSP	McMahon, Patrick	Shooting
135	7/24/68	VSP	Menard, Roland T.	Shooting
136	7/22/68	VSP	Messier, Truman and wife	Shooting
137	7/24/68	VSP	Meunier, Gerard	Shooting
138	7/20/68	VSP	Miller, Gary L.	Shooting
139	7/24/68	VSP	Moore, John J.	Shooting
140	Undated	VSP	Morley, Nancy E.	Shooting
141	7/23/68	VSP	Nadeau's Auto Parts	Shooting
142	7/20/68	VSP	Newell, Gordon	Shooting
143	7/23/68	VSP	Neyman, William W.	Shooting/adultery
144	7/29/68	VSP	Norton, Rodney J.	Shooting
145	7/22/68	VSP	Numerous law offices	Shooting
146	7/23/68	VSP	Orleans Body Shop	Shooting
147	7/21/21	VSP	Page, Nicolette	Shooting
148	7/23/68	VSP	Parkview Shell	Shooting
149	7/20/68	VSP	Pat McMahon's junk yard	Shooting
150	7/22/68	VSP	Peavey, Rachel M.	Shooting
151	7/20/21	VSP	Peck, Milton A.	Shooting
152	7/23/68	VSP	Phillip's Gulf Service	Shooting
153	8/3/68	VSP	Phillips, Marlene M.	Shooting
154	7/19/68	VSP	Pike, Billy	Shooting
155	7/23/68	VSP	Pike, Woodrow Mrs.	Shooting
156	7/22/68	VSP	Plante, Leo	Shooting
157	7/23/68	VSP	Poitras, Claude	Shooting
158	7/23/68	VSP	Poitras, Colleen	Shooting
159	7/23/68	VSP	Poitras, Lionel	Shooting
160	7/23/68	VSP	Poitras, Marcel	Shooting

161	7/19/68	VSP	Poitras, Patricia E.	Shooting
162	7/20/68	VSP	Poutre, Fred	Shooting
163	7/20/68	VSP	Powers, Anna R.	Shooting
164	7/20/68	VSP	Pray, Richard L.	Shooting
165	7/24/68	VSP	Preseault, Alice M.	Shooting
166	7/23/68	VSP	Prue, Fred Lane	Shooting
167	7/20/68	VSP	Prue, Louis A.	Shooting
168	7/20/68	VSP	Pudvah, John R.	Shooting
169	7/20/68	VSP	Racine, Paul	Shooting
170	8/12/68	VSP	Randall, Glenn	Shooting
171	7/23/68	VSP	Ray's Texaco	Shooting
172	7/24/68	VSP	Rebai, John	Shooting/adultery
173	7/24/68	VSP	Reeves, Wright	Shooting
174	8/3/68	VSP	Richard, Delphis J.	Shooting
175	7/26/68	VSP	Rivers, Wright E.	Shooting
176	7/19/68	VSP	Robillard, Guy	Shooting
177	7/29/68	VSP	Rocheleau, Howard V.	Shooting
178	7/24/68	VSP	Routhier, Camille	Shooting
179	Undated	AG	Roy, Bernadette	Shooting
180	8/8/68	VSP	Roy, Gerard	Shooting
181	7/20/68	VSP	Royer, Chubby	Shooting
182	7/21/68	VSP	Royer, Emile P.	Shooting
183	7/20/68	VSP	Royer, Kenneth V.	Shooting
184	7/21/68	VSP	Rumsh, Pauline A.	Shooting
185	7/22/68	VSP	Scott, Daniel	Shooting
186	7/24/68	VSP	Sheehan, John	Shooting
187	7/26/68	VSP	Sheltra, Coleen J.	Shooting
188	7/19/68	VSP	Sheltra, Kenneth	Shooting
189	7/28/68	VSP	Sheltra, Larry	Shooting
190	7/19/68	VSP	Sheltra, Paul	Shooting
191	7/19/68	VSP	Sheltra, Ronald R.	Shooting
192	7/24/68	VSP	Sicotte, Albert	Shooting
193	7/24/68	VSP	Simmons, Albert J.	Shooting
194	7/24/68	VSP	Simons, Albert L.	Shooting
195	7/23/68	VSP	Skinner, Myron R.	Shooting
196	7/19/68	VSP	Skinner, Ruth	Shooting

197	7/19/68	VSP	Small, George S.	Shooting
198	7/24/68	VSP	Smith, Duffy	Shooting
199	7/22/68	VSP	Smith, Edson	Shooting
200	7/26/68	VSP	Smith, Ellison E.	Shooting
201	7/22/68	VSP	Smith, Mike	Shooting
202	7/24/68	VSP	Smith, Wayland D.	Shooting
203	7/19/68	VSP	Snider, Harold	Shooting
204	7/19/68	VSP	Snider, Pauline	Shooting
205	7/23/68	VSP	Souliere's Flying A	Shooting
206	7/23/68	VSP	Squire, David J.	Shooting
207	7/21/68	VSP	St. George, Wilfred	Shooting
208	7/19/68	VSP	St. Onge, Archie L.	Shooting
209	7/21/68	VSP	Stevens, Nelson C. III	Shooting
210	7/21/68	VSP	Taylor, Earl	Shooting
211	8/28/68	VSP	Tipton, Walter G.	Shooting/adultery
212	7/22/68	VSP	Tombs, Susan	Shooting
213	7/24/68	VSP	Trombley, Harold	Shooting
214	7/22/68	VSP	Unnamed informants	Shooting
215	7/30/68	VSP	Urie Jr., John R.	Shooting
216	7/24/68	VSP	Valley, Raymond D.	Shooting
217	7/24/68	VSP	Van Stockelburger, Marjorie	Shooting
218	7/22/68	VSP	Veysey, Beverly	Shooting
219	7/26/68	VSP	Vinton, Leon	Shooting
220	7/23/68	VSP	Webster Motors	Shooting
221	8/12/68	VSP	Wells, Percy	Shooting
222	7/26/68	VSP	Whipple, Karen Rae	Shooting
223	9/4/68	VSP	Wichelns, E.	Shooting/adultery
224	7/22/68	VSP	Wiggett, Ilene	Shooting
225	7/25/21	VSP	Willey, Laurence M.	Shooting
226	7/21/68	VSP	Williams, Hollis	Shooting

APPENDIX B

RESOLUTION

Vermont Legislature, Equal Opportunity Study Committee, May 27, 1968

Philip Hoff Papers, mss-379, Silver Special Collections, University of Vermont

RESOLVED that in order to achieve consistency when the words "Black" and "White" are used to denote a race, that they be capitalized; when either word is used as an adjective in direct connection with a descriptive phrase, such as Black Community, White Movement, it will also be capitalized; in other forms, when the terms are used as an adjective, they will not be capitalized; the word "racial" will be used to describe the four major divisions of racial color, as Black, White, Yellow, and ~~Brown~~ Red, and the word "ethnic" will be used to describe nationality, such as German-American or Italian-American. (Strikethrough in original).

APPENDIX C

RESOLUTION

Vermont Legislature, Equal Opportunity Study Committee, May 27, 1968

Philip Hoff Papers, mss-379, Silver Special Collections, University of Vermont

WHEREAS this committee is charged with defining the role of Vermont in the field of race relations; and

WHEREAS a program is underway whereby under-privileged children from New York City will assemble with a like number of children from Vermont at the Vermont State Colleges and other facilities throughout the state this summer; and

WHEREAS it is the hope and aim of this program that a "dialogue" will be commenced between different segments of our society to the mutual benefit of both; and

WHEREAS this program may well be a real contribution to an era of greater understanding and, more importantly, of positive action—of concern, plus care, plus action; and

WHEREAS the funding of this important program requires generous cooperation from many varied sources; and

WHEREAS there is still much to be accomplished despite an excellent start:

NOW THEREFORE, this committee records its faith and belief in the aims, purposes, and value of this New York City-Vermont project, and it urges everyone in all capacities be they public or private, religious or secular, corporate or individual, to join in its financial support.

APPENDIX D

REV. GORDON G. NEWELL RADIO ADDRESS, JULY 19, 1968

IRASBURG BOARD OF INQUIRY, EXHIBIT 34, PRA-00858, VERMONT STATE ARCHIVES

Good morning,

I have asked for this time on Radio Station WIKE to bring a vital message to you. May it enter the farthest reaches of your heart and conscience.

About two weeks ago Rev. David Johnson, a colored minister moved to our peaceful little town of Irasburg with his wife and four fine children, two boys and two girls.

This splendid family moved to Vermont from the far shores of the Pacific that wash the beaches of California. They came with a deep hope, a longing and a prayer moving in their hearts. They had had enough of violence, riots, clubs and guns. They came seeking peace and happiness and a chance to live with dignity and in harmony with their fellow men.

Then last night, around midnight (and without warning), the Rev. Johnson and his family were fired upon three times by some persons whose minds are poisoned with prejudice. They drove slowly by the Johnson residence in a white and red car and using a full-choke shotgun opened fire. They fired first through a downstairs window, and then they fired directly through an upstairs window where they supposed Mr. Johnson to be standing.

What kind of idiocy is this? Who would suppose that such a dastardly thing could happen here in such a town as Irasburg, Vermont? We simply don't know. But one thing is sure—before this day is over I shall contact the office of the Governor. I will call Bishop

Joyce, Rev. Roger Albright of the Vt. Council of Churches, and we will speak a message that will sear the souls of the white population in the State of Vermont and beyond.

We will not retreat, we will not compromise, we will not sit idly by. We will speak loudly and clearly. We will <u>act</u> until every white citizen in this state is moved to a new kind of morality that will restore the Johnsons to their rightful place of dignity and happiness in the State of Vermont, so help us God.

This is Rev. Gordon Newell speaking.

APPENDIX E

IRASBURG BOARD OF INQUIRY'S
WITNESSES AND EXHIBITS

Irasburg Board of Inquiry, PRA-00858, Vermont State Archives

Witnesses (Alphabetical listing)

		By FOOTE	By BROWN	By ELDREDGE	By Board
1.	ALEXANDER, Erwin A., Commissioner, VtStPol.	647-679 695-700 703-704	---	679-695 700-703	
2.	BOUFFARD, Paul (Father)	283-288		288-290	
3.	CHILTON, Billy J., Sgt.,	441-431 446-451		431-446 451-453	451-452
4.	COLLINS, Donald (Fish&Game)	557--563			
5.	CONLEY, Howard,	721-751			
6.	CRAM, Roger, Corporal	145-151	151-152		
7.	DAVIS, Natalie (Mrs). (Jay's Snack Bar Owner)	313-320 516-532			
8.	DEAN, Harold E., Captain	564-575	576-584	584	585-588
9.	GOODNOW, Dana,(Cpl)	453-475 500-504	475-484	484-498	498-500
10.	GREEN, William (Sgt)	205-213 598-595	213-216	216-218	218-219
11.	HAYES, Lloyd T.,(nwptnews)	335-352			
12.	HOGAN, James, (Corporal)	393-402	402-408		
13.	HUNT, Franz A.,(NwptNews)	321-335 408-411			
14.	IVERSON, Robert A., Lt. VSP	601-608		608-609	
15.	JOHNSON, Brenda (Daughter)	246-254	254-255		
16.	JOHNSON, David L.H. (Rev.)	4-42			
17.	JOHNSON, Ophelia (Wife)	42-56 255-257		257-260	
18.	LESSARD, Jean (Trpr1/c)	226-246			
19.	LEWIS, John C.,(VtStEmpl)	638-647			
20.	MacDONALD, Bruce, (Trpr1/c)	264-269	269-270	271-273	273-275
21.	MAHADY, Frank (Dep.Att.Gen.)	104-133 609-617	133-135 617-620	620-624 620-624	
22.	McCLAY, George, (Union Man)	275-281			281-282
23.	NEWELL, Gordon G., (Reverend)	290-313			
24.	OAKES, James L., The Atty General.	65-104 705-716	716-717		
25.	PAGE, Nicollette (Waitt.Jays)	500-516			
26.	PEARSON, Leonard, St.Atty)	532-545	545-552		
27.	POTVIN, Clement, Lt.,VSP	152-157 177-200 225	200-201 225		
28.	RACHLIN, Robert (Atty)	597-601			
29.	SHANKS, John B. (Cpl)	157-172	173-176		
30.	SMALL, George (Son D.Johnson)	56-64			
31.	WADE, Laurence A., (Cpl)	353-386	386-389	389-392	392-393
32.	WARNER, Edward F.,(Cal.Inv.)	634-637		625-634	
33.	WASHBURN, Lawrence, (Cpl).	135-145			

BOARD's EXHIBITS

#1 = Certificate of Ordination, Reverend Johnson
#2 = Preacher's License, Reverend Johnson
#3 = Ltr, JOHNSON to ALEXANDER, 7-19-68
#4 = Photograph
#5 = Photograph
#6 = Photograph
#7 = Photograph
#8 = Photograph
#9 = Photograph
#10 = Photograph
#11 = Statement, Ruth M. SKINNER, 7-19-68
#12 = Statement, Harold H. SNYDER, 7-19-68
#13 - Ltr., J.L. OAKES to F.A. HUNT, 8-27-68
#14 - Ltr., L. PEARSON to J.OAKES, 8-17-68
#15 - Ltr., OAKES to PEARSON, 8-19-68
#16 - Ltr., Newport Daily Express to OAKES, 8-16-68
#17 - Ltr., Frank G. MAHADY to Major DAVIS, 9-17-68
#18 - Ltr., Major DAVIS to MAHADY, 9-18-68
#19 - Comments OAKES, 10-16-68
#20 - Ltr., OAKES to ALEXANDER, 8-13-68
#21 - Ltr., Major DAVIS to OAKES, 8-15-68
#22 - Statement, Nancy Elizabeth MORLEY
#23 - Comments MAHADY
#24 - Inv. Rpt. of WASHBURN
#25 - Inv. Rpt. of CRAM
#26 - Inv. Rpt of SHANKS
#27 - Inv. Rpt of POTVIN
#28 - Deposition excerpts, LESSARD, 8-21-68
#29 - Deposition excerpts, LESSARD, 8-21-68
#30 - Statement, LESSARD, 7-22-68
#31 - Ltr., McCLURE to Judge GIBSON, 11-6-68
#32 - Radio Stmt, NEWELL, 1 page
#33 - Ltr., Barbara LAWRENCE to NEWELL, 10-4-68
#34 - Radio Statement, NEWELL, 4 pages
#35 - Newspaper clipping
#36 - Newspaper clipping
#37 - Newspaper clipping
#38 - Newsppaer clipping
#39 - Newspaper clipping
#40 - Seaside, Calif. Pol. Dept. Ltr., re JOHNSON, 2-18-66
#41 - Interrogation form re: Ross Lee BROWN, 7-19-68
#42 - Stmt David Lee Henry JOHNSON, Sr., 7-20-68
#43 - Interrogation form re: Larry Gene CONLEY, 7-20-68
#44 - Interrogation form re: Kenneth Victor ROYER, 7-20-68
#45 - Interrogation form re: Gary David MARCOTTE, 7-20-68
#46 - Investigation report, John P. HEFFERNAN, 7-21-68
#47 - Interrogation form re: Nelson Cheney STEVENS, III, 7-21-68
#48 - Investigation report of John P. HEFFERNAN, 7-23-68

#49 - Statement, Billy J. CHILTON, 7-22-68
#50 - Letter, D.L.H. JOHNSON, to Montgomery Ward, 7-23-68
#51(1) - Memo, Attorney General's Office.
#51(2) - Letter Appreciation from JOHNSON to Whom It May Conern, 7-19-68
#51(3) - Ltr Apprec from JOHNSON re Trpr Lane MARSHALL, 7-22-68
#51(4) - Ltr., Attorney General to Rev. JOHNSON, 7-26-68
#51(5) - Ltr., Attorney General to ALEXANDER, 7-26-68
#52(1) - Warning and Waiver, 7-26-68 in re: Barbara LAWRENCE.
#52(2) - Statement, Barbara LAWRENCE, 7-26-68 (typed)
#52(3) - Statement, Barbara LAWRENCE, 7-26-68 (handwritten)
#54 - Transcript of interview of Barbara LAWRENCE by Dana O. GOODNOW,
         Robert PELLON and Lawrence A. WADE.
#55 - Ltr., Elkton, Md., Pol. Dept. to Ophelia D. GIVENS, in re
         marriage of JOHNSON to GIVENS, 7-28-68
#56 - Application for marriage license, JOHNSON-GIVENS, 8-27-51
#57 - Investigation report, Laurence A. WADE, 7-30-68 (14 pages)
#58 - Investigation report, Roger A. CRAM, 7-30-68
#59 - Investigation Report, Lawrence A. WASHBURN, 7-30-68
#60 - Report, Ronald J. WOODWARD to Lt. C. F. POTVIN, 7-30-68
#61 - Affidavit, Assistant Attorney General, 7-31-68.
#62 - Ltr., Frank C. MARINELLO, ChPol Monterey, Cal., to Major
         Glenn DAVIS, 7-31-68
#63 - Information & Warrant in re: Larry G. CONLEY, 8-1-68.
#64 - Officer's Arrest Report in re: Larry Gene CONLEY by John SHANKS
#65 - Officer's Arrest Report in re: Larry Gene CONLEY by SHANKS.
#66 - Memo, Joe HEANEY, 8-1-68
#67 - Statement, Natalie Edith DAVIS, 8-2-68
#68 - Ltr., Claire M. COMEAU to F.G. MAHADY, 8-2-68
#69 - Ltr., Evelyn E. SOMERS (Newport Daily Express) to OAKES, 8-2-68
#70 - Investigation Report of Robert M. DUHAIME, 8-2-68
#71 - Investigation Report of James A. HOGAN, 8-5-68
#72 - Investigation Report of Billy J. CHILTON, 8-5-68
#73 - Ltr., Attorney Gen. to E.E. SOMERS (NDE) 8-6-68
#74 - Ltr., Attorney Gen. (MAHADY), to SPRINGER, 8-6-68
#75 - Investigation Report of Lane F. MARSHALL, 8-7-68
#76 - Notice of Alibi in re: CONLEY by M.E. BATON, 8-8-68
#77 - Stmt of B.A. LAWRENCE and O. JOHNSON, 8-8-68
#78 - Information & Warrant, in re: JOHNSON, 8-9-68
#79 - Warrant in re: Barbara Anne LAWRENCE, 8-12-68
#80 - Investigation Report of James A. HOGAN, 8-9-68
#81 - Officer's Arrest Report in re: D.L.E. JOHNSON, 8-12-68
#82 - Officer's Arrest Report in re: Barbara Anne LAWRENCE
#83 - Conviction Report in re: Barbara Anne LAWRENCE by Claire COMEAU
#84 - Ltr., MAHADY to BATON, 8-12-68
#85 - Request Assignment Counsel in re: B.A. LAWRENCE, 8-12-68
#86 - Investigation report of J.A. HOGAN, 8-12-68
#87 - Transcript Docket #508-68 Oscr 8-12-68 in re: B.A. LAWRENCE
#88 - Post Office Certified Mail Receipts.

#89 - Investigation Report of Lane F. MARSHALL, 8-12-68
#90 - Statement, Earl D. LeCLAIRE, 8-13-68
#91 - Ltr., MAHADY to BATON, 8-14-68
#92 - Ltr., MAHADY to Edward F. KEHOE, 8-14-68
#93 - cc Ltr., State's Atty Orleans, to Robert D. RACHLIN, 8-14-68
#94 - FBI statement in re: JOHNSON military svc, FBI #550926B
#95 - Notice of appearance, Robert A. GENSBURG, 8-15-68
#96 - Notice of appearance, Peter Forbes LANGROCK & Mark L. SPERRY
#97 - Ltr MAHADY to BATON, 8-15-68
#98 - Ltr MAHADY to Lee E. EMERSON, 8-15-68
#99 - Annonymous letter, 8-15-68
#100 - Ltr., Carmenlee CROTEAU to MAHADY, 8-16-68
#101 - Ltr., Andrew B. CURRIER (Chestertown, Pa., Comm. Church) to
        E.A. Alexander, 8-16-68
#102 - Ltr., Robert D. RACHLIN to Leonard PEARSON, 8-16-68
#103 - Investigation Report of Dana O. GOODNOW, 8-17-68
#104 - Investigation Report of Dana O. GOODNOW, 8-17-68
#105 - Ltr., MAHADY to BATON, 8-19-68, re: CONLEY
#106 - Ltr., MAHADY to SPRINGER, 8-19-68, re: CONLEY
#107 - Telegram fr RACHLIN to ALEXANDER
#108 - Inv. MacPherson Tvl Bur of Vt.,8-20-68,tickets sent to B. ROY.
#109 - Ltr., Lt.Robt.H.IVERSON to ChPol St.Petersburg,Fla.,8-20-68
#110 - Telegram, MAHADY to Bernadette ROY, 8-20-68
#111 - Ltr., MAHADY to SPRINGER, 8-21-68
#112 - Subpoena Richard E. LaCLAIR, 8-26-68
#113 - Subpoena Donald COLLINS of Barton, 8-26-68
#114 - Subpoena Harold Henry SNYDER, Irasburg, 8-26-68
#115 - Subpoena Bernadette ROY of Newport, 8-26-68
#116 - Subpoena Earl D. LaCLAIR of Barton, 8-26-68
#117 - Subpoena Ruth Marion SKINNER of Irasburg, 8-26-68
#118 - Subpoena Nancy Elizabeth MORLEY, Newport, 8-26-68
#119 - Ltr., Edward F. KEHOE to MAHADY, 8-21-68
#120 - Conviction Report, re: L.G. CONLEY, 8-20-68
#121 - Warrant re: L.G. CONLEY, 8-22-68
#122 - Transcript proceedings, CONLEY trial (19 pages)
#123 - Motion by State's Attorney, 8-23-68
#124 - Order, L.E. SPRINGER, 8-23-68
#125 - Request Attendance of witness, L.E. SPRINGER, 8-23-68
#126 - Ltr., C.O. GRANAI to MAHADY, 8-23-68
#127 - Motion for change of venue, 8-23-68
#128 - Investigation report of Clement F. POTVIN, 8-28-68
#129 - Ltr., Chief of Police, Walter G. TIPTON to ALEXANDER, 8-28-68
#130 - Receipt telegraphic money order, 8-29-68
#131 - Mtn to Dismiss, 8-29-68
#132 - Motion to Quash information, 8-29-68
#133 - Transcript, proceedings, 8-30-68, Orleans Docket 507-68
#134 - Ltr., David Henry GILL to Leonard PEARSON, 8-30-68
#135 - Ltr., MAHADY to EMERSON, 8-30-68

#136 - Memo of Law in support of respondent's motion to quash 9-1-68
#137 - Memo of Law in re: Respondent's Motion to Quash, 9-3-68
#138 - Memo of Law in re: Respondent's Motion to Dismiss, 9-3-68
#139 - Memo of Law in re: Respondent's Motion for change of venue, 9-3-68
#140 - Ltr., Robert H. BAUS, ChOfPolice Columbus, Ohio to VtStPol, 9-4-68
#141 - Ltr., fr. E. WICHELNS to Det. L. WADE, 9-4-68
#142 - Motion, State's Attorney, 9-5-68
#143 - Motion for continuance, 9-5-568
#144 - Hearing on continuance, 9-5-68
#145 - Findings of Fact on Respondent's Motion for Change of Venue, to Dismiss and Quash, 9-6-68 (9)
#146 - Ltr., RACHLIN to ALEXANDER, 9-6-68
#147 - Motion, 9-9-68
#148 - Memo to Motion, 9-10-68
#149 - Hearing on Motion to Continue, 9-10-68
#150 - Ltr., Lt. IVERSON to John REVAI, U.S. Army Intell,9-10-68.
#151 - List of Jurors, 9-11-68
#152 - Investigation Report, Robt. M. DUHAIME, 9-12-68
#153 - Memo fr Sgt W.A. GREEN to Captain DEAN, 9-13-68
#154 - Investigation Report, Laurence A. WADE, 9-13-68
#155(1 & 2) Investigation Report, John F. ELWELL, 9-13-68
#155(3) - Investigation Report, James A. HOGAN, 9-13-68
#156 - Investigation Report, Laurence A. WADE, 9-13-68
#157 - Ltr., EMERSON to OAKES, 9-17-68
#158 - Ltr., Attorney General to Major Glenn DAVIS, 9-18-68.
#159 - Telephone Memo fr Maj. DAVIS, 9-19-68
#160 - Ltr., Mary H. PERKINS to Lee E. EMERSON, 9-20-68
#161 - Ltr., Governor HOFF to James L. OAKES, 9-27-68
#162 - (1 & 2) - Ltr., OAKES to ALEXANDER, 10-4-68
#162(3) - Ltr., Ernest W. GIBSON to ALEXANDER, 10-2-68
#162(4) - cc of (3) above
#162(5 & 6) - Ltr., ALEXANDER to OAKES, 10-1-68
#163 (1) - Ltr., Ernest W. GIBSON to Governor HOFF, 10-11-68
#163 (2) - Ltr., Governor HOFF to Ernest W. GIBSON, 10-8-68
#163 (3) - Ltr., Governor HOFF to Bobby L. JACKSON, 10-8-68
#163 (4) - Ltr., Bobby J. JACKSON to Governor HOFF, undated.
#164 - Ltr., OAKES to Philip A. ANGELL, Jr., Leonard PEARSON and Detective Laurence A. WADE, 10-30-68.
#165 - Memo Interview with Philip ANGELL, Jr., 10-30-68
#166 - Ltr., L. PEARSON to J.L. OAKES, 11-2-68
#167 - Ltr., Philip A. ANGELL, Jr., to Oakes, 11-3-68
#168 - Ltr., Laurence A. WADE to J.L. OAKES, 11-5-68
#169 - Comments MAHADY, 11-7-68, 6 pages (Duplice #23, removed)
#170 - Ltr., Monterey Peninsula Herald, Fred SORI to L.T.HAYES,7-30-68
#171 - Ltr, Dept.OfTheArmy, LTC Harry A. HEATH to HAYES, 10-25-68

#172 - Ltr., Madalyn S. DAVIDSON, StTreasurer to OAKES, 11-7-68, with attachments, CASH REQUISITION and Promissory Note.
#173 - Newspaper clipping, Newport Daily Express, 2 pages.
#174 - Statement, Jean LESSARD, 7-22-68, 1 pg, photostat
#175 - Original, inked statement, ROGER T R. FORTIN, 7-30-68, 1 pg.
#176 - Blank Travel Request Form, DA-F-6A, 1 page.
#177 - Bulletin #37.3 from Commissioner of Administration, William F. KEARNS, Jr., to All State Agency Heads, 7-1-66, subj: "Signatures on Purchasing & Financing Documents," 1 page.
#178 - Ltr., William F. KEARNS, Jr., to Erwin A. ALEXANDER, 8-2-68
#179 - Ltr., William H. BAUMANN to Governor HOFF, 1-8-63
#180 - Inked statement of Barbara A. LAWRENCE, 11-14-68 and 2 pages /photostat of statement, Barbara LAWRENCE, 7-26-68.

APPENDIX F

DOROTHY COLLINS, IRASBURG BOARD OF INQUIRY

M. Jerome Diamond Notes, 1968–1969, MSA 418:12 Vermont Historical Society

Hyde Park, Vt.
Nov. 24, 1968

To Judge Gibson
Mr. Wick

In the accompanying report I have tried to cover the results of the investigation as I would to a group of Vermont men and women. I can't help but reflect how disappointed they would be at some of my omissions. But I do not feel they could call it biased though it certainly points to some hazy understandings of legal procedure, and a less than perfect record for racial prejudice. I believe it answers the questions in the minds of most people.

Perhaps it offers some slight insight into the probable reaction to our findings and recommendations. Anyway, here it is from a woman's point of view.

Dorothy M. Collins

REPORT

The Vermont Community takes a look at itself motivated by its concern over the recent shooting into a house occupied by a negro man and his family. The Governor's appointed Board of Investigation has heard the evidence, and the press has kept the public informed.

There were three questions most often asked. The first queried –

Was some organization, person, or subversive affiliation responsible for the Rev. David Johnson's move to Irasburg? Careful investigation of records through the Armed Forces, from police files in communities of previous residence and documents show no such influence. It is clear that he moved to Vermont seeking a better life for his family.

The second question asks—Is there evidence of racism in this case? If by racism one means a militant majority of the population is out to drive away our colored citizens, the answer is No. Racism in varying measure does exist in Vermont to a degree that encourage the lawless to violence, even felonious action, and court officers to subscribe to a double standard in the prosecution of adultery cases. It seems to be difficult for a community to accept a man as a man, Black or White, without discrimination. The people of good will with a Christian sense of responsibility tend to bend over backwards in helping a colored family. Yet a community in which a young man of military age can honestly ask a friend, who works in a state agency whether the police may be expected to take action if he "bothers the negros" and later shoots into an occupied dwelling in which a little Black child lives must characterize its educational program at home, school and church as unfinished business. Organized harassment of the Johnsons by individuals from surrounding towns, and the remarks made by a police officer indicate an underlying prejudice. The influence of some members of the Press was of questionable value to unbiased action of officers.

The third question has to do with the quality of police protection afforded. Evidence points again and again to hard work and long hours put in by individual officers, but it also shows time wasted due to poor communication, loose organization, some uncertainty about laws, and reluctance on the part of citizens to become involved. The zeal and speed with which adultery charges were pressed by officers contrary to the generally accepted custom of leaving such cases to the civil courts contrasted sharply with the slow action in the harassment case. The racist comments of at least one officer does not give confidence in the equal justice before the law which we cherish. The fact that protection was offered immediately, that those who threatened or used physical violence have been apprehended, and, where found guilty, punished added to the Rev. Mr. Johnson's confidence that his family will be safe here as he feels himself to be the target for discrimination makes the image somewhat less bleak. It must be remembered that the Board is not investigating a case in which police indulge in the brutality of gun and club, but the potential danger of thought and word. The apparent lack of stability in the emerging personality of the Rev. Mr. Johnson tended to confuse the issue for officers and public alike.

Recommendations should include a warning to the Vermont community to avoid complacency and watch carefully the influences at work within itself especially in its responsibility for the values of its young people. That whatever measures necessary be taken to so organize the forces in the state responsible for the safety of its inhabitants that they may act swiftly, justly "without fear or favor of any man," with knowledge of proper authority and procedure, channels of command, and a high degree of informed cooperation. That additions to law enforcement personnel whether by appointment or recruitment through other means be carefully screened to insure the high standards evident in most of its present members.

BIBLIOGRAPHY

MANUSCRIPTS

George A. Aiken Papers, Silver Special Collections, University of Vermont, Burlington.

Benjamin Collins Papers, Silver Special Collections, University of Vermont.

Deane C. Davis Records, Vermont State Archives and Records Administration, Middlesex, Vermont.

Thomas C. Davis Papers, Silver Special Collections, University of Vermont.

M. Jerome Diamond Notes, Vermont Historical Society, Barre, Vermont.

John Easton Records, Vermont State Archives and Records Administration.

Philip H. Hoff Papers, Silver Special Collections, University of Vermont.

Investigation of the Irasburg Affair Records, Vermont State Archives and Records Administration.

Keyser Commission Records, Vermont State Archives and Records Administration.

James L. Oakes Papers, Vermont Historical Society.

Richard A. Snelling Records, Vermont State Archives and Records Administration.

NEWSPAPERS

Boston Record American

Brattleboro Reformer

Burlington Free Press

Caledonian-Record (St. Johnsbury)

Essex County Herald (Island Pond)

Herald and News (Randolph)

Montpelier Monitor

Newport Daily Express

Rutland Herald

St. Johnsbury Republican

Seven Days (Burlington)

Times Argus (Barre)

United Opinion (Bradford)

Vermont Farm Bureau News (Essex Junction)

BOOKS

Cheney, Kimberly B. *A Lawyer's Life to Live: A Memoir.* Montpelier: Rootstock Publishing, 2021.

Davis, Hamilton E. *Mocking Justice: America's Biggest Drug Scandal.* New York: Crown Publishers, 1978.

Department of Public Safety. *Vermont State Police, Twenty-Fifth Anniversary, 1947–1972.* Montpelier: State of Vermont, 1972.

_____. *Vermont State Police, Thirty-Fifth Anniversary, 1947–1982.* Montpelier: State of Vermont 1982.

Duffy, John J., Ralph H. Orth, Samuel B. Hand, eds. *The Vermont Encyclopedia.* Hanover: University Press of New England, 2003.

Eleventh Biennial Report 1969–1970 Department of Public Safety State of Vermont. Montpelier, 1970.

Hand, Samuel B., *The Star that Set: The Vermont Republican Party, 1854–1974.* Lanham, MD: Lexington Books, 2002.

_____, Anthony Marro, and Stephen C. Terry. *Philip Hoff: How Red Turned Blue in the Green Mountain State.* Castleton: Castleton State College, 2011.

_____, Anthony Marro, and Stephen C. Terry. "Civil Rights in the Whitest State," in *Green Mountain Scholar: Samuel B. Hand, Dean of Vermont Historians.* Burlington: Center for Research on Vermont, 2017.

Lee, Harper. *To Kill a Mockingbird.* New York: HarperCollins, 1960.

McKibben, Carol Lynn. *Racial Beachhead: Diversity and Democracy in a Military Town.* Stanford: Stanford University Press, 2012.

Resch, Tyler. *The Bob Mitchell Years: An Anthology of a Half Century of Editorial Writing by the Publisher of the Rutland Herald.* Rutland: Rutland Herald, 1994.

_____. *The Rutland Herald History: A Bicentennial Chronicle.* Rutland: Rutland Herald, 1995.

Sherman, Michael, Gene Sessions, and P. Jeffrey Potash, *Freedom and Unity: A History of Vermont* (Barre: Vermont Historical Society, 2004.

Shenon, Philip. *A Cruel and Shocking Act: The Secret History of the Kennedy Assassination.* New York: Henry Holt and Company, 2013.

Stackelberg, John Roderick. "The Irasburg Affair: A Case Study of Racial and Ideological Conflict in Vermont. Burlington: University of Vermont, 1972.

Tenth Biennial Report Department of Public Safety, 1967–1968. Montpelier, 1968.

Thomas, Marlo. *The Right Words at the Right Time.* New York: Atria Books, 2002.

Wrinn, Stephen M. *Civil Rights in the Whitest State: Vermont's Perceptions of Civil Rights, 1945–1968.* Lanham, MD: University Press of America, 1998.

Photos

Images courtesy of the Vermont State Archives and Records Administration, the Vermont Historical Society, and the Howard Gould family.

NOTES

1   John H. McKenzie Jr. to Governor Deane C. Davis, April 5, 1969, Correspondence with Governors Deane Davis and Philip Hoff and others, 1968–1969, Investigation of the Irasburg Affair records, 1968–1969, PRA-00858, Vermont State Archives and Records Administration (hereafter VSARA).

2   Sten Lium, Caledonia County State's Attorney, "The Vermont Department of Public Safety, 1947–1968, The Birth, Flourishing, and Degeneration of an Institutionalized Ideal," December, 1968, Deane Davis Papers, A181-0046, VSARA; *Burlington Free Press*, 2 May 1972, 9 June 1972.

3   Kimberly B. Cheney, *A Lawyer's Life to Live: A Memoir* (Montpelier: Rootstock Publishing, 2021), 186.

4   *Burlington Free Press*, 8 October 1980.

5   *Rutland Herald*, 29 August 1979; *Times-Argus* (Barre-Montpelier), 19 July 1988.

6   Vermont Public Radio interview with Tom Slayton, May 2, 2011, https://archive.vpr.org/commentary-series/slayton-irasburg-affair-remembered/

7   Mark Davis, *Seven Days*, 25 November 2015; Mark Bushnell, *VTDigger*, 31 May 2020.

8   Robert B. Eldredge, RE IRASBURG MATTER, Chronology of Investigation of Adultery Charge, March 25, 1969, Correspondence, PRA-00858, VSARA.

9   Frederick M. Reed to Governor-Elect Deane C. Davis, Jan. 2, 1969, ibid.

10 See, e.g. State of Vermont Human Rights Commission, *Dr. Lydia Clemmons v. Vermont State Police & Vermont Department of Public Safety*, HRC Complaint No. PA18-0017 & HRC Complaint No. PA19-0006, March 25, 2021; Report on Investigation, HRC investigator Nelson M. Campbell, July 16, 2020; Follow-up Discussion with Human Right (sic) Commission (HRC) Chair, VSP Commissioner Michael Schirling, April 14, 2021; Statement of the Department of Public Safety on Findings of the Human Rights Commission in March 2021, https://vsp.vermont.gov/public/June2021statement.

11 Samuel B. Hand, Anthony Marro, and Stephen C. Terry, "Civil Rights in the Whitest State," in *Green Mountain Scholar: Samuel B. Hand, Dean of Vermont Historians* (Burlington: Center for Research on Vermont, 2017), 186–208; Samuel B. Hand, Anthony Marro, and Stephen C. Terry, *Philip Hoff: How Red Turned Blue in the Green Mountain State* (Castleton: Castleton State College,

2011), 141–146; John J. Duffy, Ralph H. Orth, Samuel B. Hand, eds., *The Vermont Encyclopedia* (Hanover: University Press of New England, 2003), 168; Samuel B. Hand, *The Star that Set: The Vermont Republican Party, 1854–1974* (Lanham, MD: Lexington Books, 2002), 265; Michael Sherman, Gene Sessions, and P. Jeffrey Potash, *Freedom and Unity: A History of Vermont* (Barre: Vermont Historical Society, 2004), 541–543; Stephen M. Wrinn, *Civil Rights in the Whitest State: Vermont's Perceptions of Civil Rights, 1945–1968* (Lanham, MD: University Press of America, 1998), 69–76.

12   https://digitalvermont.org/files/original/42/1932/FindingsRecommendationsIrasburgAffair.pdf

13   Keyser Commission records, 1979–1980, A-003-00001, VSARA.

14   M. Jerome Diamond Notes, MSA 418:12, VHS.

15   "Young Turks" Reunion Papers, 1964–2000, MSA 544, VHS.

16   Tanya Marshall, "History and Mystery of Vermont Governors' Records," *Burlington Free Press*, 19 February 2017.

17   Hoff to Davis, Feb. 10, 1969, PRA-00858, VSARA.

18   Christopher Burns to author, email exchange Nov. 24, 2020.

19   Grier D. Martin, Public Records Request Specialist, Vermont Department of Public Safety, Nov. 26, 2019 email response to author's request for access to the Howard Gould investigation and papers of Department of Public Safety commissioners Francis Lynch and Warren Cone, and Major James Ryan.

20   VSP attorney Brooke Pearson to William McCarty, Esq., Nov. 15, 1982, *Charlene Gould, et. al. v. Vermont Attorney General, et. al*, Docket No. S377-81Rc, VSARA.

21   Montpelier Police Chief Tony Facos Nov. 18, 2019 email response to author's public records request, pursuant to Vermont's Public Records Act, 1 V.S.A. § 315, *et. seq.*

22   Michael J. Carpenter, *Green Mountain Troopers: Vermont and Its State Police* (Shaftsbury: P. T. R. Publishing, 1997), 27–28.

23   Inaugural address of Philip H. Hoff, Jan. 7, 1965, https://sos.vermont.gov/media/ldxpfkvo/hoff1965.pdf.

24   *Rutland Herald*, 16 July 1965.

25   *Tenth Biennial Report Department of Public Safety, 1967–1968*, 7–10.

26   *Rutland Herald*, 28 November 1968.

27   Carpenter, *Green Mountain Troopers*, 87.

28   *Caledonian-Record* (St. Johnsbury), 11 November 1949.

29   Angela Evancie and Erica Heilman, "Is the NEK Really So 'Different'?," March 9, 2018, https://www.vpr.org/post/northeast-kingdom-really-so-different#stream/0

30   *The Eighteenth Decennial Census of the United States, Census Population: 1960*, vol. 1, Part 47 Vermont (Washington, D. C.: U. S. Department of Commerce, 1961);

Population and Housing Unit Counts Vermont, *1990 Census of Population and Housing* (Washington, D. C.: U. S. Department of Commerce, 1992).

31 *Burlington Free Press,* 10 June 1869.

32 *Brattleboro Daily Reformer,* 19 April 1967.

33 *Jacobellis v. Ohio,* 378 U.S. 184, 197 (1964).

34 Edwin Alexander testimony, Stenographic Record, State of Vermont Executive Department Board of Inquiry into the So-Called Irasburg Affair, 7, 8, 15, 16, 22 November 1968, PRA-00858, VSARA.

35 Gene Sessions, "The KKK in Vermont, 1924," VHS, https://vermonthistory.org/kkk-in-vermont-1924

36 *Caledonian-Record,* 15 June 1923.

37 Ibid., 23 July 1924.

38 *Vermont Standard,* 17 July 1924.

39 *Caledonian-Record,* 31 July 1924.

40 *United Opinion* (Bradford), 15 August 1924.

41 *Essex County Herald* (Island Pond), 24 July 1924.

42 *Herald and News* (Randolph), 11 September 1924.

43 Sessions, "The KKK in Vermont."

44 *Caledonian-Record,* 20 September 1924.

45 United States Census, 1920.

46 United States Census, 1960, Vermont Part 47, General Population Characteristics, https://www2.census.gov/library/publications/decennial/1960/population-volume-1/24989706v1p47ch3.pdf

47 Hand, *Philip Hoff,* 128.

48 Ibid., 26.

49 Ibid., 31.

50 *Montpelier Monitor,* 17 August 1961.

51 *Burlington Free Press,* 17 August 1961.

52 Stoyan Christowe to "Dear Fellow Young Turks and Old Turks," May 17, 1978, MSA 544:1, VHS.

53 "Young Turks' Round Table Discussion at Bill Billings," MSA 544:3, VHS.

54 Sherman, *Freedom and Unity,* 503.

55 Ibid.

56 *Burlington Free Press,* 7 November 1962.

57 Hand, *Philip Hoff,* 43.

58 Ibid., 125–134.

59 *Brattleboro Reformer,* 4 December 1968.

60   Ibid., 26 March 1969.

61   Ibid., 134–138.

62   Ibid., 138.

63   *The United Opinion* (Bradford), 7 March 1968.

64   *Brattleboro Reformer,* 7 March 1968.

65   *Rutland Herald,* 11 March 1968.

66   Ibid., 13 May 1968.

67   *Burlington Free Press,* 27 May 1968.

68   Sherman, *Freedom and Unity,* 541.

69   Ibid., 24 May 1968.

70   "Equal Opportunity in Vermont, Report of the Committee to Study Proposal No. 31," November 1968, Legislative Council of the State of Vermont, Vermont-New York Youth Project, Civil Disorders, 1968, MSA 307:03, VHS.

71   *Montpelier Evening Argus,* 20 June 1945.

72   *Burlington Free Press,* 21 July 1944.

73   *St. Johnsbury Republican,* 21 July 1944; *St. Albans Daily Messenger,* 21 July 1944.

74   Hoff to Mrs. Ann Raynolds, May 20, 1968, Benjamin Collins Papers, mss-094, Silver Special Collections, University of Vermont (hereafter UVM).

75   Legislative Council Equal Opportunity Study Committee, Meeting of May 27, 1968, Hoff Papers, UVM.

76   Benjamin Collins to Raymond L. Bady, January 28, 1969, George Aiken Papers, mss-172, UVM; "Equal Opportunity in Vermont," November 1968, MSA 307:03, VHS.

77   *Burlington Free Press,* 20 September 1968.

78   *Times Argus,* 12 June 1968.

79   Benjamin Collins Papers, UVM.

80   Ibid.

81   Statement of Mayor John V. Lindsay, undated, Hoff Papers, UVM.

82   Vermont Council of Churches Board of Trustees, June 7, 1968, Thomas C. Davis Papers, mss-428, UVM.

83   *Burlington Free Press,* 30 April 1968.

84   Ibid.

85   Ibid., 2 May 1968.

86   Davis "Hunger and Malnutrition in Orleans County" memorandum to Hoff, May 9, 1968. Thomas Davis Papers, UVM.

87   The Governor's Committee on Hunger in Orleans County, June 4, 1968, Thomas Davis Papers, UVM.

88   Jonathan P. A. Leopold, M.D. to Hoff, June 11, 1968, Hoff Papers, UVM.

89 Thomas J. Hahn to Lt. Gov. Daley, June 5, 1968, Hoff Papers, UVM.

90 *Rutland Herald,* 13 June 1968.

91 *Burlington Free Press,* 10 June 1968.

92 *Rutland Herald,* 18 June 1968.

93 Ibid., 20 June 1968.

94 Ibid., 24 June 1968.

95 Ibid., 16 July 1968.

96 William F. Kearns Jr. to Hoff, June 10, 1968, Hoff Papers, UVM.

97 The Governor's Committee on Hunger in Orleans County, June 12, 1968, Thomas C. Davis Papers, UVM.

98 William F. Kearns Jr., et. al., to Hoff, June 14, 1968, Benjamin Collins Papers, UVM

99 *Times Argus,* 4 September 1970.

100 Terry and author email exchange, July 8, 2021.

101 Ibid., 1 May 1968.

102 J. O. Kilmartin, Department of the Interior to Frank T. Adams Jr., March 12, 1968, Benjamin Collins Papers, UVM.

103 *Rutland Herald,* 31 May 1968.

104 Ibid., 13 May 1968.

105 Hand, *Philip Hoff,* 140.

106 Ibid., 178.

107 Carpenter, *Green Mountain Troopers,* 67.

108 *Report of the Commission on A State Police for Vermont to the Legislature, 1937,* 6–7, 31. No. xx-558873, Vermont Historical Society.

109 Carpenter, *Green Mountain Troopers,* 80; *Rutland Herald,* 2 January 1935.

110 Carpenter, *Green Mountain Troopers,* 90.

111 Inaugural Address of Ernest W. Gibson, Jan. 9, 1947, https://sos.vermont.gov/media/3w2jqvvq/gibson1947.pdf

112 Carpenter, *Green Mountain Troopers,* 97–101.

113 Commissioner Alexander to Governor Davis, Dec. 6, 1968, Deane Davis records, PRA181-00046, VSARA.

114 A Crime Control Program for the Vermont State Police, Prepared by: The Department of Public Safety, State of Vermont, Aug. 1, 1968, Vermont Governor's Commission on Crime Control and Prevention, Commission records, 1967–1972, PRA-00837, VSARA.

115 Alexander to Hoff, Oct. 20, 1966, Hoff Papers, UVM.

116 Ugo J. Sartorelli, Chief of Statistics for Departments of Motor Vehicles & Public Safety to Attorney General James Oakes, July 25, 1967, Governor's Commission on Crime Control, PRA-00837, VSARA.

117 *Rutland Herald,* 12 December 1968.

118 *Burlington Free Press,* 30 October 1959.

119 *Brattleboro Reformer,* 21 March 1967.

120 Ibid., 30 December 1967.

121 Oakes testimony, PRA-00858, VSARA; *Burlington Free Press,* 23 November 1968.

122 *Burlington Free Press,* 21 June 1968.

123 *Brattleboro Reformer,* 5 March 1968; *Times Argus,* 17 February 1968; *Rutland Herald,* 20 May 1968; *Burlington Free Press,* 11 July 1968.

124 *Brattleboro Reformer,* 12 May 1967.

125 Hand, *Philip Hoff,* 141.

126 *Burlington Free Press,* 11 March 1968.

127 Ibid., 18 January 1968.

128 Mrs. E. Sheridan Case to Governor Deane Davis, Jan. 16, 1969, Governor Deane C. Davis records, 1969–1972, A181-00046, VSARA.

129 Correspondence, Orville R. Dunn and Frederick Reed, Aug. 6 and 18, 1969, ibid.

130 Reed and Maj. Davis, July 24, 1969; Departmental Memorandum, Sergeant Gordon J. Mooney to Maj. Glenn Davis, Aug. 5, 1969, ibid.

131 *Times Argus,* 22 May 1967.

132 *Times Argus,* 21 October 1966; correspondence, Nelson Hayes to Oakes, Nov. 10, 1966, James L. Oakes Papers, MSA 535:01, VHS.

133 *United Opinion,* 6 April 1967.

134 J. Sydney Stone to Governor Davis, Oct. 2, 1969, Deane Davis records, A181-00046, VSARA.

135 *Brattleboro Reformer,* 29 July 1969.

136 "The Land: Cry, Vermont," *Time* magazine, Sept. 26, 1969.

137 *Tenth Biennial Report,* 27: *Brattleboro Reformer,* 11 May 1968.

138 Crime Control Program, PRA-00837, VSARA.

139 Major Glenn E. Davis to Governor Deane C. Davis, April 2, 1969, A181-00046, VSARA.

140 Alexander to Hoff, Oct. 20, 1966, Hoff Papers, UVM.

141 *Burlington Free Press,* 4 September 1968.

142 *Tenth Biennial Report,* 59.

143 Crime Control Program, PRA-00837, VSARA.

144 Hoff Papers, UVM.

145 Statement of E. A. Alexander, Commissioner of Public Safety, November 22, 1968, exhibit 187, PRA-00858, VSARA.

146 Crime Control Program, PRA-00837, VSARA.

147 *United Opinion,* 25 April 1968; *Tenth Biennial Report,* 58; *Eleventh Biennial Report 1969–1970 Department of Public Safety State of Vermont,* 38.

148 *Brattleboro Reformer,* 20 October 1967.

149 *Burlington Free Press,* 8 February 1968.

150 Lium, "The Vermont Department of Public Safety," Deane Davis Papers, A181-0046, VSARA.

151 Governor Davis records, PRA A181-00046, VSARA.

152 *Rutland Herald,* 10 March 1967.

153 Hoff Papers, UVM.

154 Right-Wing Extremists, 1966, Benjamin Collins Papers, UVM.

155 C. V. McQuide and Shawn Bryan, Cost Control Council, to Richard W. Mallary, July 5, 1978, Governor Richard A. Snelling Papers, A184-00053, VSARA.

156 *Report of the Commission on a State Police,* 12.

157 *Brattleboro Reformer,* 1 April and 9 May 1947.

158 Cost Control Council, A184-00053, VSARA.

159 Alexander to Commissioner William F. Kearns, Department of Administration, Nov. 10, 1965, Hoff Papers, UVM.

160 Memorandum David M. Otis to John T. Gray, Budget & Management Division, Nov. 24, 1965, ibid.

161 Carpenter, *Green Mountain Troopers,* 99.

162 *Rutland Herald,* 12 August 1948.

163 *Burlington Free Press,* 10 November 1967; *United Opinion,* 16 November 1967.

164 *Burlington Free Press,* 8 February 1968.

165 Oakes to Alexander, Dec. 13, 1967, Vermont Governor's Commission on Crime Control, PRA-00837, VSARA.

166 Alexander to Oakes, Dec. 26, 1967, ibid.

167 *Brattleboro Reformer,* 19 June 1968.

168 Correspondence, Aiken Papers, UVM.

169 *Rutland Herald,* 30 March 1968; *Burlington Free Press,* 19 June 1968.

170 *Findings and Recommendations,* 29.

171 *Tenth Biennial Report,* 46.

172 *Rutland Herald,* 19 November 1966.

173 *Tenth Biennial Report,* 29.

174 *Rutland Herald,* 7 November 1967.

175 *Burlington Free Press,* 16 January 1968.

176 Ibid., 9 June 1968.

177 "State of Vermont, A Study of Services and Practices of the Vermont Department of Public Safety, Appendices," *Vermont Governor's Task Force for the Management Study of the Department of Public Safety,* A300-00001, VSARA.

178 A. G. Fisher to Reed, Aug. 31, 1969, Governor Davis records, PRA181-00046, VSARA.

179 *Burlington Free Press,* 27 October 1967.

180 Dean and Alexander testimony; Alexander to Hoff, Jan. 2, 1969, PRA-00858, VSARA.

181 *Findings and Recommendations,* 30.

182 A Drug Abuse Control Program for the State of Vermont," Aug. 1, 1968, PRA-00837, VSARA.

183 James M. Jeffords to Governor Deane Davis, July 25, 1969, ibid.

184 *Rutland Herald,* 30 October 1968.

185 *Rutland Herald,* 7 March 1970.

186 Terry interview and email exchange with author, July 12, 2021.

187 M. Jerome Diamond Notes, MSA 418:12, VHS.

188 *Findings and Recommendations,* 7.

189 Ibid., 29.

190 Philip Shenon, *A Cruel and Shocking Act: The Secret History of the Kennedy Assassination* (New York City: Henry Holt and Company, 2013), *passim.*

191 Alexander testimony, PRA-00858, VSARA.

192 Undated correspondence, Philip Hoff Papers, mss-379, Silver Special Collections, UVM.

193 *Burlington Free Press,* 2 August 1968; Howard Conley testimony, ibid.

194 *State of Vermont vs. Larry G. Conley,* transcript of change of plea, exhibit 122, Board of Inquiry, PRA-00858, VSARA.

195 *Burlington Free Press,* 2 August 1968.

196 Radio Statement, Reverend Newell, exhibit 34, PRA-00858, VSARA.

197 *Rutland Herald,* 20 July 1968.

198 *Burlington Free Press,* 20 July 1968; *Brattleboro Reformer,* 22 July 1968.

199 Investigation report, Clement F. Potvin, Lieutenant, Aug. 21, 1968, exhibit 27, PRA-00858, VSARA.

200 Dean testimony, PRA-00858, VSARA.

201 Lt. Robert H. Iverson to Chief of Police, St. Petersburg, Florida, Aug. 20, 1968, exhibit 109, ibid.

202 David Johnson testimony, ibid.

203 Department of the Army, Ltc. Harry A. Heath to Hayes, Oct. 25, 1968, exhibit 171, PRA-00858, VSARA.

204 *Findings and Recommendations,* 22.

205 Memo, Joe Heaney, 8-1-68, exhibit 66, PRA-00858, VSARA.

206 FBI statement in re: Johnson military svc, FBI #550926B, exhibit 94; Letter, Walter G. Tipton, Captain of Detectives, St. Petersburg Police Department to Alexander, 8-28-68, exhibit 129, ibid.

207 Fred Sorri to Lloyd T. Hayes, July 30, 1968, exhibit 170, ibid.

208 Carol Lynn McKibben, *Racial Beachhead: Diversity and Democracy in a Military Town* (Stanford: Stanford University Press, 2012), *passim.*

209 Ibid.

210 Billy J. Chilton memorandum and investigation report, July 22, 1968 and Aug. 5, 1968, exhibits 49 and 72, ibid.

211 Laurence A. Wade investigation report, Sept. 13, 1968, exhibit 156, ibid.

212 Johnson testimony and Certificate of Ordination, exhibit 1, PRA-00858, VSARA.

213 Ibid.

214 *Findings and Recommendations,* 10.

215 Father Paul Bouffard testimony, PRA-00858, VSARA.

216 Kenneth E. Cline, Patrolman, Elkton Police Dept. to Dana Goodnow, July 28, 1968, exhibits 55 and 56; Tipton to Iverson, exhibit 129, PRA-00858, VSARA.

217 Transcript of interview of Barbara Lawrence by Dana O. Goodnow, Robert Pellon and Laurence A. Wade, exhibit 54, ibid.

218 Johnson testimony, ibid.

219 *Burlington Free Press,* 11 February 1967.

220 Ibid., 29 December 1967.

221 Newell testimony, PRA-00858, VSARA.

222 Ibid.

223 *Burlington Free Press,* 14 November 1968.

224 Mrs. Albert W. Howard to Hoff, Jan. 7, 1969, Correspondence with governors, PRA-00858, VSARA.

225 Heffernan investigation report, exhibit 48, PRA-00858, VSARA.

226 *Vermont Farm Bureau News* (Essex Junction), 1 August 1968.

227 Undated correspondence, Hoff Papers, UVM.

228 *Times Argus,* 19 July 1988.

229 Investigation report, Laurence A. Wade, July 30, 1968, exhibit 57, PRA-00858, VSARA.

230 *Burlington Free Press,* 30 July 1968.

231 *Rutland Herald,* 17 September 1968.

232 Memorandum, Sgt. William A. Green to Captain Harold E. Dean, Sept. 13, 1968, exhibit 153, PRA-00858, VSARA.

233 *Burlington Free Press,* 27 September 1968.

234 *Rutland Herald,* 27 June 1968.

235 Ibid., *United Opinion,* 27 June 1968.

236 Vermont State Police Operations Plan, International Motorcycle Scramble, Grafton, July 10–11, 1965, Hoff Papers, UVM.

237 Mr. & Mrs. Albert P. Smith to Hoff, July 19, 1968, Hoff Papers, UVM.

238 Lium, "The Vermont Department of Public Safety," Deane Davis Papers, A181-0046, VSARA.

239 *Times Argus,* 23 July 1968.

240 *Brattleboro Reformer,* 15 July 1968.

241 *Rutland Herald,* 15 July 1968; *Burlington Free Press,* 15 July 1968.

242 "A Report Relative to the 1968 Grafton Scrambles submitted to the Hon. Philip H. Hoff and the General Assembly of the State of Vermont," Hoff Papers, UVM.

243 Hoff Papers, UVM; *Burlington Free Press,* 1 July 1965.

244 Alexander to Attorney General Ramsey Clark, Aug. 13, 1968, Hoff Papers, UVM.

245 Ramsey Clark to Hoff, Sept. 5, 1968, ibid.

246 *Rutland Herald,* 7 September 1968.

247 Deane Davis papers, A181-00046, VSARA.

248 New York-Vermont Youth Project Status Report, June 10, 1968, MSA 307:04, VHS.

249 Benjamin Collins papers, UVM.

250 Mrs. William G. Blodgett to Vt. Youth Project, October 16, 1968, Collins Papers, UVM.

251 Report and Evaluation, March 1969 of The Vermont-New York City Cooperative Youth Project, Summer 1968, Thomas C. Davis Papers, UVM.

252 Investigation report, Laurence A. Wade, exhibit 154, PRA-00858, VSARA.

253 Statements of Nancy Elizabeth Morley and Vickie Raye Beaton, exhibits 22 and 154, ibid.

254 *Findings and Recommendations,* 19.

255 *Rutland Herald,* 4 April 1968.

256 *Brattleboro Reformer,* 25 June 1968.

257 *Burlington Free Press,* 23 July 1968.

258 Ibid., 7 June 1968.

259 *Rutland Herald,* 23 August 1968.

260 *Brattleboro Reformer,* 10 July 1968.

261 Ibid., 17 July 1968.

262 *United Opinion,* 4 July 1968.

263 *Times Argus,* 17 July 1968.

264 Potvin investigation report, exhibit 27, PRA-00858, VSARA; Donald Collins' testimony, ibid.

265 Collins' testimony, ibid.

266 Potvin investigation report, exhibit 27, ibid.

267 Investigation report, Laurence A. Wade, Sept. 13, 1968, exhibit 154, ibid.

268 Ophelia Johnson testimony, ibid.

269 Potvin investigation report, ibid.

270 Ibid.

271 Statement, Ruth Marion Skinner, July 19, 1968, exhibit 11, ibid.

272 Statement, Harold Henry Snider, July 19, 1968, exhibit 12, ibid.

273 Major Glenn Davis to Mahady, Sept. 18, 1968, Hoff Papers, UVM.

274 Investigation report, James A. Hogan, Aug. 9, 1968, exhibit 80, PRA-00858, VSARA.

275 Investigation report, Lane F. Marshall, Aug. 12, 1968, exhibit 89, ibid.

276 *Times Argus,* 8 April 1967.

277 *Burlington Free Press,* 19 Aug. 1967.

278 Marshall investigation report, exhibit 89, PRA-00858, VSARA.

279 Newell testimony, ibid.

280 Laurence Wade testimony, ibid.

281 Rev. David L. H. Johnson letter, July 19, 1968, exhibit 51, ibid.

282 Johnson testimony, ibid.

283 Brownell memo and correspondence between Johnson and Oakes, exhibit 51, ibid.

284 Potvin investigation report, Aug. 28, 1968, exhibit 128, ibid.

285 Conley change of plea hearing, exhibit 122, ibid.

286 *Findings and Recommendations,* 22–23.

287 Ibid., 14–15.

288 *Boston Record American,* 20 July 1968.

289 *Times Argus,* 19 July 1968.

290 *Bennington Banner,* July 20, 1968; *United Opinion,* 25 July 1968.

291 Ed Barnard to Hoff, July 21, 1968 and Hoff to Barnard, Aug. 11, 1968, Hoff Papers, UVM.

292 Charmion to Hoff, July 20, 1968 and Hoff to Charmion, Aug. 11, 1968, ibid.

293 Mr. & Mrs. Patrick Chicoine to Hoff, undated, Philip Hoff Papers, UVM.

294 Correspondence, Hoff Papers, UVM.

295 Newell statement, exhibit 34, PRA-00858, VSARA.

296 Alexander testimony, ibid.

297 Lawrence Washburn testimony, ibid.

298 Wade investigation report, July 30, 1968, ibid.

299 Potvin testimony, exhibit 133, ibid.

300 Lium, "The Vermont Department of Public Safety," Deane Davis Papers, A181-0046, VSARA.

301 John Shanks testimony, PRA-00858, VSARA.

302 Wade testimony, ibid.

303 Oakes testimony, ibid.

304 James Malloy to James Oakes, Nov. 14, 1968, James Oakes Papers, MSA 535:11, VHS.

305 Oakes to Malloy, Nov. 22, 1968, ibid.

306 Brenda Johnson testimony, ibid.

307 Wade testimony, ibid.

308 Marshall investigation report, 7 August 1968, ibid.

309 *Rutland Herald,* 22 July 1968.

310 Potvin investigation report, PRA-00858.

311 Wade and Washburn investigation reports, ibid.

312 *Findings and Recommendations,* 6; Wade testimony, ibid.

313 Wade and Washburn testimony, ibid.

314 Dean testimony, ibid.

315 Mahady testimony, ibid.

316 *Burlington Free Press,* 19 July 1968.

317 *Rutland Herald,* 1 May 1968.

318 Oakes testimony, PRA-00858, VSARA.

319 RE IRASBURG, COMMENTS OF ATTORNEY GENERAL JAMES OAKES, Oct. 18, 1968, exhibit 19, ibid.

320 Alexander testimony, ibid.

321 Wade investigation report, July 30, 1968, ibid.

322 Oakes notes, MSA 535:11, VHS.

323 Oakes testimony, PRA-00858, VSARA.

324 *Findings and Recommendations*, 23.

325 *Burlington Free Press*, 20 July 1968.

326 James A. Hogan investigation report, Aug. 9, 1968, PRA-00858, VSARA.

327 Wade testimony, ibid.

328 Shanks testimony, ibid.

329 Oakes testimony, ibid.

330 *Burlington Free Press*, 19 July 1968.

331 *Rutland Herald*, 27 July 1968.

332 Alexander to Hoff, PRA-00858, VSARA.

333 Potvin investigation report, ibid.

334 *Brattleboro Reformer*, 22 July 1968.

335 Roger A. Cram investigation report, July 30, 1968, exhibit 25, PRA-00858, VSARA.

336 Washburn investigation report, ibid.

337 Wade investigation report, ibid.

338 Chilton and Iverson testimony, ibid.

339 Chilton testimony, ibid.

340 Oakes testimony, ibid., *Burlington Free Press*, 8 November 1968.

341 *Findings and Recommendations*, 23–24.

342 *Times Argus*, 26 July 1968.

343 Wade investigation report, PRA-00858, VSARA.

344 *State of Vermont v. David L. Johnson*, Findings of Fact on Respondent's Motion for Change of Venue, Motion to Dismiss and Motion to Quash, District Judge Lewis E. Springer, Sept. 6, 1968, exhibit 145, ibid.

345 David Henry Gill to State's Attorney Leonard Pearson, Aug. 30, 1968, exhibit 134, ibid.

346 Lawrence statement, July 26, 1968, exhibit 53; Lessard statement, July 22, 1968, exhibit 174; Lessard deposition, Aug. 21, 1968, exhibit 29; Lessard and MacDonald testimony; Wade investigation report, exhibit 57, ibid.

347 Lessard deposition.

348 Chilton and Wade investigation reports, ibid.

349 Robert B. Eldredge, RE IRASBURG MATTER, March 25, 1969, Correspondence with Governors Deane Davis, Philip Hoff and others, 1968–1969, ibid.

350 Oakes and Dean testimony, ibid.

351 *Findings and Recommendations*, 11.

352 *Brattleboro Reformer,* 24 July 1968.

353 Mahady memorandum to Board of Inquiry, exhibit 23, PRA-00858, VSARA; James Oakes Papers, MSA 535:10, VHS.

354 Comments of Attorney General James Oakes, exhibit 19, PRA-00858, VSARA.

355 Mahady memorandum, ibid.

356 Wade investigation report, exhibit 57, PRA-00858, VSARA.

357 Johnson testimony, ibid.

358 *Findings and Recommendations,* 25.

359 *St. Albans Daily Messenger,* 29 July 1968.

360 *Findings and Recommendations,* 24.

361 Goodnow testimony, exhibit 133, ibid.

362 *Findings and Recommendations,* 13.

363 Ibid., 25.

364 Wade investigation report, exhibit 57, PRA-00858, VSARA.

365 Shanks investigation report, exhibit 26, ibid.

366 Ibid.

367 Ibid.

368 Information, exhibit 63, ibid.

369 Pearson testimony, ibid.

370 *Findings and Recommendations,* 26.

371 Mahady testimony, ibid.

372 Terry interview with author, July 9, 2021.

373 *Times Argus,* 2 August 1968.

374 *Rutland Herald,* 2 August 1968.

375 *Burlington Free Press,* 2 August 1968.

376 *Rutland Herald,* 4 September 1968.

377 Arthur A. Ristau to Ralph A. Foote, Nov. 13, 1968, Hoff Papers, UVM.

378 *Brattleboro Reformer,* 2 August 1968.

379 Alexander testimony, PRA-00858, VSARA.

380 Alexander to Governor Hoff, Jan. 2, 1969, ibid.

381 *Findings and Recommendations,* 29.

382 Alexander to Hoff, PRA-00858, VSARA.

383 Statement of Attorney General James Oakes, exhibit 19, ibid.

384 *Rutland Herald,* 31 August 1968.

385 Potvin testimony, exhibit 28, PRA-00858, VSARA.

386 Newell radio address, exhibit 34, ibid.

387 Newell testimony, ibid.

388 Bottum testimony, exhibit 133, ibid.

389 Mahady memorandum, exhibit 23, ibid; ; MSA 535:10, VHS.

390 Claire M. Comeau, Clerk to Frank C. Mahady, Aug. 2, 1968, exhibit 68, PRA-00858, VSARA.

391 Richard LeClair statement, Aug. 2, 1968, exhibit 27, ibid.

392 Earl LeClair statement, Aug. 13, 1968, exhibit 90, ibid.

393 James A. Hogan investigation report, Aug. 5, 1968, exhibit 71, ibid.

394 Lawrence statement, Aug. 8, 1968, exhibit 77, ibid.

395 Robert E. Rachlin testimony, ibid.

396 Newell statement, exhibit 34, ibid.

397 Pearson testimony, ibid.

398 Potvin testimony, ibid.

399 Mahady memorandum, exhibit 23, ibid; MSA 535:10, VHS.

400 *Daily Express,* undated, exhibit 36, PRA-00858, VSARA.

401 *Findings and Recommendations,* 17.

402 Ibid.

403 Ibid.

404 *Daily Express,* exhibit 36, PRA-00858, VSARA.

405 Newell statement, exhibit 34, ibid.

406 Terry and author email exchange, July 8, 2021 and interview, July 9, 2021.

407 *Rutland Herald,* 16 August 1968.

408 *Findings and Recommendations,* 18.

409 *In Re: Barbara Ann Lawrence,* Docket No. 508-68 Oscr, exhibit 87, PRA-00858, VSARA.

410 Mahady testimony, ibid.

411 Ibid., 14 August 1968.

412 *Burlington Free Press,* 27 September 1968.

413 Franz Hunt testimony, PRA-00858, VSARA.

414 Franz Hunt to Oakes, Aug. 16, 1968, exhibit 16, ibid.

415 Leonard Pearson to Oakes, Aug. 17, 1968, exhibit 14, ibid.

416 Oakes testimony, ibid.

417 Oakes to Pearson, Aug. 19, 1968, exhibit 15, ibid.

418 *Burlington Free Press,* 22 August 1968.

419 Oakes to Hunt, Aug. 27, 1968, exhibit 13, ibid.

420 Conley change of plea transcript, exhibit 122, ibid.

421 David Gill to Pearson, Aug. 30, 1968, exhibit 134, ibid.

422 *Findings and Recommendations,* 27.

423 Ibid., 30.

424 *United Opinion,* 26 December 1968.

425 *Rutland Herald,* 14 December 1968.

426 Wick Memorandum, undated, exhibit 165, PRA-00858, VSARA.

427 Wade to Oakes, Nov. 6, 1968, exhibit 168, ibid.

428 Baumann to Hoff, Jan. 8, 1963, exhibit 179, ibid.

429 Commissioner William F. Kearns Jr. to Alexander, Aug. 2, 1968, exhibit 178, ibid.

430 Dean testimony, ibid.

431 *Rutland Herald,* 12 September 1968.

432 Ibid.

433 Newell statement, exhibit 34 and Trooper John F. Elwell investigation report, Sept. 13, 1968, exhibit 155, PRA-00858, VSARA.

434 *Rutland Herald,* 6 and 7 September 1968.

435 Telegram, Rachlin to Alexander, undated, exhibit 107, PRA-00858, VSARA.

436 Mahady to Hoff, Sept. 6, 1968, M. Jerome Diamond's Notes, MSA 418: 09, VHS.

437 *Rutland Herald,* 5 September 1968; *Brattleboro Reformer,* 14 September 1968.

438 *Rutland Herald,* 1 November 1968.

439 Mahady memorandum, exhibit 23, PRA-00858, VSARA; MSA 535:10, VHS.

440 *Times Argus,* 19 July 1988.

441 *Rutland Herald,* 2 November 1968.

442 *Rutland Herald,* 13 September 1968.

443 Ibid., 14 September 1968.

444 *Burlington Free Press,* 18 September 1968.

445 *Times Argus,* 11 September 1968.

446 *Burlington Free Press,* 20 September 1968.

447 Executive Records, volume 34, 1967–1968, A189-00036, VSARA.

448 *Rutland Herald,* 4 October 1968.

449 *Brattleboro Reformer,* 5 November 1968.

450 Stenographic Record, PRA-00858, VSARA.

451 *Burlington Free Press,* 6 November 1969.

452 *Bennington Banner,* 6 November 1969; Sen. Aiken to Ralph E. Becker, November 21, 1969.

453 Oakes to Aiken, November 5, 1969, Aiken Papers, UVM.

454 *Rutland Herald,* 6 November 1969.

455 Bennett Evans Greene to Aiken, November 8, 1969, Aiken Papers, UVM.

456 Hand, *Philip Hoff,* 21–22.

457 Marlo Thomas, *The Right Words at the Right Time,* (New York: Atria Books, 2002), 159.

458 *Findings and Recommendations,* 30.

459 Gibson statement, Stenographic Record, PRA-00858, VSARA.

460 Gibson to Hoff, Dec. 12, 1968, Hoff Papers, UVM.

461 Tyler Resch, *The Bob Mitchell Years, An Anthology of a Half Century of Editorial Writing by the Publisher of the Rutland Herald* (Rutland: Rutland Herald, 1994), 28, 99.

462 Ibid., 99.

463 Terry interview with author, July 9, 2021.

464 *Rutland Herald,* 31 May 1968.

465 Resch, *The Bob Mitchell Years,* 104.

466 *Times Argus,* 16 December 1968.

467 Oakes to Wick, July 19, 1966, Hilton Wick Papers, mss-586, UVM.

468 Wick to Oakes, Oct. 30, 1967, ibid.

469 Wick to Theodore Corsones, May 15, 1968, ibid.

470 *Burlington Free Press,* 12 June 1981.

471 Hoff to Oakes, Sept. 27, 1968, MSA 535:08, VHS.

472 Hoff to Alexander, Oct. 4, 1968, exhibit 185, PRA-00858, VSARA.

473 Gibson to Alexander, Oct. 2, 1968, exhibit 183, ibid.

474 Statement of E. A. Alexander, exhibit 187, ibid.

475 *Findings and Recommendations,* 4.

476 Gibson to Collins and Wick, Oct. 23, 1968, MSA 535:18, VHS.

477 Correspondence, exhibit 163, PRA-00858, VSARA.

478 Ibid.

479 *Brattleboro Reformer,* 2 October 1968.

480 Gibson to Oakes, Oct. 9, 1968, MSA 535:18, VHS.

481 Memorandum, Priscilla Laplante to William F. Kearns Jr., Dec. 27, 1968, Hoff Papers, UVM.

482 Gibson to Hoff, Dec. 23, 1968, ibid.

483 Oakes to Gibson, Oct. 15, 1968, MSA 535:18, VHS.

484 *Findings and Recommendations*, 30.

485 http://www.vermonttroopers.com/

486 Oakes to Gibson, Oct. 15 and 22, 1968, MSA 535:18, VHS.

487 Exhibit 19, PRA-00858, VSARA.

488 Gibson to Collins and Wick, Oct. 23, 1968, MSA 535:18, VHS.

489 Gibson to Alexander, Oct. 28, 1968, exhibit 186, PRA-00858, VSARA.

490 Diamond notes, MSA 418:12, VHS.

491 *Rutland Herald,* 15 November 1968.

492 James McClure to Gibson, Nov. 6, 1968, exhibit 31, PRA-00858, VSARA.

493 Vermont-New York Youth Project, Retrospective 1989, MSA 307:09, VHS.

494 Barbara Lawrence statement, Nov. 14, 1968, exhibit 180, ibid.

495 *Findings and Recommendations,* 16.

496 Alfred B. Rollins Jr. to Hoff, Dec. 17, 1968, Hoff Papers, UVM.

497 Eldredge to Hoff, Dec. 17, 1968, ibid.

498 Alexander Statement, exhibit 187, PRA-00858, VSARA.

499 *Brattleboro Reformer,* 29 November 1968.

500 Arthur A. Mooney to Oakes, Nov. 30, 1968, MSA 535:11, VHS.

501 Oakes to Mooney, Dec. 5, 1968, ibid.

502 John H. Downs to Aiken, December 5, 1968; Rachlin to Aiken, March 6, 1969, Aiken Papers, UVM.

503 *Times Argus,* 16 December 1968.

504 Osmer Fitts to William Rogers, Jan. 9, 1969, Davis Papers, A181-0046, VSARA.

505 William Rogers to Fitts, Jan. 17, 1969, ibid.

506 Statement of James L. Oakes, April 8, 1970, Aiken Papers, UVM.

507 Aiken to Nixon, November 11, 1969, ibid.

508 Background on the Judgeship, March 5, 1970, ibid.

509 Oakes to Aiken, April 1, 1970, ibid.

510 *Rutland Herald,* 12 November 1969.

511 *Burlington Free Press,* 17 December 1968.

512 *Brattleboro Reformer,* 30 December 1968.

513 *Rutland Herald,* 18 December 1968.

514 Eldredge to Hoff, Dec. 17, 1968, Hoff Papers, UVM.

515 *Rutland Herald,* 31 December 1968.

516 Hoff to Alexander, Dec. 19, 1968, PRA-00858, VSARA.

517 Alexander to Hoff, Jan. 2, 1969, ibid.

518 *Burlington Free Press,* 6 January 1969.

519 *Rutland Herald,* 7 January 1969.

520 Eldredge to Davis, Jan. 31, 1969, Correspondence, PRA-00858, VSARA.

521 Correspondence, Hoff Papers, UVM.

522 Ibid., 7 January 1969.

523 *Rutland Herald,* 7 January 1969.

524 Memorandum, Reed to Davis, Jan. 2, 1969, Correspondence, PRA-00858, VSARA.

525 Memorandum, Major Glenn E. Davis to Lieutenant Clement F. Potvin, Feb. 27, 1969, Deane Davis papers, A181-00046, VSARA.

526 *Findings and Recommendations,* 29.

527 Ibid.

528 Ibid., 15 November 1968.

529 *Findings and Recommendations,* Ibid., 30.

530 Alexander to Davis, March 12, 1968, Correspondence, PRA-00858, VSARA.

531 Shenon, *A Cruel and Shocking Act, passim.*

532 *Times Argus,* 25 February 1969.

533 Correspondence between Mrs. E. C. Royce and Reed, Feb. 13 and March 5, 1969, PRA-00858, VSARA.

534 Davis to Alexander, March 27, 1969, ibid.

535 Ibid., 23 September 1968.

536 Alexander to Governor Davis, June 5, 1969, Deane C. Davis records, PRA-A181-00046, VSARA.

537 PRESS RELEASE, DEPARTMENT OF PUBLIC SAFETY, May 12, 1969, ibid.

538 VERMONT DEPARTMENT OF PUBLIC SAFETY, Major Offenses Known to State Police, 1 January–31 August, 1969, ibid.

539 "A Drug Abuse Control Program," PRA-00837, VSARA.

540 Eleventh Biennial Report, 11.

541 Lium, "The Vermont Department of Public Safety," Deane Davis Papers, A181-00846, VSARA.

542 Senate Committee on Highways and Traffic, Jan. 20, 1978, PRA-01088, VSARA.

543 William F. Kearns Jr., et. al., to Hoff, June 14, 1968, Benjamin Collins Papers, UVM.

544 Ibid., 16 January 1971.

545 *Burlington Free Press,* 3 January 1974.

546 William L. Meyer to Deane Davis, Governor, Nov. 7, 1969, Deane Davis Papers, A181-00846, VSARA.

547 Eldredge to Davis, June 4, 1969, ibid.

548 *Rutland Herald,* 15 August 1955.

549 *Rutland Herald,* 16 April 1970.

550 Lium "The Vermont Department of Public Safety," Deane Davis Papers, A181-00846, VSARA.

551 Carpenter, *Green Mountain Troopers,* 27–28; 105.

552 Ibid.

553 *Burlington Free Press,* 2 June 1975.

554 Performance Audit, 3.

555 *Rutland Herald,* 9 November 1975.

556 Ibid., 25 July 1979.

557 Governor Richard A. Snelling records, 1977–1985, A-184.

558 Ibid.

559 *Rutland Herald,* 14 October 1975.

560 *Eleventh Biennial Report,* 33.

561 *Burlington Free Press,* 2 May 1972; *Rutland Herald,* 9 June 1972.

562 *Burlington Free Press,* 30 May 1976.

563 *Burlington Free Press,* 1 November 1989.

564 *Rutland Herald,* 4 January 1977.

565 Report of Laurent Guillot, Oct. 1, 1979, Keyser Commission, A-003, VSARA.

566 *Brattleboro Reformer,* 1 December 1979.

567 *Rutland Herald,* 5 October 1971.

568 Hamilton E. Davis, *Mocking Justice: America's Biggest Drug Scandal* (New York: Crown Publishers, 1978), 42–43; 233–235.

569 Cheney, *A Lawyer's Life,* 186.

570 *Rutland Herald,* 3 August 1974.

571 Cheney, *A Lawyer's Life,* 186.

572 R. Paul Wickes, general counsel to Governor Snelling, memorandum of conversation with William Gray, May 19, 1980, Snelling papers, A184-00053, VSARA.

573 *Brattleboro Reformer,* 1 December 1979.

574 Report to Governor Thomas P. Salmon by The Special Committee to Review All Vermont Criminal Convictions Involving Evidence Produced by Former Law Enforcement Officer Paul Lawrence and to Recommend in Which Cases Pardons Should be Granted, Dec. 15, 1976, Box A003-00001, VSARA.

575 *Fourteenth Biennial Report 1975–1976,* Department of Public Safety, State of Vermont, 5; 45; 47.

576 Richard W. Mallary to Governor Richard A. Snelling, July 31, 1978, Governor Richard A. Snelling Papers, A184-00053, VSARA.

577 C. V. McQuide and Shawn Bryan, Cost Control Council, to Mallary, July 5, 1978, ibid.

578 Cost Control Council, 4–7.

579 Criminal Justice Agencies in Vermont 1971, *National Institute of Law Enforcement and Criminal Justice Statistics Division* (Washington: GPO, 1972).

580 *Rutland Herald,* 14 October 1975.

581 Ibid.

582 Davis interview, Sept. 21, 1979, Keyser Commission.

583 Performance Audit of the Department of Public Safety, December 1975, *passim.*

584 "Confidential" Department of Public Safety Rules and Regulations, signed by Commissioner Edward Corcoran and Governor Thomas Salmon, Feb. 13, 1976, Keyser Commission.

585 *Rutland Herald,* 9 September 1976.

586 Ibid., 10 September 1976.

587 *Burlington Free Press,* 2 February 1977.

588 Ibid., 20 June 1978.

589 *Brattleboro Reformer,* 28 May 1981.

590 Preliminary Report of the Committee to Inquire into the Organization, Structure and Administrative and Management Polices of the Department of Public Safety, April, 1980, *passim,* LC-002, Box LC-01053, file 32, VSARA.

591 *Rutland Herald,* 5 August 1979.

592 *Burlington Free Press,* 31 January 1975.

593 *Brattleboro Reformer,* 20 May 1976; *Rutland Herald,* 3 June 1976.

594 Inaugural address of Richard A. Snelling, Jan. 6, 1977, https://sos.vermont.gov/media/dk1bpdn2/snelling1977.pdf.

595 *Rutland Herald,* 8 December 1976.

596 William H. Bauman interview, Oct. 11, 1979, Keyser Commission.

597 Gregory A. McKenzie, Deputy Attorney General, *A Report of an Investigation of the Practices, Procedures and Personnel within the Department of Public Safety,* June 1979; ibid.

598 Lieutenant Richard C. Curtiss to Baumann, Feb. 18, 1977, ibid.

599 Memorandum, Baumann to Merriam, March 3, 1977, ibid.

600 McKenzie, *A Report,* Keyser Commission.

601 *Rutland Herald,* 15 October 1978.

602 Executive Department, "For immediate release," June 20, 1977, Snelling Papers, A184-00053, VSARA.

603 *Rutland Herald,* 15 October 1978.

604 Robert Gensburg, Giroux Report to Governor Salmon, 1976, recited in Cheney, *A Lawyer's Life,* 235.

605 *Burlington Free Press,* 8 October 1980.

606 McKenzie, *A Report,* Keyser Commission.

607 Ibid., 81.

608 Davis interviews, Sept. 21, 1979 and October 2, 1979, ibid.

609 Lynch interview, Sept. 17, 1979, ibid.

610 *Report of the Keyser Commission Regarding Certain Alleged Irregularities in the Vermont Department of Public Safety,* April 1, 1980, 42, Keyser Commission.

611 Davis interview, Sept. 21, 1979, ibid.

612 *Rutland Herald,* 16 March 1980.

613 Ibid., *Cornelius F. Reed v. Department of Public Safety,* 137 Vt. 9 (1979).

614 Oral Affidavit of Dennis E. Bouffard, March 3, 1980, Keyser Commission.

615 Senate Committee on Highways and Traffic, Jan. 20, 1978, *passim.*

616 *Burlington Free Press,* 28 July 1984.

617 Ryan interview, Nov. 2, 1979, Keyser Commission.

618 Lynch interview, Sept. 11, 1979, ibid.

619 Ibid.; *Report of the Keyser Commission,* 97–98; *Investigation into the Activities by the Office of the Attorney General, 1980, passim,* Attorney General John Easton records, 1981–1985, SE-114-00004, VSARA.

620 Davis interview, Sept. 21, 1979, Keyser Commission.

621 Lynch interview, Sept. 11, 1979, ibid.

622 *Rutland Herald,* 21 November 1979.

623 McGee and Gray to Snelling, May 1, 1978, ibid.

624 *Rutland Herald,* 6 May 1978.

625 DPS memorandum, Fish to Ryan, April 14, 1978, Keyser Commission.

626 Kenneth Strong interview, Sept. 19, 1979, ibid.

627 McKenzie, *A Report,* 44, ibid.

628 McGee to Strong, Dec. 30, 1977, ibid.

629 DPS memorandum, Merriam to McGee, Jan. 6, 1978, ibid.

630 McGee to Merriam, Jan. 13, 1978, ibid.

631 Fish to McGee, Jan. 16, 1978, ibid.

632 McGee to Lynch, Jan. 17, 1978, ibid.

633 Senate Committee on Highways and Traffic, Jan. 20, 1978, 39.

634 Morse interview, Aug. 28, 1979, Keyser Commission.

635 Lynch interview, Sept. 11, 1979, ibid.

636 McGee to Merriam, Jan. 30, 1978, ibid.

637 McGee to Merriam, Feb. 7, 1978, ibid.

638 McGee "Chronology of Events—Merriam Polygraph," and interview, Sept. 5, 1979, ibid.

639 McKenzie, *A Report,* 32–38, ibid.

640 Ibid., 84–85.

641 McGee to Merriam, April 13, 1978, ibid.

642 McGee, "Chronology," Keyser Commission.

643 Ramey interview, Aug. 29, 1979, ibid.

644 Lt. John F. Bardelli report, Oct. 25, 1979, ibid.

645 *Rutland Herald,* 25 August 1978.

646 *Investigation into the activities,* 67–68; 183, Easton records, SE-114-00004, VSARA.

647 McKenzie, *A Report,* 59–60, ibid.

648 Adams interview, Sept. 25, 1979, ibid.

649 McKenzie, *A Report,* 53, ibid.

650 Ibid., 52.

651 McGee, "Chronology," ibid.

652 McKenzie, *A Report,* 61, ibid.

653 Ibid., 66.

654 Ibid., 83.

655 Ibid., 67.

656 McGee Memorandum, June 25, 1979, ibid.

657 Diamond affidavit, June 21, 1979, ibid.

658 Lynch to Diamond, May 1, 1978, ibid.

659 McGee Memorandum, ibid.

660 Bardelli report, Oct. 2, 1979, ibid.

661 *Rutland Herald,* 5 May 1978.

662 Ibid., 6 May 1978.

663 Lynch to Hudson, May 11, 1978, ibid.

664 *Brattleboro Reformer,* 5 October 1978; *Rutland Herald,* 8 October 1978.

665 Ibid., 14 October 1978.

666 *Brattleboro Reformer,* 15 July 1978; *Rutland Herald,* 16 July 1978.

667 Lynch to Snelling, Sept. 29, 1978, Snelling Papers, VSARA.

668 *Rutland Herald,* 14 October 1978.

669 Lynch to Snelling, Sept. 29, 1978, Snelling Papers.

670 Gilbert to Snelling, Oct. 2, 1978, ibid.

671 Vrest Orton to Snelling, Oct. 4, 1978, ibid.

672 Gray to Snelling, Oct. 5, 1978, ibid.

673 Ryan to VTA, *The Vermont Trooper* (Winter 1978), author's collection.

674 J. Robert Grimes, Office of Criminal Justice Programs, LEAA, Oct. 30, 1978, Snelling Papers, VSARA.

675 *Burlington Free Press,* 10 May 1977.

676 Lynch to Gilbert, Nov. 22, 1978, Snelling Papers.

677 Ryan to Lynch, Nov. 22, 1978, ibid.

678 Statement by Governor Richard A. Snelling, Jan. 16, 1979, ibid.

679 *Burlington Free Press,* 18 January 1979.

680 *Burlington Free Press,* 26 April 1979.

681 Transcript, Governor's Press Conference, Feb. 23, 1979, ibid.

682 Diamond to Lynch, Feb. 27, 1979, Keyser Commission.

683 Lynch to Diamond, May 28, 1979, ibid.

684 Diamond to Lynch, May 31, 1979, ibid.

685 *Rutland Herald,* 1 August 1979.

686 Gilbert to Baumann, June 19, 1979, ibid.

687 Snelling to Senator Harry Lawrence, May 18, 1979, ibid.

688 Lynch to Snelling, April 13, 1979, ibid.

689 *Rutland Herald,* 31 May 1979.

690 *Burlington Free Press,* 7 February 1979.

691 *Brattleboro Reformer,* 8 February 1979.

692 *Rutland Herald,* 22 April 1979.

693 Ibid., 16 April 1980.

694 Ryan interview, Aug. 30, 1979, Keyser Commission.

695 *Investigation into the Activities,* 1, Easton records, SE-114-00004, VSARA.

696 Attorney General John Easton response to Governor Snelling's question: "What evidence exists which would meet the standard of proof required to support a disciplinary dismissal of Major Ryan?," Jan. 28, 1981, ibid., 18.

697 *The Talisman,* Rutland High School Year Book, 1959.

698 *Rutland Herald,* 4 December 1959.

699 Ibid., 8 June 1960 and 24 February 1962.

700 Ibid., 7 March 1964.

701 *Brattleboro Reformer,* 18 October 1966.

702 *The Talisman,* 1964.

703 Albert Ravenna interview with author, April 13, 2020.

704 *Rutland Herald,* 12 June 1970.

705 Lay interview, Aug. 29, 1979, Keyser Commission.

706 Hebert interview, Aug. 21, 1979, ibid.

707 Truex interview transcript, undated, Keyser Commission.

708 *The Vermont Trooper* (Winter 1980), 2–3.

709 Edward Prescott interview, Sept. 26, 1979, Keyser Commission.

710 Thomas Truex statement, undated, ibid.

711 Charlene Gould interview, ibid.

712 Jason Gould interview with author, Feb. 28, 2020.

713 Theriault interview, Sept. 10, 1979, ibid.

714 Investigation into the Activities, 13, Easton records.

715 AJ Ravenna and author interview, April 13, 2020.

716 Bouffard interview, Aug. 16, 1979, ibid.

717 Ibid; Truex interview, Aug. 15, 1979, Keyser Commission.

718 *Burlington Free Press,* 5 August 1977; Easton response to Snelling request re: Ryan dismissal, 27, Easton records.

719 *Investigation into the Activities,* 59, Easton records.

720 David Reed deposition, Aug. 31, 1978, 36, Keyser Commission.

721 Reed Investigation Report, no. 525–573, March 8, 1978, ibid.

722 Reed deposition, 32, ibid.

723 *Investigation into the Activities,* 75, Easton records.

724 Reed deposition, Keyser Commission.

725 Reed investigation report, ibid.

726 Ryan interview, ibid.

727 Reed investigation, ibid.

728 Reed deposition, 26–27, ibid.

729 *Investigation into the Activities,* 24, Easton records.

730 Charlene Gould interview, Keyser Commission.

731 Ibid.

732 *Burlington Free Press,* 24 January 1980.

733 Charron to Gould, March 15, 1978, ibid.

734 Reed to Ramey, Departmental Memorandum marked "Confidential," March 13, 1978, Keyser Commission.

735 Reed to Lynch, March 13, 1979, ibid.

736 Reed deposition, 33–34, ibid.

737 Lt. Laurent Guillot report, Aug. 23, 1979, ibid.

738 *Rutland Herald,* 25 July 1979.

739 Charlene Gould interview, ibid.

740 Bouffard interview, ibid.

741 *Rutland Herald,* 30 December 1979.

742 *Vermont Trooper* (Spring 1979), 2.

743 McKenzie, *A Report, passim.*

744 *Rutland Herald,* 1 July 1979.

745 *Burlington Free Press,* 25 July 1979.

746 *Burlington Free Press,* 12 August 1979; Lynch interview, Keyser Commission.

747 Snelling to Gilbert, July 19, 1979, Snelling papers.

748 *Burlington Free Press,* 12 August 1979.

749 *Rutland Herald,* 25 July 1979.

750 Robert D. Rachlin and William W. Pearson, "Report to the Commissioner Department of Public Safety 16 April 1981," 21, Keyser Commission.

751 *Rutland Herald,* 25 July 1979.

752 Ibid.

753 Ibid.

754 *Investigation into the Activities,* 107–108, Easton records.

755 Easton records.

756 Ryan to Snelling, July 24, 1979, Keyser Commission.

757 Easton records.

758 *Report of the Keyser Commission,* 69.

759 Ryan interview, Keyser Commission.

760 *Investigation into the Activities,* 113, Easton records.

761 Ibid, 108–109.

762 *Burlington Free Press,* 29 August 1979.

763 Truex interview, undated, Keyser Commission.

764 *Investigation into the Activities,* 67–68; 183, Easton records.

765 Kostelnik interview, Aug. 15, 1979.

766　Charlene Gould interview, Keyser Commission.

767　*Rutland Herald,* 26 July 1979.

768　*State v. Lynch,* 137 Vt. 607, 409 A.2d 1001 (1979).

769　*Rutland Herald,* 27 July 1979.

770　Charlene Gould interview, Keyser Commission.

771　Bouffard interview, Aug. 16, 1979, ibid.

772　Truex statement, undated, ibid.

773　Charlene Gould interview, ibid.

774　Truex statement, ibid.

775　Statement, John Palmer, undated, ibid.

776　Donald Ravenna to author email, Nov. 7, 2019.

777　Kostelnik statement, Aug. 16, 1979, ibid.

778　Paul Goguen interview, Sept. 26, 1979, ibid.

779　*Burlington Free Press,* 6 August 1979.

780　Prescott interview, Keyser Commission.

781　Harold Kinney statement, Oct. 11, 1979, ibid.

782　Charlene Gould interview, Sept. 6, 1979, Keyser Commission.

783　*Rutland Herald,* 2 February 1980.

784　*Rutland Herald,* 31 July 1979.

785　Albert Ravenna and author interview, April 13, 2020 and email, April 14, 2020;
　　　Bardelli report, Oct. 4, 1979, Keyser Commission.

786　*Rutland Herald,* 1 August 1979.

787　*Brattleboro Reformer,* 31 July 1979.

788　*Rutland Herald,* 31 July 1979.

789　Martin interview, Aug. 29, 1979, and Gould Certificate of Death, Aug. 1, 1979,
　　　Keyser Commission.

790　Patch interview, Aug. 30, 1979, ibid.

791　*Burlington Free Press,* 1 August 1979.

792　*Investigation into the Activities,* 68, Easton records.

793　Easton records.

794　Mallary to Gilbert, Aug. 23, 1979, Snelling papers.

795　Albert Ravenna and author interview.

796　*Investigation into the Activities,* 142, Easton records.

797　Ibid.

798　Ibid., 44.

799 Preferral of Charges, Philbrook to Ryan, April 23, 1981, Easton records.

800 Departmental Memorandum, Ryan to File, Aug. 2, 1979, Keyser Commission.

801 *Rutland Herald,* 3 August 1989.

802 *Report of Commissioner Warren M. Cone, Department of Public Safety to Governor Richard A. Snelling,* undated, LC-01053, VSARA.

803 *Burlington Free Press,* 1 August 1979.

804 *Brattleboro Reformer,* 31 July 1979.

805 Ibid.

806 *Rutland Herald,* 31 July 1979.

807 *Burlington Free Press,* 1 August 1979.

808 Ibid.

809 *Rutland Herald,* 1 August 1979.

810 Ibid.

811 Ibid.

812 Ibid.

813 Ibid., 5 August 1979; *Burlington Free Press,* 1 August 1979.

814 *Rutland Herald,* 1 August 1979.

815 Ibid, 3 August 1979.

816 Ibid.

817 *Burlington Free Press,* 3 August 1979.

818 Governor Richard A. Snelling to Vermont State Troopers, August 2, 1979, author's collection.

819 *Rutland Herald,* 7 August 1979.

820 Benson Scotch, Assistant Attorney General to Gregory A. McKenzie, Deputy Attorney General, August 3, 1979, Easton papers.

821 "CONFIDENTIAL: Random Notes Not Appearing Elsewhere in the Report," *Report of Commissioner Warren Cone,* 1–3, VSARA.

822 *Rutland Herald,* 16 January 1980.

823 David Putter interview with the author, Feb. 12, 2021.

824 Memorandum, Ryan to Cone, August 8, 1979, Keyser Commission.

825 "Random Notes," 4.

826 Keyser Commission, 98.

827 Ibid., 87.

828 Ryan to Cone, August 8, 1979.

829 Easton papers.

830 *Burlington Free Press,* 7 August 1979.

831 Baumann to Gilbert, June 28, 1979, Snelling papers.

832 Gilbert to Snelling, August 6, 1979, ibid.

833 Thomas M. Crowley to Snelling, August 3, 1979, ibid.

834 *Rutland Herald,* 21 November 1979.

835 Bardelli report, August 14, 1979, ibid.

836 Bardelli to Cone, August 20, 1979, Interdepartmental Message, State of Connecticut, ibid.

837 *Rutland Herald,* 21 November 1979.

838 Ibid.

839 Keyser Commission, 38.

840 Gilbert to Snelling, Nov. 8, 1979, Snelling papers.

841 Snelling to Keyser, August 10, 1979, Snelling papers.

842 Keyser Commission, 59.

843 Ibid.

844 Charles H. Zimmerman, Chief Examiner, Scientific Security, Boston, MA, August 16, 1979, Keyser Commission.

845 *Investigation into the Activities,* 67, Easton records.

846 "Random Notes," 5–6.

847 Keyser Commission, 74.

848 Ibid, 62.

849 *Rutland Herald,* 2 February 1980.

850 Ibid.

851 "Random Notes," 4–5.

852 Palmisano to Cone, Oct. 2, 1979, Keyser Commission.

853 "Random Notes," 6–7.

854 *Report of Commissioner Warren A. Cone,* A-7.

855 Confidential, Department of Public Safety, State of Vermont, Rules and Regulation, approved by Gov. Thomas Salmon, Feb. 13, 1976, Keyser Commission.

856 Cone to Ryan, 11 October 1979, ibid.

857 *Investigation into the Activities,* 147, Easton records.

858 *Report of Commissioner Warren Cone,* C-36.

859 Gilbert to Snelling, Oct. 18, 1979, Snelling papers

860 Paul S. Gillies and Henry Bailey to Warren Cone, Dec. 31, 1979, ibid.

861 *The Vermont Trooper* (Winter 1980), 1.

862 Palmisano statement, Dec. 20, 1979, *State Police v. Sergeant Reed, 1979,* A341-00001, VSARA.

863 Phillip C. Linton, Assistant Attorney General to John J. Easton, Attorney General, April 17, 1981, Snelling papers.

864 "Scandal," Merriam-Webster Dictionary.

865 *Rutland Herald,* 16 November 1979.

866 *Burlington Free Press,* 16 November 1979.

867 *Rutland Herald,* 14, 15 December 1979.

868 Ibid., 8 April 1980.

869 *The Vermont Trooper* (Winter 1980), 3.

870 Email exchanges with author, Dec. 24, 2019.

871 *Brattleboro Reformer,* 1 December 1979.

872 Brooke Pearson to Philbrook, June 19, 1980, Snelling papers.

873 *Burlington Free Press,* 9 October 1980.

874 *Brattleboro Reformer,* 1 and 14 December 1979; *Rutland Herald,* 1 December 1979.

875 *Burlington Free Press,* 27 January 1980; *Brattleboro Reformer,* 5 March 1980.

876 *Burlington Free Press,* 18 November 1979.

877 *Rutland Herald,* 9 October 1980.

878 Valsangiacomo to Cone, Jan. 7, 1980; to Gilbert, Jan. 10, 1980, Easton records.

879 *Rutland Herald,* 21 December 1980.

880 Valsangiacomo statement, *State Police v. Reed.*

881 *Rutland Herald,* 22 January 1980.

882 Ibid., 7 March 1980.

883 *Brattleboro Reformer,* 22 January 1980.

884 *Rutland Herald,* 23 and 24 January 1980.

885 *Burlington Free Press,* 25 January 1980.

886 *Rutland Herald,* 24 January 1980.

887 *In re: David A. Reed, Disciplinary Panel Findings and Conclusions Constituting Recommendations to the Commissioner,* 14–15, Keyser Commission.

888 *Burlington Free Press,* 12 February 1980.

889 *Rutland Herald,* 31 January 1980.

890 *Investigation into the Activities,* 118–119, Easton records.

891 *Rutland Herald,* 12 February 1980.

892 *Investigation into the Activities,* 119, Easton records.

893 Nickerson testimony, Easton records.

894 *Rutland Herald*, 9 February 1980.

895 *Burlington Free Press*, 12 February 1980.

896 *Rutland Herald*, 14 February 1980.

897 Preliminary Report of the Committee, 8.

898 *Rutland Herald*, 6 February 1980.

899 Ibid.

900 *Brattleboro Reformer*, 6 February 1980.

901 *Rutland Herald*, 29 February 1980.

902 *Burlington Free Press*, 23 February 1980.

903 *Rutland Herald*, 21 March 1980.

904 Ibid., 7 March 1980.

905 Preliminary Report of the Committee, 1.

906 *Burlington Free Press*, 15 October 1980.

907 *Rutland Herald*, 7 March 1980.

908 *Burlington Free Press*, 8 May 1980.

909 *Rutland Herald*, 15 February 1980.

910 Ibid., 17 February 1980.

911 Ibid.

912 Ibid., 2 April 1980; 25 April 1980.

913 Ibid., 3 April 1980.

914 *Burlington Free Press*, 3 April 1980.

915 James Douglas to Tom Sykras, April 24, 1980, Snelling records.

916 Title 20, VSA § 1923.

917 *Rutland Herald*, 19 July 1980.

918 Ibid., 14 July 1980.

919 Lt. Gordon J. Mooney transcript, Easton records.

920 *Rutland Herald*, 2 April 1980.

921 Report of Keyser Commission, 4.

922 *Rutland Herald*, 27 April 1980.

923 Ibid., 23 April 1980.

924 *Brattleboro Reformer*, 21 April 1980.

925 *Rutland Herald*, 27 April 1980.

926 *Burlington Free Press*, 18 May 1980.

927 *Rutland Herald*, 26 October 1980.

928 *Brattleboro Reformer*, 8 October 1980; *Rutland Herald*, 9 and 12 October 1980.

929 *Burlington Free Press*, 8 October 1980.

930 *Rutland Herald*, 12 October 1980.

931 *Brady v. Maryland*, 373 U.S. 83 (1963).

932 Spear testimony, Snelling records.

933 *Burlington Free Press*, 8 October 1980.

934 Rachlin, *Report to the Commissioner*, 1, Keyser Commission.

935 *Burlington Free Press*, 22 April 1981.

936 Preferral of Charges, Easton records.

937 *Burlington Free Press*, 20 July 1984.

938 *Brattleboro Reformer*, 17 July 1984.

939 *Charlene Gould, et. al. vs. Vermont Attorney General's Office M. Jerome Diamond, et. al.*, Rutland Superior Court, Docket No. S377-81Rc, VSARA.

940 General Release, Nov. 28, 1983, ibid.

941 *Rutland Herald*, 16 July 1978.

942 Ibid.

943 Hand, *Philip Hoff*, 179.

944 Baredlli report, Oct. 4, 1979, Keyser Commission, author's emphasis.

945 *Report of Commissioner Warren M. Cone*, F-4-5.

946 *Report of the Keyser Commission*. 93.

947 *Investigation into the Activities*, 165, Easton records.

948 *Burlington Free Press*, 6 January 2020.

949 *Rutland Herald*, 21 July 1938.

950 *Burlington Free Press*, July 19, 1982; *Rutland Herald*, 29 July 1990.

951 *Rutland Herald*, 14 May 1983.

952 Michael Schirling and author email exchange, April 27, 2020.

953 https://vsp.vermont.gov/memorial/yeaw

954 Jason Gould and author email exchange, Feb. 25, 2020.

955 https://callforbackup.org/about/

956 Governor Philip B. Scott to David Edwards, Sept. 1, 2019, correspondence in possession of Jason Gould.

INDEX

ABOUT THE AUTHOR

GARY G. SHATTUCK IS A NEW HAMPSHIRE NATIVE who served in the Vermont law enforcement community for over three decades. He received his B. A. degree from the University of Colorado, a Juris Doctor degree from the Vermont Law School, a Master's degree in Military History concentrating on the Revolutionary War and attended post-graduate courses in Archaeology and Heritage at the University of Leicester (UK). He served for many years as a patrol commander with the Vermont State Police and assistant Attorney General for the State of Vermont prosecuting Vermont Drug Task Force cases. Gary went on to become an assistant United States attorney with the U. S. Department of Justice where, in addition to prosecuting criminal offenses and acting as the District of Vermont's anti-terrorism coordinator and arguing cases before the U. S. Court of Appeals in the Second Circuit, he also worked as a legal advisor in Kosovo and Iraq. Since leaving government service, he has written six books and many articles on early Vermont history. Gary also serves on the Board of Trustees of the Vermont Historical Society, is a member of the University of Vermont's Center for Research on Vermont and former member of the Vermont Historical Records Advisory Board (Vermont State Archives and Records Administration) and the Fort Ticonderoga National Council.